The Army of George II

The Soldiers who Forged an Empire

Peter Brown

Helion & Company

Helion & Company Limited
Unit 8 Amherst Business Centre
Budbrooke Road
Warwick
CV34 5WE
England
Tel. 01926 499619
Email: info@helion.co.uk
Website: www.helion.co.uk
blog.helion.co.uk/

Published by Helion & Company 2020
Designed and typeset by Mach 3 Solutions Ltd (www.mach3solutions.co.uk)
Cover designed by Paul Hewitt, Battlefield Design (www.battlefield-design.co.uk)

Text © Peter Brown 2020.
Colour plates by Patrice Courcelle © Helion & Co. 2020; other images as credited.

Cover: Private Gentleman of the Third Troop of Horse Guards during the War of the Austrian Succession. Original artwork by Patrice Courcelle © Helion & Co. 2020

Every reasonable effort has been made to trace copyright holders and to obtain their permission for the use of copyright material. The author and publisher apologise for any errors or omissions in this work, and would be grateful if notified of any corrections that should be incorporated in future reprints or editions of this book.

ISBN 978-1-913118-96-9

British Library Cataloguing-in-Publication Data.
A catalogue record for this book is available from the British Library.

All rights reserved. No part of this publication may be reproduced, stored in a retrieval system, or transmitted, in any form, or by any means, electronic, mechanical, photocopying, recording or otherwise, without the express written consent of Helion & Company Limited.

For details of other military history titles published by Helion & Company Limited, contact the above address, or visit our website: http://www.helion.co.uk

We always welcome receiving book proposals from prospective authors.

For my wife Sarah and my daughter Ciara, who have had to put up with me whilst I have been writing this.

And for my Mum; from the wee boy who never went anywhere without a book.

Contents

Introduction		vi
1	The Sinews of War	7
2	The King's Shilling	15
3	Gone for a Soldier	31
4	Crime and Punishment	55
5	Officers and Gentlemen	60
6	The Infantry	78
7	The Cavalry	104
8	The Board of Ordnance	126
9	Colours and Standards	136
10	Volunteers, Subjects, and Mercenaries	143
11	Physicians and Surgeons	150
12	The Train	158
13	The Army on Campaign	169
14	The Experience of Battle	188
15	'The Butcher's Bill'	209
16	'La Guerre Sauvage': The Army in the American Colonies	219
17	John Company: Service in India	244
18	Colonial Regiments in the Rest of the Empire	260
19	Leaving the Army	265
Epilogue		271

Appendices		
I	Infantry Uniforms 1742-1760	273
II	Infantry Regiments Raised During the Seven Years War	276
III	British Regiments Serving in North America	279
IV	American Provincial Regiments	281
V	Special Distinctions and Badges Displayed on Regimental Colours	282
VI	Heavy Cavalry Uniforms	283
VII	Dragoon Uniforms	286
VIII	Light Dragoon Uniforms	288

Colour Plate Commentaries	289
Bibliography	294

Introduction

The army of King George II is in many ways the forgotten army of the eighteenth century, falling as it does between the very successful campaigns of the Duke of Marlborough, at the beginning of the century, and the even better-known successes of the Duke of Wellington at its end. When it is remembered in the National consciousness it is usually through individuals, such as 'Wolfe of Quebec' or 'Clive of India', or as the villainous redcoats who crushed the gallant Scots Highlanders at Culloden.

Yet in many ways this army did more to establish Great Britain on the global stage than either the Duke of Marlborough or Wellington. As well as fighting two wars in Europe, its soldiers would see action in the far corners of the world, including North America, India, the Caribbean, Cuba, and Africa.

George II (1683-1760), engraving by and after J.E. Nilson. (Anne S.K. Brown Collection)

It would also face rebellion at home and fight a civil war that secured the Hanoverian succession and hence guaranteed British opposition to French dominance in Europe. The story of this army is both the story of the birth of the British Empire and also the creation of the legend of the invincible British redcoat.

In compiling the information contained in this book, I found many sources to be contradictory, incomplete, and often speculative. The information presented here is gleaned from the best sources available at the time of writing: where information is contentious or contradictory, I have indicated that to be the case. This book is intended to provide a rounded picture of the British soldier during the reign of George II, from his recruitment, through training, on campaign and into battle before his eventual retirement. It is, I believe, the most detailed account of a soldier's life in this time period currently available and has been something of a labour of love. I do hope you enjoy it.

Peter Brown, August 2020

1

The Sinews of War[1]

Anyone buying a book about the Army of George II did not do so to read a long chapter about eighteenth-century politics and finances. However, if we are to understand the many failings of the army described later, it is important that we first understand the relationship between the army and Parliament, or more specifically between Parliament and the King. What follows is a necessarily brief summary of the political situation during this period.

When George II came to the throne, in October 1727, it was not to lead Great Britain as an absolute monarch, but rather to be the figurehead of a Parliamentary democracy. Although the King could influence the appointment of cabinet ministers and would make his feelings known about issues such as foreign policy or domestic law, it was Parliament that actually drafted legislation, enacted laws and decided on key issues.

The one area where the King had sole control was over the army. The Bill of Rights, passed in 1689, stated that the monarch would retain 'the Government, Command and Disposition of the army'. The soldiers within the army swore loyalty to the crown whilst their colours, standards, and emblems displayed the Royal Arms. However, the Bill of Rights had also made clear that 'the raising of a standing army within the United Kingdom in time of peace, unless it be with the consent of Parliament, is against the law'.[2] In other words, the army only existed so long as Parliament allowed it to do so. Under the terms of the Mutiny Act, every year the King, through the War Office, would put estimates for the cost of the army before Parliament for approval. It was up to Parliament to agree to pay the estimated costs and to pass the Act, which allowed the British army to exist for another twelve months. Although the King controlled the army, Parliament retained control of the purse strings.

To the modern reader, the passing of the Mutiny Act would seem to be a foregone conclusion, as the existence of a national army is a necessity, not

---

[1] Summarized from Col. H.C.B. Rogers, *The British Army of the Eighteenth Century* (Oxford: Allen and Unwin, 1977), and Rex Whitworth, *William Augustus, Duke of Cumberland* (London: Leo Cooper, 1992).

[2] Rogers, *British Army of the Eighteenth* Century, p.18.

THE ARMY OF GEORGE II

George II in uniform wearing Garter sash. Colour mezzotint by W. Dickinson after Pine. (Anne S.K. Brown Collection)

HRH Prince William, Duke of Cumberland, favourite son of George II, depicted in an engraving commemorating his defeat of the Jacobites in 1745-1746. Engraving after Thomas Hudson. (Anne S.K. Brown Collection)

a luxury, especially during the turbulent times of the eighteenth century. However, this was not the case for one main reason: Parliament did not trust the King. This distrust originally stemmed from the English Civil War when King Charles had used the army to enforce his will against Parliament and this was something that Parliament was determined would never happen again. Given that the Monarchy had been restored in 1660, the fact this attitude continued into the reign of the new Hanoverian kings may seem a little paranoid. However, we must remember that Europe was still dominated by absolute monarchs, such as Louis XV in France or Frederick the Great in Prussia, and democracies were very much the exception rather than the norm. That the King could use a standing army to reassert his authority and once again rule by Divine Right was a genuine argument put forward by Members of Parliament at the time and is often seen in populist literature and hand bills designed to create distrust of the monarch. How far this fear that the King could use the army in this manner was a genuinely-held belief amongst Members of Parliament is a moot point. However, it was a useful argument to use to place restrictions on the size of the army, and hence for Parliament to tangibly display its control to the King.

In times of war, Parliament rarely opposed the raising of new regiments but equally rarely gave the Commander in Chief everything he asked for. As soon as the crisis passed or the war ended, Parliament would quickly move to cut funding and reduce the size of the army again.

The factions within Parliament further complicated the issue. The King was estranged from his first son, Frederick, Prince of Wales, with the two barely on speaking terms. Frederick held a separate Court at Leicester House and attracted to him ambitious young noblemen and Members of Parliament who were keen to associate with the future King. The situation was not helped when the Kings second, and favourite, son, William, Duke of Cumberland, was made Commander in Chief of the Army. Bills introduced by Cumberland to reform the army could be blocked by the 'Leicester House Set' simply to frustrate him, and indirectly the King, and to win favour with Frederick.

The King, for his part, had to allow Parliament to have its way. Not too long ago, William of Orange had replaced the Stuart monarchy in a bloodless coup with the help of Parliament, whilst the ascension of his own father to the throne of England as George I had been met with rioting in many towns across England. He was acutely aware of the exiled Stuart Prince waiting in the wings for a chance to take back his throne. George II could not afford to rock the boat, as his hold on the throne was far from secure.

The Military Establishment

The practical result of all the political shenanigans in the Houses of Parliament was that the amount of money granted to pay for the army was always insufficient.[3] In times of war, Parliament could be generous and invested heavily in raising new regiments and funding overseas expeditions. However, as soon as the war was over, the army would be rapidly reduced in size and funding would once again be cut. This is reflected in the numbers on the 'Military Establishment'.

The 'Military Establishment' refers to the total number of men in the army, divided between the infantry and cavalry arms. The artillery, engineers and support arms came under the strength of the Board of Ordnance and had a separate budget. Originally, regiments were posted to the strength of the Irish, Scottish or English establishments, with the Government of each expected to cover the costs of their upkeep. Following the Act of Union, regiments were shown on the British Establishment – which covered England, Wales, and Scotland – or on the Irish Establishment, which was still paid for from the Irish exchequer and then reclaimed from the British Government. The number of men on the Irish Establishment was set at 12,000 by the 'Disbanding Act' of 1699 and remained so until 1769. The number of men on the British Establishment varied depending on the political situation in Europe and the whim of Parliament.

If a regiment was taken from Ireland to supplement the British Establishment or to be sent overseas, it either had to be replaced with another regiment from the British Establishment or a new regiment would be raised in its place. In this way, the 12,000-man establishment was maintained. Often, regiments from the British establishment would be circulated around the United Kingdom, spending some time in Ireland as well as on the mainland, and we see some regiments appearing on the British Establishment one year and the Irish the next. This was simply to keep the regiments from becoming too established in one area of the country and also because some districts, especially in Ireland, had better provision of barracks and hence regiments were moved to ensure they all benefitted from good accommodation as well as the not so good. Having 12,000 men in Ireland acted as a general reserve to the Commander in Chief and was a cushion of troops he could call on if needed. Regiments on the Irish Establishment tended to be only about 300 men strong, consisting of a nucleus of veteran soldiers, trained NCOs and officers. The idea was that, on the outbreak of war, new recruits could be drafted into these regiments and be quickly trained by the experienced troops already there. This was deemed to be better than raising a new regiment from scratch.

In 1715 the number of men on the British establishment was recorded as 8,000. Following the Jacobite rebellion in 1719, this was raised to 12,000. In

---

3   Summarized from Tony Hayter (ed.), *An Eighteenth Century Secretary at War* (London: The Bodley Head The Army Records Society 1988) with statistics and summary from J.A. Houlding *Fit for Service* (New York: Oxford University Press, 1981) and Rogers, *British Army of the Eighteenth Century*.

1720, following the birth of Charles Edward Stuart, a further Jacobite attempt on the throne was expected and hence the establishment was raised again to 18,000. From this, the army was expected to garrison the various forts and magazines in Britain, the Channel Islands, the Mediterranean, and Colonial plantations as well as troops raised as marines or drafted to support the fleet. This number also included Invalids, men retained on the books on half-pay, and also new recruits in training. Consequently, the 18,000 men were spread very thin. During the 1730s the threat of war with Spain prompted the raising of the establishment to 26,000 and this was raised again when the War of the Austrian Succession broke out in Europe. That said, the 18 battalions and 29 squadrons that Britain sent to support their Dutch and Austrian allies at the beginning of the war amounted to less than 16,000 men, which was a tiny army by European standards.

The Parliamentary penny-pinching on the military establishment almost led to disaster for the King. Following the defeat of a predominantly British and Dutch army at Fontenoy in 1745, the French realised that most of the British trained battalions were in Europe and took the opportunity to invade. French troops were embarked on ships and an escort fleet of warships had left port before bad weather scattered the invasion fleet and put paid to the plan for that year. However, the invasion had been a very real threat and its failure did not stop the French supporting the subsequent landing of the Jacobite Prince, Charles Edward Stuart, in Scotland to raise the Highland clans in rebellion later the same year. At that time there were fewer than 3,000 trained troops in Scotland to face him, which were easily routed at the Battle of Prestonpans. Parliament was forced to recall the Duke of Cumberland from Flanders along with 10 of the best battalions to face the threat and was also forced to pay for Dutch and Hessian troops to come to Britain to provide much-needed assistance.

When the rebellion was crushed at Culloden in 1746, one might have expected that the near success of the enterprise would have encouraged Parliament to vote for a large increase in the size of the army, and to a certain extent it did. However, the new figure was agreed at only 30,000 men of whom 20,000 were to be stationed in Britain and the rest in the overseas possessions. The Irish Establishment remained at 12,000. When the War of the Austrian Succession ended, Parliament agreed to keep the establishment at this level but even this small number was bitterly disputed by MPs with some even proposing the disbanding the army altogether and relying on the Militia instead!

In 1756 the threat of French invasion once more raised its head as hostilities had broken out between France and Britain in America and war in Europe was expected imminently. Once again, the numbers of men on home service was considered to be too small and Parliament was forced to ask for the loan of Hanoverian troops from the King's German possessions and to hire 8,000 mercenary troops from the German state of Hesse-Kassel. At the outbreak of the Seven Years War the British establishment was raised to 49,000 men, of which 30,000 were designated for home defence and 19,000 for service in the colonies. By 1758 the establishment was increased to 54,000, but even this number proved to be insufficient, such was the demand for extra troops to be deployed overseas to meet the armies growing commitments in various theatres of war.

By 1759 there were 22,000 troops in America; 20,000 in Germany, under Prince Ferdinand; and 13,000 overseas in the West and East Indies, Gibraltar, West Africa and the Caribbean. By 1762 there were 111,553 soldiers around the world in the pay of the British Government, which included locally-raised troops in the colonies and mercenary and allied troops in Europe.[4]

Once again, the establishment at home was neglected. On paper, it looked to be around its 30,000-man total, but a close examination of these numbers shows that the effective force was much less. Many of this number were Invalids, men in training, drafts waiting to go overseas to join their regiments, and soldiers unfit for general service. The Commander in Chief, Lord Ligonier, assessed that there were fewer than eight trained regiments of infantry and two of cavalry available for home defence, a total of 8,530 men, most of whom were new recruits. This review had been carried out as there were rumours of yet another French plan to invade England and once again the defences were found wanting. For the first time, the Militia had to be turned out in significant numbers to garrison defences and free up regular troops. This period also saw the first formation of Fencible Regiments, which were essentially regular soldiers but who were only available for service at home.

When the Seven Years War ended, despite repeated threats of invasion from France and the need for garrisons to protect the substantial land gains made in the colonies, Parliament once again called for the army to be reduced to its 1749 level of 30,000 men. Lord Ligonier argued to retain a small number of men in 85 infantry regiments, to act as a nucleus of regiments on which a new army could be built, rather than disband them all. However, in a now predictable pattern, Parliament approved the request but only for 70 regiments. Whilst these regiments would remain in existence, they would be cut back to a couple of hundred men each, usually the veterans and grenadiers, with the surplus officers retained on half pay.

The British Army was constantly overstretched throughout this period as a suspicious parliament viewed it as a threat and would not grant the funds to recruit and equip it adequately to do the job they wanted it to do. Despite one full-scale French invasion attempt in 1744-1745 and the threat of others in the following years, there never appeared to be enough troops in Britain to adequately defend it, with Parliament more willing to hire mercenaries or to look to their allies for support than to raise the troops themselves. Lack of funding is a theme we will return to often in this work.

The War Office

The War Office was the Government department that dealt with military matters and from 1721 it was based at Number 7 Whitehall on Horse Guards Parade. The Secretary at War (sometimes called the Secretary of War) was

---

4 Additional statistics summarised from Hayter (ed.), *Eighteenth Century Secretary at War*, pp.352-354.

the head of the department and he was assisted both by a Deputy Secretary and a First, or Senior, Clerk. There are very few records detailing how many other staff were employed, but a surviving wage bill for September 1759 shows only 11 further Clerks in the office even at the height of the Seven Years War. Given that they looked after recruitment, training, promotion, supply and all other aspects of the day to day running of the army, they must have been rushed off their feet!

The Secretary at War was a civilian post and had originally been the clerk to the Commander in Chief of the Army. He was not a politician and was often not even invited to cabinet meetings, unless his advice was specifically required. However, he did have direct access to the King, with scheduled weekly meetings to discuss matters pertaining to the army, and was thus a politically powerful and influential individual. The Secretary at War was only responsible for the administration and organisation of the army, not military strategy, which was the responsibility of the Commander in Chief in consultation with the cabinet. The Secretary at War could influence strategy, however, by discussing what was, and was not, possible with the resources available.

Sir William Yonge held the post from 1735 to 1741, when Thomas Winnington succeeded him. Henry Fox took over in 1746 and held the position until 1755 when William Wildman, Viscount Barrington took it on. He was to hold the post throughout the Seven Years War and was appointed to the role again in July 1765 until December 1778. It is from his surviving correspondence that we have gleaned much of how the War Office operated.[5]

The Secretary at War, through the War Office, would produce a series of estimates that would be put before Parliament early in the Autumn session. These would estimate how much each regiment was expected to cost the exchequer in the year to come. Some would cost more than others, due to their size, overseas posting and so on. The estimates did not break down the costs but simply gave an overall figure for each regiment with a total cost for the entire army for the year ahead. This estimate was not set in stone and the War Office could return to Parliament to ask it to vote for more money in unforeseen circumstances, such as the declaration of war. However, Parliament liked the War Office to stick within budget and, where possible, save money!

Once parliament had passed the estimate, it was the job of the War Office Clerks to draw up the establishments. These represented a far more detailed breakdown of the costs and expenses for each of the regiments for the coming year. Each regiment was required to undergo an inspection by the Commissary General of the Musters, not only to ensure that it was ready and trained for war but also to assist in estimating how much the regiment would cost to run. Using these muster rolls, the Clerks at the War Office would estimate how much each regiment was likely to cost in the year ahead.

---

5   For more details on the working of the War Office see Hayter (ed.), *Eighteenth Century Secretary at War*.

Pay and subsistence could vary a great deal depending on whether the regiment was in quarters, barracks or under canvas, posted overseas or in garrison. The estimate also had to include one shilling in the pound for the Paymaster Generals fee, one day's pay a year from all the officers and men for the maintenance of Chelsea Hospital, allowances for officers' servants, and the cost of clothing and other items lost to deserters. Money also had to be estimated for recruiting, and costs or fees for the regimental agent and for the support of officers' widows and so on. Once these were all drawn up, they were put before the King for approval. Assuming the King signed the Establishment, it was then taken to the Treasury for approval. The treasury then drew up the necessary paperwork that could then be presented to the Paymaster General in exchange for cash or promissory notes. The money could now be passed to the regiments.

Regimental Agents[6]

Colonels of regiments were generally well-heeled individuals, often landed gentry or members of the aristocracy, and certainly not the kind of gentlemen who would want to become involved with the day-to-day book keeping required for the successful running of a regiment. Instead, they employed a regimental agent.

Agents were civilian contractors who took on the financial management of the regiment in exchange for a fee. Usually based in London (or Dublin in the case of the Irish Establishment) these men were more than just accountants, but well-connected merchants and middlemen. They undertook sourcing cloth for uniforms, dealt with sword cutlers, gunsmiths, and farriers as well as arranging the purchase of wagons or horses and other necessaries for the men. When the soldiers were in billets the agent often settled the bill for their stay as well as making arrangements for food supply when they were in barracks. To do all of this, the agent often employed clerks and runners himself to work for him and to make the whole arrangement more efficient. They were required to keep accurate accounts that had to be produced to the treasury at the end of the financial year to ensure that they were spending the Governments money correctly and not embezzling it.

The position of agent was not just one of buying and selling. Often, the agents worked on behalf of the colonel, using their connections at the War Office to lobby on their patron's behalf, persuading them to give his regiment a plum posting, for example, or pressing for it not to be disbanded when the war ended. If there was any money left from the annual allowance, this was considered to be a bonus that could be split between the colonel and the agent. One of the most famous Agents during this period was John Calcraft, some of whose accounts are still held in the National Archives. Over the years he built up a business that employed numerous other Agents and by 1761 he

---

6 Information on regimental agents summarised from Alan Guy, (ed.), *Colonel Samuel Bagshawe and the Army of George II 1731-1762* (London: The Bodley Head for the Army Records Society, 1990).

had 52 different regiments on his books. By using economies of scale, he was able to bulk purchase items for the majority of his regiments, which reduced costs and hence left more money in the coffers.

With the administration of the regiment being taken care of by the agent, this left the colonel and his officers free to take care of the day-to-day running of the regiment. First amongst these chores, was recruitment.

2

The King's Shilling

The ranks of the army of George II were, for the most part, filled with volunteers. To the modern reader, this seems unlikely, as we imagine life in the eighteenth-century British Army to be a harsh one, with few luxuries and a short life expectancy. In fact, many occupations in England during this century fitted this description, with most working men employed in jobs that involved hard manual labour, long hours and low pay. The army, on the other hand, provided a young man with a regular wage, daily food, a roof over his head and medical care should he fall ill, all of which had a lot to be said for during a time when starvation and destitution were very real threats. Indeed, the soldiers themselves felt they were better off in their job than in many others. One contemporary, Sergeant Stevenson, wrote: 'we always looked on soldiers as being in better circumstances than any country labouring men and we have considered ourselves to be much better off than we should have been had we remained at home'.[1]

Despite this, many historians are of the view that many 'volunteers' joined the army simply to avoid starvation. As Daniel Defoe famously wrote: 'In winter the poor starve, thieve or turn Soldier'.[2] These were certainly hungry times, with crop failures and food shortages occurring at different times throughout the reign of George II. Having been sent to quell a food riot in Gloucester in 1756, James Wolfe certainly thought that starvation might be a factor in gaining some new recruits, writing: 'I hope it will turn out a good recruiting party, for the people are so oppressed, so poor and so wretched, that they will perhaps hazard a knock on the pate for bread and clothes, and turn soldiers through sheer necessity'.[3]

However, despite Wolfe's optimism, there is no clear correlation between food shortages and a rise in recruitment. For example, 1755 and 1756 saw extensive crop failures and food shortages across the country. This period also coincided with the beginning of the Seven Years War and was one of increased recruitment by both the Army and the Royal Navy. One would imagine that with widespread poverty and starvation,

---

1 Ilya Berkovich, *Motivation in War* (Cambridge: Cambridge University Press, 2017), p.159.
2 Berkovich, *Motivation in War*, p.128.
3 Beckles Willson, *Life and Letters of James Wolfe* (London: William Heinemann, 1909), pp.304-5.

THE ARMY OF GEORGE II

'The Recruiting Sergeant'; A new recruit takes the King's shilling against his sweetheart's wishes. Engraving by J. Goldar after John Collet. (Anne S.K. Brown Collection)

people would flock to the recruiting parties, but this turned out not to be the case. In fact, recruiting into the army was so low that the Government was forced to introduce Recruiting Bills that allowed magistrates to force vagrants and minor offenders into the ranks. It appears that whilst some recruits undoubtedly did join the army to escape poverty, many more did not, and the idea that the ranks were filled with those driven into the army through hunger is demonstrably not the case.

So, what did drive young men to join the army? Most recruits seem to have volunteered for the same reasons that young people volunteer for the armed forces today, and have done for centuries. Bored with their prospects at home, they wanted to leave the community they grew up in, and where they would no doubt spend the rest of their lives, to get out and see the world. The recruiting sergeants in their well-turned-out red uniforms cut a handsome figure and the tales told over a mug of ale of battles won in faraway places no doubt inspired their imagination. John Haime, for example, stated he joined the Queens Regiment of Dragoons 'in search of adventure', whilst Duncan Wright, who joined the 10th Foot in 1754, stated that he did so because he had always wanted to be a soldier. Thomas Payne wrote that he wanted 'to see the world' and attempted to join Burgoyne's 16th Light Dragoons in 1759. When he was rejected for being too short, he instead joined the East India Company. A group of dragoons who were billeted in Dunbar hired a room at the home of Thomas Rankin, who at that time was only a boy. He was greatly influenced by their appearance and demeanour and as a result, decided to join up when he was old enough.[4]

An examination of the handbills and recruiting posters of the day reinforce this idea of joining the army for a life of adventure. A recruiting poster for the East India Company appeals to those whose 'ambition is above Slavery and Mean Employment, or to be subject to Masters or Mistresses tempers'. Young men who had debts, or perhaps had an affair ending in an unwanted pregnancy, could also use the army as a means of escape. The Prince of Wales' Dragoon Guards poster appealed for recruits using just this kind of language. It promised they would enter 'a Life of ease and Jollity *(for any young)* Man troubled with Inquietude of Mind, from Connections with the Fair Sex or any uneasy Circumstance whatever'.[5]

During times of war, it was also possible that men joined for patriotic reasons, wanting to do their bit for King and Country. The reign of George II saw two major wars with France, and the perceived injustices and murder visited on the Kings subjects by the enemy was something that recruiters were keen to capitalise on. Joining the army gave potential recruits the opportunity to strike back against the enemy, protect their loved ones and their country. For example, in 1759 the dean of Gloucester offered an extra bounty to men who would: 'compose a body of Light Infantry the most capable of annoying our enemies in their present desperate design against the protestant religion and British Liberties'.[6]

Sometimes, men joined for more personal reasons. For example, Peter Williamson joined the Rangers during the French and Indian War to take revenge on the French and Indians who had killed his family and who at one stage had held him prisoner. When the recruiters came by he wrote: 'never did I go to any enterprise with half that alacrity and cheerfulness I now went with this party'.[7]

The soldiers bearing, their smart uniforms and the inclusion of a sword on their belt showed them to be part of a group set aside from normal society. Many recruiting posters of the time called for 'young gentlemen' to answer the King's call to arms, implying that those who did so would be socially elevated. It is perhaps more difficult for us in modern times to identify with this, but at the time British society was divided along very clear class lines and the Army may well have been seen as an opportunity to better oneself. This might especially be true if you were to join a cavalry regiment or one of the older infantry regiments, such as the Guards. Private John Shaw states his reason for joining was to: 'be clear from work and [become] a gentleman at once'.[8]

Not everyone who joined the army was an unskilled labourer. A look through the professions of new recruits reveals trades such as cottar,

---

4   V. Neuberg, 'The British Army in the Eighteenth Century', *Journal of the Society for Army Historical Research*, No 245 (Spring 1983) pp. 44-45.
5   Berkovich, *Motivation in War*, p.136.
6   Berkovich, *Motivation in War*, p.137.
7   Berkovich, *Motivation in War*, p.154.
8   Berkovich, *Motivation in War*, p.149.

weaver, tailor, cooper, blacksmith and other tradesmen. Whilst in Leeds, Captain Archibald Grant 'inlisted four very good recruits, in my opinion, all shoemakers in this town, they came together in a body and told me that if I would take them all they would inlist but they are determined not to separate'.[9]

A look through the list of men notified as having deserted the army in Ireland shows most were previously employed in the textile industry and nearly 25 percent in Farming with only one percent showing their trade as 'none'. This demonstrates that the lure of adventure, patriotism, social advancement, or simply to escape life in one's home town, for whatever reason, cut across society and attracted not only unskilled men but those from all sorts of background to the colours. It is significant that whilst some of the recruiting posters mention the significant bounty gained for joining, pay and food are not mentioned, which one might expect if they were seen as significant draws to recruitment at the time. Those who volunteered to join King George's army were the kind of restless young men who have been drawn to military service for centuries.

Beating the Drum

As discussed in the previous chapter, the various regiments in the British army were reduced in size once a war had ended with many private soldiers released from service and their officers placed on half pay. During these periods of peace, recruitment would be limited. However, as soon as another war was on the horizon, orders would come for the regiments to quickly fill their ranks. In February, 1755, for example, Corporal Todd records in his diary: 'We received orders from the War Office to augment & compleat each company to 3 Serjeant, 3 Corporals, 2 Drummers and 70 Effective Man. Recruiting partys was immediately sent out into different parts of England & Scotland'.[10]

Recruiting parties consisted of one or two trusted NCOs from the regiment, usually a sergeant and a corporal, along with a drummer to literally 'drum up' support. An officer would sometimes be dispatched to oversee two or three recruiting parties that might be operating in the same area. The recruiters were given a sum of money for their daily subsistence and another, sometimes substantial, sum to provide a bounty or an initial payment to encourage new recruits to join. For this reason, the NCOs in the recruiting parties had to be trustworthy, since they would be in charge of the cash for recruiting and be given a fairly free rein in terms of how they went about their business. Occasionally, they did not live up to this expectation, as Captain Vernet Lovett attested to the War Office in March 1748:

---

9   Stuart Reid, *British Redcoat 1740-93* (London: Osprey, 1996), p.5.
10   Andrew Cormack and Alan Jones (eds) *The Journal of Corporal Todd 1745-1762* (Stroud: Sutton Publishing limited for the Army Records Society, 2001), p.12.

> Serj. Streett lost the money I gave him…to carry on the recruiting service at cards; Corp Parker his proportion spent at the ale house & some other extravagances that has obliged me to draw £40 since I left London… When I imagined (the) Serj had money to inlist men I find for many weeks they have had not a shilling.[11]

The recruiters were sent out with a very detailed instruction about who was, and who was not, acceptable as a recruit. The directions for the 93rd Regiment of Foot stated:

> All recruits are to be able bodied, Sound in their limbs, free from Ruptures, Scald heads, Ulcerous sores or any remarkable deformity. None to be Inlisted who cannot wear his hair, who is knee'd, Splay footed or subject to fits…No Strolers, Vagabonds, Tinkers, Chimney Sweepers, Colliers or Saylors to be Inlisted.[12]

As there was no set amount agreed for a bounty, recruiters were encouraged to use their discretion when deciding how much each recruit was worth. However, when the recruiting party had reached its quota, any money left over from their recruiting pot would be split between the NCO's and their officer. It was therefore not in the recruiting parties' interests to take young men who were either unwilling to join or who did not meet the criteria. If the captain of the company refused the recruit, or he deserted on his way to the regiment, any expense the sergeant had incurred up until then had to come from his 'budget', so to speak. Equally, costs incurred on any recruit turned away by the colonel when he arrived back with the regiment had to be borne by the captain. Unfit recruits would eat into any profit the recruiters hoped to make whilst, if they could recruit men by offering a smaller bounty, that was all to the better. Hence we see Corporal Todd celebrating when he 'inlisted Robert Smally upon the march at Warrington in Lancashire for £1 6s',[13] whereas Captain Verney Lovett lamented: 'I had a fine recruit to whom I gave £3 claim'd as a deserter from the Welsh Fuzileers'.[14]

The recruiting party would travel around the county, attending fairs or markets where likely young men might be in attendance. They would usually set themselves up at a local inn or public house, with the recruiter standing outside shouting that the regiment was recruiting, much like a town crier. Some recruiters used music to attract attention, often employing not just a drummer but a fifer as well. When John Grant was tasked with recruiting 25 men for the Black Watch in Scotland in 1758, he 'got a good piper and then four young men (who were) good dancers' before setting himself up in an ale house. With the piping and boisterous dancing 'this collected a crowd & drink was not scarce…I soon enlisted my number and set out for Perth'.[15]

---

11   Guy (ed.), *Colonel Samuel Bagshawe*, p.73.
12   Guy (ed.), *Colonel Samuel Bagshawe*, p.210.
13   Cormack and Jones (eds), *Journal of Corporal Todd*, p.12.
14   Guy (ed.), *Colonel Samuel Bagshawe*, p.73: Captain Verney Lovett to Major Samuel Bagshawe, 1 March 1748.
15   Ian Macpherson McCulloch, *Sons of the Mountains. The Highland Regiments in the French Indian War 1756-1767* (Fleischmanns: Purple Mountain Press Ltd, 2006), p.107.

There were certain men, however, that recruiting parties were not supposed to enlist. These included indentured servants, boys who were already apprentices, and members of the Militia. However, this did not stop unscrupulous recruiters trying their luck. For example, the War Office had to write to Colonel Montague in April, 1756, asking for the release of: 'two Apprentices in your Regiment being demanded by their masters…if upon strict examination you find the men to be regularly indented and not out of their time, you do acquiesce'.[16] Equally, Lord Strange berated Serjeant Thomas Surman of the 35th Regiment for attempting to enlist members of his Militia. Surman protested his innocence, stating that he did not know they were Militia, which Strange doubted very much, as he was caught attempting to recruit them whilst: 'in their Regimentals and performing their duty at the place appointed for annual exercise'.[17]

Men were supposed to be of the Protestant religion and this seems to have been particularly enforced when recruiting in Ireland. Should recruits turn out to be Catholic, they would be rejected upon arrival back at the regiment with all of the expense on their bounty and keep until then being lost. This did not stop some recruiters taking such men on in order to fill their quota. Lieutenant Colonel Windus complained that Lieutenant Caulfield and Ensign Cook of his regiment had acted 'in Open opposition to the first and most material article of your recruiting instructions by inlisting papists…out of the ten inlisted by Ens Cook, one, Dunn, deserted on his way here & all the rest…are Papists'.[18]

Recruits had to be 5ft 6' tall and be in good health, as shown in the directions to the 93rd Regiment above. The height requirement might be waived if the recruit was not yet eighteen as he might be expected to grow. Although there were no regulations concerning the completeness of the recruits teeth, it was essential for an infantryman to be able to bite open a cartridge, which was part of the musket firing drill, and so a man could be disqualified from joining the regiment if his teeth were bad or if he had many missing.

Recruits were supposed to be at least 16 years old, but there are many examples of much younger children being in the ranks. For many orphans or young boys whose families could not afford to feed them, the army was considered a better option than the workhouse. So long as the recruit was able to hold a musket, not too many questions would be asked by the recruiting sergeant of anyone claiming to be 16. Young men might well be taken on in the expectation that they would grow into soldiering. For example, John Christopher joined the 12th Foot in 1756, although he was 'about 15 or 16 years of age & too weak to carry arms, our Lieutt Collonel ask'd him if he would be a drummer to which he seem'd very glad…although he always was a very bad one as he could never learn that duty to no perfection'.[19] Eight men appear in the Chelsea Hospital registers having been recruited into the Foot

---

16   Hayter (ed.), *Eighteenth Century Secretary at War*, p.231.
17   Hayter (ed.), *Eighteenth Century Secretary at War*, p.230.
18   Guy (ed.), *Colonel Samuel Bagshawe*, p.218. Lt Col Windus to Col Bagshawe, 26 March 1760.
19   Cormack and Jones (eds), *Journal of Corporal Todd*, p.204.

Guards or Marching Foot regiments at age eleven, with a further eleven men listed who had joined as twelve-year-olds.[20]

Also in the ranks were the sons of serving soldiers, who had grown up following the regiment. It was in the soldiers' interests to get them on the regimental books as soon as possible, both to start earning a living and also not to continue being counted as a 'camp follower' any more. For example, army child William Brown was pensioned from Onslow's 8th Foot in 1742 having served 32 years although he was only aged 44 at the time.[21]

Competition amongst regiments for recruits was fierce, with every regiment in the Army under pressure to bring their units up to strength before they shipped out to war, and as a result, savvy recruits could drive a hard bargain. It was not just other British regiments that they were up against. In 1757, the War Office had to ask the Secretary of State for the Northern Department not to grant permission for Dutch units to recruit British subjects, writing: 'It has been represented to me from Major Grant of the 1st Highland Battalion that the Scotch Dutch Officers, at present recruiting in Scotland, are a great hindrance to him; as they can afford to give as much money as he can and enlist only for a term of years'.[22] Although it occasionally happened, it was considered very bad form for rival recruiting parties to attempt to steal a new recruit away with a better offer.

Having identified a likely lad, the recruiters would often retire inside the hostelry to ply their prospective recruit with some ale and promises of what they could expect in His Majesty's Army. Having agreed a bounty, the recruit would be given a symbolic shilling as his first wage, which he would be encouraged to turn into ale for his new regimental colleagues as quickly as possible! The bounty was sometimes given by means of a promissory note, which could be redeemed when the recruit arrived back at the regiment, but it was just as often given in cash out of the recruiter's allowance. Some recruits frittered their bounty away, whilst others, especially amongst Highland regiments, appear to have sent their bounty money home to their families. An honest recruiting sergeant would usually advise the new recruit to save some money for a good pair of shoes, some shirts or other necessaries that he might need in his new profession. The recruit was then provided with a rosette of brightly coloured ribbons, which marked him out as the newest member of the regiment. The new soldier would be brought in front of a magistrate as soon as possible to swear an oath of allegiance, at the conclusion of which he was officially in the Army and would be treated as a deserter should he abscond thereafter. He would then follow the recruiting party as it went about its business, helping to persuade other young men to join the regiment and joining the recruiting party when they went drinking in the evenings with their potential new enlistees. During this period any

---

20 Andrew Cormack, *'These Meritorious Objects of the Royal Bounty' The Administration of the Out-pension of the Royal Hospital, Chelsea in the early Eighteenth Century*. (Thesis for the degree of Doctor of Philosophy (History) 2016), p.139.
21 Cormack, *'These Meritorious Objects of the Royal Bounty'*, p.139.
22 Hayter (ed.), *Eighteenth Century Secretary at War*, p.42. Barrington to William Pitt, 14 February 1757.

expenses incurred by the recruit were borne by the recruiting sergeant from his allocation of money. One can see why, having shelled out a sizable bounty and spent money on his recruits' ale, food, and accommodation for a few days, the sergeant would not like to see his potential soldier turned away. One can also see why it was in the sergeants' interests not to fool young men into joining, or to take unwilling recruits, as the opportunities to abscond from the small recruiting party were many. Not only would the recruiters have to travel around the county until they had reached their quota, they would then have a long journey back to their regiment, which was often undertaken on foot and could take several days.

That said, pressure to fill the ranks often led recruiting sergeants to use many underhand tactics to fool naive young men into inadvertently joining up. Many are the tales told of men being bought a drink by a recruiting sergeant only to find a shilling in the bottom of it, or, having been made drunk by the recruiting party, woke up the next day to find he had enlisted. Many of these tales are apocryphal, being more common in popular fiction than in real life. However, it is true that some such incidents did occur. Corporal Todd wrote of one occasion where he saw a recruiting party getting William Kerby drunk in order to recruit him 'so I inlisted him to hinder the Serjeant…as he was but a poor labouring man & (I intended to) set him at liberty when he was sober for nothing'.[23] One recruiting sergeant went round the town of Preston in November 1758 with 'a fiddler instead of a Drummer, & we went about and he made his speech & offer'd 2 1/2 Guineas for any Young fellow that was 5 foot 7 inches High'. Having no luck, he spotted a young man stood by a doorway 'One of the Serjeants Recruits went to the door & asked the young man to shake hands with him & left a shilling in his hand, calling out to us in the room that he had inlisted a man. Where upon the Serjeant & the rest of the recruits rush'd out & brought the Young fellow into the room amongst us'.[24] The War Office wrote a stinging letter to Lieutenant Sharpe of Lord George Beauclerk's 19th Foot in January, 1756, concerning the recruitment of Joseph Roberts, stating that: 'your Serjeants giving Roberts a shilling more in his Change in order to Inlist him…was an unfair way of proceeding…I desire that you will give no further molestation to the said Roberts as it may greatly hurt the service'.[25]

Having taken the 'King's shilling', all was not lost for an unwilling recruit or anyone who suddenly thought better of his actions in the cold light of day. If someone was prepared to pay back any bounty that he may have been given, along with a sum of money to cover the recruiting expenses, he could be discharged straight away. Sometimes a distressed mother or other family member would approach the sergeant of the recruiting party to make such a payment before they left town. Corporal Todd recruited Henry Cook and his servant into his Regiment but was met soon after by Henry Cook's mother and his brother, as well as 'Mr Robert Wright, Proctor, with them to assist them to get Clear'd'. Todd agreed to release them as they were not yet sworn

---

23   Cormack and Jones (eds), *Journal of Corporal Todd*, p.109.
24   Cormack and Jones (eds), *Journal of Corporal Todd*, p.109.
25   Hayter (ed.), *Eighteenth Century Secretary at War*, p.229.

in, but insisted on the return of the bounty along with 'a Guinea & a crown each, to which they consented… [I] gave them a discharge from me and then we parted, as I thought the money would look better in my pocket than in theirs'.[26] A discharge could also be obtained by writing to the colonel of the regiment or even to the War Office directly, especially if the recruit's family had connections and could pull some strings. Thomas Levett, a regimental agent, wrote to the War Office to support:

> [A]n application from Major Sawyer for the discharge of one Robert Thomas, who is one of Lt Lewis last recruits, listed at Hereford, and whose father is a tenant of the Majors and is willing to pay any listing charges as far as five pounds…I hope you will be so kind as to comply with the Majors request as the man is but a recruit that has just joyn'd the regiment.[27]

Not all such appeals succeeded, however. A petition from a master craftsman to release two of his apprentices from the 19th Regiment of Foot was dismissed stating: 'If apprentices and Servants weary of their masters service, present conditions of life, can't enlist, ther's an End to Recruiting the army since no Man is born a soldier but enters into it at the Time he's found fit and willing for service'.[28]

As can be seen, recruitment into the Army was generally by consent, and if one was fooled into joining or was an unwilling recruit, there were ways of being released. However, this is not to say that there were no 'pressed men' in the Army. Far from it. A lack of willing volunteers often forced the government into taking drastic action to boost numbers. During the Jacobite Rebellion in 1745, for example, Parliament passed two acts encouraging Magistrates to conscript: 'all such able bodied men…who cannot, upon examination prove themselves to exercise any lawful trade or employment'.[29] For every man so recruited, the parish constables received a bounty of £3 into the vestry account, hence these recruits received the nickname 'Vestry Men'. A similar act for the 'Speedy and Effectual Recruiting of his Majesty's Land Forces and Marines' was passed on 9 March 1756 and was renewed on 15 February the following year. It allowed Magistrates and lesser local officials to 'search, apprehend and secure…for listing…such able bodied men as do not follow or exercise any lawful calling or employment, or have not some other lawful and sufficient support and maintenance'.[30] Men still had to be between the age of 17 and 45, be at least 5 feet 4 inches and 'be of the Protestant religion'. In 1757, any 'idle and disorderly persons' were added to the list of those who could be impressed.[31]

However, contemporaries were aware of exactly the kind of men this sort of policy produced. One wrote that by the use of this act: 'the country gets

---

26   Cormack and Jones (eds), *Journal of Corporal Todd*, p.114.
27   Guy (ed.), *Colonel Samuel Bagshawe*, p.80.
28   Berkovich, *Motivation in War*, p.130.
29   Houlding, *Fit for Service*, p.118.
30   Richard Middleton. 'The Recruitment of the British Army 1755-1762', *Journal of the Society for Army Historical Research* Vol. 67, No. 272 (Winter 1989), p.229.
31   Middleton, 'The Recruitment of the British Army 1755-1762', p.229.

clear of their banditti and the ranks are filled up with the scum of every county, the refuse of mankind. They are marched loaded with vice, villainy and chains to their destined corps where, when they arrive, they corrupt all they approach and are whipped out or desert in a month'.[32] Court records are full of men who elected to enlist rather than face gaol. In St Albans in 1759, a man arrested for threatening another 'was discharged out of custody on his enlisting as a soldier' whilst William Desborough escaped the hangman for theft of a sheep in 1760, also by enlisting. Another record from Stevenage in 1757 shows that a man fined for two cases of assault was: 'discharged, the Defendant having inlisted into Lord Robert Manners Regiment of Foot'.[33] John Baker, Jeremiah Smith, Charles Dailey, and Thomas Elliott, were all sentenced to death for Highway Robbery at Maidstone in November 1760 but received pardons when they volunteered to join the 49th Foot, then in Jamaica.

In April 1758, Corporal Todd wrote:

> We got a great number of impressed men into our Regiment for the constable brings them in every Saturday, the market day, where we have an Officer & a Serjeant & Corporal & 12 men waiting at the Towns Hall where a bench of Justices of the Peace sits… Any young fellow that's out of place, or has got a girl with child, or has any loose (character) is sure of being brought, for the Constables receives one pound for every man they take up & several of them will take up anyone…[34]

This was sometimes the only means of reconstituting depleted regiments. Following the heavy casualties sustained by the Royal Welch Fusiliers at Fontenoy and their subsequent capture at Ghent, the regiment was sent back to England to recover in October 1745. A small detachment of two sergeants and two corporals were sent to Kensington 'to receive such recruits as shall be delivered to them from time to time from the vestrys of St Martins and St James's parishes'.[35]

There was another form of conscription practiced in the British army which was not driven by the government but by a different kind of loyalty altogether. There is strong evidence amongst the Highland regiments, especially the 78th Foot, that landlords coerced tenants to enlist their sons to avoid eviction from their farms, with one widow who lost all four sons to the Frasers' recruiting party against their will. One private in the 77th described his battalion as 'mostly composed of impressed men from the Highlands'.[36]

In addition, there were those families still suffering due to the role they played in the Jacobite rebellion that hoped now to show their loyalty to the

---

32 Peter Way, '"The scum of every county, the refuse of mankind": Recruiting the British Army in the eighteenth century' in Erik-Jan Zürcher (ed.), *Fighting for a Living: A Comparative Study of Military Labour 1500-2000* (Amsterdam University Press, Amsterdam, 2013), p.8.
33 J.E.O. Screen, 'The Eighteenth Century Army at home as reflected in Local records', *Journal of the Society for Army Historical Research Vol. 88*, No. 355 (Autumn 2010), p.225.
34 Cormack and Jones (eds), *Journal of Corporal Todd*, p.38.
35 A.D.L. Cary (ed.), *Regimental Records of the Royal Welch Fusiliers* (Uckfield: Naval & Military Press, 2015), p.112.
36 McCulloch, *Sons of the Mountains*, p.31.

crown by sending their sons to fight for the King. Archibald MacDonald volunteered from his cell in Edinburgh Castle where he had been imprisoned since taking part in the rebellion. Lord Beauclerk, the Commander in Chief in Scotland, supported his application stating: 'it were right that he, and some other of his tribe, were so employed to scalp and have their chance of being scalped…. so as not to be a mere burden for life upon the Government'.[37]

Barrington, as Secretary at War, did not approve of the conscription acts and felt that these sorts of recruits were not suitable for the army. In 1759 he wrote: 'I can not advise a recruiting Bill this session, Those Bills always produce trouble & tyranny in the country. Those pass'd in 1757 and 1758 produced little more than 200 men each year & in all probability produce fewer this'.[38] Although his numbers seem small compared to contemporary accounts, it is possible he was playing down the number of recruits these Acts produced in order to prevent a further Bill being extended. What does come across in his writing, and those of contemporary military commanders, is that the men recruited through conscription did not make good soldiers and were generally the first to be dismissed when peace was concluded. The core of the army throughout this period consisted of willing volunteers, which was, as we shall see, essential to its success.

The System of Drafts

Whilst direct recruiting was the most obvious way to bring a regiment up to fighting strength, another system existed known as drafting. In these cases, an understrength regiment that was due to be posted overseas might receive drafts of men from other regiments in order to bring it up to strength. For example, the 44th and 48th Foot received drafts from the other regiments stationed in Ireland before departing for America in 1755. The draft system was unpopular amongst the other regimental colonels, as it often resulted in them losing their best men along with their uniforms and equipment!

To begin with, regiments staying at home that had been asked to provide drafts would, not surprisingly, offer their worst recruits, the troublemakers, awkward marchers and so on, in an effort to retain their best troops. The War Office quickly identified this dodge and gave permission for the regiment which was due to receive the drafts to choose the men they wanted from the home regiment when it was on parade. As a result, regiments often lost their best troops to the draft and were sometime denuded of good men altogether. In Nov 1760, for example, the 93rd Foot lost 109 of its best men to a draft and in Feb 1761 lost another 109. The lieutenant colonel stated that this draft, along with natural wastage, 'tore the regt to pieces'.[39] In March the 93rd lost a further 297 men so that by April they could only muster 188 rank and file of whom 45 were recorded as sick.

---

37 McCulloch, *Sons of the Mountains*, p.24.
38 Hayter (ed.), *Eighteenth Century Secretary at War*, p.54.
39 Guy (ed.), *Colonel Samuel Bagshawe*, p.203.

Soldiers lost to the draft took all of their uniform and kit with them. This represented a substantial financial loss to the regiment, who often had to apply to the War Office, or to the regiment that was receiving the draft, for recompense. This money was slow to arrive, if it arrived at all, and left the Regiment out of pocket. As Colonel Bagshawe of the 95th complained:

> [T]he cloathing detained by those regiments with the drafts may be returned, or a sufficient recompense made for such cloathing and that the debts of the drafts may be paid, or that your excellencys will be pleased to consider in what manner the Captains of the 93rd may be indemnified as it is a loss they cannot well sustain…[40]

Finally, officers drafted with their men could often find themselves at a financial disadvantage as well. Some might find that commissions in the regiment they were drafted to were worth less than they had paid for a commission in their original regiment. For example, one officer of the Royal Fusiliers wrote a furious letter to the War Office when he, having paid £1,000 for his commission, found himself drafted into a younger regiment,[41] whilst 2nd Lieutenants from the same Fusilier Regiment found they had become Ensigns, a commission worth much less both to buy initially and in daily wages.

Unpopular or not, the draft system was practised throughout the eighteenth century as a quick and easy way of bringing a battalion up to strength before it was sent overseas, despite the harm it did to those regiments who had to provide the drafts.

Deserters

There is a view that life in most 18th-century European armies was extremely harsh and as a result desertion was very high. This is certainly true of armies that employed conscription, such as the Prussian army, with Regiment Jung-Braunschweig Nr.39 losing 1,650 men to desertion during the course of the Seven Years War, which was more than its entire complement![42]

However, desertion was not as serious an issue for the British army. In 1758, at the height of the Seven Years War, only 3.9 percent of men stationed at home deserted the colours. This compares favourably with the (admittedly much larger) French army where, on average, 20 percent of troops deserted every year. Between 1756 and 1762 just under 2,000 men deserted in America, during one of the harshest and most bitterly fought campaigns of the war, which still represents only 4.5 percent of the total number of troops deployed there. The British army, it appears, did not suffer from the high desertion

---

40   Guy (ed.), *Colonel Samuel Bagshawe*, p.236: Col. Bagshawe to the Lord Justice General and General Governors of Ireland 21st April 1761.

41   C.T. Atkinson, 'The Army under the early Hanoverians: More gleanings from W.O.IV and other sources in the public records office', *Journal of the Society for Army Historical Research*, Vol.21, No.83 (Autumn, 1942), p.3.

42   Christopher Duffy, *The Army of Frederick the Great* (Newton Abbott: David and Charles, 1974), p.67.

rates that plagued many other European armies at the time. However, it is true to say that desertions did occur, although a close examination of the records left by absconders shows that low pay, hard living, or harsh discipline were not the main reasons given for deserting.

If a man was going to desert the colours he generally did so soon after joining, usually when he sobered up and the reality of military life dawned on him. Those who had no friends or family to pay back their bounty, or had no contacts in high places that could intercede for them, were usually left with no choice. As discussed above, deserting was often not very difficult, as not all the recruits could be guarded day and night during their return trip to the regiment and most were placed solely on their honour not to abscond. For example, Lieutenant Francis Flood complained that Thomas Carroll and Pat Higgins had escaped from his recruiting party in Ballinakill in Ireland: 'I can assure you I gave each of the deserters two guineas as they were really fine fellows'.[43] There also appear to have been those who took the recruiting sergeant's bounty with the sole intention of deserting as soon as possible afterwards. The *Belfast Newsletter* reported that Henry McCarland allegedly went to Coleraine 'on purpose to cheat the recruiting party there' by taking his enlistment money and then absconding.[44] Indeed, there are a number of cases of individuals being serial deserters. Peter Henly, if he is to be believed, deserted from seven British regiments, three times from the marines, twice from the Royal Navy and once from the Dutch East India Company! On the sole occasion he was caught, whilst deserting the 60th Foot, he was brought back and received 200 lashes but successfully deserted again soon after.[45] In 1763, Daniel McLean claimed he had 'enlisted in most of his Majestys regiments both on the British and Irish Establishments and deserted them all'.[46]

Once the recruit made it to his regiment, was sworn in, issued his uniform and had begun his military life, the likelihood of him deserting was actually much reduced. However, there were still many reasons why a man would desert. Some soldiers left because they had a sense of grievance against the regiment, or they received harsh treatment at the hands of a particular officer or NCO. Corporal James Hardy, for example, deserted two days after being court martialled and reduced to the ranks.[47] Just as many left because they had a wife or family that were being left behind when the regiment was being posted overseas, or for other similar family reasons. In March 1762, Lieutenant Flood of the 93rd Regiment was arrested having been absent from his post as he had gone to see his wife who at that time was very ill.[48] There were also some rather more unusual deserters. Private Thomas Watson was encouraged by his own officers to desert, as he was a Quaker and they were afraid that his pacifist beliefs were having undue influence on his fellow

---

43 Guy (ed.), *Colonel Samuel Bagshawe*, p.215.
44 Neal Garnham, 'Military Desertion and Deserters in Eighteenth-Century Ireland', *Eighteenth-Century Ireland / Iris an dá chultúr*: Vol. 20 (2005), p.93.
45 Berkovich, *Motivation in War*, p.64.
46 Garnham, 'Military Desertion and Deserters in Eighteenth-Century Ireland', p.93.
47 Cormack and Jones (eds), *Journal of Corporal Todd*, p.319.
48 Guy (ed.), *Colonel Samuel Bagshawe*, p.258.

soldiers. As he did not drink and was well-behaved, they could not court martial him and instead allowed him to quietly desert with their blessing.[49] In 1762 an angry crowd attacked a recruiting party of the 62nd Foot in Carrickfergus, Northern Ireland, and forcibly liberated a recruit, which is probably the only recorded time that a soldier deserted against his will.

A significant cause for desertion was news that the regiment was being posted to the colonies. Most men expected to go to Europe to fight the French and the idea of going on campaign per se did not seem to cause many desertions. However, being posted to an overseas colony involved a lengthy sea journey in insanitary conditions, after which the men would land in hot climates where they generally died in droves from disease. To many, a posting to the colonies was practically a death sentence and there was a corresponding jump in desertions as soon as the regiment's destination was announced. In 1754, for example, drafts were ordered: 'to fill up Collonel Adlercorns regiment to 800 strong, who is ordered for the East Indies. Numbers of the Draughts diserted before they Embarked'.[50] It was the threat of an overseas posting that caused the biggest single instance of desertion in the British army. In 1743 the Black Watch, at that time numbered the 43rd Foot, was stationed in London awaiting deployment to Flanders. However, a false rumour spread amongst the men that their destination was actually the West Indies, which caused consternation in the ranks, and overnight two corporals, one piper and 190 private men deserted. All the men were recaptured and condemned to death, although this punishment was rescinded for all except Corporals Malcolm and Samuel McPherson, and Private Farquhar Shaw, who were considered to be the ringleaders and executed. Ironically, 38 of those men who were pardoned were removed from the Black Watch and sent to join regiments that were being posted to overseas colonies.[51]

Men deserting when their posting was made known became such a problem that regiments were often not told their destination until they were camped and under guard in a secure location from which desertion could be prevented. One such example occurred in March 1756 when Corporal William Todd 'was ordered upon command with 4 men to conduct a deserter to the Savoy in London & soon after I went with another to the same place where there is upwards of 8 hundred confin'd bound for the Indies etc'.[52]

If a soldier wanted to desert it was relatively easy to do so. The billeting in small groups in inns or on the local populace rather than in barracks, allowed a soldier simply to walk away at a time that suited him. Most attempted to do so in civilian clothes so as not to draw attention to themselves, with some even going in disguise. Corporal William Harris, for example, who deserted the Carrickfergus Garrison in 1759 was 'supposed to be travelling in women's apparel'.[53] The regiment did make some efforts to recover deserters. If an initial search of the area did not recover him, announcements could be made

---

49 Berkovich, *Motivation in War*, p.64.
50 Cormack and Jones (eds), *Journal of Corporal Todd*, p.10.
51 McCulloch, *Sons of the Mountains*, p.107.
52 Cormack and Jones (eds), *Journal of Corporal Todd*, p.14.
53 Garnham, 'Military Desertion and Deserters in Eighteenth-Century Ireland', p.95.

in the town square or from the church pulpit, adverts taken out in local papers or handbills produced and rewards offered for anyone passing information that led to his arrest. These would often provide some descriptive details of the deserter to help the populace identify him. For example, deserter James McHatten was described as having a 'clownish stoop' whilst Ambrose McLivany had 'remarkable black teeth'. Barnett Blake, we are informed, was prone to 'turn out his toes very much in walking' whilst Patrick Hughes had a 'remarkable cut' on his head that would 'probably find him out'. How anyone is expected to recognise Ambrose McKeown is less clear, however, as he is simply described as having 'much the appearance of a blackguard'.[54]

Between 1756 and 1762 there were only 455 court martials for desertion amongst the home battalions, which suggests that most deserters got away. However, it is possible that the figures for men recaptured are skewed, as they might not always have been dealt with by way of court martial. The recognised penalty for desertion was death, which would generally have to be the sentence if the case were referred to a court martial, and so instead the deserter was charged with being absent without leave and dealt with by a Regimental Court Martial. This often suited the colonel, as the formation of a General Courts Martial was not only troublesome but also embarrassing for the regiment. In some cases, if the regiment was based in England, the punishment was often reduced or overlooked altogether, especially if there were mitigating circumstances. If it was believed that the man had reason to desert, to see sick relatives or to provide for family, the Army was not without sympathy. For example, John Downs and John Grace were deserters from the 69th Foot who were captured and detained in the goal in Haverfordwest. The Secretary at War wrote to the local Justice of the Peace to let him know that a party of the 69th was currently in Gloucester and asked the Justice to:

> [A]cquaint them that in case they join the party at that place there is great reason to believe that their desertion may be pardoned. I must likewise beg that you will be pleased to advance each of these men 7s to carry them to Gloucester...[55]

An analysis of the statistics for the period suggests that as many as 60 percent of cases where the deserter was caught either went unpunished or had a substantially reduced sentence, probably because they were dealt with at a regimental level.[56]

Of those who were tried and found guilty by court martial, most were sentenced to death, as this was the legislated punishment for the offence. However, all sentences of death had to be placed before the King to be ratified. At this point, regiments would take the opportunity to mitigate for the defendant, stating his previous good conduct, bravery in battle, youth or just plain stupidity. For example, the court martial of William Manning

---

54   All examples from Garnham, 'Military Desertion and Deserters in Eighteenth-Century Ireland', p.95.
55   Hayter (ed.), *Eighteenth Century Secretary at War*, p.35.
56   Berkovich, *Motivation in War*, p.74.

suggested clemency as he 'is sometimes crazy'.[57] The King could then choose to reduce the sentence to corporal punishment or even to pardon the defendant, which appears to have happened in over half the cases the King examined.

When on campaign, however, desertion was more often than not punished by death as an example had to be made of those deserting in the face of the enemy. This would be by hanging and was generally carried out in front of the regiment. However, even in these cases senior officers were loath to pass a death sentence unless absolutely necessary. A good example of this can be seen in the letters of Major General Jeffery Amherst who had to order the death of a deserter in June 1759. In his order to the duty officer, Colonel Montgomery, he stated that: 'the sentence to be put in execution before Colonel Fitchs regiment. I hope in God this is the last example of this kind that I shall be forced to make & that I shall never send you again on so disagreeable a service'.[58]

Although the British Army did suffer from desertion, the numbers were very low compared to other contemporary European armies. When the men did desert, it was usually for reasons unconnected to their pay and living conditions and was more often for personal reasons, such as family needs or disagreements with officers. The most common cause of desertion was knowledge of a potential deployment to the colonies, but, even then, numbers were few. When caught, deserters were not always executed out of hand and more often than not their sentence was reduced or they were pardoned altogether. The fact that desertion was not a significant problem for the British Army reinforces the view that this was a volunteer force whose ranks were filled with men who wanted to be there.

---

57   Berkovich, *Motivation in War*, p.134.
58   Richard Middleton (ed.), *Amherst and the Conquest of Canada: Selected papers from the Correspondence of Major-General Jeffrey Amherst 1758-1760* (Stroud: Sutton Publishing Limited 2003), p.68.

3

Gone for a Soldier

Barracks and Billets

Having joined his regiment, the new recruit would now begin his life in the military.

The first thing he would be allocated would be his billet. As the Army in Ireland was permanently established, barracks had been built to accommodate them. However, in the rest of Britain purpose-built barracks were hard to find. Since Parliament believed the Army to be a temporary institution it did not vote the necessary money required to build permanent barracks to house them. Instead, the regiments were moved around the country, spending no more than a couple of months in any one location, and were billeted on the local populace.

The Mutiny Act, passed in 1689, prohibited the quartering of soldiers in Private Houses unless the owner consented. 'Private Houses' were defined as any building other than victualing houses, houses of public entertainment, and houses in which wine or liquor was sold.

This meant that the regiment was broken down into its constituent companies and squadrons and billeted in public houses and inns in the local area. Initially, this was done on an ad hoc basis, with the regimental quartermaster approaching a local magistrate who could decide which premises were to be used and raising an order permitting the soldiers to do so. The quartermaster would then march the said number of men round to the premises to speak to the licensee, who would have to house the men or face prosecution. In 1756, the War Office asked the Excise Office to compile a list of all the market towns and villages across the country and provide an account for each of 'the number of beds, and stable room for horses which the Publick Houses and Inns within their sundry districts can… accommodate guests… by which means the Troops may be more commodiously Quartered'.[1] By using this list the War Office were able to order regiments to particular areas and then identify the premises in which they were to stay. This aimed

---
1 Hayter (ed.), *Eighteenth Century Secretary at War*, p.223.

to share the burden amongst the various public houses and ensure no one premises was used too often.

The innkeepers would be paid by the regimental agent, or the quartermaster, for the soldiers' food and lodgings during their stay. The cost of accommodation and subsistence had been allowed for in the yearly cost of the regiment, calculated by the War Office and approved by Parliament. Rates to be paid to innkeepers were listed in the Mutiny Act. The daily payment for 'diet and small beer' was 4d, for a dragoon it was 6d whilst a further 6d was allowed for hay and straw for the dragoons' horse. In 1756, for example, there is a parish record showing that 'innholders and other public house-keepers in Hertford, Ware and Hoddesdon' were supplied with £1,600 to be distributed 'in proportion… to the several numbers of soldiers quartered on them respectively'.[2] Soldiers were spread out as much as possible so as not to unduly effect any one business. When a detachment of the Royal Horse Guards were quartered in Nottingham, for example, the 97 men were distributed between 30 public houses, with the most men in one place being six and the average three.[3]

However, innkeepers did not like having soldiers billeted on them. The money paid by the regiment for the subsistence of soldiers quartered in inns and alehouses was deemed insufficient in 1689 when the Mutiny Act was passed and it only became more so as the cost of food and supplies began to rise after the middle of the century. The Bishop of Bath and Wells petitioned the War Office on behalf of the town of Bath, stating, 'several innkeepers have been forced to leave their businesses and shut up their houses' as the inhabitants would not frequent Inns where the soldiers were billeted whilst the Innkeepers received insufficient recompense from the regiment for their keep. He asked that the town 'be excused at any rate for a time from quartering any more' as they have been 'overburdened for several years past'.[4]

As a result, owners of licensed premises began to refuse to have soldiers billeted on them. The orders of the magistrates then had to be enforced by the local constables, who were allowed to claim back any expenses they incurred during the course of this duty. Hence, in January 1754, there is a record of the Constables in Manchester receiving one shilling expenses for 'quartering soldiers…Hay very dear and Landlords extremely troublesome'.[5] In Leicester, in 1756, a warrant was issued for the owner of 'the White Horse who refused to receive three soldiers Billeted on him by Mr Mayor' whilst in 1758 a woman in Manchester received a summons 'for refusing a billet'.[6] Some towns were asked to billet soldiers only on an occasional basis, whilst others were regularly used. Guildford, for example, was centrally placed between London, Portsmouth and a permanent barracks at Chatham and had a constant stream of soldiers, marines, sailors, camp followers, sick and wounded passing through it. As a result, the local people petitioned the

---

2   Screen, 'Eighteenth Century Army at Home', p.219.
3   Screen, 'Eighteenth Century Army at Home', p.222.
4   C.R.B. Barrett, *The 7th Queen's Own Hussars* (London: Leonaur Ltd, 2008) Vol.I, p.101.
5   Screen, 'Eighteenth Century Army at Home', p.221.
6   Screen, 'Eighteenth Century Army at Home', p.219.

Government to have a barracks built in their town as the constant billeting of soldiers was ruining their business. In their petition they stated that of the 27 publicans in the town, 15 had gone out of business in the previous three or four years due to debts incurred from billeting soldiers.

When posted to Ireland, the soldiers tended to stay in purpose-built barracks or in garrison in places like Dublin Castle. This was as a result of an act passed in 1707 that permitted no quarters to be provided in private homes or inns except for parties of soldiers on the march, in a seaport awaiting transportation, or in an emergency. This rule was flexible, as, in 1725, we find the Corporation of Kinsale, whose members were all Protestant, agreeing to provide quarters for soldiers 'in the public houses and houses inhabited by Papists'.[7]

Troops were often moved to Ireland before onward transportation to the colonies or to Europe, and so billeting on local people did occur as these troops were both 'on the march' and often 'in a seaport awaiting transportation'. However, as this was not a common occurrence, the soldiers were not always unwelcome. Sergeant Thompson of the 78th Highlanders records that when they arrived in the town of Donaghadee, near Belfast, in 1757, he noted it: 'had only one principal street, it was supposed there would not be accommodation for us all'. However, he soon found that the population began to argue about who should be allowed to house the troops, with those not being given soldiers to look after feeling very hard done by. Thompson was getting settled in his billet when he heard an argument between his new landlord and another resident: 'I overheard a female voice saying "You have got upwards of twenty of the Scotch soldiers to your share and I have not been able to get one; this is treating me very ill"'.[8] This lady insisted on two soldiers going to her house next door to be quartered.

Postings in Lowland Scotland, especially in Glasgow or Edinburgh, were not considered too bad, but postings in the Highlands were not at all popular. The troops were often housed in cold and ill-maintained barracks and castles, far from urban centres and with little to do. In 1745, Captain Martin, who was resident at Fort William on the north west coast of Scotland, near Ben Nevis, expressed a view held by many: 'we are miserable, ill lodged and ill fed. No fire or provisions…No books and so raining for 40 days I have been here – not one dry'.[9]

Moving between Billets

The troops were moved from their lodgings every couple of months so as not to overburden one area. For example, on th18 September 1751, the 7th Dragoons were posted 'two troops to Shrewsbury and one each to Stafford, Burton-on-Trent, Walsall and Ashburn'. On 10 October they were moved,

---

7   Screen, 'Eighteenth Century Army at Home', p.219.
8   McCulloch, *Sons of the Mountains*, p.36.
9   Rex Whitworth (ed.), *Gunner at Large: The Diary of James Wood RA 1746-1765* (London: Leo Cooper 1988), p.72.

with 'four troops at Worcester and one each at Pershore and Bromsgrove'. They were then moved to Birmingham on 2 November to be reviewed after which they returned to 'Shrewsbury, Stafford, Burton-on-Trent and Walsall' with the Ashburn troop remaining in Birmingham. They remained in these quarters until the end of February 1752.[10] Soldiers could be moved from their lodgings more often in certain circumstances. It was deemed prudent, for example, to remove troops from towns where fairs, horse races or circuses were due to take place, to 'prevent accidents which probably would otherwise happen from Riotts & Drunkeness generally attending fairs'.[11] An Act of Parliament forbade troops to be garrisoned in a borough where an election was due to take place, in case anyone alleged that the presence of the military influenced the result, which also applied to any town holding Assizes for the same reason.

When a regiment was required to move to its next billets, local magistrates were expected to raise the funds for wagons to help transport the regiment's equipment and belongings. The magistrate would then send the constable to find local people willing to rent their wagons for use by the army. One such order from a Nottingham magistrate to the constable made in 1742 commanded him:

> [T]o cause one cart with four able horses and ropes to be at the old town hall by four of the clock tomorrow morning to take up part of the baggage belonging to Brigadier General Braggs regiment of foot and carry it to Derby. Hereof fail not at your peril.[12]

The costs for this undertaking were paid to the contractor and reclaimed by the magistrate from the regiment or the War Office. The tariff for England and Wales was laid down in the Mutiny Act and is listed as 9d per mile for a cart and four horses. This was considered inadequate by mid-1750s and local authorities had to make up the difference out of the rates, which the Mutiny Act provided for. Payment in Scotland was 3s per two miles per man and horse. In Ireland the rates were 1 or 2d, depending on the size of vehicle, per mile but this was raised to 3d in 1729. If transport was not forthcoming, wagons could be pressed into service, but this was avoided if at all possible, so as not to antagonise the local people.

Pay and Conditions

A soldier was generally paid his wages in cash, although how often he was paid depended on circumstances. If he was posted to a remote location, his pay might take longer to reach him than if he were near an urban centre, and he could wait a considerable amount of time if he were posted overseas. Infantry soldiers were paid 8d per day with cavalry soldiers being paid

---

10 Barrett, *7th Queen's Own Hussars*, p.167.
11 Hayter (ed.), *Eighteenth Century Secretary at War*, p.219.
12 Screen, 'Eighteenth Century Army at Home', p.224.

slightly more. Of this, the first 2d was classed as 'off reckoning' and went to pay off the soldier's debt to the regiment, which usually involved paying back the cost of his uniform. It was very rare for soldiers to ever completely pay back this debt, as they were encouraged to buy new shirts or replacement items from the regiment and to simply have them added to their debt, whilst the annual reissue of clothing meant that those who had managed to pay off their arrears found themselves back in debt again. The remaining 6d went toward the soldier's keep and was considered subsistence money. From the weekly subsistence money, the Captain of the company was allowed to deduct sixpence for: 'shoes, stockings, gayters, medicines, shaving, mending of arms',[13] and other necessaries supplied by the army. When in barracks or living under canvas, the soldier was entitled to receive one pound of bread, or the equivalent in flour to make his own, and either one pound of beef or nine ounces of pork every day. This might be supplemented with additional items such as butter or cheese. Soldiers might also be issued an allowance of rum or beer depending on their posting. It was not always possible to issue this food directly, such as when the men were on transport ships, and, sometimes, meals were provided on board ship or at the inn were the men were billeted instead. In this case, further deductions were made from their pay to cover this cost.

Soldiers often used their remaining cash to supplement their diet with locally purchased food. The cost varied depending on demand and where the men were posted in the country. Those posted to rural communities or coastal towns and villages found that they could easily supplement their rations, whereas those closer to urban centres, or held in camp awaiting deployment, found supplies reduced and prices higher. For example, when Corporal Todd was posted to Limerick in 1750, he recorded that 'Salmon is very cheap and the other provisions very reasonable' whereas when he was posted to Canterbury in 1756 he found 'everything is unreasonable dear… Potatoes is 3 1/2d per pound…men live very hard'.[14]

Food was usually cooked communally, with the men in a billet sharing their allowances to make it go further. Often the cooking was undertaken by one of the soldiers' wives who lived with the men in the same billet. If the soldiers were billeted on private houses, as they sometimes were in Ireland and very often had to be when on campaign, they would give their daily food allowance to their host, who would cook it for them and the host family as well. Sergeant Stevenson gave his allowance to his host when billeted on a family in Ireland who had six children to feed on only 10d a day. His host was astonished to see how generous the allowance of food was for each soldier compared to what he and his family had to get by on.[15] Equally, Corporal Todd gave his issue white bread to his host family whilst posted in Germany and ate their local black bread as the children thought white bread to be a luxury. He remembered:

---

13 Reid, *British Redcoat 1740-93*, p.8.
14 Cormack and Jones (eds), *Journal of Corporal Todd*, pp.3 & 17.
15 Berkovich, *Motivation in War*, p.159.

The poor children of my Ospass [host] running about me crying out "Weiss Brod (white bread) Corporal"… I took my knife & cut the loaf all a' pieces & divided it amongst them, but my Ospass & Frow would a'had me to a'kept some for myself, but I told them I could eat their bread very well & therefore the Children should have mine.[16]

Any cash remaining after food and necessities were taken care of was often spent on alcohol. Where possible, the men were given their subsistence money daily by their sergeant of corporal to prevent them blowing a whole week's allowance on one night out!

The Daily Grind

The day generally began as it ended, with a parade and a roll call. The first order of the day, especially if war was on the horizon, would then be to teach the men their drill and the handling of their weapons. Even veteran troops appear to have been put through their paces in order to make the response to the word of command second nature to the men. Corporal Todd recorded just such an early start in 1761:

> At half an Hour after 5 o'clock in the morning we peraded & fell into the ranks… we march'd off to the field of exercise were we went through the firings and the different evolutions…We march'd back to the perade about 11 o'clock & was dismiss'd to return to our quarters.[17]

Drill would not go on all day, unless the men were very new recruits or were being punished for some reason. Lieutenant Colonel Windus wrote to his commanding officer in 1760 outlining the need to provide extra drill for his men, especially those he felt were malingering:

> We go on very well with our drilling, twice a day and the very awkward are out 3 times a day…all malingerers or any who misbehave…are confin'd & exercised 3 times a day, kept on half diet, washed & kept clean & made Sick of the Hospital not Sick *in* the Hospital.[18]

When it came to the cavalry, the drill regime was not as harsh, with much of the training time spent teaching the men to ride and to look after their mounts. To achieve this, many of the troopers were trained to ride by a Riding Master employed specifically for the purpose. In 1746, both Richs 4th Dragoons and Cope's 7th Dragoons show riding masters on their regimental

---

16 Cormack and Jones (eds), *Journal of Corporal Todd*, p.253.
17 Cormack and Jones (eds), *Journal of Corporal Todd*, p.133.
18 Guy (ed.), *Colonel Samuel Bagshawe*, p.226.

returns whilst Lord Stair's 2nd Dragoons showed a 1d stoppage from the troopers' wages to cover the costs of a riding master.[19]

Once they had paraded, drilled, and cleaned their equipment to their NCOs' satisfaction, much of the rest of the day was the men's own. For some, this free time was an opportunity to earn a little extra cash. Musicians could give local performances, men from the artillery organised firework displays, and even the pioneers could earn money by cutting and collecting firewood for the men and officers. Those with a trade could practise it to earn money, either from the other men in the regiment or from local people, with tailors, cobblers, and barbers in high demand. Those who could read and write could help with the regimental paperwork, or find work locally teaching children as Corporal Todd did when he was posted in Ireland. His commanding officer was approached by Madam Castleton of Ballyhack, who required a teacher for the school in her town and heard that one of the soldiers could read and write. With his commanders permission, Todd spent his free time holding classes and 'had 22 scholars the first day & every day they increasing until I had 38 great and small & many of them paid weekly so that I liv'd well'.[20]

However, just as often, the men could find little to entertain them locally and spent this free time in idleness. Not surprisingly, the combination of bored soldiers and the easy availability of alcohol in their lodgings often led to trouble, with drunken fights, damage, and riotous behaviour regularly reported. Leicester Quarter Sessions contained cases of profane swearing by soldiers and also cases of soldiers fathering illegitimate children and refusing a monetary surety. The Convention of the Royal Burghs of Scotland made representations in July 1739 about a riot committed at Linlithgow over two days 'by some of the souldiers of Briggadeer Barrells regiment'.[21] In 1755 the Council of Cork asked for Fowke's 2nd Foot to be removed from the city because of a 'terrible affray…in which two soldiers were greatly wounded and one townsman killed on the spot and several others desperately cut and a very ill blood has been bred between the soldiers and the townspeople'.[22]

Bored soldiers also got up to mischief, which did little to endear them to the local populace. A Mr Legge wrote to the War Office to complain about Sergeant John Mills who fished trout from a stream without permission and, when challenged, said: 'he was the Kings servant & I was no more & that he would go a fishing & sporting wherever he pleas'd'.[23] Poaching, however, was not the worst offence bored soldiers committed. A letter from the War Office to George Stone, an innkeeper from Cobham in Surrey, in 1756, had to include: 'Forty seven pounds to make good the loss you sustained by having your apartment blown up by the Light Dragoon[s]'![24]

---

19 Sumner, Percy, 'Uniforms and Equipment of Cavalry Regiments from 1684 to 1811', *Journal of the Society for Army Historical Research* Vol.14, No.55 (Autumn, 1935), p.99.
20 Cormack and Jones (eds), *Journal of Corporal Todd*, p.11.
21 Both from Screen, 'Eighteenth Century Army at Home', p.226.
22 Screen, 'Eighteenth Century Army at Home', p.227.
23 Hayter (ed.), *Eighteenth Century Secretary at War*, p.228.
24 Hayter (ed.), *Eighteenth Century Secretary at War*, p.227.

THE ARMY OF GEORGE II

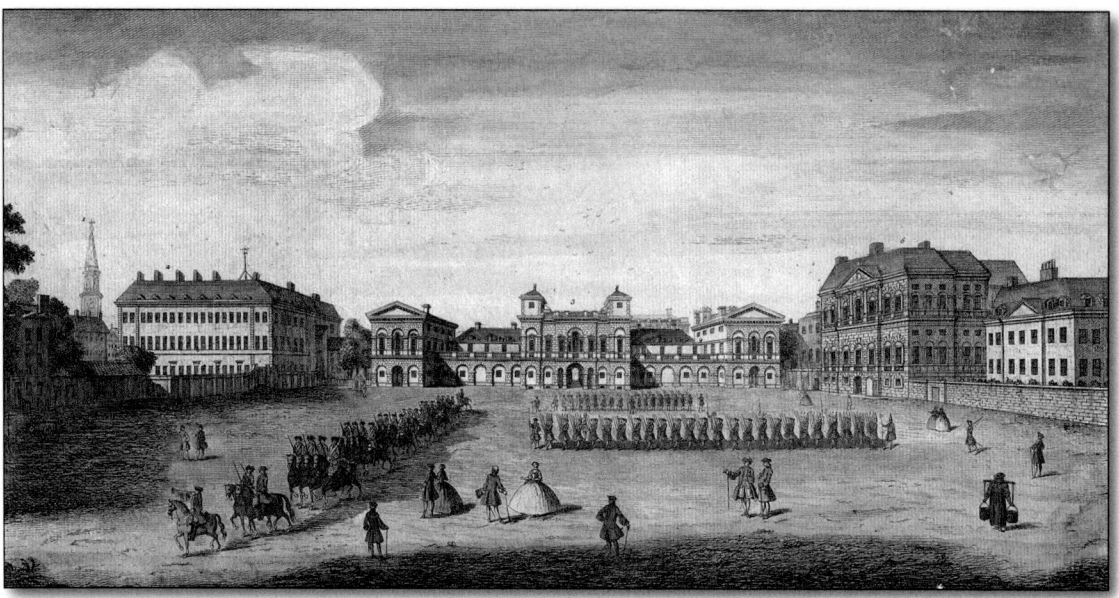

'A perspective view of the parade in St. James's Park'; note the grenadiers on either flank of the infantry formation. Engraving by and after John Maurer. (Anne S.K. Brown Collection)

Reviews

The practice of dispersing the soldiers of a regiment to billets in different locations made it difficult for the men to drill as a complete company, and it was extremely rare for them to drill together as a regiment. The War Office recognised that extended periods of inactivity or lack of meaningful drill would make the regiments ineffective when the time came for them to march to war. To ensure that they were fit for purpose, the King proposed that they be regularly reviewed. These were essentially tests, where the regiment would come together and parade before an appointed general officer who in turn would ensure that they were trained and could perform their drill to the required standard. The instructions to the general officer from the War Office were clear:

> [T]hat you do cause them to Pass in Review before you, and take an exact account of their numbers, with the goodness, size, age and make of their men and horses, the condition of the clothing, accoutrements and horse furniture…that you cause the Division or troop to be exercised before you and carefully observe whether the officers as well as the serjeants and private men are perfect in the manual and evolutions according to our book of exercise… and this service being performed you are to make a just an impartial report in writing…[25]

The then-Lieutenant Colonel Humphrey Bland had published *A Treatise of Military Discipline* in 1727, which outlined all of the exercises that should be undertaken by both horse and foot and this was widely used as a drill book by officers throughout this period. Both infantry and cavalry regiments were

---

25   Hayter (ed.), *Eighteenth Century Secretary at War*, pp.114-116.

1745 Bayonet Drill, with the musket being used to thrust like a pike. Etching by and after William Baillie. (Anne S.K. Brown Collection)

expected to perform their drills and manoeuvres, changing formation from column of march into a battle line, advancing and retiring in front of the enemy, and so on. Drill manuals such as Kane's *System of Military Discipline for a Battalion of Foot* gave the army guidance as to the orders that were to be given and the various evolutions the infantry were expected to perform. Infantry officers shouted out their orders, which were then followed by a drumbeat that corresponded to that order. Each command, be it 'Bayonets to be fixed', 'Shoulder', 'Take post in battalion', 'First caution', 'Recover your arms', 'to the Right-about', and so on, were expected to be carried out competently by the regiment under the watchful eye of the reviewing officer.

Whilst marching, changing formation, and deploying into battle lines was extremely important for the infantry, the real focus was on firing as this was deemed to be a battle-winner. During the War of the Spanish Succession, the Duke of Marlborough had adopted the Dutch system of platoon firing, whereby the battalion was divided into 18 different sections, named platoons, placed alternately along the three ranks and who each fired in a proscribed sequence. This had the effect of creating a rolling fire along the line and proved most effective during Marlborough's wars. The Duke of Cumberland was a believer in this system and ordered all the infantry regiments to practise it. However, whilst the platoon firing system was undoubtedly effective it required constant drill and practise to get it right. Following their experiences during the War of the Austrian Succession, many British officers began to adopt a simpler system of firing, called the 'alternate fire' system. Instead of a complicated pattern of firing by platoons, alternate firing used the existing company as the designated firing unit. The company was numbered according to the sequence in which they should fire, either from right to left, or from the flanks to the centre, and each fired in turn. This was a much simpler system, as every soldier knew which company he was in and hence only had to remember the firing sequence. James Wolfe was a believer in the alternate fire system, writing: 'As the alternate fire by platoons…or by companies, is the most simple plain and easy and used by the best disciplined troops in Europe, we are at all times to imitate them in that respect'.[26]

Reviewing officers reported the adoption of the alternate fire system back to the Duke of Cumberland and he was clearly not impressed, putting his foot down in written orders dated 1757:

> I am surprised to hear that my orders as to the Fireing and Posting of the officers, approved and confirmed by his Majesty, are changed according to the whim & supposed improvements of every fertile genius; and therefore it is my positive order that …they conform exactly to those standing orders.[27]

Despite this, alternate firing persisted, with some regimental colonels keeping platoon firing for reviews whilst practising alternate firing on campaign. For example, prior to departure from the Isle of Wight for raids in France, Lieutenant General Mordaunt drilled his force in the alternate firing system, of which the Duke of Richmond wrote:

> General Mordaunt…has dared to follow common sense…He has abolished the manual exercise both old and new and draws up all the regiments as Kingsleys used to do, by companies with their own officers. This is truly great and you have no idea how much it has already improved the other regiments.[28]

The debate about the best firing system would continue throughout the period.

Cavalry reviews, it appears, were much simpler affairs. Whilst they would still be expected to deploy from march columns, wheeling each troop into its squadrons and then into line, the manual of exercise for the cavalry stated:

> [I]t is sufficient for them to ride well, to have their horses well managed and train'd up to stand fire…That they march and wheel with a grace and handle their swords well, which is the only weapon our British horse make use of when they charge the enemy; more than this is superfluous.[29]

Although they might not have had as much to do on the day as the infantry, the cavalry certainly had a good deal of preparation to undertake. Prior to a review on in October 1742, Lord Stair ordered:

---

26   David Blackmore, *Destructive and Formidable: British Infantry Firepower 1642-1765* (Barnsley: Frontline Books, 2014), p.122.
27   Blackmore, *Destructive and Formidable*, p.123.
28   Blackmore, *Destructive and Formidable*, pp.132-133.
29   Richard Kane, *A New System of Military Discipline for a Battalion of Foot* (Uckfield: The Naval and Military Press, 2012), p.110.

The Horse and Dragoons to take all their small accoutrements to pieces and see that they are very well cleaned and blacked, and then put them together again. The bosses, bits and curbs to be as bright as hands can make them. The boots to be as black as possible, and their knee pieces not to appear above three inches above the boot-top. All their arms to be as bright as silver. The whole buff accoutrements to be of one light buff colour, the swords to be all brightened. The hats new cocked. 3 straps to each cloak…Officers to wear their sashes over their shoulders.[30]

In 1726 there was a written request for more powder for Dragoon regiments for musketry practice: 'as their firing in the exercise is the same as the foots'[31]. It appears from this and other evidence that the Dragoons were expected to dismount and then go through the same firing drills as the infantry until quite late in the period, even though their battlefield role had actually moved away from that of mounted infantry.

The artillery were expected not only to deploy their guns expertly, but also to fire them efficiently and accurately. Gunner James Wood recorded being reviewed by the Duke of Cumberland on 28 May 1747, deploying eight short 6-pounders in support of four infantry regiments, which were also being put through their paces. During this review, Woods claims to have 'fired a short 6 pounder ten times in a minute'.[32] On 31 May the Duke returned and on this occasion the artillery fired at targets, alongside their Austrian counterparts. The targets were set at 800 yards and both Austrian and British teams fired two pieces of cannon. Woods records; 'The English knocked the target down the second fire; the Austrians fired but did not come up to us in firing…The Duke and the Prince of Hesse seemed very well pleased with the performance'.[33]

Not all reviews went well. If the men had not been doing their drill whilst dispersed in billets, or their officers had been slack at learning their manual of exercise, then things could easily go wrong. Kane wrote:

> I was once at a review when the commanding General of the Troops was reviewing a Regiment of foot, where were present the Colonel, Lieutenant Colonel, Major and most of all the Captains and yet not one of them capable of going through the discipline of the Regiment, of which the General, very justly took publick Notice.[34]

One description of a review which took place in Kilkenny in 1750, simply stated that it was so bad it 'would make a dog spew'.[35] Often the expectation to perform the firing drills quickly put undue pressure on the men, which could lead to accidents. Gunner Woods recorded one accident at a review in 1747:

---

30   Percy Sumner, 'Uniforms and Equipment of Cavalry Regiments from 1684 to 1811', *Journal of the Society for Army Historical Research* Vol.14, No.55 (Autumn, 1935), p.99.
31   Atkinson, 'The Army under the early Hanoverians', p.6.
32   Whitworth (ed.), *Gunner at Large*, p.40.
33   Whitworth (ed.), *Gunner at Large*, p.40.
34   Kane, *New System of Military Discipline*, p.115.
35   Garnham, 'Military Desertion and Deserters in Eighteenth-Century Ireland', p.91.

The Duke was reviewing some of the foot regiments and the gunner in ramming up the charge of one of the short sixes, it went off and blew off the arm that rammed home and the end of the ramrod struck a foot soldier in the head and killed him on the spot and wounded several others.[36]

After the review, the regiment would once again disperse to its billets. Going back to the 7th Dragoons, they were reviewed by Lieutenant General Campbell in Gloucester on 18 October 1750, after which they marched 'three troops to Worcester, one to Pershore and two to remain in Gloucester'.[37] On 13 April 1751 they were gathered at Gloucester, where Lieutenant General Onslow reviewed them before they were once again dispersed to new billets, and so it went on until such time as the regiment was deployed on active service.

Policing Actions

Although there were parish constables who enforced the rulings of local magistrates, there was no 'police force' in Britain to deal with more difficult public order situations that arose at the time. Throughout the reign of George II there were occasional crop failures, which in turn led to food shortages and riots. Disputes about working conditions and wages were also common, and this also led to riots and public disorder aimed at those seen to be the cause of the problem. There were widespread food riots in 1756 and 1757, for example, and further similar riots in 1766. As early as 1728, records show soldiers being sent to Lawfords Gate in Bristol and Bedminster to suppress 'tumultuous weavers and other persons'.[38] On 17 December, 1740, a troop of the 7th Dragoons was ordered to march immediately to Evesham 'to assist in putting down the riots in that neighbourhood'.[39]

Occasionally, soldiers present in a town would volunteer to assist the local magistrates if public disorder occurred. For example, three recruiting parties present in Nottingham in 1766 helped with the suppression of a riot that broke out during the course of a local fair.[40] However, the correct approach was for the local magistrate to write to the Secretary of State to officially request assistance. If the Secretary of State was satisfied as to the seriousness of the situation, he would write to the Secretary at War asking him to order troops to assist. The War Office would then approve the deployment of troops and send a message to the nearest regiment to turn out. When Viscount Barrington was Secretary at War, he ensured that this was strictly enforced, as the Kings enemies in Parliament would jump on any suggestion that the military was being used illegally to repress the people.

---

36 Whitworth (ed.), *Gunner at Large*, p.53.
37 Barrett, *7th Queen's Own Hussars*, p.166.
38 Barrett, *7th Queen's Own Hussars*, p.101.
39 Barrett, *7th Queen's Own Hussars*, p.107.
40 Screen, 'Eighteenth Century Army at Home', p.225.

Indeed, the Mayor of Cork complained to the Government in December, 1758, about Captain Robert Jephson, whom he had directed:

> [T]o give a detachment of soldiers to aid the civil officer in arresting some persons in the town of Cove, charged with felony, and who allegedly had refused to obey it, and in a very contumelious manner declared he would wipe his britch with twenty such orders.[41]

Although he was being a little overdramatic, Captain Jephson was quite correct, as he could not turn out his troops to arrest criminals or supress riots without the permission of the War Office. Not surprisingly, this created a huge delay, as it could take days for the request from the magistrates to reach London and then for the marching orders for the regiment to be conveyed to them and for the regiment, in turn, to travel to the place of the disturbance. As a result, many riots went unchecked and had often burned themselves out or had moved to a different area before troops arrived. For example, in 1740 in Newcastle-upon-Tyne there were extensive corn riots which raged around the city from the 7-25 June before they were brought under control, during which extensive damage had been done to buildings, public records had been burned, and over £1,800 worth of goods looted from shops.

In an attempt to offset this, orders to the troops became quite broad with regard to geographical areas and gave the commander some freedom to act on his initiative in case the rioters had moved on to a different parish. For example, the orders given to Lieutenant Colonel Harvey of the 6th Inniskilling Dragoons in August 1756, asked him to take three troops and to march with all haste to Leicester 'or to any other place or places as you shall be informed the rioters to be at' in order to assist the Magistrates in 'Suppressing any riots and disturbances that may happen and in apprehending the said Rioters'.[42]

The army was often also employed in support of the revenue men. One of the main losses to the coffers of the British Government was that lost in tax revenue as a result of smuggling. Smuggling goods, especially brandy, from France was big business, as import taxes were excessive and many people in coastal communities turned a blind eye to a trade that brought much-needed money into the local economy. Local revenue men were employed to patrol the coast, collect the tax revenue from imported goods, and to arrest anyone involved in smuggling. However, the smuggling gangs were usually more numerous and better armed than those sent to arrest them. Take the case of John Buckley, the Excise Officer of Hastings, who had apprehended a known smuggler named Stephen Bourner. In his report, Buckley states Bourner:

> [W]ho had been arrested and carried to the excise office, was rescued out of the hands of the said Buckley by the said smugglers [who were] enabled to carry off the prisoner, which they did in triumph, firing several pistols as they went along [before they] went in Triumph on board a Cutter and set sail for France.[43]

---

41   Screen, 'Eighteenth Century Army at Home', p.227.
42   Screen, 'Eighteenth Century Army at Home', p.227.
43   Hayter (ed.), *Eighteenth Century Secretary at War*, p.269.

Not surprisingly, regiments of infantry and cavalry were called upon to take their turn patrolling coastal areas to apprehend smugglers and to support the revenue men. They were usually deployed as a company or a troop to a particular location, although infantry could be scattered across an area in groups of 12 men, which were referred to as a 'corporal's guard'. This was the minimum number of soldiers expected to escort the revenue men about their business. Records for the Queen's Dragoons found them in November 1749, to be 'on the smuggling duty' whilst in 1751 the 6th Dragoons had three troops based in Colchester working against the smugglers, whilst the other three were in Kent on similar duty. Cavalry regiments were more likely to be assigned to anti-smuggling duty, as the horsemen could cover more ground in the pursuit of fugitives. Infantry were more likely to be used as a garrison in a peacekeeping or law enforcement capacity in towns or villages suspected of housing smugglers. For example, in 1760 troops were deployed to support the Revenue collector of the Loughrea district in Ireland, as he had been attacked by a mob whilst going about his duty. Later that year a number of corporal's guards were deployed in towns and villages along that part of the coast that were suspected of being involved in smuggling, such as Ballybay which was considered, 'a nest of lawless people'.[44]

In November, 1753, Corporal Todd was involved in a raid on a small settlement in County Kerry 'to take Murphy O'Sullivan, a great Smugler, who was outlaw'd by killing an Officer of the Custom, where by £500 was offered for the Apprehending & takeing him Dead or Alive'. Todd and his men surrounded the house O'Sullivan was in and called for him to surrender. Instead, O'Sullivan and his men fired on the soldiers and 'wounded two of our men out of the windows with blunderbusses'. The soldiers set fire to the house forcing the smugglers to make a run for it. The soldiers killed two as they tried to escape and then O'Sullivan 'came out last with a loaded blunderbuss & it missing fire we shott him dead at his door'.[45] Todd and his men recovered some silver spoons from the house which they divided amongst them and were further rewarded with £4 12s each reward money when they brought O'Sullivan's body back to Cork.

When working in these coastal communities, the soldiers did not always receive a warm welcome. Many people relied on smuggling to support their living and the soldiers were an obvious symbol of Government oppression. This situation was made worse when the soldiers were ordered to apprehend Naval deserters and escort them back to their ships, as these were often local men. When employed searching wagons leaving Portsmouth for contraband and deserters in 1745, Captain Bagshawe found himself 'been called Scoundral, villain, thief, told I should be broke like a Scoundral, challenged to fight, threatened to have my head broke, to be shook out of my laced cloaths, sticks lifted at me and attempts made to strike me' from a local population that did not appreciate his efforts. He elsewhere wrote that: 'when we take sailors to Portsmouth it is rather like conveying prisoners through an

---

44 Aaron Graham and Patrick Walsh (eds), *The British Fiscal-Military States, 1660-c.1783* (Oxford: Routledge: 2016), p.155.
45 Cormack and Jones (eds), *Journal of Corporal Todd*, pp.7-10.

enemies country…such numbers of sailors assemble to attack the guard and rescue their comrades'.[46]

Soldiers who fired on smugglers did not always find themselves supported by the law. In 1732 Excise Officers and the soldiers accompanying them were fired on at Macroom in County Cork, forcing the soldiers to return fire. Two of the 'assailants' were killed in the exchange but soon after two soldiers and an Excise man, one Hercules Harding, were arrested and placed before Cork assizes accused of murder. Although they were acquitted, it shows that soldiers could not act with impunity when on employed on policing actions[47].

Aboard Ship as Marines

Six infantry battalions, the 44th through to the 49th, had been raised as marines for the War of Jenkins Ear in 1739, and were subsequently joined by the 50th to 53rd, all of these regiments being dispersed to perform this duty around the fleet. In 1747, what remained of these men were transferred to the Admiralty and then disbanded in 1748. Although 50 new marine companies were raised in 1755, they remained under Admiralty control and did not appear on the Army musters. Despite having dedicated troops working as marines, they were never enough: regular infantry regiments were therefore expected, from time to time, to provide companies to serve aboard ship. Although the men could expect extra pay for undertaking this duty, this was not a popular posting. First of all, the men had to purchase items required for sea service, which included bedding, a canvas jacket, trousers, check shirts, a cloth cap, shoes, and linen, and to pay for packing costs. The extra stoppages from their wages to cover these costs could be as much as £2 9s 8d a man which is often much more than they could expect to make in extra pay. Additionally, soldiers did not enjoy life at sea and repeated posting to marine duties was the cause of much complaining to the War Office. The men would often be put under the command of naval officers, and the harsher discipline and more rigid rules aboard ship were often much worse than they were used to. It did not help that many men became very seasick. In 1757, having not long put out to sea, one soldier recorded: 'Serjeat Tongue & most of our Soldiers was very sick that they could not stand the deck but was oblig'd to lay in there hammock & could eat or drink nothing'.[48]

It was not all bad news, as the soldiers did get to see a bit of the world. In 1731, soldiers from Kirke's and Clayton's Regiments were required to 'serve on board the fleet in Mediterranean during summer'.[49] During this posting they were responsible for escorting the 15-year-old son of the King Philip of Spain, Don Carlos, to take possession of his new Duchy of Parma, which he had been awarded as part of the Treaty of Vienna. This no doubt provided a welcome interlude to an otherwise very dull posting.

---

46   Guy (ed.), *Colonel Samuel Bagshawe*, p.45.
47   Graham and Walsh (eds), *British Fiscal-Military States*, p.151.
48   Cormack and Jones (eds), *Journal of Corporal Todd*, p.27.
49   Atkinson, 'The Army under the early Hanoverians', p.145.

Promotion

Promotion from private to corporal and on to sergeant was achieved by serving your time, learning your trade, and waiting for the man in the rank above you to die, retire, or move on. When a vacancy did occur, the captain of the company would recommend his preferred choice of replacement to the colonel, who would usually confirm the appointment. In making his choice, the captain would look at the length of the man's service, his disciplinary record, and his ability to gain the respect of his peers (which would be crucial if he were to keep the men in line).

The only other means of promotion was by transfer. When a new battalion was being formed, as happened frequently in time of war, volunteers would be called for from experienced men in existing regiments. These generally had to be men of at least a years' experience: 'expert in their exercise, can read and write well, are sober and well behaved, strong and active and in every respect qualified to be Serjts or Corporals in the Regt'.[50] Selected privates would go to the new battalion as corporals, and existing corporals as sergeants. This provided a core of trained and experienced troops who could then drill the new recruits to get them to the required standard.

When the new Highland regiments were to be raised in 1757, the requirement was not just for experienced men. The Secretary at War wrote to the officer commanding the Foot Guards asking for 25 men who were ready to be sergeants 'who can speak the Highland language, ten of whom are to be turned over to Lieut Col Montgomery's battalion and the remaining fifteen to Lieut Col Frasers battalion…to be draughted of their own consent and approved of by the said Lieut Col appointed for that service'.[51] The same letter went out to eight other regiments, of which the 25th Foot provided 10, as did the 32nd, and the 26th nine with a total of 80 Gaelic speaking NCOs drafted from the nine foot regiments. This demonstrates just how many Gaelic speaking, or highland, Scots were already serving in the ranks of the 'English' and lowland Scottish regiments.

A Soldier's Life

During peacetime, the various regiments of the army were not overworked. Surviving records for the 16th Foot, between 1737 and 1743, shows that it spent 63 percent of its time dispersed in billets or marching between them. When it comes to other uses, 17 percent was spent in anti-smuggling operations and only two percent in riot control. Only 13 percent of its time was spent together as a complete regiment, probably at reviews, whilst five percent was spent working with other regiments at a higher level of organisation.[52]

---

50   Guy (ed.), *Colonel Samuel Bagshawe*, p.201.
51   McCulloch, *Sons of the Mountains*, p.25.
52   Summarised from Houlding, *Fit for Service*, pp.398-405.

The first thing this data demonstrates was that a soldier's life was not a particularly hard one, especially when compared to the daily life of other eighteenth century professions, such as that of a tin miner or farm labourer of the time. Soldiers spent much of their time in idleness, using their free time as they wished. Although pay was low, the men did not go without food or shelter, which is significant at a time when there were regular riots due to food shortages and when income from other forms of employment was uncertain or seasonal.

Secondly, the lifestyle the men lived contributed to a sense that they were set apart from society and that the regiment was their home. The men moved billet regularly and never settled for long in any one place, and when billeted in a new area the local population rarely welcomed them. Equally, when deployed to suppress a riot or to arrest smugglers and deserters, hostile locals saw them as the tools of a repressive Government. The soldier thus began to see himself as set aside from society with the regiment as the only permanency in his life. He spent the vast majority of his waking day in the fellowship of the other men of his company or troop, eating, sleeping and, when suppressing riots, fighting together. This created a bond between the men and a loyalty to the regiment, which, as we shall see, stood them in good stead when war finally came.

The attitude of the general public toward the common soldier during this period was ambivalent. On the one hand, their being constantly billeted on communities, or being used to suppress dissent or enforce unpopular tax laws, made them hated by the common man. John Hervey, First Earl of Bristol, a close confident of Queen Caroline and a noted political pamphleteer, wrote to King George II in 1735, stating:

> [T]here is nothing so odious to men of all ranks and classes in this country as troops; That people who had not sense enough to count up to twenty, or to articulate ten words together on other subjects had their lessons so well to heart that they could talk like Ciceros on this topic and never to an audience that did not chime in with their arguments.[53]

On the other hand, when victories were won in Europe, or in the colonies, and celebratory bells rung in churches across the country, the people were happy to drink the health of the soldiers who had won it. They also turned out in their thousands to see lines of finely dressed troops parade their enemies' captured colours along Whitehall. Horace Walpole wrote after the Battle of Dettingen:

> I expect to be drunk with hogsheads of the Mayne-Water and with odes to his Majesty, and the Duke, and Te Deums…We are all mad – drums, trumpets, bumpers, bonfires! The mob are wild and cry "Long Live King George and the Duke of Cumberland, and Lord Stair and Lord Carteret, and General Clayton that's dead!"[54]

---

53 Guy (ed.), *Colonel Samuel Bagshawe*, p.1.
54 Michael Orr, *Dettingen 1743* (London: Charles Knight & Co, 1972), p.72.

When the Jacobites retreated north in 1745 after their failed march on London, Cumberland's pursuing army was welcomed as it passed through English towns and cities on their trail. When the Duke of Cumberland asked for replacement shoes and stockings for the men, as theirs had worn out in the harsh winter weather, not only were these supplied but the citizens of London started a fund which raised £18,910 and ultimately provided 10,000 woollen caps, 16,500 pairs of woollen gloves, 9.000 pairs of woollen ankle spatter dashes, 4,500 paillasses, 810 watch coats and 1,200 blankets to keep the men warm in the wintry conditions.[55] Hardly the actions of a population that hated soldiers?

Perhaps this ambivalence has always existed between the public and the army. As Rudyard Kipling was to write about the public's attitude toward the army in the Victorian era:

> For it's Tommy this, an' Tommy that, an' "Chuck him out, the brute!"
> But it's "Saviour of 'is country" when the guns begin to shoot.

The Army Wives

If the commanders of the Army could have their way, the men would stay single, childless, and celibate for their entire army career. Still, however much they disapproved, it was recognised, not unreasonably, that the men would have relationships with the opposite sex and that allowances had to be made.

The women who followed the army were in many ways the unacknowledged and invisible logistical support arm of the regiment, without whom the soldiers found it difficult to operate. They are unacknowledged because, on paper, there were very few of them with the regiments, although their actual numbers were much greater. They are almost invisible because historical records of the time make little mention of them, or only mention them in passing, and rarely recognise the contribution they made to the Army's success.

The high command viewed soldiers' wives as something to be tolerated but not encouraged. Wives, and especially children, were seen as a burden on the regiment and an added logistical problem the officers could do without. James Wolfe reminded NCOs: 'to discourage Matrimony amongst the men as much as possible, the Service Suffers by the Multitude of women already in the Regiment'. He forbade any man to get married without asking an officer first, 'that the woman's character can be enquired into'. He also wrote:

> The Lieut Colo. Further recommends to the soldiers not to marry at all. The long march and embarkation that will follow must convince them that many women in

---

55   W.A. Speck, *The Butcher; The Duke of Cumberland and the Suppression of the '45* (Cardiff: Welsh Academic Press, 1995), p.95.

the Regts are very inconvenient, especially as some of them are not so industrious, nor so useful to their husbands, as a Soldiers wife ought to be.[56]

Despite all this discouragement, not surprisingly, men did have relationships, and most did get married. Soldiers sometimes married local girls in the area where they were stationed, whilst others took wives whilst campaigning overseas, especially if they were placed in garrison in one area for a long time. For example, whilst in America Moses Dorr recorded in 1758 that an Iroquois woman had married a soldier and remained in camp as 'her husband has gone with the army'.[57] A surviving record for a regiment returning from Holland in 1748 shows that of the 69 women accompanying them, 52 were married to soldiers in the ranks whilst only 17 remained unmarried, suggesting that most soldiers did marry their sweethearts rather than 'living in sin'[58].

Regulations stated that only six women could be returned on the regimental roll for each company within the regiment. These women could draw two-thirds daily rations for themselves and half a full ration for their children when on campaign but received no free rations when in garrison. That is not to say that there were only six women attached to each company, but rather that this was the number shown on the returns. There were often many more wives and girlfriends who followed the regiment and did not appear on the rolls, as well as their children. As one Commissariat return states:

> In the computation is included the Women and Children belonging to each Regiment, which are indeed very numerous beyond any idea of imagination; and although the former are victualled at the rate of a moiety of each mans allowance and the latter at a fourth only, yet the expence is very considerable.[59]

These extra women could not draw regimental rations for themselves or their children. Instead, they had to earn money by doing chores around the camp, cooking for the men, baking and selling their wares, mending clothes or doing laundry. Some worked as servants to the officers and others as Sutlers, selling whatever goods the soldiers needed. If there were no opportunities to make money, then it fell to the soldier to divide his rations with his wife and family. Dr John Pringle, who was to become Physician General to the British Army during the War of the Austrian Succession, wrote that 'The greatest impediments to messing are the wives and children, who must often be maintained on the pay of the men. In such circumstances it is not improper food but the want of it that may endanger a soldiers health'.[60]

---

56 Paul E. Kopperman, 'The British High Command and Soldiers Wives in America 1755-1783', *Journal of the Society for Army Historical Research* Vol.60, No.241 (Spring 1982), p.22.
57 Sarah Fatherly, 'Tending the Army: Women and the British General Hospital in North America, 1754—1763', *Early American Studies*, Vol.10, No.3 (Fall 2012), p.587.
58 Kopperman, 'The British High Command and Soldiers Wives in America', p.1.
59 Kopperman, 'The British High Command and Soldiers Wives in America', p.20.
60 Kopperman, 'The British High Command and Soldiers Wives in America', p.24.

Even on campaign, when some of the regimental women could draw rations, there was never enough to go round. Corporal Todd recorded in his diary during the campaign in Germany during the Seven Years War:

> HSH Prince Ferdinand was pleas'd to order a present of one Barril of brandy & 600 pounds of rice and pease to each battalion & every four squadrons & each Soldiers wife one pound of bread & every child half a pound per day during his highness pleasure. This order was very acceptable as the bread we receive is not near sufficient for several men, much less for them that has wifes & children.[61]

When the regiment was deployed overseas, the women already on the regimental returns could expect to go with them. Those not on the returns might very well be left behind if there was not enough room on the ships. There are many examples of abandoned wives having to look to local parish councils for charity to help them get by. In 1744, for example, Nottingham town council provided 2 shillings to '4 soldiers wifes left in Town; after the regiment has gone' whilst in 1757 Cork Council paid £70: 'for sending to their respective homes the wives and children of the Soldiers gone on the late expedition' to Louisburg. [62] Just as often this happened in reverse, when soldiers were bound for home and had to leave their wives and children behind in the theatre of war. In 1745 several battalions were sent home from Flanders to deal with the Jacobite rebellion and Lord Ligonier recorded that he had: 'to hire a ship to carry 270 ladies, yet I fear many of the miserable devils will be left behind'.[63] However, if there was room on board, it appears as though other wives could be allowed to travel with the army, as Major General Braddock recorded in 1755: 'A greater number of women have been brought over than those allowed by the Government'.[64]

Highland soldier, with wife and child. Hand-coloured engraving c.1742. (Anne S.K. Brown Collection)

Wives and children accompanied their regiment on even the most dangerous of expeditions. During the raid on St Malo in 1758, Corporal Todd recorded the death of a young boy aboard ship who was crushed by a dislodged cannon. 'He belonged to a soldier in Captain Wrights company …His father and Mother being aboard was very sorrowful, as he seemed a promising boy'.[65] What is startling about this tragic story, is that even on an expedition expected to be away for days and perhaps only weeks

---

61 Cormack and Jones (eds), *Journal of Corporal Todd*, p.217.
62 Screen, 'Eighteenth Century Army at Home', p.236.
63 Rex Whitworth, *Field Marshal Lord Ligonier* (Godmanchester: Ken Trotman, 2006) p.107.
64 Kopperman, 'The British High Command and Soldiers Wives in America', p.26.
65 Cormack and Jones (eds), *Journal of Corporal Todd*, p.60.

at most, soldiers still had their wives and family with them on board ship. Indeed, so essential were the women to the daily running of the regiment that they were included on even these short raids, with the general orders stating: 'Only two women per company to be allowed on board to wash for the men & to have provisions the same as the men'.[66]

When on campaign the women marched alongside the men, sometimes letting the children ride in the wagons and occasionally carrying their husband's musket when he was tired. Women were also employed herding the sheep or cattle that often accompanied the regiment. Hannah Winthrop, who accompanied Braddock's column in America in 1755, says the women:

> [S]eemed to be the beasts of burthen, having a bushel basket on their back by which they were bent double; the contents seemed to be Pots and Kettles, various sorts of furniture, children peeping through grid irons and other utensils, some (with) very young infants who were born on the road.[67]

When the regiment went into camp at the end of the day, the women would be employed cooking, mending clothes, cleaning utensils and doing the laundry. Life on campaign does not appear to have been easy, and women were expected to carry out this hard physical labour often whilst pregnant or looking after small children. Despite all the dangers and hardships, army women seemed determined to stay with their men and suffer whatever the army had to offer.

Women were expected to take orders just as the men were, and to help out were necessary, carrying supplies, helping to dig defences, bringing water to the men on piquet duty or any other role the officers devised. For example, one surviving order reads: 'Ten women per regiment are ordered immediately to join the artillery; they will be employed in sewing up sandbags, and making wads from old junk for the guns'.[68]

Bad as some of these jobs were, the role the women hated the most was to work in the hospital as nurses. This required the emptying of bedpans, laundering spoiled bedclothes, looking after the sick and injured and often becoming exposed to the illnesses that were rife in the hospital environment. Not surprisingly, unless their husbands were ill in the hospital at the time, women were not keen to do the work. To encourage women to take on the role, the Army paid sixpence a day to its nurses but still many women found that they could make more doing much easier work around the camp. As a result, many had to be ordered to attend. In 1758, for example, each company of the 42nd Foot was ordered ' to send a woman to the hospital tomorrow as a Nurse',[69] whilst on another occasion women were forbidden to draw rations unless they agreed to take on a job as a nurse. If they refused they would be: 'cut of from provisions & drumm'd out of the corps or garrison &

---

66 Cormack and Jones (eds), *Journal of Corporal Todd*, p.20.
67 Kopperman, 'The British High Command and Soldiers Wives in America', p.30.
68 Kopperman, 'The British High Command and Soldiers Wives in America', p.16.
69 Fatherly, 'Tending the Army', p.584.

never suffer'd to return'.[70] Indeed, during the Quebec campaign, Brigadier General Robert Monckton had to resort to forcing women to work as nurses. He ordered two women per company to attend the temporary hospital and wrote:

> If any Woman refuse to serve as Nurses in the Hospital, or after having been there leaves it without being regularly dismissed by order of the Director she shall be struck off the provision roll & if found afterwards in any of the camps shall be turned out immediately.[71]

Widows of those men killed in action were often offered the opportunity to serve as nurses as a way to continue receiving provisions and remaining with the army.

All of the army wives were subject to army laws whilst with the regiment and if they broke them could be liable to regimental punishment. Minor offences were dealt with in the traditional army manner: the lash. This punishment could be administered for theft or other minor offences committed in camp, or for looting or marauding whilst marching through friendly territory. Surviving records show that in 1758 an unnamed woman was 'whipt 70 stripes and drummed out of camp' whilst another was sentenced to '2 [hundred] & 50 lashes on her bear [sic] rump'.[72] In November 1759, twice within 10 days, pairs of women were whipped through the streets of Quebec for selling liquor to the troops, which had been strictly forbidden by the general commanding.

The worst punishment was being drummed out, or expelled from the regiment. This removed the offender from the regimental roll and disqualified them from receiving rations or travelling with the regiment. If in Europe or based at home, the woman would have to fend for herself and if she wanted to continue to follow her husband, she would have to do so with the rabble of camp followers that followed in the army's wake. If based overseas, being drummed out could have terrible consequences. During the campaign on Lake George in America, for example, strict camp rules were imposed, with the addition that: 'Any woman found evading this order will be sent to the Provost, Drumm'd out of the line & sent away without an escort'.[73] This was essentially a death sentence, as any women leaving camp would have to make her way across miles of dense forest to get back to civilisation and may very well meet hostile Native Americans or French troops along the way.

When campaigning in Europe, women were usually ordered to stay with the baggage train when battle was expected or the train was moving through enemy territory, and could no longer expect to march alongside their men. This was ostensibly to keep them safe, but it also prevented them getting in the way as the officers began to get their men into position for the coming battle. During these campaigns, light troops sometimes attacked the baggage

---

70 Fatherly, 'Tending the Army', p.584.
71 Fatherly, 'Tending the Army', p.584.
72 Fatherly, 'Tending the Army', p.591.
73 Fatherly, 'Tending the Army', p.598.

train, but usually the women and camp followers were not put in danger by enemy action. Corporal Todd recorded one incident in 1761:

> The Enemys Hussa's, Pandores etc greatly Harrass'd our rear, & took our regiment Baggage Waggon & several others…John Rose wife & two children of our company was taken & she having 9 Duckets, it being all the stock they had, about her…the enemy Hussars when they took them let the Women & children go without searching them…She came up with her children & her money safe to her husband, whereof John Rose was so glad that he would give every man in our company a double box of Geneva.[74]

It is not made clear whether John Rose was more pleased to see his family or his money!

When on campaign overseas, however, especially in America, women shared the dangers of campaigning alongside their men. After the siege of Fort William Henry, for example, the surrendered British garrison were set upon by North American Indians whilst believing themselves to be under the protection of the French. One witness wrote; 'In going Over the River there was an Indian shot one of our wimen and began to scalp her. Her husband being a little before her shot the Indian dead'.[75] In 1755, the baggage train of Major General Braddock's column was also attacked and overrun by Native Americans, with only four women surviving the subsequent massacre of the 50 that originally set out. As they were not all noted on the regimental returns, often the true number of casualties amongst women and children during incidents like this cannot accurately be calculated, and is often much higher than listed on official returns.

The fate of women whose husbands or lovers were killed in action was not clear. If she was recognised on the regimental role then she would be entitled to collect any outstanding pay owed to her husband before his death. However, the Army did not make this easy to collect and women often had to preserver to get what was owed to them. Take for example the wife of Private Anthony Thomas, who died whilst serving as a marine aboard ship. She was entitled to his outstanding pay and to the bonus he would have collected but the officer in charge delayed giving her the outstanding balance as he could have pocketed it himself if it went unclaimed. In the end, her constant badgering made the officer capitulate, writing that he found it: 'very hard that an officer must be eternally plagued with such strumpets…'[76] Even officers wives had trouble recovering money owed to them by the army. Mrs Catherine Bagshawe, the wife of Colonel Thomas Bagshawe, was forced to write to the King in 1762, following her husband's death. He had expended a great deal of their money in the raising and equipping of a regiment which she hoped to recoup, along with a pension as she had no means of income. She outlined the expenditure in her letter stating:

---

74   Cormack and Jones (eds), *Journal of Corporal Todd*, p.207.
75   Kopperman, 'The British High Command and Soldiers Wives in America', p.31.
76   Guy (ed.), *Colonel Samuel Bagshawe*, p.85.

> [T]hat the sum for which his Lieutenant Colonelcy would have sold for being £5000 added to the £3000 which he expended in raising and accoutreing his Regiment make a neat loss upon his death to his family of no less than £8000… (the applicant) most humbly hopes that your Majesty will be most graciously pleased to take the case of herself and Orphans into your Royal consideration.[77]

Those not recognised on the regimental rolls, or, worse, not even married to the soldier, found it even harder to collect any outstanding pay. The widows of the troops killed during the French Indian War in America, for example, were each given only half a guinea to support themselves and to make their way back to England.

The women of the army provided indispensable logistical support to the men. This was recognised at the time by senior officers, who allowed them to accompany the army even on short raids and expeditions. When in garrison or on campaign, the wives and girlfriends of the soldiers endured hardship alongside their men and deserve to be recognised for it, rather than continuing to be the invisible logistical support arm.

---

77 Guy (ed.), *Colonel Samuel Bagshawe*, p.270.

4

Crime and Punishment

There is a long-held view that the officers and NCOs treated eighteenth-century soldiers cruelly. Floggings were administered for minor offences whilst the death penalty was inflicted at the drop of a hat for those found guilty of more serious crimes. It was hence a fear of their officers and their NCOs, the story goes, that drove the men forward in battle, as the penalty for retreating was just as severe as going on.

A close examination of daily life in the eighteenth-century British Army does not seem to bear this out. British officers were expected to lead their men from the front when going into battle and they were very unlikely to have the support of their troops if they had treated them harshly. As one contemporary pointed out: 'even the rawest and the most arrogant of subalterns was unlikely to rejoice at the prospect of marching into battle in front of a hundred loaded muskets carried by men who hated him'.[1]

To begin with, all military punishments have to be seen in the light of contemporary civilian punishments. This was an age where criminal punishment included branding, whipping through the streets, and use of the stocks or pillory for public shaming. The death penalty could be handed out for theft of livestock or property worth 40 shillings or more, and often was, with the crowds at Tyburn enjoying up to 40 executions in a single day.

Within the military, there were three levels of courts that passed judgement on soldiers deemed to have committed an offence. The first was the company court, which was usually chaired by a sergeant, assisted by a corporal and three private soldiers. These courts ruled on very minor matters such as personal disputes, internal thefts between soldiers, or similar petty crimes. They would be formed on an ad hoc basis and were used as a means of dealing with minor infringements within the company. The most severe sentence it could pass down were beatings, which were usually administered by NCOs. These were the sort of barrack room trials and 'Kangaroo Courts' familiar to anyone who has served in the military and were designed more to humiliate the offender than to punish, both in order to prevent them making the same mistake again and acting as an example to others. Some NCOs

---

1   Dennis Showalter, *Wars of Frederick the Great* (London: Frontline Books 2012), p.23.

could be inventive with their punishments, as two soldiers taking part in the Quebec campaign found out in 1759. Whilst on sentry duty they 'behaved in a scandalous and unsoldierlike manner upon their post, the first screaming out and firing his piece and both by giving the most evident tokens of fear'. As punishment they were made to 'stand an hour at the necessary house [the latrine] each with a womans cap upon his head as a small punishment for the dishonour they have brought upon the Corps…' Additionally, they were had to lead the company advance, and to 'march in front of all parties without a grain of powder in their pieces, where they may have the opportunity to wipe off the infamy they now lie under'.[2]

The next court was the regimental court martial. Chaired by a senior officer of the regiment who was assisted by a further four officers, this court ruled on more serious matters for which corporal punishment was the likely outcome. The articles of war, established in 1728, stated this court had to be called 'within the space of eight days at the farthest after confinement of any such offender'.[3] This stipulation was introduced to prevent long periods of confinement for soldiers who may be innocent of the offence, as was the further amendment of 1735 which allowed for only three officers to preside if five could not be found. The decision of the court had to be approved by the colonel of the regiment before being carried out. The colonel was supposed to act as an independent arbiter who could overrule the court if he found their decision to be incorrect, but in practice this rarely happened.

Although the regimental court martial had the appearance of a court, the defendant had no legal advice, was not represented, except by himself, and those judging him were army officers who were not legally trained. In truth, they were a device for punishing soldiers, often extremely cruelly, without any proper legal structure and represented an extremely arbitrary system of punishment. This court was only supposed to rule on minor offences such as being absent without leave, neglect of duty, ill-discipline or brawling. The punishments which could be inflicted upon the guilty party could include: the gauntlet, where the accused was forced to walk between two lines of his fellow soldiers who each beat him with a stick as he passed; the horse, which resembled a carpenter's saw-horse with the crossbar carved into a sharp edge which the accused would straddle for a period of hours; and piqueting, where a suspended prisoner was made to balance on a sharp tent peg or stake. There is a record, for example, of a Private Samuel Bull who was made to 'ride Wooden Horse for one hour' for the offence of 'insolence to an officer'.[4]

However, by the middle of the century the lash, or 'flogging', was by far the most common form of punishment. There does not appear to have been a clear set of military laws alongside which was a set number of lashes. Rather, the colonel of the regiment or the regimental court martial set the punishment to suit the occasion. The number of lashes inflicted on the

---

2 Fred Anderson, *A People's Army: Massachusetts Soldiers and Society in the Seven Years War* (Chapel Hill: University of North Carolina Press, 1996), p.239.
3 Arthur Gilbert, 'The Regimental Courts Martial in the Eighteenth Century British Army', *Albion: A Quarterly Journal Concerned with British Studies*, Vol. 8, No. 1 (Spring, 1976), p.53.
4 Gilbert, 'Regimental Courts Martial', p.51.

offender could vary depending on the severity of the offence, if there were aggravating circumstances, or if the commander simply wanted to make an example of the offender to discourage others. Although the court did not have the authority to order more than 100 lashes, this was regularly exceeded. For example, 'Sergeant William Brittin was given 500 lashes for being absent from quarters, selling his arms and embezzling the pay of his men'.[5] whilst 'Edward Hurst, Sergeant, was broke to a mattross and received 400 lashes by order of a Regimental Court Martial for striking Lieutenant Barrett of the RA'.[6]

Floggings were carried out in front of the whole regiment, usually on parade. The victim was tied to a stake, or the wheel of a gun, and the requisite number of lashes administered, usually by a drummer from the regiment. If the sentence required a large number of lashes, it would not be uncommon for the victim to be cut down after a certain number had been given and allowed to recover before the remainder of the sentence was carried out. One contemporary wrote: 'Three men, from some trifling offence which I do not recollect, were tied to be whipped. One was to receive 800 lashes, the others 500 apiece. By the time they had received 300 lashes the flesh appeared to be entirely whipped from their shoulders'.[7]

The highest court was the general court martial, which adjudicated on capital offences. It consisted of thirteen senior officers drawn from different regiments from that of the offender. Where possible, it was chaired by a Deputy Judge Advocate who ensured that the proceedings were fair and carried out within the law. If a death sentence was passed, this would then be sent to the Judge Advocate General who then presented the case to the King, as the final arbiter. Only when the King confirmed the death sentence was it carried out.

It appears that soldiers who had committed capital offences were often charged with more minor offences in order to keep the proceedings within the regimental court system. For example, a deserter might be charged with being 'absent without leave' rather than desertion in order that the regiment can deal with him rather than calling a general court martial. However, having found him guilty, the punishment could often exceed that which the general court martial would have handed down. For example, Corporal Duncan Sheriz of the Foot Guards wrote a letter to the colonel accusing his sergeant of fraud, for which he was 'stript and the Drums with switches whipped him 200 lashes, and as I am informed a few days after 200 more and a few days after 200 more; in all 600 executed by ten drums'.[8] Compare this to the case of a William Clarke who, for 'a high offense against his Royal Family' was found guilty by a general court martial and sentenced to 900 lashes, which was reduced to 600 by the King.[9] The sentences are nearly identical, with the punishment for treason at a general court martial being the same as making an allegation of fraud against an NCO at a regimental court.

---

5   Gilbert, 'Regimental Courts Martial', p.54.
6   Whitworth (ed.), *Gunner at Large*, p.106.
7   Anderson, *A People's Army*, p.138.
8   Gilbert, 'Regimental Courts Martial', p.52.
9   Gilbert, 'Regimental Courts Martial', p.52.

The Duke of Cumberland attempted to reform the regimental courts system in 1749 and made it clear that: 'Members of Courts Martial are not judges. A CM is a Court of Honour and Equity'. He wanted to ensure that officers did not abuse their power, and whilst the soldier had to obey 'any lawful command of his superior officer' for the officer to have protection under the law he had to be acting 'in the execution of his office'. He also proposed that: 'no one may be prevented from bringing his grievance even to the King after he has first properly and quickly applied to his particular superior'.[10] This opened the door for soldiers who felt aggrieved by their sentence from a regimental court martial to appeal to have their case heard by a general court martial instead.

Although a soldier was perfectly within his rights to do so, the senior officers of the army generally discouraged appeals, as they did not want to waste time dealing with frivolous or unnecessary cases. Research shows that in about 80 percent of appeal cases the sentence was actually increased by about 212 lashes on average, for making 'vexatious and groundless' appeals.[11] The act of going to appeal also brought embarrassment to the regiment, and sometimes the senior officers were prepared to negotiate in order to prevent an appeal taking place. For example, in February 1750, Sergeant Samuel Burgoyne successfully appealed his 100-lash sentence for being absent without leave and 'drawing a hanger on John Day in his house',[12] and instead received a reduction in rank rather than put the case before a general court martial.

On campaign there was often no time to go through the above procedures. Instead, courts martial could be called in camp with the commander-in-chief of the army acting in the King's place as final arbiter of the sentence, including the death penalty. For example, after the battle of Fontenoy there were a number of general courts martial for soldiers accused of cowardice which the Duke of Cumberland chaired and confirmed the sentence of the court.

Punishment on campaign was often harsh and swiftly enforced. During the Raid on St Malo in 1758, Corporal Todd records: 'General orders that no man presume to stir out of the camp or Marraud or to go upon the outside of the line… the Captain of the Provost Guard having received orders to hang any man he catches out of the line'. Soon after, William Cross, a grenadier, heard a cry from the woods and went to investigate, finding a local woman being attacked by a British soldier. He chased off the attacker and set the woman free whereupon the provost captain:

> [D]irectly came up to the place & took William Cross & hang'd him up in one of the trees without anymore to do… Our Colonel went to the General directly with the woman … & told the General the whole affair whereby orders was sent to the Captain of the Provost Guard that all men he takes to confine them for future … All our army was very glad this order was countermanded.[13]

---

10   Whitworth (ed.), *Gunner at Large*, p.137.
11   Gilbert, 'Regimental Courts Martial', p.61.
12   Gilbert, 'Regimental Courts Martial', p.58.
13   Cormack and Jones (eds), *Journal of Corporal Todd*, p.47.

Although punishments were harsh for private soldiers, they were often no more harsh than they might expect in civilian life. Officers needed recourse to corporal punishment in order to keep those men pressed into military service, from prisons or through the impressment act, in line. If, however, one followed the rules and did as one was told, it was possible to go one's entire military life without being flogged or being subject to corporal punishment, as most of those whose diaries have survived managed to do.

5

Officers and Gentlemen

There is a joke often told in military circles, which states that British officers are drawn from the cream of society, in the sense that they are both rich and thick. This stereotype is often laid at the door of officers from the eighteenth-century Army, implying that the officer class were drawn from the wealthiest in society, were often not very bright and who lacked military skill and empathy with their troops. As with any stereotype, examples of this sort of officer can be found in the army of George II, but they are very much the exception rather than the rule. As we shall see, officers were generally middle-class individuals who began their military career as junior ranks and worked their way up through dedication and ability, although in many cases a wealthy financial backer did not do their career any harm either.

A Pair of Colours

It is true to say that any young man who aspired to become an officer in the British army during the eighteenth century would have to possess the money to do so, as commissioned rank was generally only gained through purchase. The new recruit would be expected to join as an ensign or cornet, the lowest officer ranks in the infantry and cavalry respectively, and gain experience before being allowed to progress up the ranks. It has been estimated that around 20 percent of officers came from the aristocracy and that these were disproportionately concentrated in the Household regiments. However, the majority of candidates were just as often from 'well off' middle class families and were usually second or third sons, who were not likely to inherit the family business or estate and were required to find gainful employment elsewhere. They might be the sons of businessmen, local officials or magistrates, or even the sons of clergy. For example, in 1760 Lord Hillsborough sent a list of recommendations to the War Office which included: 'Jaspar Waring, eldest son of Mr Thomas Waring, Minister of the Church of England' and 'Alexander Colvill, son of Doctor Colvill, a Presbyterian Parson…a pretty young fellow & fit for the service'.[1]

---

1 Hayter (ed.), *Eighteenth Century Secretary at War*, p.286.

OFFICERS AND GENTLEMEN

'The military nurse, or Modern officer'; this satire from c.1750 jokes that the officers of the army are so young that they have to be nursed by the NCOs. Engraving by and after R. Attwold. (Anne S.K. Brown Collection)

Once created an officer, the applicant joined a very exclusive club where social class was no longer an issue. The men saw themselves as brother officers and, in most cases, the social standing of their family was forgotten. In Richbell's 39th Foot during the Jacobite rebellion, for example, the Hon. John Sempill, who would later become the 12th Lord Sempill in 1746, held the same rank as Roland Lewis, whose brother was an apothecary on Tower Hill in London.[2] With regard to recruiting, the War Office stated that 'Two invariable & indispensable rules of the army are that every man shall begin

---

2 Guy (ed.), *Colonel Samuel Bagshawe*, p.14.

Military Life with the lowest Commission, and that he shall be at least 16 years of age before he obtain any'.³

The first rule was generally adhered to. Candidates could only buy a commission higher than that of cornet or ensign when a new regiment was being formed from scratch, and, even then, these posts were offered first to existing officers in other regiments or to those held on the establishment on half-pay. The second rule, that candidates had to be at least 16 years of age, appears to have been regularly overlooked. In an age were boys were often apprenticed as young as 11 or 12, there was often pressure to get them into the ranks before they were fully 16. Just as with the private soldiers, some families were happy to disguise their son's age to gain a vacant commission that might be gone by the time he was 16.

Assuming the family of our new recruit had the cash to purchase him a position as an ensign in the infantry, or a cornet in the cavalry, it was not as easy as simply presenting oneself to the colonel of the regiment and expecting to be employed. Vacancies did not occur often, especially in peacetime when the size of regiments was usually reduced, and existing positions might only fall vacant when officers retired or died. Thus, when a post did become available, competition to obtain it was fierce. It was at this point that the better-connected families might prevail over those without influential friends. Families would approach well-connected patrons, such as their local MP, a peer of the realm, or someone already established within the military, such as a friendly general. A patron could choose to support such a candidacy for altruistic reasons, to help the family out, or could perhaps be related to the candidate in some way. Many families sent second or even third generations into the army, and it did the new candidate no harm if his father or grandfather had served in the ranks before. Ensigns were asked to take an oath upon appointment declaring that they had not paid anyone to gain them their commission and so a direct bribe to a patron, whilst not unheard of, was unlikely. Instead, patrons could be secured by the promise of political or social advancement or assistance. For example, one candidate was recommended by his MP as his father is a 'firm friend of the administration' whilst another MP recommended a young man be given a position as his father is 'essential to my interest in Devonshire'.⁴ In 1761 Lord Anson wrote to the Secretary at War to obtain a commission for the son of a client that he hoped 'may be done before the election',⁵ in the hope of winning his support. The 4th Duke of Marlborough called in a favour with the Secretary at War in 1760, applying for 'a troop of Dragoons; or a Company in an Old regiment for a Gentleman whose name is Travell; his Father was a very zealous friend to us in the late Oxfordshire Election which makes me interest myself for his son'.⁶

All applicants had to apply to the War Office, where the application would be considered and those selected put before the King for approval, as he was the ultimate arbiter on commissions. Hence, all attempts at influence tended

---

3   Hayter (ed.), *Eighteenth Century Secretary at War*, p.317.
4   Hayter (ed.), *Eighteenth Century Secretary at War*, p.275.
5   Hayter (ed.), *Eighteenth Century Secretary at War*, p.275
6   Hayter (ed.), *Eighteenth Century Secretary at War*, p.285.

to be toward individuals who worked at the War Office or to the Secretary at War directly, as they were the gateway to the King. However, if one was particularly well connected it was possible to bypass the War Office altogether.

Obviously, in time of war commissions were easier to come by and new regiments were often raised quite quickly to meet the need for men. The King would grant permission for well-off individuals to raise their own regiments and it was then in the gift of this new colonel to recommend individuals for commissions. Unscrupulous colonels could recommend the commissions to the sons of friends, business partners, or to petitioners to advance their business or political aims. For example, in December 1757 Lieutenant Colonel Thomas Gage submitted a proposal to raise, at his own expense, a 500-man regiment of 'light armed foot' to operate in America as light infantry. When the new regiment was formed in May 1758 only four of its 19 officers had any previous light infantry experience, with the majority being friends or associates of Gage. However, no-one raising a new regiment would want it to be a laughing stock when it went to war, and so whilst some commissions no doubt were distributed for nepotistic reasons, colonels of new units also looked to fill the more senior commissioned posts with experienced men.

When the regiment was deployed on campaign, casualties inevitably occurred either through illness, accident or as a result of battle. This created vacancies at an alarming rate and officers soon became in short supply. At the Battle of Fontenoy in 1745, for example, Duroure's 12th Foot lost its colonel and lieutenant colonel killed and its major wounded, with four captains killed or wounded along with eight lieutenants and four ensigns. When a vacancy occurred on campaign, officers were often temporarily promoted to fill the role, obtaining a 'brevet' or temporary promotion until a suitable candidate could be found. It is worth noting at this stage that those granted brevet rank, would not be granted this rank permanently unless he had the means to purchase it. The awarding of a brevet was a temporary stopgap measure to continue the effective running of the regiment and was not a permanent 'battlefield promotion'. As a result, 'gentlemen volunteers' often accompanied regiments on campaign. These were young men who lacked the cash to purchase a commission and who accompanied the regiment to learn its ways whilst waiting for a non-purchase vacancy to occur.

Officer of the 5th Royal Irish Dragoons, c.1760. Watercolour by R.A. Wymer. (Anne S.K. Brown Collection)

The final route for a young man to gain a commission was by direct promotion through patronage. This could be simply an act of kindness performed by the King or the Commander in Chief. For example, the Duke of Cumberland: 'gave an Ensigncy to the Orphan son of an officer who lost his life in the service; but finding the boy not to be of the proper age, recalled his commission, educated and maintained him till he was turned of 16, & then gave him a new one in another Regt'.[7] Equally, the colonel or some other notable within the army could recognise potential in a young soldier and look to elevate him from the ranks. This was rare but it did happen and was encouraged when Viscount Barrington was Secretary at War. In 1760 Lord Hillsborough recommended: 'a Private man in Ld Loudons regiment, & Ld Barrington said he liked to promote such a person if his character justified it, for which Ld Loudon is referred to'.[8]

Promotion for valour on the field of battle was also rare but not unheard of. During the Battle of Dettingen in 1743, trooper George Daraugh of Rich's 4th Dragoons rescued the guidon of his regiment after it had been captured by a French Officer, riding after him and cutting the Frenchman down. For this act of gallantry, George II personally granted him a cornetcy in the Regiment along with a purse of guineas. Following the Battle of Fontenoy in 1745, the Duke of Cumberland promoted two individuals from the ranks, namely Sergeant Peter Hewitt and Trooper Thomas Stevenson both of whom had performed acts of bravery during the battle. Hewitt proved himself to be very capable, gaining promotion to lieutenant in 1748 and then to captain in August 1756.

Promotion, Purchase and Patronage

As discussed elsewhere, each infantry regiment had three officers allocated to each company. The first company was commanded by the colonel, the second by the lieutenant Colonel, the third by the major, with captains commanding the remaining companies. Each company also had a lieutenant as the second in command and an ensign as the junior officer. If the regiment were based at home and at full strength, then this would be the accepted organisation. However, in times of peace, regiments were often reduced to half strength or even smaller, with the private men being paid off and released from service. The officers of these companies were held on the establishment on half-pay, and were released back into civilian life. If war was to break out, as it invariably did during this period, the half-pay officers would be recalled to the colours and take charge of the new recruits who would soon fill up the ranks. This system ensured that experienced officers were not lost to the army by the reduction process but could be immediately recalled when required.

In order to be promoted to the next rank, the candidate would have to wait for a vacancy to become available. In the first instance, a vacancy would be offered to the man with the most seniority in the junior rank below. So,

---

7   Hayter (ed.), *Eighteenth Century Secretary at War*, p.316.
8   Hayter (ed.), *Eighteenth Century Secretary at War*, pp.285-286.

if a captain was promoted to major, for example, the captain's vacancy was usually offered to the lieutenant with the most seniority. If he moved up, this created a vacancy for a lieutenant, which, in turn, should be offered to the senior ensign. The ensign's post so created would be open for applicants from outside. This system was designed to ensure that only experienced men were promoted through the ranks and that each man served in the rank below for a reasonable amount of time and consequently learned his trade.

It was not sufficient, however, for the candidate to simply hold the most seniority. Each rank had a set monetary value, which the candidate had to pay in order to gain the post. The same rank could cost a different price dependant the regiment, with older, more established regiments costing more than the same rank in a newly raised regiment. The most expensive commissions were those of the thee foot guards regiments, with the 1st Foot Guards being the most prestigious, and the similar household cavalry regiments. Major Robert Preston valued the ensigncy in such an old regiment at £450 and 'the difference from Lieutenant to Captain Lieutenant at £200 and from Captain Lieutenant to Captain at £350'.[9] Commissions in cavalry regiments were considered to be more prestigious than infantry and had a correspondingly higher cost. In 1720, a captain's commission in the Royal Regiment of Dragoons cost £1,800, a major's commission £3,200, whilst anyone hoping to obtain the colonelcy would have to find £7,000[10].

Assuming the applicant had the cash, he would make his ambition known to the colonel who would in turn recommend him for the post to the War Office, where it would then be put before the King. The applicant would deposit the cost of the position with the Regimental Agent, who would retain it until the post was approved. An officer promoted to the next rank would not expect to pay the full sum for his new post, as he expected to sell his own position and so only had to find the difference between the two. However, this could still be a substantial amount. In 1756 Bulleine Fancourt paid 360 Guineas (£367) for his ensigncy in the 14th Foot, with a relatively modest sum of roughly 470 guineas (£500) changing hands for his lieutenancy. In this case he had only to find the difference of £133. However, he subsequently paid 1,600 Guineas (£1,680) for his position as captain in the 56th: a massive difference of £1,180.[11] Usually, officers had to have a patron from whom they could borrow the money or, more often than not, they had to turn down the offer of promotion as they simply could not afford it.

If the vacancy could not be filled from the existing officers, it would then be offered to officers of the regiment who were currently out on half-pay. This was clearly written into the War Office Rules of Service, which stated: 'unless on very extraordinary occasions all the Regimental Vacancies shall be filled from the Half Pay'.[12] After all, it did not make sense to have qualified men being paid to kick their heels whilst at the same time employing new

---

9 Guy (ed.), *Colonel Samuel Bagshawe*, p.241.
10 Richard Cannon, *Historical Record of the First, or Royal, Regiment of Dragoons* (London: Clowes and Sons, 1840), p.59.
11 Hayter (ed.), *Eighteenth Century Secretary at War*, p.309.
12 Hayter (ed.), *Eighteenth Century Secretary at War*, p.293.

THE ARMY OF GEORGE II

Officer of the 10th Dragoons, c.1760. Watercolour by R.A. Wymer. (Anne S.K. Brown Collection)

men into the service. If the post could not be filled here either, it might then be opened up to applicants from other regiments who were on full or half-pay who, perhaps, had no possibility of advancement within their own units for the foreseeable future. It would only be then, if the post could not be filled by any other means, that the colonel of the regiment could recommend someone new to the army for the commission.

Officers were not allowed to sell their commission for more than they bought it for, and were not allowed to auction it or sell to the highest bidder. In addition, they were forbidden from taking bribes or incentives to sell to a particular person. The Notes on the Purchase of Commissions from 1759 makes it very clear that: 'In all instances where it shall be found that any Money, or other consideration, has been given for a Commission, not openly sold with the Leave of His Majesty, the Person obtaining such a commission will be superseded'.[13]

Although not unheard of, it was thus very difficult for an individual to buy their way straight into a regiment at a senior post, as there was usually a long list of individuals waiting for a vacancy to become free. It was more usual for applicants to enter as an ensign and then work their way up the ranks either within their own regiment or by transferring between them. During his tenure as Commander in Chief, the Duke of Cumberland was acutely aware that if inexperienced men were allowed to purchase senior positions in the infantry and cavalry regiments it would greatly reduce the effectiveness of the army. Although he recognised that it did happen, he wrote to the Secretary at War stating: 'I am not fond of bringing officers into our service over the heads of those who have done their duty well'.[14]

King George II took a very active interest in promotions and commissions, as he did with all military matters. The King, along with the Secretary of War and the Commander in Chief, each kept a book containing the names of all the officers in the army, alongside which were notes about

---

13 Hayter (ed.), *Eighteenth Century Secretary at War*, p.293.
14 Whitworth, *Duke of Cumberland*, p.143.

Cumberland as captain-general of the allied forces in Flanders. Hand-coloured engraving by Louis-Simon L'Empereur after David Morier. (Anne S.K. Brown Collection)

each. Details such as their patron, if any, was listed, their length of service and often some opinions about them, which had come to the King's ears through trusted sources. For example, Lieutenant Bosomworth was noted for being 'perfectly acquainted with the manner of Wood Fighting' whilst John Playter 'attends his duty and is of sound principles'. Some notes were more politically motivated, with one officer noted for being 'A Whig gentleman & his family always in the Government interest' whilst others showed the favour of one patron or another, with notes such as: 'Col Mordaunt recommends him earnestly'.[15] This ensured that the King, the Commander in Chief and the Secretary of War were sighted on the ability of the men they were about to confirm in post and this acted as a block to those being promoted beyond their ability or purely for nepotistic reasons. Such notes could be the difference between the confirmation of a promotion or wasting one's career away in the Indies.

Good officers who did not have the money to obtain promotions could appeal to the War Office for dispensation, either directly or through a patron. In these instances, if the Secretary of War thought the case justified, perhaps in consultation with the King or the Commander in Chief, he could pay the promotion cost on the applicant's behalf or stand as guarantor for a loan to secure it. It is not clear how often such petitions were granted but many of them still exist. For example, in 1758 Lord Tyrawley wrote to the War Office to highlight the case of Sir William Wiseman, who had purchased the position of captain lieutenant in the Coldstream Guards, although 'Captain Clarke and Captain Rainesford' were senior. Wiseman, it appears, 'bought his Lieutenancie over their heads, as they had not Money to purchase'. He bemoaned the fact that this was allowed stating: 'he that has most money must soon outstrip all his brother officers. And I am of the opinion that Clarke has the undoubted right to the Captain Lieutenancie …and I do recommend him to you as such'.[16]

The ability of younger wealthier men to leapfrog the older and more experienced officers simply because they had the money to do so was identified by the War Office as a problem. Lord Barrington wrote in 1759:

> Men who come into the army with the warmest dispositions to the Service, whose business becomes their pleasure, who distinguish themselves on every occasion that offers, are kept all their lives in the lowest ranks because they are poor. These meritous Officers have often the cruel mortification of seeing themselves Commanded by Young Men of opulent families who came much later into the service…and the Commission is purchased perhaps by the Youngest, least steady & least experienced of that Corps or of some other to the infinite distress of many deserving Men and to the great scandal and Detriment of the Service.[17]

The King, along with the Commander in Chief and the Secretary of War, did attempt to offset this by granting promotions to those who deserved

---

15 All from Hayter (ed.), *Eighteenth Century Secretary at War*, p.277.
16 Hayter (ed.), *Eighteenth Century Secretary at War*, p.286.
17 Hayter (ed.), *Eighteenth Century Secretary at War*, p.287.

them, either through experience or seniority, but there was only so much even they could do. That said, the system did ensure that wealthy young men still had to serve their time and promotions could be delayed or even refused if the War Office did not feel they were merited or that the officer was not yet experienced enough. In June 1759, for example, an application was received for a promotion for the nephew of Lieutenant General Humphrey Bland, who was then one of the most senior officers in the army. The request asked for him to be promoted to the rank of captain, even though he lacked seniority and 'has not been long in his present rank and is but nineteen years of age'. It was refused by the War Office, with the Secretary of War writing:

> The truth is that the Lieutenant Colonel, the Major and all the Captains agree that Lt Bland is not fit to be rais'd to the rank of Captain or to be trusted with the command of a troop, and this opinion of their's is confirmed by the Major General of the Brigade…I hope you will recommend Lt Lovibond for the purchase of the Troop as I am told…that he is a very diligent and intelligent officer.[18]

The proof that experience was required before promotion could be gained can be seen in the amount of time served by officers of different ranks. Records from 1740 show that lieutenant colonels of Foot had served on average 27 years in the army before they attained their rank, with majors serving on average 26 years before gaining theirs. Lieutenants could expect to serve 19 years on average before being promoted to captain, whilst ensigns served 11.5 years each before being promoted. These figures were compiled after a long period of peace, when there was not much movement amongst the ranks.[19] However, even at the height of the Seven Years War, when many officers were killed or injured in battle and demand for replacements was high, the average for the same ranks was still significant. Lieutenant colonels and majors were still serving 13 and 17 years respectively, whilst captains could still expect to serve 10 years as a lieutenant before being promoted. The only rank where the time served dropped dramatically is for ensign to lieutenant, which drops to only two years in 1759. This could be due to a high mortality rate amongst lieutenants during this period, but resignations and transfers can also skew the statistics. For example, when the 39th Foot was posted to Jamaica, many officers sold their commissions rather than go overseas, meaning that the 10 Lieutenants who did travel had served only 3.5 years each as ensigns and over half had served less than a year before being promoted. Still, even these statistics show that most officers were very experienced before they were promoted and the idea that the majority of British officers only held their positions because they had purchased them and none of them had any practical military experience is false.

---

18 Hayter (ed.), *Eighteenth Century Secretary at War*, p.287.
19 Houlding, *Fit for Service*, pp.108-109.

THE ARMY OF GEORGE II

'The Right Honble John Lord Viscount Ligonier, One of His Majesty's most Honble. Privy Council, Knight of the Most Honble. Order of the Bath: Colonel of His Majesty's First Regimt. of Foot Guards Field Marshal & Commander in Chief of His Majesty's Forces, & Master General of the Ordnance &c. &c.' Mezzotint by Edward Fisher after Joshua Reynolds. (Anne S.K. Brown Collection)

A Matter of Honour

Unlike the artillery school at Woolwich, there was no training college for junior officers in the infantry or cavalry. In fact, compared to the qualifications required for similar supervisory roles in the Civil Service, the Royal Navy, or even the legal profession, prospective officers needed no identifiable qualifications other than to be of good character. With no exam qualification system, an officer could only rely on his seniority and good name to assist him in gaining promotion. With it widely known that the King himself kept a book with detailed notes about each individual, a British officer's good name and reputation were all the currency he had to trade. Consequently, they went to great lengths to defend it.

The officer class had a very clear idea of what was, and was not, acceptable behaviour for an officer and a gentleman, as one contemporary wrote:

> There are offences which admit of no precise definition and yet which in the military profession are of the most serious consequence, as weakening and subverting that principle of honour on which the proper discipline of the army must materially depend.[20]

---

20 Alexander Tytler, *An Essay on Military Law and the Practice of Courts Martial* 3rd Ed. (Edinburgh: T. Egerton, 1814), p.117.

Any actions outside of this code could result in action being taken by the other officers of the regiment. Initially, this might take the form of peer group sanctions being brought to bear in the form of social and professional ostracism, until the offender cleared his name by removing the blot on his honour. If this did not work, the officer would be brought before a regimental court martial, charged with the catch all offence of 'Conduct Unbecoming of an Officer'. This action would be taken against those suspected of telling lies, stealing, slandering other officers or, in the worst cases, for cowardice. Some of these offences could be fairly clear-cut. For example, Ensign Charles Nethercoat was accused of overcharging the Board of Ordnance for supplies whilst Ensign Peter Cockey was dismissed under the 'conduct' regulation when it was discovered that he had two wives. Often the military charge of 'conduct unbecoming' was used as a means of protecting officers from facing criminal charges at local magistrates' court. Major Ralph Correy of the 28th Foot was accused of buying and selling goods illegally, for which he was found guilty and suspended from the army for six months. Some charges show that officers could be just as ill-behaved as their soldiers. On 3 August 1760 Lieutenant Thomas Hopson was charged with either urinating or spilling water, it was never established which, through the floorboards of his quarters and wetting Captain Thomas Faulkner who was lying in bed in the room downstairs.[21]

There were no floggings or hangings for officers committing these offences. Instead, those found guilty were sentenced to reductions in pay, suspension from their position for a period of months or, in the worst cases, cashiering. For most though, the real damage was caused to their honour and their standing amongst their peers. In an organisation as small as the eighteenth-century British army, word of misdemeanours or indiscretions travelled fast and would affect how you one received by other ranks. For this reason, officers could not afford to have their honour questioned and often took any allegation straight to a regimental court. A good example of this occurred in 1761, when Lieutenant Maxwell Boyle told the other officers of the Regiment that he had seen Lieutenant George Orpen 'stoop' at the battle of Minden, which he took as an act of cowardice. Boyle challenged Orpen in front of his fellow officers and Orpen called him a liar. Orpen was subsequently placed before a regimental court martial for 'Conduct Unbecoming through Cowardice' and for accusing another officer of being a liar. Orpen stated he had not stooped 'excepting to get his watch out of his breeches, which having fallen down to his knees he stopped to get it out'. Orpen was subsequently acquitted of both charges.[22]

However, the most common way for an officer to defend his honour was not to take the case to regimental court but rather to fight a duel against the person who had caused the offence. The 1737 Articles of War were very clear about the fighting of duels. They state that:

---

21 All examples from Arthur Gilbert, 'Law and Honour amongst Eighteenth Century British Army Officers', *The Historical Journal*, Vol. 19, No. 1 (Mar., 1976), pp.75-87.
22 Gilbert, 'Law and Honour', p.84.

> [No] officer or soldier presume to send a challenge to any other officer or soldier to fight a duel, upon pain of being cashiered if he is an officer, or suffering the severest corporal punishment if a non-commissioned officer or private soldier... Nor shall any officer or soldier upbraid another for refusing a challenge.[23]

That all seems pretty clear. Duels were forbidden and officers who took part in them, or who disparaged fellow officers for refusing one, would be guilty of an offence. It would appear, however, that of all the articles of war, this was the one not only ignored by officers but where the opposite was openly practised! For example, Lieutenant Eubule Ormsby was put before a Regimental Court Martial for cowardice when he did not show up for a duel with Lieutenant Cornelius Lysaught. The other officers of the regiment refused to continue to serve with Ormsby because of his perceived cowardice and Ormsby was only cleared of the charge as he stated he had been on his way to the duel but had been stopped by another lieutenant who threatened to arrest him if 'he did not desist'. Another example is the case of Captain Benjamin Beilby. His regiment was posted to Minorca, where he appears to have fallen out with a fellow officer, Captain Robinson. Apparently, Robinson verbally abused Beilby in front of the troops, shouting things like: 'Is that the way you march your guard, you shitten dirty fellow' and 'Is that the way you make your men slope their arms, you dirty dog'. Far from his regiment taking action against Robinson for abusing a fellow officer, as outlined in the Articles of War, Beilby's lack of action resulted in him being ostracised by the other officers, who felt that he was duty bound to defend his honour. When Beilby still refused to challenge Robinson to a duel he was brought before a regimental court martial by the senior officers of his Regiment, accused of: 'having repeatedly received from Captain Robinson...language unbecoming the character of an officer and a gentleman without taking proper notice of it'. He was found guilty and sentenced to a year's suspension from pay and duty! It took the intervention of the Judge Advocate in England to reinstate Beilby, who, it was found, could not be guilty of 'neglecting to seek a method of redress forbidden as well by the military as the common law'.[24]

Duels, it seems, were fought so routinely that they are barely deemed worthy of a mention by people at the time. Gunner Wood, whilst on board ship bound for India, wrote: 'A duel was fought with sword and pistol between Captain Lieutenant Jones, an artillery officer in the Dodington, and another gentleman passenger in the said ship. Nothing of consequence happened.'[25] Indeed, Woods writes more about the weather and the ships heading than he does about this incident or its causes, which, given it happened on an otherwise dull sea voyage, shows how common these events must have been.

Duels could only be fought between officers and gentlemen. They were not a course of action open to the other ranks, who, it was thought, should not presume to have the social status to even have any honour, let alone the ability to challenge others in order to defend it. When a surgeon's mate

---

23   Gilbert, 'Law and Honour', p.79.
24   Gilbert 'Law and Honour, p.80.
25   Whitworth (ed.), *Gunner at Large*, p.78.

from his regiment, assaulted Lieutenant Strode in 1762, he was placed in a quandary. The surgeon's mate had refused to apologise and instead challenged him to a duel to settle the matter, but the surgeon's mate was not an officer, nor was he considered a 'gentleman' being, in essence, a private soldier. Hence Strode refused the duel but subsequently found himself in front of a regimental court martial for 'Conduct Unbecoming through Cowardice' for failing to accept it![26]

Although duels could be fought in many ways, and with different weapons, one account of a duel will be sufficient to inform the reader as to what exactly went on. In 1762, Lieutenant Robinson challenged Lieutenant Conors to a duel for a reason that is not recorded. On the morning of the duel, Conors went to Robinson's tent and they loaded their pistols in front of each other. Accompanied by their seconds, and by other officers from the regiment who had come to watch the spectacle, they went to the location where the duel was to take place. Conors then recorded:

> We then went together to the ground, shook hands and took five paces, we then faced about and fired at each other, which missed. Lieutenant Robinson then presented a second pistol, which flashed in the pan after a long aim; I then fired my second pistol, but did not hit him; on which he was priming again, and just as he was going to present, Lieutenant Maine came up, saying for shame Gentlemen, desist etc and seized the pistols in Lieutenant Robinsons hands. [27]

Prevented from shooting Conors, Robinson drew his sword, which was also seized by the seconds, after which Robinson took to assaulting Conors with a stick. The men were separated and later forced by their commanding officer to shake hands in the officers' mess.

Leading by Example

Eighteenth century British officers are often depicted as remaining aloof from the other ranks, looking down on their lower social class. Officers are also characterised as a caring little about the suffering of their men or about their basic living conditions. Again, however, a close examination of contemporary records does not bear this out.

It is true that the ranks within the British Army were very clearly defined. Officers did not fraternise with the men, and this continued into the NCO ranks, as Corporal Todd explained: 'Major Chapman gave orders that no serjeant should drink with the Corporals, nor Corporals to drink with the Private Soldies [sic] nor Soldies [sic] to drink with Drummers neither to keep company with each other'.[28] This was strongly enforced, to the point that officers caught drinking with private soldiers could face a regimental court martial. In 1762, for example, Lieutenant Richard Rose was accused of

---

26   Gilbert, 'Law and Honour', p.83.
27   Gilbert, 'Law and Honour', p.82.
28   Cormack and Jones (eds), *Journal of Corporal Todd*, p.14.

drinking with the common soldiers but he successfully argued that he had: 'approached one William Hinxter in a punch house to inquire about a silver sword Hinxter wanted to sell, and sat down only because he had something in his shoe. It was at that moment that he was "caught" by another officer'.[29] In 1760, Ensign Hill was also tried for 'drinking and lying with the private men' which he admitted but stated that: 'tho I condescended to drink with them, Yet it has appeared by the evidence of the Kings witnesses that the men continued to preserve that respect which is due to an officer and look'd upon and behaved to me as such during the whole time of my being with them'.[30]

Even so, these cases were rare and Officers and NCOs ensured that a clear divide was maintained between the different ranks. The reason for this is clear. Officers and NCOs could not go drinking and socialising with the men and the next day order them to be flogged for a minor offence. Socialising with the men would reduce discipline and these sorts of rules are still common in the military today. However, keeping a clear distinction between the ranks is not conclusive evidence that the officers looked down on the men or treated them badly. Contemporary diarists record instances where senior officers have taken an interest in the private soldiers under their command, making time for them to learn new skills or recommending them for promotion. Corporal Todd was allowed a leave of absence to visit ill relatives whilst Colonel Bagshawe's correspondence contains many examples of his interest in his soldiers' wellbeing. Officers had to enforce discipline in their regiment and this sometimes called for men to be flogged, but British officers were not, on the whole, unnecessarily cruel to the men under their command.

When it comes to officers sharing the hardships of army life, the case is less easily made. Daily life for an officer was certainly a good deal easier than that of a private soldier. Although often billeted in the same town as their soldiers, officers could have the pick of the billets and would also expect to have their own quarters. Many kept servants or employed a private soldier from the regiment as a batman, to clean their clothes or look after their kit. The extra costs incurred by Lieutenant Colonel Bagshawe, listed in a letter written in 1750, outline just some of the benefits of being an officer. For example, he details the costs of shoeing and stabling his own horse; the costs of hiring a coach to take him into town, no doubt for a night out; a new suit of regimentals and a frock coat for duty wear; books, pens, ink, paper, and other 'trifling articles' that indicate that he was living pretty well. Those officers without an independent income did often struggle to survive on their pay alone. Having to purchase so many items, such as dress uniform, horses and so on, soon accounted for much of an officer's pay, especially amongst the junior ranks, and many officers writing at the time bemoan their lack of spare cash. Whilst they were unlikely to ever make a fortune, however, it was certainly the case that army officers were never going to starve. As we shall see, when on campaign many officers continued to enjoy a good standard of living, bringing a lot of creature comforts with them from home to make the burden of campaigning a little easier. It would not be unusual for an officer to

---

29 Gilbert, 'Law and Honour', p.86.
30 Gilbert, 'Law and Honour', p.86.

have a number of 'Bat' horses with him on which he would have loaded fine wines, bedding, his own tent and equipment, as well as those of the servants who inevitably accompanied the senior ranks. It would thus be untrue to declare that officers shared the all of the 'hardships' of campaigning.

That said, many features of campaign life were unavoidable for all those involved. The particularly harsh weather conditions experienced in Canada, for example, where winter temperatures fell well below zero, the lack of supplies in all theatres or disease, be it a tropical fever in the Indies or dysentery in Flanders, affected all the men of the regiment regardless of rank. These hardships were borne by the officers alongside their men, with many even, amongst the senior ranks, leading by example. Whilst on campaign in Germany in 1761, Corporal Todd wrote:

> About midnight HSH Prince Ferdinand with the Marquis of Granby & several other generals came along the line to view the situation we were in & gave instructions how are generals and officers were to behave in case the enemy stand another attack in the morning, & ordered cannon to several places where they were thought most proper. After this Lord Granby wrapt'd himself in his great coat and lay down upon the ground amongst us, which greatly encouraged our men, although we were in the greatest want of all sorts of necessarys at this time and expecting to engage every moment.[31]

Lord Howe, who commanded the 55th Foot in America, was an exceptional officer who instigated many of the changes to the men's uniforms and equipment to make it better suited for fighting during the French Indian War. One soldier wrote of him:

> Lord Howe was the idol of the army; in him they placed the utmost confidence, from the few days I had to observe of his method of conducting, it was not extravagant to suppose that every soldier in the army had a personal attachment to him, he frequently came among the carpenters and his manner was so easy and familiar that you lost all that constraint and diffidence we feel when addressed by our Superiors whose manners are forbidding.[32]

When an order was imposed sending the women back to camp and forcing the soldiers to do their own washing, one Massachusetts officer wrote: 'Lord Howe has already shown the example by going to the brook and washing his own'.[33] To be fair, Howe was recognised as an exceptional case amongst the British officers, even at the time, with many others not engaging with the men or accepting the rough living conditions just as gracefully.

However, the idea of leading by example and having empathy with the men under one's command came right from the top. The Duke of Cumberland was much loved by his men, who cheered when they heard he was taking over command during the Jacobite campaign. One soldier wrote that the

---

31 Cormack and Jones (eds), *Journal of Corporal Todd*, p.165.
32 E.C. Dawes (ed.), *Journal of General Rufus Putnam* (Albany: J. Munsell's Sons, 1886), p.66.
33 Francis Parkman, *Montcalm and Wolfe* (Boston: Little Brown and Company, 1902), p.345.

reason for this is: 'for they see he does whatever the meanest of them does and goes thro' as much fatigue'.[34] A story is told that Cumberland personally carried the musket of one of his sergeants who was obliged to relieve his wife of her baby.[35] On another occasion, during the Battle of Fontenoy, Cumberland approached the men of the Black Watch, who were waiting to be deployed from a sunken lane onto the battlefield, and enquired if they had everything they needed. When they asked for more ammunition, as they had been skirmishing with the enemy throughout the previous evening, he immediately called for a tumbril to be brought up and the men were re-supplied, a simple act but one that the men did not forget. The Marquis of Granby was also very careful to look after the troops under his command. After the Battle of Minden, for example, he ensured the men were fed, bringing up a bullock and bread for each regiment, as well as other home comforts; 'Lord Granby order'd all the British troops engaged there in half a pint of Brandy per man, & we drank His Majestys health, & Lord Granbys!'[36]

Senior officers also shared the danger of enemy action. Colonels and lieutenant colonels physically led their regiments forward into battle, whilst officer casualties in battle were proportionally higher than those of the men, especially in battles in America, where enemy sharpshooters targeted officers. Both cavalry and infantry officers had to lead from the front and put themselves in as much danger as the men in order to inspire them and to lead through example. It was this sort of 'leading from the front' that led to the death of Lord Howe at Bernitz Brook in 1758 whilst in 1761 Corporal Todd recorded:

> This afternoon happened a sharp skirmish between the Black Prussia Hussars, the Hanoverian Hunters & a considerable body of the enemy in which little or no advantage was gain'd upon either side. In this encounter, Prince Henry of Brunswick was mortally wounded & died soon afterwards.[37]

The Duke of Cumberland was famously, and sometime ill-advisedly, always in the thick of the fighting. He was wounded at Dettingen, and led his men from the front at Fontenoy, where many of his aides were killed and wounded around him. Cornet Philip Brown witnessed his bravery and wrote 'His Highness the Duke was never excelled by any hero whatever. He exposed his person everywhere the same as the most private soldier'.[38]

Authority in the eighteenth-century British Army was far from absolute. Officers needed to earn the respect of their men and this could not be beaten into them by endless floggings. Instead, officers had to treat the men at least tolerably well and be seen to be fair in their treatment of them. On campaign and in battle he had to lead them through example. These are still desirable leadership traits in the British Army today, and it was just as readily

---

34 Whitworth (ed.), *Gunner at Large*, p.64.
35 Whitworth (ed.), *Gunner at Large*, p.81.
36 Cormack and Jones (eds), *Journal of Corporal Todd*, p.175.
37 Cormack and Jones (eds), *Journal of Corporal Todd*, p.172.
38 Jeremy Black, *Britain as a Military Power 1688-1815* (London: Routledge, 2016), p.67.

recognised and encouraged by the leadership in the eighteenth century. Clearly, not every officer in the army reached this high bar, but the need to strive to achieve it was clearly recognised, with Richard Kane writing in his *New System of Military Discipline*:

> I cannot but take notice of some Gentlemen, who, instead of treating their men with Good Nature, use them with Contempt and Cruelty; by which those Gentlemen often meet their Fate in the day of battle from their own men; when those officers who, on the other hand, treat their men with Justice and Humanity, will be sure, on all Occasions, to have them stand fast by them, and even interpose between them and death.[39]

---

39 Kane, *New System of Military Discipline*, p.117.

6

The Infantry

The infantry regiments of the British Army consisted of the line infantry and the three regiments of Foot Guards.

For most of this period the Guards regiments each had multiple battalions, with the second battalion being used as a training or depot battalion. Before the first battalions went off to war the second battalions would be stripped of their men to ensure the first battalions were up to strength. The second battalions would continue to recruit and send trained recruits to the first battalions to replace losses. For this reason, Foot Guards battalions beginning a campaign in Flanders would be guaranteed to be up to strength.

As we shall see, this is more than can be said for the regular battalions. During times of peace, the line regiments would be run down to a couple of hundred officers and men. As war approached, they would go into overdrive, recruiting as many men as they could, only to have the regiment reduced again once peace was brokered. In these instances, officers would be placed on half-pay and returned to civilian life until recalled to the colours, whilst the private men were given their back pay along with a small sum for their trouble and then let go. As discussed in Chapter 2, when a regiment was given its orders to go on campaign, if would once again set about recruiting, or receive drafts from other regiments to make up its numbers.

The Regiments of Foot

At the beginning of the period, infantry Regiments were named after their colonel, with officers referring to them as 'Barrell's Regiment' or 'Munro's' for example. As the colonel had paid to raise and clothe the regiment, they were allowed to put their own coat of arms or individual regimental symbol on the colours carried by the regiment and the badges on the caps of the grenadiers and musicians. For example, the Colonel of the 3rd Foot (The Buffs) in 1725 was Sir Charles Wills. At this time the grenadier caps and regimental colours carried the coat of arms of the Wills family, being a 'demi-griffin azure, a coronet… holding in its claws a battle axe…' whilst the 25th Foot carried the image of a Lion's head on colours and caps, being the coat of arms of its 'owner', Colonel Shannon.[1] George II disliked this practice, as it lacked uniformity but also because it implied that the regiments belonged to the colonels and not to the King. In 1745, the Duke of Cumberland introduced a series of reforms designed to solve both problems. To begin with, the colours and standards were from now on only the King's Colour (a Union flag) and a Regimental Colour, which could no longer bear images except those approved by the King (see Chapter 9 for further details). The reforms also attempted to do away with the practice of naming regiments after their colonels and instead introduced a numbering system, with the oldest regiments on the establishment receiving the lowest, most senior, numbers. The 1st (Royal) Regiment, for example, had originally been raised in 1625 and claimed the longest service on the British establishment, whilst the regiment designated as the 2nd Foot could trace its formation back to the garrison of Tangiers in 1680. It is interesting to note that many officers and men continued the practice of calling regiments by the name of their colonel throughout the period with Cumberland himself occasionally doing so in his written orders and orderly book.

Battalions in a Regiment

For the majority of eighteenth century, most British infantry regiments consisted of only one battalion, except for the three Foot Guards regiments and the 1st (Royal) Regiment. In these cases, one battalion was available to be deployed overseas on campaign with the other remaining at home as a 'depot' battalion, which constantly went through a cycle of recruiting and training the men who were then drafted into the first battalion to make good any losses. With the huge increase in recruiting demanded by the Seven Years War, 15 regiments found themselves with enough recruits to constitute a second battalion. The War Office did not consider that this was the best use for these men, however, and in June 1758, the second battalions of these 15 regiments were separated and formed into completely new regiments instead. It was not common for the second battalions to be deployed overseas but it did occasionally happen, with the 2nd Battalion of the 1st (Royal) Regiment sent independently to fight in America in 1757, for example, or the 2nd Battalion of the Black Watch, which had been raised in 1758, being sent to campaign in Martinique.

Companies in a Battalion

In 1714, at the end of the War of the Spanish Succession, British infantry battalions consisted of 13 companies, one being a Grenadier company and the rest composed of musketeers or 'hatmen', so named as they wore the normal 'tricorne' cocked hat rather than the grenadiers' distinctive mitre. In 1717 the

---

[1] W.Y. Carman, *British Military Uniforms from Contemporary Pictures* (London: Leonard Hill Books Ltd, 1957), p.57.

number of companies in a battalion was reduced to 12, although many of the regiments had already been reduced to a skeleton staff anyway, so this did not have a great effect on physical numbers. A return for Handasyd's Regiment for 12 August 1725, for example, records only 26 officers and staff, 50 NCOs and drummers, and 290 men, which is only 24 men per company, whilst the Royal Welch Fusiliers returned 396 NCOs and men in twelve companies in February 1727.[2] The extended period of peace resulted in continued cuts to the army and in November 1729, orders were received for the: 'two youngest companies' of all 'marching regiments of foot to be broke' and the remaining ten companies to be reduced by 10 privates. An order dated January 1736 called for regiments based in Ireland to be further reduced to '2 sgts, 2 cpls, a drummer and 43 privates per company' which almost halved the original company strength.[3]

With the outbreak of the War of the Austrian Succession, each battalion was still made up of ten companies, with each company notionally consisting of: 1 captain, 1 lieutenant, 1 ensign, 3 sergeants, 3 corporals, 2 drums and 70 private men. On paper, the battalion at full strength should therefore have consisted of 814 all ranks. When the war ended the numbers of men in the battalions was once again reduced but the notional strength of the battalion remained at ten companies.

At the beginning of the Seven Years War, new regiments were raised which appear to follow this pattern: 'His majesty having thought fit to order ten regiments of foot…to be forthwith raised and consist of ten companies of three Sergts, three Corporals, two Drummers and 70 effective Private men besides commissioned officers'.[4] The full complement of officers is listed as: '1 Colonel, 1 Lt colonel, 1 Major, 9 Capt, 11 Lieuts, 9 Ensigns, 2 Surgeons mates 30 Serjts 30 Corpls and 20 Drums' although occasionally two fifes are swopped for drummers. Added to this would be one surgeon and one chaplain. The administration of the regiment is detailed below, but it can be noted here that there were only nine ensigns as the grenadier company usually had two lieutenants instead of a lieutenant and an ensign. However, these numbers were the ideal strength of the battalion, and very few managed to recruit enough men to reach this target before departing on campaign. When the 44th Foot sailed for America from Cork in 1755 it numbered only 500 men and had been forced to receive a draft of men from each of the other regiments in Ireland at the time just to make it up to this number. The 35th Regiment had similar problems when it was ordered overseas in 1756, numbering only 496 men and only making this number up to 900 by receiving a draft of prisoners and condemned men who were pardoned if they volunteered to join the colours! Some regiments, however, had less trouble recruiting, such as the 77th Highlanders who landed in America substantially over strength with 1,170 men. As a rule of thumb, taking

---

2　Atkinson, 'The Army under the early Hanoverians', p.143.
3　Atkinson, 'The Army under the early Hanoverians', p.145.
4　Hayter (ed.), *Eighteenth Century Secretary at War*, p.158.

account for sickness and casualties, most regiments departing on campaign rarely numbered over 500 men.[5]

Just to complicate matters further, in 1757 a decision was taken by the War Office to reduce those foot regiments based in Britain and Ireland to nine companies. The officers of the tenth company were put on half pay until a vacancy came up within their regiment, which they were then recalled to fill. The War office records state that: 'During the war, Regiments consisting of 10 companies frequently came home. On their arrival here they were constantly reduced to nine'.[6] This reduction was confirmed when the 93rd Foot was raised in Ireland in January 1760, the raising order stating it was to be: 'Of able bodied Protestants. To consist of nine companies. Each Company of 3 Serjeants, 3 Corporals, 2 drummers and 70 Private men'.[7] This meant that some regiments serving abroad retained the 10-company organisation whilst others, based at home, now consisted of nine. However, some of those reduced to nine were then deployed overseas, such as the 90th and the 91st, which would thus have served alongside regiments who retained the original 10 companies. This is what makes pinpointing exactly what the make-up of any particular regiment was at a given time such a tricky business.

When the Seven Years War ended, the regiments were returned to England and once again were reduced to a minimum of staff as a cost saving measure. Those sent to join the Irish Establishment were particularly harshly reduced. One record from the War Office required that: 'the 53rd and 54th Regiments of Foot shall be reduced to the same numbers as the other Regiments of Foot serving on the Irish Establishment viz 2 Serjeants, 2 Corporals, 1 drummer and 28 private men in each company besides the usual Commissioned officers'.[8] The British Army ended the reign of George II numbering not a great deal more than it did at the beginning.

Administering the Regiment

The regiment was commanded by a colonel, with a lieutenant colonel as his second in command followed by a major. These three officers were the field officers, but they also commanded the first three companies of the battalion, with the first company being the Colonel's, the second the Lieutenant Colonel's and the third the Major's. The remaining companies were commanded by captains, and, although numbered, were generally referred to by their commander's name, such as 'Captain Shelby's company' for example. Second in command for each company was a lieutenant. As the colonel was often away on business or working as a staff officer, the lieutenant in his company often ended up running it in his absence, essentially doing the job of a captain. As a result of this, the lieutenant in the Colonel's Company

---

5 Lee McCardell, *Ill-Starred General: Braddock of the Coldstream Guards* (Pittsburgh: University of Pittsburgh Press, 1986), p.136. See also McCulloch, *Sons of the Mountains*, p.35.
6 Hayter (ed.), *Eighteenth Century Secretary at War*, p.152.
7 Guy (ed.), *Colonel Samuel Bagshawe*, p.206.
8 Hayter (ed.), *Eighteenth Century Secretary at War*, p.160.

was referred to as the captain-lieutenant. Although he continued to be paid as the junior rank, this was considered to be the senior lieutenant's position and he generally was the first to be offered the next captain's position when one became available.

At the beginning of this period, every company carried a company colour or standard. It was the ceremonial role of the third officer in each company, the ensign, to carry the colour, but on a practical level he was the junior officer of the company. Fusilier regiments, which had originally been raised to guard the artillery and may have inherited traditions from the Ordnance Board, used the term second lieutenant instead of ensign, but there was no practical difference.

One of the company lieutenants would be made regimental adjutant and to him fell the mundane paperwork created by the day to day running of the regiment, including liaison with Agents, sorting accommodation, replacing lost or damaged equipment and so on. Taking on the role of adjutant could be a thankless task but if done well it placed the officer in good standing for promotion.

The regiment would also appoint a quartermaster. This role could be held by a lieutenant but was just as often held by a senior sergeant, whose role was to go ahead of the regiment and secure its accommodation, allocating billets and ensuring they were of suitable quality. The remaining officers in the regiment were the surgeon and the chaplain, both of whose roles are discussed elsewhere.

1st Foot Guards, Grenadier, 1726. Watercolour by Charles Lyall. (Anne S.K. Brown Collection)

One company in each battalion was designated as grenadiers, and this was the only company the regiment tried to maintain at full strength, usually not reducing it during peacetime. Contrary to popular myth, it did not consist of the tallest or largest men, but rather it was made up of veterans and men who had proven their worth. Being moved from a standard company to the grenadier company was considered to be a 'promotion' by the private soldiers and the source of great pride. Grenadiers considered themselves to be better than the other private soldiers and they were issued distinctive 'mitre' caps which set them apart. In battle, the men of this company were either placed together on the right of the line, the position of honour, or split equally and placed at each end of the line, to stiffen the resolve of the rest of the men.

Occasionally, if there was a particularly difficult job to do, the grenadier companies could be separated from their parent battalions, either to act as independent companies or brought together to form a makeshift battalion entirely of Grenadier companies. For example, during the French Indian War in Canada, Major General

Wolfe's formed the 'Louisbourg Grenadiers' from the grenadier companies of the 22nd, 40th and 45th Regiments during the Quebec campaign. In this case, the hat companies of the three regiments were left behind in garrison at Louisbourg with the detached grenadiers acting as a single battalion in the attack on Quebec. Examples of this practise can also be found during the Seven Years War campaign in Germany. At Vellinghausen in 1761, for example, Lord Granby refered to two British battalions of Grenadiers, one of which was identified as 'Grenadiers of the Guards', suggesting that it might have been made up of Grenadiers from the three Foot Guards battalions.

Earlier, however, during the War of the Austrian Succession, the use of combined grenadier battalions was not encouraged as it was not believed by the King to be a good use of these excellent troops. In 1743, for example, during the Dettingen campaign, Lord Stair agreed with his Austrian allies to push a force of grenadiers ahead of the main army to seize the town of Mayence. To carry out this task, all the grenadier companies, including those of the Foot Guards, were detached and formed into makeshift battalions. After the incident, Lord Carteret wrote a stern letter to Stair:

> His Majesty does not approve of your separating the Grenadiers from their respective Corps, which has not formerly been practised amongst our troops and His Majesty thinks may be attended with several ill consequences viz: Their not being in the same good order when joyned again to their Corps…the fatigue they must undergo by their frequent separation must occasion sickness and when there happens to be real service there must be losses of killed and wounded which the company cannot support.[9]

Clearly, if this was the King's view then this will have filtered down to other general officers who consequently did not separate out their grenadiers.

Also within each regiment, eight men would be designated as pioneers and were placed under the command of a corporal. They were distinguished by wearing forage caps, usually decorated with crossed axes or a similar design on the front. These caps were considered more practical than the cocked hat, given the type of manual labour the men were required to do. They marched at the head of the regimental column when on exercise, and on parade drew up behind the colour party. On campaign, these troops would go ahead of the regiment, with the vanguard, and were expected to repair roads, cut holes through hedgerows or clear any obstacles that might impede the progress of the regimental column. In camp they would cut firewood, make tent pegs to replace lost ones, and perform other manual chores as the officers required. One officer described the perfect Pioneer: 'As Pioneers are a good deal employed in works of labour and fatigue, it is absolutely necessary that they should be remarkably strong and well set, to be the better enabled to undertake both'.[10]

---

9   C.T. Atkinson, 'Grenadier Companies in the British Army', *Journal of the Society for Army Historical Research*, Vol.10, No 40 (October 1931), p.227.
10 Cormack and Jones (eds), *Journal of Corporal Todd*, p.125.

In addition, 'a man of [every] company is appointed Camp Colour men, those carry spades to level the roads under the command of the Quartermaster Serjeant of each Regiment. And the Quartermaster commands both the Pioneers & the Camp Colour men'.[11] The camp colour men also assisted the Quartermaster with marking out the regimental camp grounds, which were usually indicated by 'Camp Colours' or flags in the regimental facing colour with the regimental number on it.

Pioneers carried axes and saws in equal amounts whilst camp colour men carried spades. Their arms would be stowed whilst on this duty. Since the role of pioneer involved a good deal of much harder work than the regular infantryman, it was not a particularly popular duty. Corporal Todd was assigned the duty and explained his reluctance: 'for the Pioneers oftentimes is Ordere'd out in front to cut down wood & make facines, Bridges & Roads through woods before the army can march & is continually skirmishing with the enemy when the Regiment has nothing to do of that kind'.[12] Being out in front with the vanguard was clearly not always desirable. However, he also records being the first to discover enemy stashes of food or wine, which his men were able to help themselves to before the rest of the army came up, so it did have its advantages.

Chaplains

Along with surgeons, who are dealt with elsewhere, chaplains were the only other officers in the regiment. Although members of the officer class and allowed to mess with the officers, they were technically civilians and were appointed to their position, rather than having to purchase a commission. Although regimental colonels could put forward their candidate for the position, it remained within the gift of the Secretary at War and the War Office to approve it. This power was quite jealously guarded to ensure the right kinds of people, with the correct qualifications, were appointed. Chaplains were then, as they are now, expected to look after the spiritual wellbeing of the men, holding regular services for them in camp as well as officiating at weddings and funerals. Chaplains are mentioned as being present on campaign both in Flanders and Germany. Gunner Woods, for example, records in his diary: Order for all the soldiers to appear clean on the Parade in order to go to church at 10:30am. Marched all to the 'great church'. Prayers and sermon were read by one of our English ministers'.[13] However, they seemed less inclined to accompany the army when it went further overseas. The Secretary of War highlighted this during the French Indian War when he realised: 'there was only one Clergyman (beside the Chaplain of Artillery) to officiate in the whole British army in Canada'. He ordered the: 'reporting to his majesty the names of those chaplains who appear neither

---

11 Cormack and Jones (eds), *Journal of Corporal Todd*, p.143.
12 Cormack and Jones (eds), *Journal of Corporal Todd*, p.125.
13 Whitworth (ed.), *Gunner at Large*, p.48.

to have joined or provided proper Deputies by the time the next returns are received from Canada.[14]

Chaplains were not expected to join the regiment when it went into battle, although this did not stop some from doing so. The chaplain of the Black Watch, Laurence Macpherson, appeared at the head of the regiment at Fontenoy with broadsword in hand. When he was asked by the colonel to retire to the rear as his commission did not entitle him to stand in the ranks, he is reported to have said: 'Damn my Commission!' and subsequently charged with the regiment. He was afterwards seen giving last rites to dying men on the battlefield.

Infantry Uniforms

During the reign of Queen Anne, when the British army fought the War of the Spanish Succession, the design of the clothing worn by the various regiments was very much up to the whim of its colonel. Although the national colour of the jacket was red, the colour of the lining and cuffs, the addition of lapels or collars, as well as the coats of arms on the grenadier caps and the regimental standards, could all be very different. When George I came to the throne in 1714 he began to introduce some uniformity in their appearance, most notably by the addition of a black cockade onto the cocked hat, which was already used in the Hanoverian army as a national distinction. The King also ordered the inclusion of the white horse, which was part of the Coat of Arms of Hanover, onto head dresses, regimental colours and standards. However, it was not until the reign of George II that we begin to see real efforts at introducing uniformity amongst the various regiments. In October 1727 an order was issued stating that:

> [T]he King being desirous that all his regiments should have a fixed clothing and that each regiment should differ in their facings or otherwise…the several Colonels to consult together and prepare patterns before they make up the next clothing which they are to show His Majesty and then orders will be given that the regiments continue that clothing and that they do not presume to make any alteration whosoever shall come at the head of the corps.[15]

This order shows not only the keen interest that George II was taking in his army, but the level of control and management in which he wanted to be involved. After all, not many monarchs prior to this took an interest in the lining of jackets and the colour of a regiment's lace! The new uniforms were expected to be complete and 'put on' by the army by 11 June 1728, being the anniversary of the King's Accession Day. However, not every regiment managed to do so, as uniforms were not replaced until the old ones wore out, which could take some time. For example, in February 1728 the colonel of the 29th Foot wrote: '[Y]ou want directions about

---
14 Hayter (ed.), *Eighteenth Century Secretary at War*, p.331.
15 Carman, *British Military Uniforms*, p.58.

the next clothing. I thought that matter was so plain that you needed no directions but to go on this year and show patterns as you did for last; for we shall not want to make a real clothing until the year 1729, for what we have will do till then.[16]

A further warrant was issued in October, 1737, 'to regulate the cloathing of Horse, Dragoons and Foot' which further detailed what the infantry regiments should wear, the design of their clothing and the colour of their facings and linings. This was reinforced again by the clothing regulations of 1747, which specifically detailed which regiments could display special badges and which could only display the King's arms. By this stage there was no scope left for Colonels to 'personalise' their regiments.

New clothing was to be provided to the infantry every year. The colonel, or his agent, contracted with a supplier to provide the cloth, which was then cut and fitted by the regiment's own tailors or by local tailors employed to do the job. The new supply of clothes was supposed to be issued to the men on 11 June every year to celebrate the anniversary of George II's ascension, but it was often delayed if the regiment was overseas or on campaign. For many new recruits, this was often the first set of 'new' clothes they had ever owned and certainly the smartest. Newly appointed Sergeant James Grey of the 51st Foot wrote home excitedly, 'I have two Holland shirts, found me by the king, and two pairs of shoes and two pairs of worsted stockings: a good silver-laced hat (the lace I could sell for four dollars): and my clothes is as fine scarlet broadcloth as ever you did see'.[17]

The uniforms had to be tailored to fit the men so that they looked smart in their appearance and this tailoring appears to have been taken very seriously. Corporal Todd recorded in his journals the arrival of their new cloth whilst on campaign in Germany:

> [T]his day our new cloaths came & were served out at roll calling. And all Taylors and others that can be assistant in making them up to fit the men are to be duty free & work upon the cloathing… A house was clear'd for them to work in & a centry order at the door not to let any of the Taylors out to drink and Neglect their work…as the cloaths is so much wanted before we take the field…[18]

The King's son, William Augustus, Duke of Cumberland, ordered that a pictorial record be made of all the regiments in the army and employed the renowned painter David Morier to undertake the work. A series of copper plates were engraved and hand coloured to represent a man from each regiment of horse and infantry and bound into a book entitled 'A Representation of the Cloathing of his Majestys Household and all the Forces upon the establishment of Great Britain and Ireland' which was completed in 1742. In addition, sometime around 1751, a series of oil paintings were completed that also recorded the appearance of all of the foot and horse

---

16 Carman, *British Military Uniforms*, p.70.
17 Parkman, *Montcalm and* Wolfe, p.191.
18 Cormack and Jones (eds), *Journal of Corporal Todd*, p.141.

regiments in the army. We thus have a reasonable idea of how each regiment appeared when on parade during this period.

Surviving portraits painted of officers tend to show that prior to 1746 they continued to dress as they pleased, and although the coat remained red some are shown with full skirts rather than turnbacks, deep cuffs which were often not of the regimental colour, and with gold lace adornments to the hat and jacket designed to suit themselves. After 1746, officers appear to have purchased an expensive regimental uniform, adorned with gold or silver lace and buttons, which was reserved for parade. On campaign, they appear to have worn a simple red frock coat and short, knee length boots that were often privately purchased. Otherwise their uniform is as described below.

The regulations for 1729 stated that each foot soldier was to have 'a good full bodied cloth coat, well lined [which was to act as a waistcoat in the second year] a waistcoat, a pair of breeches, a pair of stockings, a pair of strong shoes, two good shirts and two neck cloths, besides a hat, well laced'.[19] We shall discuss each in turn.

Headwear

Most infantry soldiers wore the ubiquitous 'tricorne' cocked hat that makes this period so instantly recognisable. It was made from thick black felt and had a wide brim that was pinned to the crown on three sides to form the tricorne shape. It was worn with the front point over the left eye and generally pushed forward to keep it in place. Fashions changed through the period and the front point was sometimes 'pinched' together for a smarter appearance. The brim of the hat was edged with one and a quarter inches of white lace for the common soldiers and silver or gilt for the NCOs and officers. The officers' edging colour was also the colour of their buttons and uniform braid, being silver or gold. On the left of the hat a black cockade of woven horsehair that was held in place by a loop of material and a regimental button.

Due to the similarity in coat colour amongst many units in opposing armies of the period it was not uncommon for soldiers to place additional identifying markers in their hats to ensure they were not the victims of friendly fire. Although an example exists of this at Minden, in 1759, where British infantry allegedly placed roses in their hats, this was not a common practice amongst British soldiers.

On campaign it was common for the men to unpin the sides of their hats and let the brim down. This would keep rain from going down the collar of the jacket in bad weather but it would also keep sun off the face in very hot weather. Dr Buchanan records that during the campaign in Germany in 1743 the men un-cocked their hats for just this reason, as the days were very hot. The officers, however, refused to do so: 'None of the Officers were sicke, but

---

19 Carman, *British Military Uniforms*, p.70.

their faces were red & hot, the skin peeling off. Uncocking the hat would have proved a good preservative but was [deemed] unmilitary…'[20]

The other form of headgear worn during this period was the 'mitre'-style cap. At the beginning of the century, this was little more than a stocking cap with a stiff front piece that displayed the regimental arms. However, as the century wore on the mitre front became larger and more decorative and the cap acquired a shaped back. It had a small turned up flap at the front and the material was also turned up at the back of the mitre and edged with lace.

Originally, the front of the grenadier cap would have carried a coat of arms or a similar device at the whim of the colonel of the regiment. However, the colours of grenadier caps were set out in the 1747 regulations, which stated: 'The front of the Grenadier caps to be of the same colour with the facing of the regiment with the Kings cypher and crown over it embroidered with colours'. The small flap at the front of the cap was to be 'Red with the white horse and motto over 'Nec Aspera Terrent;' whilst the back of the cap was to be red. The turn up at the rear was to be the facing colour with 'the number of the Regiment in the middle'. An image of a flaming grenade is often depicted on the rear flap of the mitre as well, usually between the two digits of the Regimental number where applicable.

It is interesting to note that in the Morier paintings, grenadiers of the 43rd, 45th, 46th and 48th Foot do not have their regimental number shown on the back turn-up of their mitre, which shows the grenade and embroidery only. It is not clear why they did not conform to the regulations, but clearly some regiments chose not to.

At the top of the cap was a white woollen tuft with a centre of coloured threads that usually matched the facing colour of the regiment. As with cocked hats, caps were usually fitted with tapes sewn into the lining, which were secured to the soldier's hair to prevent it blowing off. The caps of the officers from the grenadier companies were usually decorated with silver or gold thread and were generally much more lavish in appearance. Those regiments granted special badges or distinctions were allowed to display them on the front of their grenadier caps. The rest of the cap remained the same. Grenadier caps were expensive and canvas covers were sometimes issued to preserve them in inclement weather. These covers were occasionally painted with the regimental arms.

In 1747, a warrant was issued which specified fur caps of bearskin for the grenadiers of Highland regiments. At the time this applied primarily to the Black Watch. These were to be made of the blackest bearskin available and were to be twelve inches in height. The helmet plate on the front of the cap was copper painted red and white, and it was worn without plumes or tassels. This existence of this warrant is often used as evidence that subsequent Highland regiments raised for the war in America, such as the 77th and 78th, also had bearskin grenadier caps, which appears to have been the case.

---

20 Dr John Buchanan, *Regimental Practice or A Short History of Diseases common to His Majesties own Royal Regiment of Horse Guards when abroad (Commonly called the Blews)* (Aldershot: Ashgate, 2012) p.251.

There has been some debate as to whether the grenadiers would have worn their mitre caps whilst on campaign, preferring to keep them for parade or ceremonial use. However, it is clear that they were such a symbol of pride to the officers and men that it is unlikely that they would not be worn into battle. It is possible that other headgear, such as a stocking cap, was worn day to day, but this would be substituted for the mitre when action was expected. During the French Indian War in Canada, for example, when all superfluous equipment was being left in stores, Major General Jeffrey Amherst wrote in 1759: 'I would leave the swords of the several regiments behind as they will be an impediment to the marching of the men in this woody country: the Grenadiers must take their caps with them'.[21]

It is perhaps worth noting here one other distinction worn by grenadiers at the time. During previous wars, grenadiers had actually carried small grenades for throwing at the enemy. To light these, they kept a slow match in a small brass case, drilled with holes to let the air circulate and keep the match lit. Although grenadiers had not carried either grenades or slow matches for some time, they retained the small brass case attached to their shoulder belt as a mark of their status.

Regiments of fusiliers also wore a version of the cap, which looked for all intents and purposes like the grenadier mitre. Whilst it carried the same design on the front, it did not have had the grenade embroidered on the back, although the regimental number does appear. The fusilier cap did not have the woollen tuft at the top of the mitre. Grenadier companies in Fusilier regiments wore the standard grenadier caps exactly as described above.

The final type of headgear worn by the infantry was the forage cap. This was generally red in colour, being made from uniform offcuts. It was a simple stocking design and had the look of an old-fashioned sleeping cap. It was worn when the men were relaxing in camp or when doing manual labour. It

Off-duty private of 23rd Royal Welch Fusiliers, c.1745, showing waistcoat and forage cap. (Reconstruction by Richard Marren Craft Workshop – photograph © Alan 'Kael' Ball)

---

21   Middleton (ed.), *Amherst and the Conquest of Canada*, p.74.

was sometimes the preferred headgear of the pioneers from each regiment, as it was comfortable and did not restrict them when chopping wood and carrying out manual labour.

Hair

Hairstyles did not change a great deal during this period. At the turn of the century, it was fashionable for the upper classes and officers to shave their heads and wear elaborate wigs, which had as much to do with controlling head lice and the like as to fashion. Wigs could be a variety of colours, even grey for the more distinguished gentlemen. As the period progressed, the smaller powdered wig began to become more fashionable and is in general use by the time of the War of the Austrian Succession. The officers' wigs were powdered white, curled at the sides and had a small 'queue', like a pigtail, at the back which was generally tied up with black silk. An existing order for the 20th Foot, dated June 1748, required officers to mount guard with queue wigs or their own hair done in the same manner.[22] As the Prussian army began to have military success it became fashionable for the officers to have long thin 'queues', which reached down between their shoulder blades, in the Prussian fashion. If wigs were not worn, officers styled their own hair in the same way, but powdering would only occur for parades or review.

In February 1748 a general order was issued stating: 'no soldier will be permitted to wear a wig after March 25th next' which suggests that private soldiers might occasionally have worn them before this date. An exception was made for men who have no hair, due to age or infirmity, who were required to provide themselves with a wig styled in the military fashion.[23]

For private soldiers, the hair would be scraped back away from the face and formed into a pigtail at the nape of the neck. Often all manner of slimy concoctions were applied to the hair to keep it in place. The 'pigtail' would then be folded over on itself to form what was known as a 'club' which was then turned up under the hat and pinned. Tabs inside the hat were then attached to the hair to stop the hat falling off. The sides would then be curled with tongs. In 1755 Sergeant Grey of the 51st Foot stated: 'one day in every week we must have our hair or wigs powdered' which was probably for parade.[24] Musicians had their pigtails plaited and folded in half with just the end of the pigtail folded up under the hat. This left much of the plaited hair visible for purely aesthetic reasons. It is possible that this style was adopted by private soldiers in the later period as Lieutenant Colonel Windus wrote of his new recruits in 1760: 'We begin to get their hair in tolerable order, which I see every morning, that it be well combed, tyed and oil'd to make it look smooth & well & before the next review it will be long enough to plat & turn up under their hats'.[25] Whether soldiers bothered to powder their hair

---

22   B. Smyth, *A History of the Lancashire Fusiliers* (Dublin: the Sackville Press 1903), Vol.I, p.80.
23   Smyth, *Lancashire Fusiliers*, Vol.I, p.80.
24   Parkman, *Montcalm and Wolfe*, p.191.
25   Guy (ed.), *Colonel Samuel Bagshawe*, p.226.

on campaign is a moot point, but it seems unlikely as they were not generally required to do so at home except for parades and reviews.

Moustaches were not encouraged in the British Army, although the Morier prints show some Grenadiers with beards. Rules about this may well have been relaxed on campaign but a clean-shaven appearance was certainly the preferred option for both officers and men.

Shirt

The soldiers were generally issued two shirts, which had a simple frill at the neck and cuffs. Officers shirts often bore more elaborate frills and were also much better quality. That said, the soldiers' shirts were clearly not cheap. When James Wolfe was employed along with his men in mending roads, in 1749, he gave orders for the issue of a coarse shirt for each man to work in 'to preserve this better linen'.[26]

Shirts do seem to have worn out before they were due for replacement and the need for them seems to be a common complaint. In 1758 Corporal Todd wrote: 'We have fine and pleasant weather & very hot, & we are in great wants of Linnen to shift us with, but one of my tent mates happened to light upon some shirts and gave me one. They are course but do very well at this time'.[27] Along with shoes, shirts were the most common item to need replacing, at the soldiers' own expense, through the year.

Waistcoat

Underneath the coat was worn a waistcoat. Unless newly issued, the waistcoat was made from the previous year's coat. The coat was unpicked, then recut and turned around to use the side that had been protected by the lining. The damaged, faded side that had been the outside of the coat was now the interior of the waistcoat. The surplus material was then made into a foraging cap. When troops served overseas in hot climates, they are sometimes shown without their heavy woollen jackets but in 'waistcoats' that have sleeves of the coat attached to them instead. Sometimes the waistcoats are shown without sleeves as well, depending on the climate.

The Uniform Coat

These heavy woollen coats were full length, coming down to cover the thighs, for which the troops were thankful in cold weather. There was a generous amount of material used, allowing pleats to be formed on both sides and it was individually tailored to fit each man, so that it came to his knee when

---

26   James Wolfe, *General Wolfe's Instructions to Young Officers* (London: Franklin Classics, 2018), p.11.
27   Cormack and Jones (eds), *Journal of Corporal Todd*, p.79.

in the 'kneeling firing' position and did not trail in the mud. It was lined with a cloth of a distinctive regimental colour, and when the generous cuffs were turned back, this colour would be visible, allowing each regiment to be distinguished from those around it.

The coats had brass or pewter buttons, which were plain and did not display the regimental number until 1767. As well as closing the coat, these allowed the cuffs to be buttoned back and, when necessary, the lapels of the coat to be buttoned across. The coat was split at the back, which also allowed the hem to be turned back and buttoned up. This also exposed the coloured lining making the regiment identifiable from behind as well. Depictions of the Guards regiments during this period show them without the hems turned back, which they may have done as a regimental distinction.

Each coat was further distinguished by lace on the sleeves and lapels. Each of the regiments had a distinctive regimental lace pattern, usually incorporating a unique colour mixed with the white lace as a means of identifying it from those who shared the same facing colour. The coloured lace used by the various regiments are listed in the appendices.

The regulation of 1729 allowed for the coats to be 'faced on the breast and sleeves' and that the collar was to be turned down two inches. This suggests that lapels were introduced about this time along with collars. However, by 1742 the colour plates illustrate only the Royal Invalid regiment with a collar, although most regiments have adopted wide lapels on their jackets. This was confirmed by the 1749 order which stated 'that all the coats of the infantry to be lapelled that are not already so'. Pockets were also to be standardised: 'that all the coats be made with the same sort of pocket as the Scotch Fuzileers vizt in the plaits of the coat'.[28]

Clearly, this took time to enforce. Those regiments already issued with new clothing would not implement the changes until the following year whilst those posted overseas or on campaign might not have received the order or have access to the material to implement it. By November 1751 the orders were still having to state: 'The soldiers coats of the infantry … to be lapelled on the breast and fully looped, the form of the loops being left to the colonel. The same is now to be observed and carried into execution'.[29] This clearly suggests that some regiments still had no lapels on their coats even by this late date.

There appears to have been much debate about adding additional padding or 'wings' to the shoulders of the infantry coat. This helped to make the men look broader and also assisted in preventing the cross belts slipping off as the soldier moved around. In May 1730 an order was issued stating: 'on viewing the patterns of clothing, we caused such as had wings or lacings on their sleeves to be taken off and made plain'.[30] However, this order appears to have been largely ignored as the Morier pictures show 19 regiments still wearing them. In December 1752 a general order was made allowing the grenadier coats of marching regiments to have 'the usual little ornament' on the point

---

28   Carman, *British Military Uniforms*, p.71.
29   Carman, *British Military Uniforms*, p.71.
30   Carman, *British Military Uniforms*, p.70.

of the shoulder, but no mention is made of the common infantry coat. The wings on the grenadiers' coats were usually edged with lace.

The soldier's coat was an intensely practical garment. In inclement weather, the hem could be dropped, the cuffs turned down and the lapels buttoned across to protect the soldier's whole body. The lining and waistcoat also provided extra warmth. In hot weather, the lining could be removed and the coat cut short or the coat sleeves removed and sewn onto the waistcoat, which would be worn instead.

Breeches

Breeches were made of the same woollen cloth as the coat and were short in the leg, generally coming to just below the knee. They were red for all regiments except for Royal regiments, which were permitted to wear blue. Officers are sometimes shown wearing breeches that were the same colour as the regimental facings. The breeches had a four-button fly and were gathered by drawstrings at the waist. They had two pockets and also had buttons and a buckle at the knee to prevent them riding up the leg. Stockings were then worn to cover the lower leg.

The red breeches would quickly wear out if worn every day, and so soldiers often had a separate pair of non-regulation breeches to wear when 'off duty'. Corporal Todd and another corporal from his regiment salvaged some 'bed-tick', which is generally blue and white stripped material, whilst foraging in France, and: 'Thomas Poyne & Goerge Darker, Taylors in our company, made them up for us…we have each of us two pair so we think ourselves well laid in for breeches…as the most of us are very badly of for Breeches by tearing them so on board [ship] etc'.[31]

In hot climates, men could also be issued with linen breeches to help them cope with the hot weather. In most cases these were red or blue to match the issued woollen breeches, but this was not always possible. Those men serving in Braddock's column during the French and Indian War, for example, wore breeches and waistcoats of Osnabruck linen, which was buff in colour.

Shoes and Stockings

Shoes were not standardised until 1749, when a design with high quarters then worn by the fusilier regiments was adopted. Made from black leather, they were not shaped to fit left and right but were of a simple square-toed design that fitted either foot and were held on by a strap attached to each upper, which were held together by a brass buckle. Generally, a one-size-fits-all approach was taken, but soldiers with a trade as cobblers, or local cobblers in the area the soldiers were posted to, no doubt cut the issue shoes to size for a small consideration.

---

31 Cormack and Jones (eds), *Journal of Corporal Todd*, p.55.

On campaign, shoes wore out quickly and the men were in constant need of re-supply.

During the Jacobite campaign, for example, the Duke of Cumberland's army: 'marched from Lichfield hither in two days which is fifty measured miles and over a most dreadful country',[32] which wore out many of the men's shoes and stockings, so much so that Cumberland applied directly to the King for replacements.

When their own army did not supply replacement shoes, the soldiers were not shy about taking them from the enemy. Corporal Todd recorded:

> Serjeant Miller found a large pair of Frenchmans shoes & he would not sell them until he brought them to me to see whether they would fit or no, as most of us was in great wants of shoes at this time. I was very glad of them. They were a little two large for me but I liked them no worse for that, as they were a pair of very good calf leather shoes & well made (they) had a deal of work in them by being seam'd twice round the tops etc. I gave him half a dollar for them & thought they were very cheap bargain as they were very easy.[33]

Officers tended to wear knee high boots, usually of the type worn for hunting, which were made of soft leather and privately purchased. Many contemporary portraits show this type of boot being worn on campaign, either in plain black or black with a tan leather top, in the classic hunting design.

Gaiters and Spatterdashes

Gaiters were leg covers that stretched from the mid-thigh down to the foot. Originally, they had been designed to prevent stones and dirt getting into soldiers' shoes when they were on the march, and as such they covered the top of the shoe and the buckle. They then extended up the leg to just above the knee, being secured by buttons up the outside. The tops were sometimes stiffened with leather to make sure they held their shape and also to prevent wear, as one officer testified before going on campaign: 'I have ordered tops of leather to be put on the gaiters when they go out to exercise & save the knees of breeches & stockings'.[34]

Gaiters also protected the breeches and stockings from mud and wear whilst on the march or carrying out manual chores. Most soldiers had two pairs. One white pair was retained for use on parade whilst another, darker coloured, pair was used for day-to-day wear. These were often dark grey or black, although other colours, such as brown, have been suggested. There appears to have been no set colour for the second pair of gaiters and it was left to the colonel, or his agent, to purchase whatever may be available at the time. Gaiters were normally made of linen, but wool gaiters were issued for

---

32   Speck, *The Butcher*, p.95.
33   Cormack and Jones (eds), *Journal of Corporal Todd*, p.158.
34   Guy (ed.), *Colonel Samuel Bagshawe*, p.228.

winter use, as they were during the winter campaign against the Jacobites in 1745.

Soldiers also wore half-gaiters or spatterdashes during spells of hot weather, when the full gaiter was too warm. This covered the top of the shoe in the same way as the gaiters but only came up to the knee, or the 'swell of the calve', hence protecting the hose but joining the bottom of the breeches. These were never worn for parade and were solely for daily wear and as such were always of a dark colour, usually black. For example, in 1761, Corporal Todd records the: 'Orders for a field day tomorrow…To be in black spatterdashes and buff garters'.[35]

NCO and Officer Distinctions

Corporals were distinguished by having a plain white aiguillette, or shoulder knot, on the right shoulder. This is said to have derived from the extra length of slow match issued to corporals during the 17th century.

Sergeants were distinguished by the wearing of a sash. At the beginning of the period it was worn over the right shoulder, but by the time of the War of the Austrian Succession it was being worn around the waist. Sashes for sergeants were crimson worsted with a central stipe of the facing colour. The sashes of NCOs of the Foot Guards had: 1st Regiment, crimson sash white stripe; 2nd or Coldstream Regiment, plain crimson sash; 3rd regiment crimson with white and blue stripe. NCOs of Highland regiments continued to wear their sashes over their left shoulder and not around their waist. Finally, the sergeants also carried a halberd as a sign of their rank. It was between five and seven feet long with an ash shaft and had a metal spike and axe blade head. It was originally held parallel to the ground and used to straighten the lines of men by walking along and pushing them into place. It was also an easy way for the officers to identify where the sergeant was during battle. There is good evidence that this weapon was carried on campaign in Europe, not least its use by the sergeants of the Royal North British Fusiliers at Dettingen to unhorse enemy cavalry. However, on raids into France or on campaign in America, it appears to have been replaced with a fusil or musket.

Officers were identified first and foremost by the use of gold or silver lace on their coats rather than the yellow or white of the men. They also had an aiguillette on their right shoulder, but this would be silver or gold, as would the lace on their hat. Officers wore a gorget of silver, for the line regiments, or gold for the royal regiments and Foot Guards. These were half-moon shaped and carried the King's Arms and, after 1746, the number of the regiment on the front. It was suspended around the neck on a ribbon that was usually the colour of the regimental facings. Finally, officers wore a crimson sash over their right shoulder, although in Highland regiments officers wore it over the left, so as not to interfere with the drawing of their broadsword.

---

35 Cormack and Jones (eds), *Journal of Corporal Todd*, p.133.

On parade, Officers carried an espontoon, or spontoon, which was a spear like weapon with a nine-foot ash shaft with a steel butt. It had a twelve- and three-quarter-inch long blade and a crosspiece designed to prevent the blade from penetrating too deeply in an enemy and becoming stuck. Once on campaign, officers appear to have left their dress uniform in store and wore much simpler plain red coats with little lace or braid. During campaigns in Europe, officers continued to carry their sword and espontoon as a sign of rank, with the use of the espontoon not being discontinued until 1786. However, in the colonies, and especially during the French Indian War, most chose to carry a fusil or a privately-purchased light musket rather than the espontoon.

Musicians

Often incorrectly depicted as young boys, the role of the drummer was crucial to the effective running of the company during this period and men could spend their whole life in the army as drummers. The only means an officer would have of conveying his orders over the din of battle would be through the sound of the drums, and so drummers had to be steady and reliable men. The same is true of other musicians, such as the Highland bagpiper, who was expected to play to encourage the troops. During the battle on the Plains of Abraham, Brigadier General Murray looked for his piper in vain as he was about to lead the Highlanders in a charge against the French, reportedly shouting 'Five pounds for a piper' so important did he think the musician was to the success of the charge.[36]

During the Seven Years War, military drummers made four pence more per day than private soldiers and were classified as non-commissioned officers. They served such an important link in the chain of command that it was crucial they be replaced when lost in action. Given their brightly coloured uniforms it is not surprising that casualties amongst musicians were high and as a result they were always in demand amongst the regiments. In November, 1755, for example, Colonel Johnathan Bagley wrote to William Johnson to replace his losses, asking him to 'Send Up [a] Good Drummer' to fill the position of Drum Major, and 'if to be had' two more drummers.[37]

The 1747 clothing regulations specifically mention musicians. All drummers were to be 'cloathed with the colour of the facing of the regiment, lined, faced and lapelled with red and laced in such a manner as the Colonel shall think fit for distinction sake, the lace… being of the colour of that on the soldiers coats'. The regulations varied for Royal regiments, stating: 'The drummers of all the Royal regiments are allowed to wear the Royal Livery vizt Red; lined, faced and lapelled on the breast with blue'. The 1751 regulations were almost a mirror of the 1747, stating:

---

36 John Chapman (ed.), *Bard of Wolfe's Army: James Thompson, Gentleman Volunteer, 1733-1830* (Montreal: Robin Brass Studio, 2010), p.198.

37 William Johnson, *The Papers of Sir William Johnson* (Albany: The University of the State of New York, 1939), Vol.IX, p.325.

The Drummers of all the Royal Regiments are allowed to wear the Royal Livery, viz., Red lined, faced, and lapelled on the breast with blue, and laced with Royal lace: The Drummers of all the other Regiments are to be clothed with the Colour of the Facing of their Regiments, lined, faced, and lapelled on the Breast with Red, and laced in such manner as the Colonel shall think fit for distinction sake, the Lace, however, being of the Colours of that on the Soldiers' coats.

In fact, the coats of musicians became very heavily laced, with vertical lines on the body of the coat and chevrons of lace along the full length of the sleeve. The Foot Guards drummers lace was blue edged with gold, and this seems to have been followed by royal regiments, with their drummer's lace blue edged white or blue edged yellow following the regimental lace. Other foot regiments followed the basic design of vertical lines on the body, usually following the seams, and chevrons on the arms in their own lace. Often the addition of lace was so elaborate that not much of the base red coat underneath remained visible. As with everything else in the army, however, musicians' lace and colours varied and it is difficult to be prescriptive about how exactly each one appeared. The drummers of the Foot Guards had hanging 'false' sleeves at the rear of the jacket and in November 1751, it was ordered that the drummers of all the foot regiments were to have the same sleeves.

1st Foot Guards, drummer, 1745. Watercolour by R.M. Barnes. (Anne S.K. Brown Collection)

The drums themselves were to display the King's cypher and crown and, after 1746, had the regiment's number painted under it with the drum case to be the same colour as the facings of the regiment. No colour is designated for the rims of the drum, both top and bottom, but they are most often depicted in red.

'Mitre' caps had been worn by drummers throughout the period, but the 1751 regulations are prescriptive about their appearance. They were to be cloth, designed along the lines of those worn by the grenadiers but not so tall. The front was to be the colour of the facings with the badge of the regiment embroidered on it or, if no distinction awarded, a 'trophy of guidons and drums'. The little flap was to be as the grenadiers, with a white horse on a red backing and the motto Nec Aspera Terrent. The back part of the cap was to be red with a tassel hanging down. The turn up was to be the colour of the facing and embroidered in the middle of the back with a drum and the rank of the regiment. By the end of the Seven Years War, many drummers' caps are shown with shaped backs just like the grenadiers, although they remained smaller overall.

The fife fell out of use in British line regiments after the English Civil War, although it remained in use amongst the Foot Guards, as shown in William Hogarth's painting of the 'March of the Guards to Finchley' in 1745 which shows a boy playing a fife. In 1747 regiments were once again permitted to have the fife, although uptake appears to have been slow. In 1748, the 38th Foot listed four fifers in place of four drummers and in 1750 three drummers of the 20th Foot were noted absent from inspection owing to the fact they were away 'learning to play on the fife'.[38] Quite how many regiments had adopted the fife by the end of the Seven Years War is unclear.

Equipment

The infantryman wore a leather belt around his waist, which was about three inches wide and from which hung the scabbard for his sword and his bayonet. Across his left shoulder he wore a shoulder strap from which hung his cartridge box that rested on his right hip. This was generally made of black leather and contained a block of wood in which had been drilled eighteen holes to take the cartridges. It was covered by a large leather flap, which buckled underneath and completely enclosed the box, keeping it dry in inclement weather. For the majority of the period, this cartridge box would be plain fronted. An alternative cartridge box could be worn on the front of the waist belt and hence was nicknamed a 'belly box'. This style of cartridge box was slightly curved to be more comfortable when sitting against the stomach of the soldier. Again, it contained a block of wood that had been drilled out to take cartridges. The number of holes varied, with some boxes holding as few as 12 and others as many as 28. This style of cartridge box was more popular with light infantry, but many of the Morier portraits show Grenadiers wearing both cartridge boxes at the same time. The inclusion of a gold 'GR' with crown above it on the leather cover was originally the preserve of the three Foot Guards regiments. The Morier paintings show the infantry regiments with plain fronted cartridge boxes except for the 42nd (Black Watch), which has a clear 'GR' on the belly box worn by the grenadier.

From the soldier's left shoulder hung his knapsack, which was made of canvas or coarse unbleached linen. It was designed to hold his rations and any other necessaries that he needed day to day and which were not packed away with his camp equipment.

Infantry carried the Long Land Pattern 'Brown Bess' musket, which weighed just over eleven pounds and was 62 inches long. The rammer for the weapon was retained within a brass pipe, which ran beneath the barrel. There were a number of variations in the design, with different patterns produced in 1737, 1748, and 1756. However, the basic design and firing procedure remained the same. The soldier carried a small picker and brush to clean the

---

38   Carman, *British Military Uniforms*, p.78.

musket lock on a chain attached to a button on his coat or behind the cross belt. This was used to clear the firing mechanism, which often fouled from repeated firing.

The musket could be carried using a buff leather sling that was one and three-quarter inches wide and up to 45 inches long, the length being adjusted using a buckle.

The Board of Ordnance issued other equipment, including a backpack, water bottle, and blanket, to each soldier when he went on campaign, as well as items to be shared between soldiers, such as a tent and cooking pots. The backpack was made of goatskin and would be worn either with one cross belt, as one might wear a modern duffle bag, or with straps across both shoulders like a modern backpack. This would be used to carry clothes or any of his camp equipment, such as firewood, cutlery or pots, bedding and so on. In European warfare, all camp equipment, backpacks and unnecessary items were stored on the regimental wagons before the soldier went into battle.

Highlanders

Independent Highland Companies had been employed to keep the peace in Scotland since 1667, but in 1739 they were brought together to form a regiment, initially known as the 43rd or Crawford's regiment, but subsequently renumbered the 42nd and coming to be known as the 'Black Watch'. Their uniform was so unusual that men from the regiment had to travel to London for an audience with the King so that he could see it before it was approved. There is an apocryphal story that the men performed a Highland sword dance for the King, which was so well received that the King gave each of the dancers a gold coin for their efforts, which apparently, they handed to the doorman on the way out. Another regiment, Loudoun's Highlanders, numbered as the 64th during its existence, were raised during the Jacobite campaign but was disbanded in 1748.

At the outbreak of the Seven Years War proposals were made to raise further Highland regiments. However, to many in the British establishment, not least the Duke of Cumberland, the memories of the Jacobite Rebellion were too recent to countenance the prospect of arming Highlanders! However, the demand for men was such that even the Duke had to relent and allow the formation of the 77th (Montgomery's) and the 78th (Fraser's) in January 1757. Following the successful recruitment of these regiments, and their excellent performance in theatre, further regiments were authorised and raised from 1759. These included Keith's 87th and Campbell's 88th Highlanders, which fought in Germany, and Morris's 89th which saw action in India.

Highland regiments were authorised to: 'consist of ten companies of four Sarjeants, Four Corporals, two drummers and one hundred effective private men in each company'.[39] Positions in the regiments appear to have been in

---

39   McCulloch, *Sons of the Mountains*, p.22.

THE ARMY OF GEORGE II

Hand-coloured engraving depicting Highland soldiers c.1742, showing the plaid worn normally and as a covering for cold or wet weather. (Anne S.K. Brown Collection)

demand, as none of the new regiments struggled to recruit. The 42nd landed in America in 1756 with 1,300 men in its ranks, the 77th landed the following year numbering 1,460 men in 13 companies whilst the 78th had to be expanded to 14 companies numbering 1,542 such was the demand.

When originally raised, the headgear consisted of the rather shapeless 'Scots Bonnet' which was generally woollen. There was no band around the edge during the early period, but by the time the additional regiments were raised in 1756 there appears to have been a white lace band added. The bonnet had a black cockade on the left side, although regiments seem to have added additional adornments to the bonnet for regimental distinction. For service in America, the 77th swopped the cockade for a black bearskin tuft whilst men of the 78th are recorded as wearing 'two black feathers in hat' to distinguish them from other highland regiments.

Grenadiers of the Black Watch were permitted in 1747 to wear black bearskin covers on their mitres, which had a metal plate on the front bearing the kings cypher and a red bag on the back. It appears that other Highland regiments raised during the Seven Years War continued to equip their grenadiers with black bearskin caps.

The coat was a short, waist length 'Highland' jacket that had turned back cuffs in the facing colour of the regiment. In December 1759 the Clothing Board censured Murray's 42nd Highlanders and Fraser's 78th for having failed to comply with 'his majesties orders' and ordered their commanders to produce new 'patterns of a clothing properly laced and lapelled' for the board. This indicates that the 42nd and 78th Highlanders had no lapels on their jackets whilst the 77th did. We can assume that regiments formed after 1759 conformed to the regulations and wore lapels. Where lapels were not present the buttonholes and area around the buttons was covered with white lace.

A neckerchief of white or black cloth was worn to stop the collar of the jacket rubbing and also to smarten up the general appearance. A short red waistcoat was worn under the jacket, which probably followed the tradition of the other regiments of foot and was replaced by using the jacket from the previous year with the sleeves cut off.

Highland soldiers did not have to be issued with the long, heavy, wool jackets that the other infantry wore, as they could rely on the plaid for warmth. This was not the short kilt of later years, but a single large piece of tartan cloth belted at the waist and with the excess gathered up and worn pinned on the left shoulder. This was the traditional highland dress and was very popular with the men, as the plaid could be unpinned and pulled up like a cloak to cover the head and shoulders in bad weather and the men rolled themselves up in the material when sleeping outside. To outsiders it always appeared strange, with one British officer describing the men as wearing: 'broad garters under the knee, and no breeches, but his plaid belted around his waist which hangs exactly like the folds of the Roman garment which we see on Equestrian statues'.[40] The plaid generally followed the Government sett, meaning that they were a field of green with dark blue stripes arranged in pairs. However, variations are recorded. The grenadiers of the Black Watch may have had an additional red stripe in their tartan, whilst pipers of some regiments were described as wearing the personal tartan of the colonel. Pipers of the 87th, for example, wore the Royal Stewart tartan, described as: 'scarlet, with medium stripes of dark green arranged in pairs, the pairs spaced widely apart. Over the green stripes were alternating thin over-stripes of yellow and white'.[41]

A sporran would be worn on the front of the plaid and took the form of a leather purse decorated on the front. The men tended to buy or ornament their sporrans themselves so there was no fixed design for this. Usually they are shown with a metal horseshoe style fitting at the bottom and a buttoned flap at the top.

Thick, knee length stockings were worn, which were usually red and white checked. They were folded over at the top, showing a ribbon of the regimental tartan on the side. In America, Highlanders often wore Indian style leggings to protect their legs from the thick undergrowth of the woodland. Highland shoes are described as: 'a sort of thin pump or brogue, so light that it does not in the least impede his activity in running: and from being constantly accustomed to these kind of shoes they are able to advance or retreat with incredible swiftness'.[42] These shoes are often depicted with brass buckles. How far these shoes remained in use on campaign is not clear, and they may have been replaced with whatever was available locally or with standard issue infantry shoes.

Pipers in the Highland regiments were dressed in coats of reversed colours, faced and lined red. They were equipped only with a broadsword for protection, but otherwise appeared as the private soldiers. The Black Watch was made a royal regiment after its heroic performance at the Battle of Ticonderoga, after which their pipers would have worn the royal livery of red faced blue. The pipes were not used to give orders, as the drums were, but instead were included to encourage and inspire the men to acts of bravery. For this reason, the pipers were expected to lead the way when the regiment was advancing and those who did not were sanctioned for it. For example, when attacking the French at Quebec in 1759, the piper of the 78th Highlanders could not be found and afterwards: 'the Piper was disgraced by the whole of the Regiment, and the men would not speak to him, neither would they suffer his rations to be drawn with theirs'.[43] The following April,

---

40 Victoria Schofield, *Highland Furies: the Black Watch 1739-1899* (London: Quercus Publishing, 2012), p.56.
41 '87th Foot', *Seven Years War*, at <http://www.kronoskaf.com/syw/index.php?title=87th_Foot>, viewed 1 October 2020.
42 Schofield, *Highland Furies*, p.56.
43 Chapman (ed.), *Bard of Wolfe's Army*, p.198.

when the French attempted to retake Quebec, the piper redeemed himself, as the regiment retreated in disorder: 'a blast of his pipes … had the effect of stopping them short, and they soon allow'd themselves to be form'd into some sort of order'.[44] Piping, it seems, was not for the faint hearted.

Highlanders carried a basket-hilted broadsword, which hung from a black leather belt worn over the right shoulder and which was kept in place by a shoulder strap on the jacket. Soldiers wore a 'belly box' style ammunition box on their front attached to their waist belt, alongside the bayonet hanger and dirk, or small knife. At least one pistol was usually carried which hung from a strap over the right shoulder, hanging mid-chest on the soldier. They were also equipped with a satchel, in which was their rations, spare shirts etc. This was a canvas bag strung from their left shoulder and which rested on their right hip.

Light Infantry

Light Infantry were employed in Europe to scout ahead of the army over broken terrain that cavalry might not be able to cross, and hence screen the army from surprise attacks by the enemy. They were also used to drive out the enemy's light infantry from areas of the battlefield where their sniping and skirmishing might hold up the advance of the main force. For example, highland troops of the Black Watch were deployed as skirmishers in an attempt to drive off the Arquebusiers de Grassin, a French light infantry unit, from a wood on the allied right flank at the Battle of Fontenoy in 1745. However, whilst the British Army often sent its infantry out to skirmish or act as picquets for the advancing main force, there were no distinct light infantry companies or trained light infantry troops at this time. As we shall see, these units were formed in America during the French and Indian War but this was in direct response to the nature of the terrain and the kind of war they were engaged in. The German states, and the Austrian and French armies, had employed 'Jaegers' and 'Pandours' in their armies to carry out this role, but it was not common practice for the British.

During the Seven Years War, the increased use of irregular light infantry by the French and their allies forced the allied army under Prince Ferdinand of Brunswick to respond in kind. The enemy light troops were not only causing difficulties in the approach to battle, by skirmishing with the advance picquets or driving in scouts, but they were also attacking the supply columns and baggage trains in the rear of the army. The British regulars hated these enemy light troops, viewing them as little more than bandits. Corporal Todd wrote:

> [They] are call'd unregular troops as they seldom or never Joyn with the army but keeps on the out skirts, either in front or upon the flanks & is under no command but their own officers…if the pandores or Yeagers be overcom'd by the enemy…

---

44 Chapman (ed.), *Bard of Wolfe's Army*, pp.199-200.

they seldom will give them any quarter upon either side, for both armies has a great aversion to them as they are counted no more on them a company of Banditti or Robbers, altho there is plenty of them both in our Army & theirs. It is those sort of people that mostly plunders the wounded or slain after a battle… so that they are dispised by all Soldiers & their officers is the same as the men.[45]

In 1761, the British were finally forced to contribute to the light infantry force:

> Prince Ferdinand gave orders for a detachment of 50 men per battalion to be appointed, with officers in proportion, for Chasseurs, under the command of General Luckner. Corporal Purton of our company turn'd out for this duty & the men all turn'd out volunteers very readily, as this party is to be mostly along with the light troops.[46]

The following year orders were issued for a battalion of Chasseurs to be formed by each allied nation in the army. An order for the British contingent, dated 23 May, 1762, calls for 30 men plus a subaltern, a sergeant, a corporal and a drummer to be detached from each of the 12 English marching regiments in Germany, along with three captains, one from each brigade. The three detachments of each brigade formed a single company divided into four sections. Orders state that only the fittest and most alert men were to be chosen and that they were to be considered 'elite' troops, being allowed to 'beat the Grenadiers march' and to form only two-deep when in line. To distinguish them, they were ordered to remove the lace from their tricornes and a green cockade was substituted for the black one, although it appears that they retained the facings of their parent regiment and did not alter the rest of their uniform in any way. No mention is made of the Guards detachment or the Highland regiments who were present with the army at this time so it must be assumed they did not provide men for this new corps. One fifer was later added to each company.

---

45 Cormack and Jones (eds), *Journal of Corporal Todd*, pp.196-7.
46 Cormack and Jones (eds), *Journal of Corporal Todd*, p.193.

7

The Cavalry

The cavalry regiments, and especially the Household regiments, were seen as the most prestigious in the army, and many men who would later rise to senior rank began their careers in them. The cavalry was split into three main groups; the Household Cavalry, who were traditionally the Kings bodyguard and who spent much of their time guarding the King or his palaces; the regiments of horse, which we might consider to be the more traditional cavalry regiments; and the dragoons, who as a type began life during the English Civil War as mounted infantry. As we shall see, the role of the dragoons was to develop substantially during this period. Finally, towards the end of the Seven Years War, light troops begin to be formed within the existing cavalry regiments before eventually becoming fully-fledged regiments of light cavalry in their own right by 1759.

When King George II took the throne, his cavalry consisted of four troops of Horse Guards, two troops of Horse Grenadier Guards, eight regiments of horse and 14 regiments of dragoons.

Organisation[1]

Just as an infantry Regiment is broken down into companies, so a cavalry regiment is broken down into troops. Typically, two troops would make up a squadron with three squadrons constituting a regiment. On campaign, the cavalry tended to be deployed in squadrons rather than individual troops.

At the beginning of the reign of King George II, the Household cavalry consisted of four troops of Horse Guards and two troops of Horse Grenadier Guards. The Horse Guards were arguably the most prestigious units in the army and demand for positions amongst social climbing young officers was fierce. This was particularly true because officers of the Guards were deemed to hold higher rank within the army than their actual rank in the

---

1 Based on information from David Blackmore, *British Cavalry in the Mid-Eighteenth Century* (Nottingham: Partizan Press, 2008) and Percy Sumner, 'Uniforms and Equipment of Cavalry Regiments from 1684 to 1811', *Journal of the Society for Army Historical Research* Vol.14, No.55 (Autumn, 1935), pp.125-142.

regiment. A lieutenant in the Guards would rank as a captain, for example. As a result, each troop, which numbered about 130 privates and NCOs, had officers who ranked as one colonel, two lieutenant colonels, two majors, four exempts (captains) four lieutenants, four sub lieutenants, and an adjutant, who was the top ranked sub-lieutenant. A list published in 1742 shows the establishment strength of the Horse Guards to be 620 all ranks.

To show that even the oldest regiments were not immune from cuts, in 1746 the Horse Guards were reduced to two troops, each of 150 private soldiers and NCOs. Although the number of officers per troop remained the same, those made redundant by the cuts were either placed on half pay until a position opened up in the existing troops or were transferred to other regiments.

The Horse Grenadier Guards continued to have two troops throughout King George's reign. Each troop consisted of a colonel, one lieutenant colonel, one major, two captains, two lieutenants and one cornet, who was the Guidon bearer and the equivalent to an ensign in the infantry.

The 1st Horse was named the Royal Regiment of Horse Guards and was also known as 'the Blues' as its troops wore a distinctive blue coat faced red instead of the usual red coat. Although called 'Horse Guards' this regiment were not considered to be part of the Household Cavalry at this time, but were rather the first and most distinguished regiment of Horse. It and the 2nd Horse, known as the King's Horse, consisted of nine troops each. Each troop contained one captain, one lieutenant, one cornet, one quartermaster, two corporals and one trumpeter. All the remaining regiments of horse had six troops, officered as above. In the 2nd–8th Horse there were 38 private soldiers per troop, but the 1st Horse had 40 private soldiers per troop.

In 1746 the cavalry was forced to undertake cost-cutting measures. As well as reducing the Horse Guards to two troops, as mentioned above, the 2nd–4th Regiments of Horse were reduced to being dragoons. This was simply a way of reducing costs by paying them less. For example, a lieutenant in a troop of horse was paid 15 shillings per day whilst the same officer in a troop of dragoons was paid 9 shillings. This difference in pay was reflected throughout the ranks, and so by simply renaming the horse as dragoons, the Government substantially reduced the wage bill. Not surprisingly, this was not popular, especially as the role of these cavalry regiments on the battlefield had not changed and that the men were doing the same job for half the pay. Partly in order to salve the men's egos but more to retain the value of the officer's commissions, the regiments were re-designated the 1st, 2nd, and 3rd Dragoon Guards. As we shall see, they were allowed to keep many of the trappings of horse and viewed themselves very much as distinct from the normal dragoon regiments.

To complete the 1746 re-organisation, or downsizing, of the cavalry the Royal Horse Guards (Blues) were moved onto the establishment of the Household Cavalry and remaining 5th–8th Horse were renumbered the 1st–4th Horse. They were then moved permanently onto the Irish Establishment and were renamed the 1st–4th Irish Horse. Again, this was simply to reduce costs as, in the first instance, horse regiments posted to Ireland were expected to reduce the number of private soldiers in a troop to around 24 whilst the

2nd Horse, 1743. Watercolour by W. Sharpe. This regiment was later redesignated the 1st Dragoon Guards. (Anne S.K. Brown Collection)

Royal Horse Guards (Blues), 1756. Contemporary watercolour by E. Fitzgerald. (Anne. S.K. Brown Collection)

overall bill for maintaining the regiments now fell to the Irish Exchequer.

For the majority of this period there were 14 Regiments of Dragoons. At the beginning of the period, each regiment appears to have had only three troops. However, in February 1727 a general order was issued for three additional troops to be added to all dragoon regiments at two sergeants and 55 men per troop. In addition, seven extra men were to be added to each existing troop. By 1742, each regiment consisted of six troops, except for the 5th, which appears to have had nine, for reasons which have never been fully explained. Each troop consisted of one captain, one lieutenant, one cornet, three sergeants, three corporals, two drummers, one hautbois and 59 private men.

When the dragoon guards regiments were formed in 1746, they reduced their establishment to match that of the dragoons and replaced their trumpeter with a drummer.

As always when discussing eighteenth century British military organisation, the numbers quoted above were purely aspirational. Outside of the Household Cavalry, many regiments struggled to maintain their full quota of men. This was not helped by the fact that, during the peace between the end of the War of the Austrian Succession and the outbreak of the Seven Years War, regiments were reduced in size, with private soldiers made redundant and officers placed on half pay. For example, the dragoon guards regiments were reduced by one sergeant, one corporal and 23 men per troop for the period 1748 to 1756. Regiments on the Irish Establishment were reduced even further. When one combines this with illness, leave, and the implementation of drafts from one regiment to another, there is no real way of saying with any certainty how many men were in any of the cavalry regiments at any one time. When trying to estimate how many men were with the regiment at any particular battle, it is best to look to the returns posted during the campaign, as these give the best idea of the actual state of the regiment rather than its aspirational strength.

Uniforms and Equipment

A Parliamentary report from 6 June 1746 states: 'The foot are clothed annually, Horse and Dragoons every two years. Horse and Grenadier Guards every three years'. The reason for this frugality when it came to clothing and equipping the mounted regiments was because their kit was very expensive! A tailor's return from 1746 shows the cost of clothes for dragoons as: 'Sergeant, Corporal or Private of Dragoons 10/- to 13/6; For a drummer, when laced in an extraordinary manner, 15/- Hautboys as drummers'. The same Parliamentary report of 1746 puts the cost of a complete set of clothes and equipment for a dragoon at: 'Sergeant £30 3s 6d; Corporal, £16 2s 6d: Drummer £18 19s 7d Private £15 6s 6d', and this before he has been provided with a horse.[2] Although the colonel of the regiment might expect to recoup some of this expense over time through stoppages from the soldiers pay, the initial outlay was still substantial. Given that dragoons would have been the cheapest form of cavalryman to outfit, anyone hoping to raise a mounted regiment for the crown had better have deep pockets indeed.

Before addressing the uniform of specific regiments, it is probably best to deal first with the items of clothing they had in common. Cavalry were generally issued with a cloth coat 'well lined' with serge, a waistcoat, a laced hat and a pair of large buff gloves. Except where noted below, hats were the standard 'tricorne' and were edged with lace. Each had a black cockade on the left side, held in place by a gilt loop and button. The hat was worn with the point of the tricorne over the left eye and was held in place by a cord attached to the lining of the hat, which was hooked through the hair to prevent it blowing off when riding.

There has been some debate about whether the cavalry continued to wear head protection under their tricornes when going into battle. The idea was that a round metal skullcap could be worn to protect the head from sword

---

2   All from Sumner, 'Uniforms and Equipment of Cavalry Regiments from 1684 to 1811', p.99.

THE ARMY OF GEORGE II

'Thomas Brown of Brigadier Blands Regiment of Dragoons. He distinguished himself at the Battle of Dettingen by retaking the Standard from the French'. Contemporary engraving after unknown artist. (Anne S.K. Brown Collection)

blows, as it had been during Marlborough's time. Often referred to as a 'secret', this would either be carried as a separate item or it could be sewn into the lining of the hat. It does not appear amongst the surviving lists of standard issue equipment for this period and this has led to speculation that it fell out of use. However, a review of dragoons for 1750 notes the men carrying 'iron skull caps' at their saddlebow,[3] whilst a Jacobite report following the Battle of Clifton in 1745, complains that their swords: 'suffered much, as there were no less than fourteen of them broke on the Dragoons skull caps'.[4] The evidence therefore suggests that they were still being used, even if they were not officially issued.

Cavalry troopers were issued with a forage cap, made from offcuts of material left over when the tailors were making the men's uniforms. They

---

3 Sumner, 'Uniforms and Equipment of Cavalry Regiments from 1684 to 1811', p.99.
4 Christopher Duffy, *Fight for a Throne: the Jacobite '45 Reconsidered* (Solihull: Helion, 2015), p.261.

were essentially a stocking style of hat, like an old-fashioned night cap, and were red turned up with the regiment's facing colour.

Hairstyles for the men were generally the same as the infantry, with the private soldiers' hair being combed back into a ponytail and then 'clubbed' under the hat. Musicians were permitted to wear their hair in a plait, which was then bent up and the end tucked under the hat but the plaiting still visible. As with the infantry, officers wore their hair tied back in a queue and curled at the sides, or a wig styled in the same manner. An article in the *Gentleman's Magazine* from February, 1739, mentions 'the soldiers powdering themselves for Reviews',[5] meaning that their hair was powdered white but only when going on parade.

All the cavalry troopers wore a neck stock of white material. All the men were issued heavy red cloaks, which were lined with material coloured to match the regiment's facings. When not being worn, the cloak was rolled and stored behind the rider, red side up but with the regimental colour showing in the rolls. These were a godsend when on sentry duty or when forced to sleep in the open, and regimental surgeons put the reduced instance of colds and flu amongst the cavalry, compared to the infantry when on campaign, down to this additional piece of clothing. Unless noted otherwise, crossbelts, for sword and ammunition pouches, and waist belts, were of buff coloured leather.

Another piece of kit unique to the cavalry was the 'frock', which often appears in returns for kit issued to the troops. This appears to have been a large, loose fitting shirt or smock that the soldier could wear over his uniform to protect it from the dust and dirt thrown up by the horses when on the march. It also appears to have been worn for fatigue duty and as a result was replaced fairly regularly. A Parliamentary report from 1746 for the 1st Dragoons states: 'Last campaign frocks to go over the men's clothes provided from stoppages. Out of the Government grant extraordinary spatterdashes and a new set of frocks provided for this regiment last year, and another set provided this year'. The men appear to have liked the comfort of the 'frock' and often wore it instead of their coat, which was packed away with their gear. This looked untidy, however, and so we find the colonels having to issue orders, such as a surviving one from May, 1745 which reads: 'None of the Cavalry to march in their frocks, all in their red clothes'.[6]

Officers were distinguished by having an aiguillette on the right shoulder of gold or silver lace whilst also wearing a plain crimson sash from their left shoulder, which was knotted at the right hip to avoid interfering with the sword hilt. They also had a length of cord as a decorative sword knot: the latter originally could be any colour according to the officer's taste, but a directive issued in 1751 called for them to be 'crimson and gold in stripes, as those of the infantry'.[7] Cavalry officers did not wear gorgets. Prior to 1751, officers in the cavalry could dress as they pleased but in that year officers'

---

5 Sumner, 'Uniforms and Equipment of Cavalry Regiments from 1684 to 1811', p.98.
6 Sumner, 'Uniforms and Equipment of Cavalry Regiments from 1684 to 1811', p.99.
7 Royal Clothing Warrant 1751, from Sumner, 'Uniforms and Equipment of Cavalry Regiments from 1684 to 1811', p.99.

uniforms were regulated and ordered to conform to match the regimental uniforms. Officers' dress coats were very elaborately braided in gold but they appear to have worn a more practical, plain red coat, when on campaign. Judging from portraits of senior officers painted at the time, there appears to have been a fashion amongst officers not to turn back the coat skirts as the men did, but this was not regulation.

Cavalry quartermasters were originally identified by the wearing of a crimson sash around their waists. After 1745, sergeants of horse grenadiers and dragoons were all ordered to wear their sashes around their waists, so how quartermasters within these regiments were then distinguished is not clear.

Cavalry boots were generally better made and of higher quality than infantry shoes, but were difficult and clumsy to run in or to walk any distance. For this reason, dragoons, who still were still expected to fight dismounted, were often issued shoes and gaiters rather than cavalry boots. This is further discussed below. White material, known as 'knee pieces', was wrapped around the knees to prevent the tops of the stiff boots wearing out the riding breeches and these are often depicted in prints for all cavalry regiments being just visible above the top of the boots. Spurs were also issued to the men.

Cavalry were generally armed with a sabre, two pistols and a carbine. As the colonel of the regiment purchased these items, there was no 'standard' weapon for the cavalry, with a number of different designs in use throughout the period.

The swords tended to be straight with a basket hilt to protect the hand. These hilts were of various designs, but generally had a leather lining and were large enough to take a gauntleted hand. Swords were worn on the waist belt on the left-hand side in the case of dragoons and from a shoulder belt on the right shoulder in the case of the horse. Horse regiments can thus be distinguished by their two belts crossing on their chest whereas dragoons had only one cross belt.

Pistols generally were of the same bore as the carbine to allow the same ammunition to be used, but otherwise could be of any type. These were carried in holsters on either side of the saddle by the rider's legs, where they could be easily accessed when required. The holsters were covered with 'holster caps' which were material embroidered with the Royal cipher on a field the same colour as the regimental facing. See notes below for variations on the design of the holster caps.

Carbines were essentially just shortened muskets. The Horse Guards used a 1737 pattern carbine, remodelled in 1748, that was 62 inches long and had a wooden ramrod. In the later period, most dragoon regiments were using a 1746 pattern dragoon carbine that was 58 inches long and had a metal ramrod. It was designed with a socket so that a bayonet could be fitted, as this was also a standard issue weapon for dragoons. They were carried in a 'bucket' style holster on the right-hand side of the rider and rested across his right leg. Ammunition for the carbine was held in an ammunition pouch which was carried on a cross belt on the soldiers left shoulder, hanging at his right-hand side.

The Horse Guards

There were four troops of Horse Guards and two of Horse Grenadier Guards at the beginning of this period. The troopers all wore red coats with no lapels, blue lining, turn backs, and cuffs. A gold shoulder knot is worn on the right shoulder. A print from 1742 shows a small blue collar also present on the jacket and elaborate gold lace on the jacket, cuffs and hat lace as befits the Household Cavalry. Waistcoat and breeches were buff.

The four troops were distinguished by the addition of two coloured stripes on their buff coloured carbine belts: red for the first, white for the second, yellow for the third, and blue for the fourth. The holster caps and housings were red with the royal cipher and gold fringe but the saddlecloth appears to have matched the colour of the carbine stripes for each troop. The pistol housings for all the Household Cavalry carried the gold GR surmounted with a crown. The saddle blanket colour varied but it had a royal seal surmounted with a crown in the corner and was edged usually with gold, which had a fine coloured stripe through it that varied for the different troops.

In 1746 the four troops of Horse Guards were reduced to two. Both retained red jackets faced and lined blue. The jackets had a gold edged blue patch at the collar. They still had no lapels but the gold shoulder knot is replaced by gold edged shoulder straps. All lace was gold for officers and men. Waistcoat and breeches remained buff.

The two stripes on the carbine belts remained red for the first troop and are shown as blue for the second troop in the Morier painting. The lace edging on the horse furniture was yellow with a red central stripe for the first troop and yellow with a blue stripe for the second. The lace on the jackets remained gold.

The Horse Grenadiers were dressed in a similar manner to the Horse Guards with red coats lined blue with blue turnbacks and cuffs, although the colour of the coats was described as 'madder red' suggesting that it was darker red than the Horse Guards. Lace was white for private soldiers and gold for officers. Waistcoats and breeches were buff with black riding boots and white knee pieces. However, instead of the black cocked hat, the Horse Grenadiers wore the grenadier style 'mitre' cap. The first troops' mitre had a high blue front, a red small flap at the front and the back all red. The second, or Scottish, troop had a red front, small blue flap and back all blue. The flap of the first troop did not have the White Horse but rather a small scroll, whilst the second had the thistle-and-motto surround seen on most Scots regiments. The high front of the mitre cap in both troops had the GR cipher inside the garter with a crown overall. The only other distinguishing features of the two troops were the cords of the powder horns that were slung over their left shoulders. The first troop had blue cords and the second red. The horse furniture, housing, and holster caps were blue for the first troop and red for the second. A 1751 oil painting shows the back of the second troop's cap as having changed to red but the turn up and small flap remains blue.

Officers and NCO's of the Horse Guards and Horse Grenadier Guards were distinguished exactly as they were in other regiments of horse, having an aiguillette of gold on the right shoulder and a crimson sash over the left.

However, an order dated 20 May 1745 directs: 'All the sergeants of Horse Grenadiers, Dragoons and Foot to wear their sashes for the future round their waists'.[8] and further clarifies 'its to be worn in the same way as before viz – Those of the cavalry [knotted] on the right side, those of the infantry on the left'.[9] We can assume that sergeants of other horse regiments continued to wear their sashes over their left shoulder.

The Horse

Horse regiments were generally dressed as the Horse Guards were. However, they wore red coats with velvet lapels in the regimental colour. The coats were also lined and had turn backs and cuffs, which were again usually in the regimental colour. The waistcoats and breeches were also generally the colour of the regimental facings. Some regiments did not follow this pattern, such as Ligoniers 8th Horse, which had black facings and lapels but buff lining, turnbacks, waistcoat and breeches. Full details of the regimental distinctions are provided in the appendices.

The 1st Regiment of Horse, or Royal Horse Guards, was distinguished by wearing blue coats with red lining, cuffs and turnbacks. The waistcoat was red, the breeches blue, with black riding boots and white knee pieces. Their cocked hat had a black cockade and was edged yellow for troopers and gold for officers and NCOs. In the Morier painting, the horse furniture appears to be red with the Royal cypher on the holster caps and housing. The regiment carried their powder flask on a red cord, which hung from their left shoulder. In 1746, the Blues joined the Household Cavalry and their uniform underwent a significant change. Whilst the coats remained blue, there were now red lapels, which extended the full length of the coat, with the coat lining red, creating red cuffs and turnbacks. The waistcoat and breeches were also red. Shoulder straps now appeared on the jacket to hold the two buff cross belts in place.

During the War of the Spanish Succession, some horse and Household regiments had worn metal cuirasses to cover their torso, and a metal skullcap under their hat, both to provide some protection against enemy sword blows. It is not clear when the practice of wearing cuirasses ended, with the assumption being that by the War of the Austrian Succession they were no longer being worn by the rank and file. However, Dr Buchanan, the regimental surgeon for the Blues, records in the aftermath of Fontenoy that 'our Cuirasses saved many lives'[10] as many men had been hit by spent musket balls which otherwise would have injured them. There is also a record from July 1758 showing that the regiment were 'issued with cuirasses and skullcaps' that year.[11] This suggests that, certainly amongst the Blues and

---

8 Sumner, 'Uniforms and Equipment of Cavalry Regiments from 1684 to 1811', p.99.
9 Sumner, 'Uniforms and Equipment of Cavalry Regiments from 1684 to 1811', p.132.
10 Buchanan, *Regimental Practice*, p.153.
11 Sumner, 'Uniforms and Equipment of Cavalry Regiments from 1684 to 1811', p.258.

possibly amongst other horse regiments, the wearing of cuirasses continued well into this period.

In regiments of Horse there were no sergeants, with corporals holding the position of senior NCO. They were identified by having an aiguillette of the regimental lace on the right shoulder.

Holster covers and saddlecloths were generally the colour of the facings of the regiment. The device on the holster covers and saddlecloths prior to 1746 varied and for many regiments appears to have been of 'drums, flags and trophies'. The saddlecloths were often edged with elaborate gold embroidery, following a scrolling pattern around the edge. After 1746 the holster covers bore the 'GR' cypher with a crown above. The saddlecloths bore the rank of the regiment ('IH', 'IIH' and so on) surrounded by a wreath of thistles and roses.

The saddlecloths were generally of the facing colour and were edged with three thin coloured lines, each distinct to the regiment and each of which made up a third of the width of the edging. For example, the 1st Irish Horse had a pale blue saddlecloth that was edged white, red and white.

Dragoon Guards

The re-classification of horse regiments as dragoon guards was purely a cost saving measure, as the troopers would now be paid as dragoons and not as horse. Here was no significant change in their equipment or battlefield role and the title of 'Guards' was simply added as a face-saving measure for the colonels and officers within them. A Royal Warrant drafted in 1747 but implemented in 1751 called for their coats to be lapelled only to the waist with the colour of the regiment rather than to the bottom, as the regiments of horse had. Dragoons had no lapels, so this was considered a halfway measure. The use of velvet for lapels and facings was a distinction of horse but was retained by the dragoon guards. The regiments were further distinguished by the cut of their pockets and by the design of their lace, which distinguished one from another.

3rd Dragoon Guards, 1760. Gouache by unknown artist. (Anne S.K. Brown Collection)

Corporals had gold lace on their cuffs, whilst sergeants had similar lace on cuffs, lapels and pockets. Sergeants also wore gold shoulder knots and had sashes around their waist, which were a combination of the facing colour and the colour of the stripes on the house furniture. This made those of the 1st Dragoon Guards blue, the 2nd buff and blue and the 3rd white and red. Officers retained the silk crimson sashes over the left shoulder.

An interesting order remains from 1765, which states that swords were to be carried by officers of dragoon and dragoon guard regiments when on foot and not fusils. This suggests that officers carried fusils, or carbines, alongside the men when dismounted and that the dragoon guards could function as mounted infantry when called upon to do so.

The Dragoons

Dragoons were originally conceived to operate as mounted infantry, riding to a point on the battlefield where they were required at which time they would dismount to fight on foot. This was opposed to the horse, who were expected to charge enemy cavalry and infantry and ride them down. However, by the beginning of the reign of George II this distinction was not clear, with many dragoon regiments fighting admirably on horseback at Dettingen in 1743 and Lauffeld in 1747. At both of these battles, dragoon regiments charged alongside the horse and overcame regiments of enemy horse. Although designated dragoons, we can see from their equipment and their battlefield performance, that their role as mounted infantry was fading.

The regulations of 1736 allowed for each dragoon to be issued with:

> A coat lined with serge, waistcoat, breeches, laced hat, large buff coloured gloves with stiff tops. Boots – every 3rd clothing. Housings and [Holster] Caps – every 5th clothing. Cloaks faced with the livery of the Regiment, every 6th clothing. New Accoutrements of the best buff viz shoulder belt with a pouch, waist belt sufficient to carry the sword, with a place to receive the bayonet and sling for the arms – every 10th clothing.[12]

Headgear was the usual cocked hat edged in the same colour as the coat lace with a black cockade on the left side, held in place a gilt loop and button. However, the 2nd Dragoons (Royal North British, or Scots Greys) wore a 'mitre' cap similar to that worn by the fusiliers or musicians, being slightly smaller than the infantry grenadier caps. Prior to 1742 the high cap front appears to have been red with the small flap in the facing colour. It bore a thistle and the motto 'Nemo Me Impune Lacessit' on the flap, with a St George's cross inside a garter on the front of the cap. After 1742, the front of the cap changed to blue with the device of the thistle and motto moved to the high flat front of the cap with the small flap now bearing the Hanoverian white horse. Senior officers in the regiment may have worn the cocked hat edged gold rather than the mitre, but officers' mitre caps from the 2nd remain in museums, so perhaps this was personal choice.

The dragoon coat was red with no lapels, lined with cloth of the regimental colour, which was turned back to show coloured cuffs and skirts. Full details of the regimental colours for the various Regiments of Dragoons, including the colour of their waistcoats and breeches, are provided in the appendices.

---

12   Sumner, 'Uniforms and Equipment of Cavalry Regiments from 1684 to 1811', p.97.

Dragoon coats had a shoulder strap on the left shoulder to help hold the cross belt in place. They also had an aiguillette on the right shoulder which was yellow or white for private soldiers, in line with the regimental lace, and consequently gold or silver for the officers and NCOs. A review of the 8th Dragoons in 1735 noted silver shoulder knots for their officers and sergeants but had yellow and silver mixed for corporals.[13] The regimental facing was yellow, so perhaps corporals of other regiments might have a mix of their lace colour and facing colour in their shoulder knots as well, although the 1751 regulations called for yellow or white silk shoulder knots in line with the lace. As with the dragoon guards, sergeants also wore gold or silver shoulder knots and had sashes around their waist, which were a combination of the facing colour with stripes matching those on the house furniture. The 1751 regulations for the 14th Dragoons, for example, states: 'Serjeants,—to have narrow silver lace on the cuffs, pockets, and shoulder-straps; silver aiguillettes; and green, red, and white worsted sashes tied round their waists'.[14] The 1st Dragoons appear to have worn their aiguillette on their left shoulder, as depicted in the Morier painting of 1742. Why this was the case is unclear. In 1764 the aiguillette was removed from dragoon guards and dragoons with the general order: 'Officers and men to have an epaulette on the left shoulder instead of the shoulder knot. Officers and men to wear boots of a light sort'.[15]

There appears to have been no consistency between the regiments with regard to the buttons and buttonholes on the coats. In 1752 an order was issued requiring dragoon coats to be double breasted, meaning: 'buttons and holes on both sides or only buttons on one side and holes on both' with the proviso that the Duke of Cumberland did not mind which 'provided the clothing of all Dragoon Regiments be alike in it'.[16] A review carried out in 1753 found that the 2nd and 3rd Dragoons varied from the rest, having 'buttons and button holes on each side'[17] and they were ordered to follow suit,

4th Dragoons, c.1751. Watercolour by Richard Simkin after Morier. (Anne S.K. Brown Collection)

---

13 Sumner, 'Uniforms and Equipment of Cavalry Regiments from 1684 to 1811', p.97.
14 Sumner, 'Uniforms and Equipment of Cavalry Regiments from 1684 to 1811', p.89.
15 Sumner, 'Uniforms and Equipment of Cavalry Regiments from 1684 to 1811', p.127.
16 Sumner, 'Uniforms and Equipment of Cavalry Regiments from 1684 to 1811', p.125.
17 Sumner, 'Uniforms and Equipment of Cavalry Regiments from 1684 to 1811', p.125.

suggesting that from then on, buttons were on one side only with holes on both for all dragoon regiments. Royal regiments were to have three buttons on the cuff and three on the sleeve above it. Breeches were red.

High riding boots and white knee pieces were worn just as they were in the horse regiments. It appears that the Dragoons were issued shoes and gaiters, as reviews of the 1st Dragoons in 1753 and 1754 noted that they did not have white gaiters as stipulated.[18] Some records show black gaiters or even brown gaiters being worn by dragoon regiments at various times. It is possible that black or brown gaiters were used for fatigue duty and the white ones, if issued, kept for parade or when performing the infantry evolutions in a review. In these circumstances, the wearing of high riding boots would be impracticable. However, it seems that when on campaign the riding boots were worn and not the gaiters, as the roles performed by the dragoons were almost identical to those performed by the horse.

On one, rather rare, occasion, the soldiers of Bland's 3rd Dragoons, alongside Cobham's 10th and Kerr's 11th, fought dismounted at the Battle of Clifton, during the Jacobite Rebellion in 1745. The Jacobites were alerted to the dragoons' approach because: 'it then being quite dark, they coming very close to us, we heard only the noise of their boots and could plainly discern their yellow belts'. Later in the battle, the heavy riding boots proved to be an encumbrance, as the men attempted to retreat from a Jacobite attack across a muddy field. Some: 'endeavored to pull off their boots, to fly the easier and some of them were killed, with one boot off and another on and some with a boot only half on'.[19] The Morier paintings also show the dragoon regiments in high riding boots and not in gaiters, suggesting that this was their normal appearance and gaiters and shoes were only worn on specific occasions. It is 1767 before we see a direct order for all dragoon guards and dragoons to have 'black gaiters in which they are to do all duties on foot'.[20]

Dragoons had only one cross belt over their left shoulder, which held their ammunition pouch on their right hip. Their sword was worn on their waist belt, at the left side, along with a hanger for a bayonet. These leather items were supposed to be coloured light buff, but an inspection of the 1st Dragoons in 1753 recorded that the buff 'accoutrements are coloured yellow' and 'much worn'.[21] In the account of the Battle of Clifton above, the Jacobites are noted as having been able to spot the Dragoons in the fading light because of their 'yellow belts'. This could be discoloration caused by wear and tear rather than a determined effort to colour the belts yellow, but on many of the Morier portraits the leather does appear yellow in colour. Clearly some regiments belts had a yellowish appearance. The 2nd Dragoons coloured their leather belts and cross belts white.

The 8th Dragoons were allowed to wear two cross belts, one for the ammunition pouch and one to hold their sword, just as the horse were. This was a battle honour awarded to them after their heroics at the Battle of

---

18   Sumner, 'Uniforms and Equipment of Cavalry Regiments from 1684 to 1811', p.90.
19   Duffy, *Fight for a Throne*, pp.260-61.
20   Sumner, 'Uniforms and Equipment of Cavalry Regiments from 1684 to 1811', p.129.
21   Sumner, 'Uniforms and Equipment of Cavalry Regiments from 1684 to 1811', p.125.

Almenara in 1710 and it appears to have survived throughout this period. A review of this regiment in 1735 noted that the drummers had 'scimitar swords',[22] which may be another honour harking back to their Spanish campaign.

At the beginning of the period, the colonel of the regiment could put whatever coat of arms he wished on the horse furniture. An image of Cobham's 10th Dragoons completed in 1742 shows a very elaborate, brightly coloured coats of arms consisting of a knight's helmet with crossed flags behind. However, Cumberland's directive to remove coats of arms meant that by the time the 1751 regulations came into force, all dragoon regiments should have the Kings cypher of a 'GR' with a crown above on their horse furniture. Some regiments, such as the 5th, or Royal Irish, were allowed to retain a regimental distinction, in this case the Harp of Ireland, which replaced the King's cypher on the saddlecloth only. That said, when the Duke of Kingston raised his regiment of light horse to oppose the Jacobite rebellion, which later became Cumberland's 15th Dragoons, the saddlecloths of his regiment bore the Lion of England within a garter with the crown above. This appears to have remained until the regiment was disbanded in 1749. Saddlecloths were edged with three thin coloured lines, each distinct to the regiment. Details of the saddlecloth colours and edging are detailed in the appendices.

Light Cavalry

Most European armies made use of light cavalry, either for scouting ahead of the army or for raiding and foraging. These began as irregular units of Cossacks and eastern European hussars, but by the Seven Years War regular units of light cavalry were common. They were usually dressed in a similar fashion to the hussars of Eastern Europe, with dashing moustaches and bright uniforms.

However, there was traditionally never much of an appetite for light horse within the British establishment, with picquets of horse or dragoons usually asked to perform this role. When deployed in Europe, the British usually worked alongside other European allies who they could also rely on to provide light horse. During the 1745 Jacobite rebellion, a unit of light cavalry was raised which was originally known as Kingston's Light Horse. It performed exceptionally well, and was one of the few regiments that the Duke of Cumberland could turn to for scouting and intelligence gathering on the enemy. As a result, he was keen to keep it on the establishment when the rebellion was over and it became the 15th Dragoons. However, it fell victim to the reduction of the army at the end of the War of the Austrian Succession in 1749 and was disbanded. Cumberland, however, was fond of light cavalry units and saw their value, employing his own unit of hussars as a bodyguard on the Culloden campaign.

---

22   Sumner, 'Uniforms and Equipment of Cavalry Regiments from 1684 to 1811', p.97.

In 1755 it was decided to add a light troop to eleven existing regiments, namely the three regiments of Dragoon Guards and the 1st–5th, 7th, 10th, and 11th Dragoons. Although sometimes referred to as hussars in the periodicals of the time they were never referred to as such by the army nor equipped as such. Each troop consisted of: 'two Sergeants, three Corporals, two Drummers and 60 private men, beside commissioned officers,'[23] with one captain, one lieutenant, one cornet and one quartermaster. Recruits were 'to be light, active young men,'[24] and, ideally, good horsemen. The warrant authorising the raising of these troops stated: 'The clothing and cloaks of these Light Dragoons to be the same as that of the rest of the Regiment, only instead of hats, the men are to have jockey caps, ornamented in the front with HM's cypher and Crown in brass.'[25]

These 'jockey' style caps had a flat front area of brass on which appeared the Royal Cypher and the regimental number. Behind the front piece there was a white ridge on which was set a tuft of horsehair which regulations stipulated should be half red and half the facing colour of the regiment. The original cap design had a small rolled leather flap at the back that could be rolled down to cover the neck and collar in bad weather. Later designs had a cloth wrapped around the base of the cap, which performed the same service. The cap was reinforced with a brass bar on top to provide some head protection.

These new troops performed well during the raids on France during 1758, and so in 1759 it was proposed to raise full regiments of light horse. The 15th Light Dragoons were raised in March 1759 and the 16th in August. By December the 17th, 18th and 19th were fully raised, with the 20th and 21st complete by April 1760. However, just to confuse matters, the 17th, 20th, and 21st were disbanded in 1763 and the 18th renumbered as 17th and the 19th as 18th. The light troops in the existing dragoon regiments were all disbanded in 1763 and returned to normal duties.

The new regiments of light dragoons wore the same jockey style helmet as described above. They had dragoon style jackets although some regiments chose to have half lapels, like the dragoon guards, whilst some went without lapels. All appear to have adopted a collar of the facing colour. All the light cavalry jackets had a white strap on the left shoulder to keep their cross belt in place. Most wore white waistcoats and breeches. Boots were to be the tight-fitting jockey style and not the bucket topped style worn by the horse. Full details of the light dragoon uniforms can be found in the appendices.

Corporals were distinguished by having silver lace instead of white and a white silk aiguillette on their right shoulder. Sergeants wore the same, except the aiguillette was silver and they also had a sash about their waists which was generally the same colour as the facing colour. Officers wore the same uniform as the soldiers but with silver lace instead of white on what were generally better-quality uniforms. Their badge of rank was the crimson silk sash that was worn over the left shoulder and tied at the right hip.

---

23   Hayter (ed.), *Eighteenth Century Secretary at War*, p.177.
24   Sumner, 'Uniforms and Equipment of Cavalry Regiments from 1684 to 1811', p.126.
25   Sumner, 'Uniforms and Equipment of Cavalry Regiments from 1684 to 1811', p.91.

THE CAVALRY

16th Light Dragoons, 1759. Watercolour by R.A. Wymer. (Anne S.K. Brown Collection)

The regulations called for belts to be: 'tanned leather shoulder belt, 3 ½ inch broad, with spring and swivel; tanned leather belt for sword and bayonet; tanned leather cartouch box with a double row of holes to contain 24 cartridges, with a tanned leather strap, 1 ½' broad'[26] Clearly, the light dragoons were to wear their sword on their belt, as the dragoons did, and also to carry a bayonet. Images painted by Morier of the regiments show most soldiers wearing the 'belly box' style of cartridge box, rather than having the cartridge box hanging at the right side, as many dragoon regiments did. This freed up the cross belt to be used to hold the carbine when not in use. Equipment issued was to be: 'Carbine with ring and bar, 4ft 3' long, with a bayonet of 17'; 1 pistol, 10' in the barrel and of carbine bore; straight cutting sword, 34' in the blade with a light hilt without a basket'.[27]

---

26 Sumner, 'Uniforms and Equipment of Cavalry Regiments from 1684 to 1811', p.91.
27 Sumner, 'Uniforms and Equipment of Cavalry Regiments from 1684 to 1811', p.126.

THE ARMY OF GEORGE II

A light dragoon skirmishing. This image likely is meant to depict the 21st Light Dragoons (Royal Foresters). Watercolour by 'N.J.' (Anne S.K. Brown Collection)

The light cavalry were expected to use their firearms on horseback as well as on foot, and as such had their horse furniture altered to allow the carbine to be more easily drawn whilst mounted. They were generally mounted on smaller horses and their equipment reduced to make it as light as possible. The saddle to be with small cantles behind as, 'as the jockey saddles are' and arranged as follows: 'on the right side of the saddle is to be the holster for the pistol and on the left a churn in which a spade and felling axe, or a spade and woodmans bill, is to be carried'.[28] Cloaks were also issued and appeared as they did for dragoons, that is, red lined with the facing colour. It is not known if 'frocks' were issued but this seems likely.

Musicians

Trumpeters signalled orders in the regiments of horse whilst drummers did so in the regiments of dragoons and dragoon guards. A hautbois, or oboist, is also shown for the dragoon troops although his role is not clear. Kettle drummers were also included for the horse.

As with the infantry, musicians wore coats elaborately embroidered with lace along the seams. Those of royal regiments were distinguished by the use of the royal lace, was yellow with a blue stripe, on their red coats, which would also be lined blue, giving blue facings and turnbacks. Waistcoats were blue as were breeches.

The Morier image of the trumpeter for the 1st Troop of Horse Guards painted in 1750, shows him in red waistcoat and breeches and with a red jacket covered in an abundance of gold lace. Interestingly, the trumpeter is of Afro-Caribbean origin in this image.

For other horse and dragoon regiments, musicians wore the reversed colours of the regiment, just as the infantry did, usually with red breeches and waistcoat.

The clothing regulations stated that drummers' caps in royal regiments be: 'As those of the infantry, with tassel hanging behind; blue front with regimental badge embroidered; little flap red, with White Horse and motto: 'Nec aspera terrent'; back also red, with blue turn up, with a drum and rank of regiment in the middle'.[29] Those of other regiments would be the same,

---

28 Sumner, 'Uniforms and Equipment of Cavalry Regiments from 1684 to 1811', p.126.
29 Carman, *British Military Uniforms*, p.77.

3rd Troop of Horse Guards, War of the Austrian Succession; see Colour Plate Commentaries for more information.
(Original artwork by Patrice Courcelle, © Helion & Company)

Sergeant, 1st Royal Dragoons, Battle of Dettingen 1743; see Colour Plate Commentaries for more information. (Original artwork by Patrice Courcelle, © Helion & Company)

15th Light Dragoons, 1760; see Colour Plate Commentaries for more information.
(Original artwork by Patrice Courcelle, © Helion & Company)

Artillery Matross, 1746; see Colour Plate Commentaries for more information.
(Original artwork by Patrice Courcelle, © Helion & Company)

Drummer of the 37th Foot, Battle of Minden 1759; see Colour Plate Commentaries for more information. (Original artwork by Patrice Courcelle, © Helion & Company)

Highlander, 42nd Foot, Ticonderoga 1758; see Colour Plate Commentaries for more information.
(Original artwork by Patrice Courcelle, © Helion & Company)

Light Infantryman, 55th Foot, North America, 1758; see Colour Plate Commentaries for more information. (Original artwork by Patrice Courcelle, © Helion & Company)

Gage's 80th Regiment of Light Armed Foot, North America, 1758; see Colour Plate Commentaries for more information. (Original artwork by Patrice Courcelle, © Helion & Company)

39th Foot, India 1757; see Colour Plate Commentaries for more information.
(Original artwork by Patrice Courcelle, © Helion & Company)

Officer, 13th Foot, War of the Austrian Succession; see Colour Plate Commentaries for more information. (Reconstruction by Pulteney's Regiment – http://www.13thfoot.co.uk/ – photograph © Cath Smith)

Stand of Colours, 13th Foot, War of the Austrian Succession; see Colour Plate Commentaries for more information. (Reconstruction by Pulteney's Regiment – http://www.13thfoot.co.uk/ – photograph © Ellie Wout)

Grenadier, 13th Foot, War of the Austrian Succession; see Colour Plate Commentaries for more information. (Reconstruction by Pulteney's Regiment – http://www.13thfoot.co.uk/ – photograph © Lucy Bamford)

Hatman, 68th Foot, Seven Years War; see Colour Plate Commentaries for more information. (Reconstruction by The Old 68th Durham Light Infantry Society and Display Team – http://www.68dli.co.uk/index.php – photograph © Ellie Wout)

Fusilier, 23rd Foot (Royal Welch Fusiliers), War of the Austrian Succession; see Colour Plate Commentaries for more information. (Reconstruction by Richard Marren Craft Workshop – photograph © Alan 'Kael' Ball)

Fusilier, 23rd Foot (Royal Welch Fusiliers), War of the Austrian Succession; see Colour Plate Commentaries for more information. (Reconstruction by Richard Marren Craft Workshop – photograph © Alan 'Kael' Ball)

Officer, 23rd Foot (Royal Welch Fusiliers) c.1740-1760; see Colour Plate Commentaries for more information. (Reconstruction by Richard Marren Craft Workshop – photograph © Maria Dare)

but the front would be the regimental facing colour and the back and turn up red also.

Drummers persisted for dragoons and dragoon guards until 1766 when trumpeters were ordered instead. The regiments of light dragoons had drummers initially when they were formed in 1759 but these were replaced the following year by French, or hunting style, horns. Musicians of the light dragoons wore the reverse of the regimental colours, with a jacket the same colour as the regiment's facings. This jacket would have red cuffs and, if worn, lapels, with the shoulder strap and lace often being red as well. If the regiment had white turnbacks then it appears as if the musicians followed suit, only having red turnbacks when the regiment had turnbacks of the facing colour. Breeches and waistcoats were white. Musicians were armed only with a sword and one pistol.

The banners on the kettledrums and trumpets for the horse were the colour of the regimental facing. Kettledrums had the regimental badge or number in the centre, which would be the same as the regimental badge or number shown on the second standard for the regiment. The trumpets had the King's cypher and crown on the banners with the rank of the regiment in numerals underneath. The drums of the dragoon and dragoon guards were of brass, painted in the colour of the facing of the regiment. The badge or number of the regiment was painted on the front.

Drummer, 2nd Royal North British Dragoons c.1756. Watercolour by A.H. Bowling. (Anne S.K. Brown Collection)

Farriers

The uniform of farriers was not regulated until the warrant of 1768, and until then the colonels appear to have been free to dress them as they pleased. That said, most appear to have worn the same uniform as the troopers. Colonel Harvey of the 3rd Horse wrote in 1768: 'I see by the Horse numbers their Farriers [cease] from being armed and accoutered, which I think quite right, and I dress mine in blue. I believe the others continue the troopers cloathing'.[30]

The farriers of the 11th Dragoons and the 21st Light Dragoons also wore a blue jacket. In Morier's painting of a farrier of the 11th, he shows a blue jacket with red cuffs and buff lining and turnbacks. It had small red patches on the collar but no lapels. Waistcoat and breeches were buff. He also wears a fur mitre with a red front flap on which is a white horseshoe flanked by what appear to be the tools of his trade, a hammer and tongs. It has a red bag at the back with a white tassel. The farrier of the 21st is dressed in the same way but his jacket has red lapels.

---

30 Sumner, 'Uniforms and Equipment of Cavalry Regiments from 1684 to 1811', p.129.

It is not clear what weapons, if any were issued to the farrier, but he must have had some at this time by 1768 as per Colonel Harvey's reference in his letter, quoted above, to farriers ceasing to be armed. It appears that they carried no firelock, pistols, or sword from this date, but what they carried as standard prior to this is unclear.

Horses

Horses had to be purchased by the regiment from the open market using the money allotted to them for this purpose by the War Office. This money was referred to as the 'stock purse'. If horses were lost in action then their cost could be reclaimed from the Government, but natural wastage of horses, through disease or accidents during peacetime, had to be borne from the stock purse.

Horses were expected to be a 'strong well-bodied… from Fifteen hands and an inch to two inches and not exceeding'.[31] Dragoon horses were expected to be no taller than 15 hands. Ideally, the cavalry were looking for the 'very nimble kind of horses that can gallop, with short backs, broad fillets for carrying forage' and not the 'hairy leg'd Cart Horse that are too commonly bought for the Dragoons'.[32] Light cavalry horses were to be '14 hands 3 inches and not under. They are to be the well turned nimble road horses as nigh to the colour of the horses of the Regiment as can be got.'[33]

Farrier of the 11th Dragoons 1751. Watercolour by G.H. Brennan after Morier. (Anne S.K. Brown Collection)

In an ideal world, the horses of the British cavalry would be black, with the musicians, and in some regiments, the farriers, mounted on grey or white horses. Obviously, there were exceptions. The 2nd Dragoons (Scots Greys) not surprisingly rode grey horses exclusively where available, whilst a review of the 2nd Dragoon Guards in 1753 found them all mounted on bays. In time of war, horses became scarcer and regiments often had to take what they could get and could end up mounted on horses of a variety of colours, as a return from 1759 states for the 11th Dragoons: 'Horses not so uniform as other Regiments from the great scarcity of the dark brown horse which the Regiment is mounted on.'[34]

Whilst black was the ideal colour, as time moved on it became more important to have unity of colour rather than for the horses to be exclusively

---

31   Blackmore, *British Cavalry*, p.65.
32   Blackmore, *British Cavalry*, p.65.
33   Rogers, *British Army of the Eighteenth Century*, p.90.
34   Sumner, 'Uniforms and Equipment of Cavalry Regiments from 1684 to 1811', p.124.

11th Dragoons 1751. Watercolour by G.H. Brennan after Morier. (Anne S.K. Brown Collection)

black. From 1760 the standing orders for the dragoon guards tried to maintain all black horses and a review of the 1st Dragoons in 1757 described them as being all mounted on black horses, which were 'very pretty ones'.[35] However, by the end of our period only the Household Cavalry were still exclusively mounted on black horses.

British cavalry horses could easily be identified, as they were one of the only European countries to dock their horse's tails. This involved cutting the tailbone off at the third joint, creating what was known as a bobtail, which

---

35   Sumner, 'Uniforms and Equipment of Cavalry Regiments from 1684 to 1811', p.125.

served no practical function and was purely aesthetic. If anything, it was injurious to the horses' health, as Dr Buchanan described when he saw the horse of the Blues on campaign in Germany:

> English horses for want of their tails are greatly tormented with flies during the warm weather; fatigue themselves with kicking & stamping, wear out their Shoes, breake & Spoyle the ground; tossing their heads backwards to beat off the flies, lose their forrage. The fatigue is so much that it makes them sweat as they stand at the picket, & fall off their flesh. None of our Allies docke their horses & are allowed a smaller ratiate than ours, by two or three pounds of hay, yet are fatter & look better than ours by the latter end of the Campn.[36]

That said, not everyone seems to have followed suit. The 1st Dragoons were inspected in 1753 and the report states: 'Horses have Hunters tails',[37] which is a fuller tail in a plait. However, it was not until 27 July 1764 that a general order was issued stating: 'Horse and Dragoons, except Light Dragoons, to have horses with full tails'.[38]

Variations and Vagaries of Cavalry Uniforms

Anyone who believes that they can say with any degree of certainty how the British Cavalry of the eighteenth century appeared on any given day is skating on rather thin ice. Whilst the regulations called for uniforms to appear in a particular way, there was no guarantee that regiments would conform to the regulations straight away, or even at all!

Those troopers who had just been issued new uniform would not expect to have it renewed for two years, whilst horse furniture was only changed every five. This led to variations in dress even amongst the regiment. For example, the 1st Dragoons were instructed in the warrant of 1751 to have a red coat with blue cuffs and turnbacks, with a blue waistcoat and breeches. They were to have red pistol housings and saddlecloth. However, when they were reviewed in 1753 the troopers were found to be wearing the correct coats, lined blue, but 'buff waistcoats and red breeches'. The same report also notes that the troopers had yellow lace on their coats but their hats are laced gold. When they were inspected again in 1754 they had received 48 new sets of horse furniture to match the proscribed red lined blue and gold. This prompted the reviewing officer to record: 'men have no gaiters. Officers remarkably well mounted – their horse furniture not all new or alike'. A review in 1755 states: 'horse furniture not according to regulation, the field officers, Captains and Subalterns not being alike'. It also records that the men still had no gaiters. It is not until October 1756 that the review records 'Horse furniture according to regulation'. We can see from this that

---

36 Buchanan, *Regimental Practice*, p.317.
37 Sumner, 'Uniforms and Equipment of Cavalry Regiments from 1684 to 1811', p.125.
38 Sumner, 'Uniforms and Equipment of Cavalry Regiments from 1684 to 1811', p.127.

even the uniforms within the same regiment did not match for a period of three years.[39]

In January, 1768, the Adjutant General, Edward Harvey, wrote to the Adjutant General in Ireland requesting a list of the clothing of the several regiments of Dragoons and Horse posted in Ireland; 'so as to prevent wanton alterations…I find gold has been changed to silver and silver to gold &c as also colours altered in some Corps… particularly those which have been on foreign service'.[40] It appears that not even the Adjutant General of the Army could keep up with the unofficial changes to the uniform brought about through resistance to change, the necessity of campaign, or the natural wastage of existing uniforms. If he could not keep up, what chance have we?

---

39 Sumner, 'Uniforms and Equipment of Cavalry Regiments from 1684 to 1811', p.126.
40 Sumner, 'Uniforms and Equipment of Cavalry Regiments from 1684 to 1811', p.129.

8

The Board of Ordnance

The post of Master General of the Ordnance was a senior governmental position with a seat on the cabinet, and could be held by a soldier or a civilian. The Master General headed the Board of Ordnance, which was responsible for the manufacture, storage and issue of all pieces of cannon to the Army, the Royal Navy and the Honourable East India Company. The Board was also responsible for the building and maintenance of all the fortresses in Great Britain and overseas, including barracks and hospitals. In time of war, it issued tents and camp necessaries to the army, including individual items to soldiers such as blankets and backpacks. Ireland maintained its own Board of Ordnance, responsible to the Lord Lieutenant, which undertook these responsibilities for regiments on the Irish Establishment.

Under the Master General were five principal Officers of the Ordnance.[1] First of these was his second in command, the Lieutenant General of the Ordnance. He was the deputy to the Master General and was in charge during periods when there was no master appointed. He was responsible for artillery, transport, and contracts. His immediate subordinate was the Master Gunner who was directly responsible to him for the manufacture and provision of the cannon. The post of Surveyor General was a civilian appointment, being in charge of all engineers and engineering works within Great Britain. His immediate subordinate was the Chief Engineer who was responsible for the upkeep of fortifications in Great Britain. If required during a campaign, this branch could also raise a corps of miners, to carry out siege works or manual labour for the army, albeit that men so engaged remained civilians and were not taken on to the army list. The Clerk of the Ordnance balanced the books whilst the Keeper of the Stores made sure that the magazines were full and that the items the Board were required to provide to the army were available. Finally, the Clerk of the Deliveries performed a role similar to a commissary, ensuring that items were delivered and that there were sufficient wagons to carry them and so on.

The Board of the Ordnance was a completely separate body from that of the army, with its own administration, staff, and budget. When on campaign,

---

1   Summary from Rogers, *The British Army of the Eighteenth Century*, p.36.

Ordnance staff would accompany the army and perform a parallel role to that of the army's staff, having its own paymaster, wagon master, to attend the artillery train, and quartermaster, to find billets for the ordnance staff. This was always the case unless Ordnance staff were attached to specific regiments, as happened during the campaign in America, where engineers or artillery officers would be fed and quartered along with the regiment they were attached to.

Although the Ordnance was a completely separate body, it is important to point out that a military man often held the role of Master of the Ordnance. For example, from 1756 to 1758 it was held by Lieutenant General the 3rd Duke of Marlborough, and from 1759 to 1763 by General Sir John Ligonier. This meant that cooperation between the Ordnance and the army was usually seamless, with both departments understanding the needs of the other. As with everything about the eighteenth-century British Army, the emphasis here is always on 'usually'. Although the Master General of the Ordnance might understand the needs of the army, providing for them was not always easy.

One thing that the Ordnance did have in common with the army, however, was its shortage of funds. Money from Parliament for this military arm seems to have been just as restricted during peacetime as it was for the infantry and cavalry, with increases during periods of war followed by cutbacks as soon as the war was over. Budgets to maintain the fortresses and defences around the coast of Great Britain, especially during peace time, seem to have been particularly stretched, which is surprising given the number of invasion scares that occurred during the reign of George II. For example, in January, 1746, during the height of the Jacobite Rebellion and following the invasion scare of the year before, it was decided to make an extensive survey of the nation's defences. The subsequent report was not good, with most fortresses surveyed found to contain 'no men and but few gunners, and those ignorant of their business'.[2] Pendennis Castle, which commanded the important harbour of Falmouth, was well equipped with 46 guns but had a garrison of one master gunner, aged 96, and one gunner. The garrison of Sandown Castle consisted of one woman who stated that 'the guns were not loaded and there was no ammunition' and whilst Chester Castle was considered blessed with its garrison of 75 men of the Invalid Regiment, it contained 'nothing but empty walls and wants all manner of necessarys'.[3] Money, as always, was constantly wanting.

The Royal Artillery

On May 26, 1716, King George I issued a Royal Warrant that created the first two permanent companies of field artillery. They consisted of 100 men each and were based at the Royal Arsenal at Woolwich. In 1722 they were increased to four companies and formally became the Royal Regiment of Artillery. From the beginning, the artillery required its officers and men to

---

2   Rogers, *British Army of the Eighteenth Century*, p.41.
3   Rogers, *British Army of the Eighteenth Century*, p.41.

have academic backgrounds and to serve an apprenticeship in the correct use of artillery. Promotion was through merit and seniority and not by purchase. A school was opened in Woolwich in 1740, which reinforced this requirement, teaching new cadets the basics of gunnery, mathematics, ballistics and the construction, and destruction, of fortifications. The cadets would then join artillery units for on-the-job training before eventually becoming artillery officers themselves.

The basic administration unit of the artillery was the company. As always with eighteenth century armies, numbers varied within each company, due to illness and losses as well as the availability of replacements. However, by the time of the Seven Years War, a company of the Royal Artillery generally consisted of a captain, with a captain-lieutenant as his deputy, and a first and second lieutenant. There followed three junior officer positions known as lieutenant fireworkers, who could be cadets or officers in training. The lieutenant fireworker was equivalent to an ensign and his duties included the preparation of munitions and 'exploding' shells. There were then three sergeants, three corporals, eight bombardiers (lance corporals) and 24 gunners. There would also be about 64 mattrosses, essentially the manual labour of the regiment, who drove the wagons and limbers, dug the defences and manhandled the guns.

Around 1740, four additional companies were added to the regiment making a total of eight. In 1744, a cadet company was added to the regiment and by the end of 1748 there were 10 companies. In 1755, six new companies were raised making a total of 16, excluding the cadet company. In 1756 Pitt ordered a further increase in the artillery and engineers to 2,000 men and in 1757 the Royal Artillery was increased to 24 companies, divided into two battalions of 12 companies each. In 1760 there was another increase in recruits and the regiment was reorganised into three battalions of 10 companies each. The demands of the Seven Years War called for more men and by 1763 the Royal Artillery stood at 46 companies.

This large increase in numbers and the establishment of three battalions had the beneficial effect of freeing up promotion between ranks. Until then it had been a case of 'dead men's shoes' within the single battalion, as officers waited for some of the more senior positions to become available. The establishment of three battalions allowed for three colonels and majors and the corresponding increase in positions as captains and so on. Officers still had to work their way up the ranks through experience and seniority, however, as it remained forbidden to purchase ranks within the artillery. The Duke of Cumberland, in particular, was keen to ensure this remained the case and when artillery officers were granted equivalency with army officers in terms of military rank in 1751, he reiterated that the artillery ranks could not be purchased and could only be gained through an apprenticeship at Woolwich.

Despite all of this organisation and re-organisation, the company and battalion structure remained for administrative purposes only. When artillery officers and men were attached to overseas expeditions or to brigades or armies, it was on an ad hoc basis with the required number of men and guns sent to complete the job in hand, rather than by company or battalion

THE BOARD OF ORDNANCE

Royal Artillery gunner, sergeant and officers. Watercolor copy by Cecil C.P. Lawson after original by Richard Wootton. (Anne S.K. Brown Collection)

formation. Hence, we see apparently random numbers in detachments sent overseas, such as the six Officers, 12 cadets and 54 men sent with the 39th Foot to India in 1754, or the two lieutenants, three fireworkers and 50 men sent with Braddock to America in 1755.

Artillerymen wore a black tricorne edged with yellow lace. Officers were advised in March 1756 not to appear on parade "with hats otherwise cocked in the Cumberland manner."[4] Hair was styled as the infantry. Neck stocks were generally black. They wore a blue coat with no collar, red cuffs, lapels, waistcoat, and breeches. In May 1756 Colonel Belford issued an order that no: 'non-commissioned officer or private man is to wear ruffles on their wrists when under arms, or any duty whatsoever for the future,'[5] suggesting that these adornments to the shirtsleeves were common at the time. The lapels and cuffs of the coat were edged with lace, which would be gold for officers and yellow for the men. A written order from February 1753 required artillerymen to have 'two pair of white and one pair of black spatterdashes'. Black gaiters were generally worn when handling the artillery, as this labour quickly ruined white ones, which were worn only on parade.[6] All leather straps and equipment were white. Until 1747, gunners also carried muskets whilst officers and NCOs carried short fusils or carbines. On 1 April 1747, Gunner Woods recorded: 'the artillery gave in their firelocks and received

---

4   Francis Duncan, *History of the Royal Regiment of Artillery* (London: John Murray, Albemarle Street, 1879), Vol.I, p.149.
5   Duncan, *Royal Regiment of Artillery*, Vol.I, p.149.
6   Duncan, *Royal Regiment of Artillery*, Vol.I, p.147.

carbines in their stead',[7] which appears to have remained the case for the rest of the period.

The Ordnance[8]

At the beginning of the eighteenth century, the calibre and size of the guns in the British army was mixed and referred to by names such as Culverin and Saker, which meant different things to different people. In 1716 the Board of the Ordnance ordered the standardisation of British artillery, with the guns now designated by the weight of roundshot (the classic cannonball of popular imagination) that they fired. When Colonel John Armstrong took over as Chief Engineer in 1714 he immediately began redesigning the British artillery to make it lighter and more effective on the battlefield. This led to modified designs being introduced in 1722 and 1724. Following the war with Spain, Armstrong learned from failures identified with his gun design, introducing a further new design in 1742. Armstrong died that same year and was replaced at the Board of Ordnance by Thomas Lascelles who also made modifications to the design of the guns, introduced in 1743 and 1744. Charles Frederick then took over the role in 1750 and further redesigned the guns, always looking to improve their design and effectiveness based on their performance in the previous conflict. This resulted in a new design being introduced in 1753 before a final gun design, known as the Armstrong-Frederick design, was introduced in 1760, which was confirmed as the army standard in 1764. The artillery of this period tends to be referred to as 'Armstrong Guns' after their initial designer, but in truth the final result included the designs and modifications of both Lascelles and Frederick as well.

The metal used to cast artillery pieces was generally bronze, but confusingly it is referred to in contemporary accounts as 'brass'. The guns were designated by the weight of shot they fired (3-, 6- or 12-pounder and so on) and also by the length of their barrel, which was either short or long. Increasing the length of the barrel increased the effective range of the gun, but it also increased its weight and sometimes range was sacrificed for mobility. Hence a contemporary account might mention a 'short six', for example, meaning a 6-pound gun with a short barrel. All the Armstrong design guns have handles on the barrel, which were used to lift it onto its carriage. Some of these are shaped to look like dolphins and are often referred to as such, rather than as handles.

In 1741 orders were issued to paint the gun carriages grey and the metalwork black. However, Morier's painting of an artillery park during the War of the Austrian Succession shows the metalwork also painted grey.

---

7 Whitworth (ed.), *Gunner at Large*, p.50.
8 Information taken from Whitworth (ed.), *Gunner at Large,* Stuart Reid, *Cumberland's Army: The British Army at Culloden* (Leigh-on-Sea: Partisan Press 2006) and Rogers, *The British Army of the Eighteenth Century*. Also see 'British SYW Artillery', *My Seven Years War,* at <http://crogges7ywarmies.blogspot.com/>, viewed 1 October 2020.

It is possible that when the soldiers were applying a new coat of paint to the carriages, rather than painting around the metalwork they have simply painted over it! Once placed on the carriage, the gun rested in grooves carved in the carriage to take the trunnion shoulders. At the beginning of the period, the guns had no elevating screw, and elevation was achieved by tapping in wedges, called quoins, under the barrel. Lifting the trail with handspikes and rotating the gun on the spot achieved changes in line of fire. The gun carriages had wheel diameters of 58 inches for the majority of the guns, even the smaller 3-pounders, and the width between the wheels was standardised at 4ft 8in.

The long 3-pounder had a barrel length of 7 feet and weighed 1,232 pounds (559kg). The short barrel version was four and a half feet long and weighed about half as much. Four horses were generally required to pull the long 3-pounder with only two required to pull the lighter gun, its carriage and limber. The short 3-pounders were the guns generally issued out to infantry battalions for close support in the War of the Austrian Succession.

The long 6-pounder had a barrel length of eight feet and weighed 2,128 pounds (965kg). It generally required between seven and nine horses to pull it, its limber and carriage when on campaign. The short barrel version of this gun had a barrel length of 4.5 foot, although examples exist in 1754 of barrel lengths of 5ft 1in as well. It weighed about 542lbs (246kg) and could be pulled by two horses. By the time of the Seven Years War, these light 6-pounder guns were the standard-issue battalion guns for British regiments, with each battalion in Germany having two such guns and 34 listed as being present with the army in 1762.

The long 9-pounder gun had a variable barrel length but could be up to nine feet with the short barrel version about seven feet long, and could weigh up to 2,800lbs (1,270kg). Gun teams were similar in size to the long 6-pounder guns, requiring up to 11 horses to pull each gun along with the carriage it was mounted on and the limber.

The long 12-pounder gun was nine feet long on the barrel and weighed 3,248 pounds (1,475kg). On campaign it required between 10 and 15 horses to pull it, its carriage and its limber. There were six such guns in service in Flanders in 1747 and eight were provided for Prince Ferdinand's army in 1761. By the time of the Seven Years War there was also a medium and light version of the standard 12-pounder. The medium 12-pounder had a barrel length of 6ft 7in and weighed 2,408lb (1,092kg). Ten pieces of this size were recorded in Prince Ferdinand's army in 1759. A light 12-pounder is also recorded with a 5ft long barrel that weighed 988lb (448kg) and could be drawn by as few as five horses. Four guns of this calibre were sent to Germany in 1759 with six being recorded with the British army in Germany by 1760.

The 24-pounder gun had a barrel length of 9.5 feet long and weighed about 5,752 pounds (2,609kg). This was essentially a siege gun and was not designed for open battlefield use.

The artillery also employed howitzers and mortars, short-barrelled guns designed to fire over an enemy line, or city wall, to hit troops behind it. One of the largest employed was the 13-inch sea service mortar which had a weight of five tons and could send a shell of 200lb up to 4,000 yards. Not surprisingly, it was used for sieges and not as a field weapon, most notably in the expedition against l'Orient in 1746. The artillery also had available a 10-inch land service mortar which weighed 10cwt, the brass 5½-inch mortar which weighed 1¼ cwt, and the lighter Coehorn mortar. Mortars were placed on fixed carriages and did not have wheels. As such, their elevation could not be adjusted and variations in the distance fired was achieved by increasing or decreasing the amount of powder used to launch the projectile.

Howitzers used the same idea, having a short barrel and were designed to fire overhead. These were essentially the same as mortars but were on wheeled carriages like cannon, and could be moved around the battlefield. The howitzers used were of 4.5-inch, 5.5-inch and 8-inch calibre and generally fired shell, a hollow iron ball with the cavity packed with explosives.

It is important to note that artillery was not deployed in huge numbers by the British Army in any of the campaigns of George II, and the loss of even small numbers of guns, at battles such as Fontenoy or Rocoux, had a significant impact on the army's firepower. For example, in 1747 during the War of the Austrian Succession, the British army had twenty-six 3-pounder guns, spread between its 14 infantry battalions, and twenty-seven 6-pounder guns. At the Battle of Lauffeld that same year it lost nine 3-pounders, six short 6-pounders and one long 6-pounder in action, being a third of its 3-pounder guns and a quarter of its 6-pounders, a significant blow and difficult for the Ordnance to replace.

The Guns in Action

At the beginning of this period, during the War of the Austrian Succession, guns were driven onto the battlefield by civilian wagon drivers. They would then be unlimbered and pushed the final few feet into their firing positions. The civilian drivers then left the field, taking the limbers for the guns with them. The first problem with this approach was that the guns became stationary, and could not be moved forward to support or exploit any advantage gained by the other arms. Worse, it meant that if the day did not go well, the guns often had to be abandoned, as the civilian drivers would not return to a battlefield where the army was retreating in order to save the guns. As a result, by the time of the Seven Years War, the artillery was driving its own limbers and remained with the guns during the battle. This had a significant impact at the Battle of Minden in 1759, where Captain Philips' battery of 10 guns was able to ride up in support of the advancing British infantry regiments, unlimber on their right flank and engage the enemy at a range of 900 metres, something which would previously have been impossible.

Having rolled the guns into place, the artillerymen might decide to 'dig in', making a defensive wall of gabions or similar earth defences in front of their guns to protect them from enemy counter battery fire. This was usually done when the British had time to prepare their position for enemy assault, such as at Rocoux in 1746, or during a siege. A laboratory tent would then be pitched nearby. This was used to prepare the fuses and different ammunition for the guns and provided cover from the weather for the fireworker and the gunpowder.

The normal crew of a gun was five. The NCO for the gun sighted it and moved the trail to lay the gun in the correct position for firing. Once he was happy, he would give the order to load. At the front, to the left of the gun, stood the loader. He placed the bagged charge in the mouth of the gun followed by the projectile. Next would step forward the sponger, who would ram both charge and projectile down the barrel with the butt of his sponge staff. Next would step forward the firer, who would touch the smouldering fuse, or port fire, to the vent in the rear of the cannon, causing it to fire. The gun could recoil as much as six feet and would have to be rolled back into place by the entire crew. Now would step forward the fifth crewmember, the ventman. With his thumb protected by a leather thumbstall, he covered the vent to make sure no smouldering remains of the charge were pushed out. After dipping his sponge in a bucket of water, the sponger would then clean out the barrel from the muzzle end, making sure that there were no glowing embers or hot remains of the last charge within that might set off the new charge when it was rammed home. When the sponger was ready, the loader would then step forward and place a new charge and projectile in the barrel, which the sponger would once again ram home with the other end of the sponge stick. Meanwhile, the ventman would place a tube containing powder in the vent to ensure the charge in the barrel fired. During all of this the NCO would have observed where the last roundshot had landed, and he would now make an adjustment if required, lifting the trail of the gun with the trailspike to adjust the direction, or calling for new wedges to adjust the elevation of the gun. He would then give the order to fire. The firer would once again step forward and, after shouting to the crew to stand clear, would once again touch fuse to the vent causing the gun to fire. A trained crew could fire their gun two or three times in a minute.

There were a variety of ammunition types. Roundshot, the classic cannonball, was the weight designated by the calibre of gun firing it, with 3-pounder cannons firing three-pound balls, 6-pounder cannons firing six-pound balls and so on. A roundshot was a deadly battlefield weapon and could kill an entire file of men in an advancing battalion. Case shot, which was often called 'Partridge Shot' by contemporaries, was just a tin case containing a number of loose bullets that scattered as the case left the muzzle, much like a shotgun. The optimum range was about 200 yards and a 6-pounder held about 85 bullets. Grape shot was in the form of nine large bullets wired together, and did considerable damage when used against infantry. During sieges the artillery might be used to fire red hot shot, which was essentially roundshot heated in a furnace before being fired and was designed to start fires, or 'Carcass Shot', a hollow ball with holes drilled in it and filled with an incendiary mix, which was designed to do the same thing.

The smaller guns were often distributed amongst the infantry regiments before going into battle, to provide close artillery support. Gunner Wood, for example, recorded before the Battle of Lauffeld: 'Two short sixes were sent to every foot regiment which lay in the field with a detachment of artillery to every two guns with one officer'.⁹ Each gun would have a trained crew to man it, but the regiment was expected to provide soldiers to manhandle the guns into place and to assist with moving them and their ammunition forward if required.

One would think that with all that firepower at the artillery's disposal, it is hard to imagine any enemy forces taking or overrunning an artillery position. However, Gunner Wood recorded at Lauffeld in 1747 that the French infantry:

> [R]eally behaved very well, though we cut them down with grapeshot from our batteries of 12 pounders yet they did not seem to mind it, but filled up their intervals that we made with grapeshot as they advanced. Being overpowered we were at last obliged to retreat something faster than we advanced…¹⁰

Engineers

Trained engineers first joined the Ordnance in 1717, as civilians attached to the army to give advice on sieges and the building of defences. With the establishment of the cadet school at Woolwich, engineers began to be trained in a proper military apprenticeship alongside their artillery counterparts, although they were still technically civilians and held no military rank. However, the number of recruits training to be engineers was always small. In 1754, for example, the engineer establishment consisted of the Chief Engineer and only 32 officers of various seniority.¹¹ When engineers were required to assist the army overseas, they were usually assigned a junior officer's rank, comparable to a lieutenant, which deprived them of many of the benefits enjoyed by senior ranks in terms of accommodation and food. This was a constant source of grievance amongst engineers, many of whom had many years' experience and held much higher comparable rank within the Ordnance. It was not until 1759 that the engineers were finally granted military rank, at which time they were re-organised with similar terms of service to the Royal Artillery. From then on, the Chief Engineer took on the equivalent rank of colonel-in-chief, with two directors as his immediate subordinates. Beneath them were four sub-directors (majors), 12 engineers-in-ordinary (captains) 12 engineers extraordinary (captain-lieutenants), 14 sub-engineers (lieutenants) and 16 practitioners (ensigns).¹² The title of 'Chief Engineer' was applied to the colonel-in-chief, but was often used to describe the most senior engineer in any given theatre.

Companies of miners were raised to carry out the manual labouring that would be required in the construction or destruction of defences. Since mining was a recognised siege tactic, these recruits were sometimes found amongst the experienced tin miners in Cornwall or the coalminers

---

9   Whitworth (ed.), *Gunner at Large*, p.51.
10 Whitworth (ed.), *Gunner at Large*, p.42.
11 Rogers, *British Army of the Eighteenth Century*, p.36.
12 Rogers, *British Army of the Eighteenth Century*, p.36.

in Newcastle. Sometimes they could be recruited to perform a specific task, such as the 100 miners recruited specifically to dismantle the fortifications of the French stronghold of Louisbourg in 1760.[13] Miners could also be recruited and remain on the strength of the artillery company to which they were attached for the duration of the campaign. For example, in 1756 a company of miners was formed for service in Minorca, but upon its return to England in 1757 it was retained with four newly raised companies for service in Europe.[14]

When it comes to uniform the engineers were, for most of this period, civilians and could dress as they pleased. Since they held no military rank until 1757, they were under no obligation to dress in military uniform. That said, it was clearly beneficial for the troops to recognise them as a member of their own forces and as an officer, and so they may well have adopted a similar dress to other officers when on campaign. This would usually be a plain red frock coat, red breeches and perhaps black gaiters in line with the artillery. Engineer uniforms of the 1780s show the adoption of a black cocked hat edged with black lace and with a black cockade. The coat remained red but with black cuffs, lapels and collar and edged with gilt lace and buttons. The waistcoat has become buff as have the breeches.[15] It is not clear when exactly this uniform was adopted and it may have been adopted for use on parades when the Engineers were granted military rank in 1757.

---

13   Duncan, *Royal Regiment of Artillery*, Vol.1, p.203.
14   Duncan, *Royal Regiment of Artillery*, Vol.1, p.159.
15   See for example the portrait of Major George Maule by Johann Zofany.

9

Colours and Standards

Since the formation of the regular British Army, regiments carried flags of a particular colour, usually painted or embroidered with a heraldic device or coat of arms, by which other regiments on the battlefield could identify them. These are generally referred to as colours for the infantry, standards for the horse, and guidons for the dragoons.

In the early years, regiments were allowed to design their own colours, standards and guidons and they usually carried a device chosen by the colonel of the regiment. Very often this was his family coat of arms or a heraldic device significant to him in some way or a symbol of significance to the regiment. For example, the 2nd Foot was the Queen's Regiment and bore on their colours the back-to-back double 'C' that was the coat of arms of Catherine of Braganza, the wife of Charles II in whose reign the regiment was raised. In addition, during their time in Tangiers, they were colloquially known as Kirke's Lambs, after their then colonel, Percy Kirke. As a result, they bore an image of a lamb resting next to a flag of St George on their colours in later years.

Not many colours survive from the early reign of George II, but from those that do we can see that this trend continued. For example, the guidons of Rich's 4th Dragoons is yellow with a silver fringe and depicts the royal cipher of George II on one side and the coat of arms of the regiment's colonel, Sir Robert Rich, on the reverse. The standard carried by Ligonier's 8th Horse at Dettingen survives and it too depicts the elaborate coat of arms of its owner, as does the colour of Scipio Duroure's 12th Foot, which was present at Fontenoy.[1]

Following the Act of Union in 1707, every regiment carried a Union flag to identify it as British, alongside the regimental colour, both of which were carried by the first, or colonel's, company. A third colour, the major's colour, would be carried by the major's company with the remaining companies carrying what were called captains' colours. Once again there appears to be no hard or fast rules about what colour a company colour should be or what should be depicted on it other than it would be similar to the regimental colour. Hence a regiment could have up to nine company colours and one colonel's, or first, colour and one Union colour when marching into battle.

---

[1] Duroure's colour can still be viewed at the Museum of the Suffolk Regiment; that of Ligonier's Horse is in private hands.

This remained the case throughout the War of the Austrian Succession with the Royal Welch Fusiliers, for example, carrying 10 company colours at Fontenoy in 1745.

In 1747, as part of his policy to reform the army, the Duke of Cumberland introduced strict rules on the appearance of the colours, standards and guidons for the army. The new regulations stated: 'No Colonel to put his Arms, Crest, Device or Livery on any Part of the Appointments of the Regiment under his command'.[2] This applied not only to the colours but also to all aspects of the uniform, such as buttons, drums, and the grenadier caps. This was not just about enforcing uniformity, but, having just put down the Jacobite Rebellion, Cumberland wanted to stamp the King's authority on the army and make it clear where its loyalties lay through the use of the regiments' most visible device.

The Regulations of 1747

The Household troops were excluded from this regulation and continued to use their own colours, which are discussed below.

Infantry Regiments were to carry one King's Colour, which was to be the Union Flag. The second, or Regimental, Colour was to be the same colour as the regiment's facings. It was to have a small Union Flag as a canton in the upper hoist corner, next to the flagstaff, whilst the centre should display the number of the regiment in gold Roman numerals surrounded by a wreath of roses and thistles on the same stalk.

As always, there were exceptions. Those regiments with white facings (17th, 32nd, 43rd, and 47th) along with the 33rd, which had red facings, would carry a Regimental Colour with the red cross of St George on a white background instead. They would retain the small Union Flag in the upper hoist corner and the regimental number and wreath just as the other regiments. This decision was taken for purely practical reasons, as a pure white flag could be mistaken for a flag of surrender whilst the Foot Guards were the only regiments who had the honour of carrying red flags into battle. Exceptions were also made for those regiments granted special badges, which could be displayed in the centre of their colours rather than the regimental number. Initially these were the 1st–8th, 18th, 21st, 23rd, 27th and 41st, which all displayed their badge in the centre of the colour but also had to display their regimental number in the upper hoist corner (next to or within the small Union Flag) and were also allowed badges peculiar to them on the remaining three corners of the colour.

The colours were to be the same size as those of the Foot Guards, whose colours at the time were 72 inches along the staff and 78 inches extended, or 'on the fly'. Tassels and cords were of crimson and gold mix. The first company would carry the King's and Regimental Colours, with the Regimental Colour always being carried to the right of the King's Colour when next to each other.

---

2   Ian Sumner, *British Colours and Standards 1747-1881 (2) Infantry* (Oxford: Osprey, 2001), p.3.

The carrying of company colours appears to have been discontinued by the 1747 regulation although they do appear to have been carried during the War of the Austrian Succession in Europe and during the Jacobite campaign. Interestingly, the 2nd Foot carried a sea green colour emblazoned with the arms of its colonel, Thomas Fowke, as a Major's Colour prior to the 1747 regulations and continued to carry this, against regulations, as a third colour alongside the King's and Regimental Colours until as late as 1750.

The regulations were reviewed in 1751 and reissued. They mirror the 1747 regulations in many respects but they now provided details for second battalions of particular regiments. Second battalions were now to add a 'pile wavy', or narrow flame shaped triangle, coming diagonally away from the corner of the small Union Flag on its regimental colour. Thus, anyone looking at the regimental colour of the first battalion and second battalion could tell them apart from the 'pile wavy' device. Provision was also made for new regiments with black facings (initially the 50th and 64th Foot), which were to carry a black colour with the cross of St George upon it in red. The other distinctions remained the same.

With regard to camp colours, used to identify which regiments had been allocated which camping areas, the 1751 regulations state: 'Camp colours to be the colour of the Regiment with the rank of the Regiment upon them.'[3]

In the 1747 regulations, cavalry regiments were to carry one King's Standard and two Regimental Standards. Regiments of horse were to carry square standards made of damask silk, fringed with gold or silver. The dragoons were to carry swallow-tailed guidons made of plain silk. The new regiments of dragoon guards were to carry both designs, with a square King's Standard, made of damask silk and fringed with silver or gold as in the horse, and swallow-tailed damask silk for the regimental guidons.

The Kings Standard or Guidon for each regiment was to be crimson. In the centre was depicted the Rose and Thistle Union badge above which was a crown and below it a scroll with the royal motto 'Dieu et mon Droit'. On the first and fourth corners was placed the badge of Hanover, a running white horse on a green mound, and in the other two corners would be the regimental number in gold or silver letters on a background colour of the regimental facings.

The second and third Standards or Guidons were to be the same colour as the regimental facings. In the centre would be the number of the regiment, in gold or silver, on a crimson badge. A wreath of thistles and roses would surround this badge. In the first and fourth corners there would once again be the running horse of Hanover on a green mound whilst there would be a badge of the rose and thistle conjoined on a crimson background on the second and third corners. Additionally, the third standard or guidon would also have the number 3 on a circular crimson badge below the central device. Tassels and cords were to be a mix of crimson silk and gold.

Note that, as with infantry regiments, some cavalry regiments were granted continued use of some regimental distinctions, which could be

---

3   The Royal Clothing Warrant 1751: see also Ian Sumner, *British Colours and Standards 1747-1881(1) Cavalry* (Oxford: Osprey, 2001), p.45.

displayed on their standards and guidons with the King's permission. These are listed in the appendices. Where the regiment was granted a regimental distinction, this would appear as the central device in the second and third standard or guidon, surrounded by the wreath of thistles and roses, whilst the devices on the second and third corners would now be the regimental number on a crimson badge. If the regiment was granted the use of a motto, this would appear beneath the central device.

The staff for all cavalry standards and guidons was to be 10 feet in length, including the spearhead or finial. The tassels and cords were to be a mixture of crimson silk and gold. No size was stipulated for standards other than that they were to conform to the standards carried by the Household Cavalry. However, in 1768 their sizes were set as 27 inches on the staff and 29 inches 'on the fly'. This regulation also reduced the length of the staff to nine feet. No size was stipulated for the dragoon regiments, whose guidons were simply to be 'smaller'.

Dragoon guidons were approximately 27 inches long along the staff and about 41 inches extended, or on the 'fly'. The swallowtail slit was 10 inches long and 4 inches wide at its widest point. It is not clear if the new regiments of light horse kept the same dimensions for their guidons, but the later *Discipline of the Light Horse*, written in 1778, states the staff for light horse was eight feet long, including the finial, and the guidon 20 inches along the staff and approximately 30 inches on the fly.[4]

The regulations of 1751 detailed the fringes of the various standards and guidons as well as confirming those regiments that were entitled to a special badge or motto. However, they made no major changes, stating: 'Those of the Horse to be square and those of the Dragoon Guards, or Dragoons, to be swallow tailed'.[5]

There seems to have been some delay in putting these new regulations into practice, especially if new colours had just been issued to the regiment prior to 1747. These were expensive items to commission and colonels would often wait until the colours became worn out or damaged before incurring the considerable cost of replacing them. Hence, we see the 1st Dragoon Guards appearing on parade in 1750 with their old colours still on display, as was the case for the 6th Dragoons the same year. The colours of the 25th Foot, which had been presented in 1743, were still being carried in 1763!

Guards Regiments

The three regiments of Foot Guards had an established tradition surrounding the colours they carried, most of which already carried the King's cypher. As a result, they were excluded from the 1747 regulations, which stated: 'The Union Colour is the first stand of colours in all regiments, Royal or not,

---

4   Sumner, *British Colours and Standards 1747-1881(2) Infantry*, p.10.
5   The Royal Clothing Warrant 1751: see also Sumner, *British Colours and Standards 1747-1881(1) Cavalry*, pp.7-8.

except the Foot Guards. With them the Kings Standard is first as a particular distinction.'[6]

The Foot Guards were not mentioned in the regulations other than this and so they continued to carry one colour per company. The first colour of the 1st Foot Guards was all crimson with a crown at the centre. The remaining colours were Union Flags, each of which bore on its centre a badge particular to each company. For example, the 9th company had a white greyhound with a gold collar whilst the 10th had a gold sun in splendour. Hence, the Guards carried the Union Flag as their Regimental and Company Colours whilst their King's Colour was crimson, a reversal of the rules for standard infantry regiments.

In 1756, a crimson colour with a Union canton was adopted for the lieutenant colonel's and the major's companies, although the central badges of their companies remained the same. The Union Flag with the company distinctions continued to be carried by the remaining companies.

The 2nd (Coldstream) and 3rd (Scots) Guards followed this pattern with regard to their colours. They also carried a crimson colour as the King's colour and Union flags for the company colours with their own distinctive badges on each. They also appear to have adopted the 1756 changes to the lieutenant colonel's and major's company colours as detailed above.

For all Foot Guards colours, the cords and tassels were gold and crimson mixed for the first colour and crimson only for the company colours.

When it came to the Horse Guards, each troop carried one Standard and one Guidon. Both were embroidered with the same devices. Each troop carried flags of its own distinctive colour, with those of the first troop being crimson, the second troop white, the third yellow and the fourth blue. In 1746, after the 3rd and 4th troops were disbanded, the 2nd troop changed its colour to blue. The standards and guidons were all embroidered with a rose and thistle entwined as the centrepiece, with a crown above it and the letters G and R, one on either side of the crown. Beneath this device was the Royal motto: 'Dieu et mon Droit' on a gold scroll. Beneath this were three crowns representing the three kingdoms. They all had gold fringes, cords and tassels.

Each of the two troops of Horse Grenadier Guards carried both a guidon and a standard. The 1st troop carried blue colours and the 2nd crimson. The royal motto was on a silver scroll beneath the central device, which was otherwise the same as the Horse Guards. They also had gold fringes, cords and tassels.

The Royal Horse Guards had three squadrons, each of which carried its own crimson damask silk standard. The first was embroidered with the royal arms, the second showed a crowned royal cypher, and the third the Union symbol of conjoined rose and thistle beneath a crown and the letters G and R either side of the crown. All had gold fringes, cords and tassels. In 1758 the second and third squadrons swopped their badges, with the Union badge becoming that of the second squadron whilst the crowned royal cypher became that of the third.

---

[6] The Royal Clothing Warrant 1747: see also Sumner, *British Colours and Standards 1747-1881(2) Infantry*, pp.3-4.

The Colours in Battle

In both infantry and cavalry regiments the colours were primarily used in battle to control the advance of the men. Both infantry and cavalry would look along the line and take their dressing from the position of the colours. As the regiment advanced, the men would keep pace with the colours and not presume to go faster than them, hence keeping the line straight and controlling the pace of the advance. Under fire, the colours were clearly visible even in the smoke and noise of battle and were a visual aid to help the men see if the regiment was advancing, retreating, or stationary. After a charge, of if the regiment was pushed back in disorder, the colours gave the men an easily recognisable rallying point around which to reform. As such, colours, standards and guidons were not simply decoration but performed an essential battlefield role and the number of occasions when they were not carried are notable by their rarity. During the Ticonderoga campaign in America during 1758, for example, Lord Howe directed that no regiments were to 'carry their colours nor camp colours to the field this campaign,'[7] as the close wooded nature of the terrain meant they could rarely be unfurled without catching on branches and could not easily be seen by the men. As such they performed no useful function and were left in camp. However, in practically all other campaigns during the reign of George II, colours were carried and were essential to regimental command and control.

That said, the flags carried by the regiments of foot and horse were more than simply tools used to control the men's movements and provide a useful rallying point in battle. The King usually presented them personally to the regiment. As such, the King's Colours were a symbol of the regiment's loyalty to the crown as well as being the Union Flag, and hence a symbol of national identity. The Regimental Colours, especially those carried through previous wars, represented the identity of the regiment itself, its history and past glories, and inspired the new recruits who saw them to fight well and uphold the martial spirit of the men who had fought under those colours before. Writing in the modern age, and for many readers who have not served in the military, it is hard to describe how important these symbols were not only to the regiment, but to the men who carried and fought under them and the lengths these men would go to in order to protect them. The loss of a colour to the enemy was a stain upon the honour of the regiment and would shame it in front of the other regiments of the army. As such, men would go to great lengths to prevent their capture.

For example, at the Battle of Dettingen, in June 1743, two troops of Bland's 3rd Dragoons were ordered to counter charge the French Maison du Roi cavalry, which they did to great effect, cutting through the French and out the other side. As they were retiring, Trooper Thomas Brown saw his regiment's guidon lying on the ground and dismounted to retrieve it. As he did so, an enemy cut two fingers from his bridle hand and made off with the

---

7   Middleton (ed.), *Amherst and the Conquest of Canada*, p.48.

guidon. Brown followed, killed the man, and then single-handed fought his way back through the French cavalry to safety. It was reported that:

> He had two horses killed under him, two fingers of ye bridle hand chopt off and after retaking the standard from ye Gend'arms, whom he killed, he made his way through the lane of the enemy exposed to fire and sword, in the execution of which he received eight cuts in ye face and neck, two balls lodged in his back, three went through his hat and in this hack'd condition he rejoined his regiment who gave him three huzzas on his arrival.[8]

For this conspicuous act of gallantry, Brown was knighted on the battlefield by the King, the last private soldier ever to be given this honour. His wounds were too severe to return to the regiment and so he retired with a pension of 30 pounds a year, which he used to drink himself to death, dying in January 1746.

The French manuscript, *Les Triomphes de Louis XV*, illustrated all the colours captured by the French during that monarch's reign and within its pages are images of colours from Rich's 4th Dragoons, Huske's 23rd Foot (Royal Welch Fusiliers), Handasyd's 31st Foot, and one other unidentified British regiment, all listed as captured 'at Fontenoy'. Huske's Regiment who took over 323 casualties at Fontenoy, including 23 officers, and could easily have lost their colours here. However, the regiment was so badly mauled that Cumberland ordered it into garrison duty at Ghent until drafts of men could be found to bring it up to strength. In the meantime, the French besieged Ghent and on 14 July 1745, the fortress surrendered. It is just as likely that the colours were taken when the garrison went into captivity. Handasyd's 31st was also mauled at Fontenoy, but were involved in an attempt to relieve the siege of Ghent where they were also heavily engaged. Rich's Dragoons were not at Fontenoy, but were also forced to surrender as part of the garrison at Ghent, albeit a cornet is recorded as slipping out of a port gate with several of his men in order to save the colours when the decision to surrender was made. The most likely solution is that their guidon was lost here too. The final colour has an unidentified coat of arms and could have been a company colour for any of the regiments at Fontenoy, but not one of the Guards regiments as these were Union flags with very distinctive company emblems. The colours of the 44th and 48th Foot appear to have been lost with Braddock on the Monongahela in 1755, but generally the loss of colours by British regiments during this period is thankfully rare.

---

8   '3rd Kings Own Hussars', at <http://british-cavalry-regiments.eu5.org/3rd.html>, accessed 26 August 2020.

10

Volunteers, Subjects, and Mercenaries

Other Military Formations in the Army of George II

As we have seen from preceding chapters, the regular army was often underfunded and understaffed for the role it was asked to perform. In many instances during his reign, George II had to look for assistance from other military sources to supplement his army, especially when unexpected threats emerged such as the Jacobite Rebellion. On occasion, the King looked to his possessions in Hanover to provide extra troops, but more often Britain turned to its Dutch allies to send aid in time of need. For example, 4,000 men in six regiments, were sent to Britain to join Field Marshal Wade's army during the Jacobite Rebellion in 1745. Mercenary troops were also hired from the German state of Hesse-Kassel, with Hessian troops supporting British forces both in Europe and at home. In 1746, for example, Hessian forces were employed to support British forces against the Jacobite rebels, whilst during the invasion scare of 1756, Britain paid for 12 Hanoverian and eight Hessian battalions to be based in the south of England. However, if foreign troops could not be obtained, the King had to fall back on help from the Militia or from Volunteers.

The Militia

In theory, a volunteer Militia was required in the various British counties to assist with local law enforcement and to provide extra assistance to the army in case of emergency. The Lords Lieutenant of the counties were required to undertake the training and provision of arms for the troops and, should they be called out, to provide their first month's worth of food and upkeep. After this, any further costs incurred whilst the Militia were out would be borne by the state. Militia regiments were under the command of the Lord Lieutenant who raised them and could be disbanded again by him when they were no longer required.

However, the Militia had been underfunded and supplied for years and when the Jacobite Rebellion broke out in 1745 the years of neglect became obvious. The Militia was badly organised, with little or no training and with some being armed only with pikes or bill hooks rather than muskets. A report to the Duke of Cumberland stated: 'Tis so long since the militia was raised that we are apprehensive the arms are either lost or in bad order'.[1] The Lord Lieutenant of Somerset had not raised the militia in so long that he had quite forgotten how to go about it, and felt that looking to the militia as a way of raising troops was 'not only the most dilatory and difficult but the most ineffectual [method] of any other'.[2] The Militia's poor performance in the defence of Carlisle further confirmed the view that they were no longer fit for purpose. After the rebellion, Parliament did look at legislation designed to reform and update the Militia. However, the King actively opposed the idea of a competent Militia, as he feared those who would use it as an excuse to further deplete the regular army. Militia units were also under the command of the local Lord Lieutenant and did not swear an oath to the King, making them a rival force to his own.

The idea of Militia reformation gained no traction until 1756 when once again Britain was faced with French invasion. The numbers of regular troops available were so low that foreign troops from Hanover and Hesse-Kassel had to be used to make up the difference. This once again showed the deficiencies in the militia system and that year a bill to reform the Militia passed the Commons but was rejected by the House of Lords. The following year an amended bill was introduced which brought the Militia into existence only for five years, to assist whilst the war continued. The bill passed the Commons and this time it was passed by the Lords as well. It called for a force of 32,000 men to be raised locally in England and Wales in the larger towns and cities in Britain and Ireland to be used for home defence and to supplement the regulars in garrison duty. The plan was for this to be staffed through volunteers but if the numbers were not forthcoming the ranks would be filled by a ballot system to which all the able-bodied men in a parish were liable.

Despite the good intentions, the Militia was slow to form. The local gentry refused to stand as officers whilst the ballot system led to local riots as men refused to do the duty. By July 1759, 13 militia battalions had been formed and were used as garrison troops in coastal fortresses and to guard French prisoners held in England. However, in some parts of the country no militia had been raised at all, with counties such as Derbyshire, Sussex, and Worcestershire instead preferring to pay the fine imposed by Parliament for not complying with the law. Those counties that had formed units rarely trained them and they appear to have been not particularly well equipped. When the Militia Act came up for renewal in 1762 William Pitt called for it to be made permanent but once again the King opposed this and a compromise was reached, extending the bill by a further seven years instead. For the

---

1   Speck, *The Butcher*, p.38.
2   Speck, *The Butcher*, p.62.

remainder of the reign of George II, the Militia Act remained contentious and only partially enforced across the country.

Outside of the Jacobite Rebellion, the only recorded instance of Militia units being involved in enemy action was at the town of Carrickfergus in Ireland in February 1760. At this time a French raiding force under the command of François Thurot landed a substantial force of French troops, numbering over 1,200 men, with the intention of seizing the castle at Carrickfergus before pushing on to attack the important trade town of Belfast. The French force was met by a small number of regulars from the 62nd Foot, who were in Carrickfergus recruiting, and the local Militia under Captain Mucklewain. The Militia had plenty of powder but lacked musket balls, resorting to firing the buttons from their tunics at one stage. Despite making a gallant stand, they were forced to capitulate, but by that time a much larger force of Militia under Colonel Robert Dalway had gathered at nearby Bellahill. This force was described as 'in good uniform and well armed',[3] and numbered nearly 500 men. This force, plus the regulars gathering in Belfast, was enough to end the French raid and force them to return to their ships. Surviving accounts of the raid paint a picture of a functioning Militia system in the province of Ulster that did not lack volunteers, but was still deficient in arms and ammunition when push came to shove.

For a short period during the Seven Years War, the Militia acted efficiently in a support role for the regular army at home. However, for the majority of the reign of George II, this body did not exist in sufficient numbers, nor did it have the training or equipment, to be an effective force in home defence or to support the regular army.[4]

Volunteers

The regular army was supposed to provide troops for home defence as well as for expeditions overseas. However, when the threat of invasion loomed the numbers of regular troops trained and in a position to deploy to repel any foreign force was often woefully weak. At times like these, wealthy patrons often offered to raise regiments of infantry or cavalry at their own expense and maintain them until the immediate danger had passed. For example, Sir James Caldwell offered to raise 'an independent troop of Light Horse in the nature of Hussars' in 1759 when the threat of French invasion was at its height.[5] This was accepted in December 1759 and the regiment was employed mainly on Revenue enforcement and peacekeeping in Ireland, freeing up regular cavalry to return to the mainland.

During the Jacobite Rebellion, wealthy patrons also raised regiments to support the Government cause. The so-called 'Noblemen's Regiments' came

---

3   Charles McConnell, *The French are Landing: The Forgotten Invasion of Carrickfergus in 1760* (Carrickfergus: Carrickfergus Publications, 1995) p.37.
4   Summary based on Speck, *The Butcher*, and Rogers, *British Army of the Eighteenth Century*.
5   Richard Canon *Historical Record of the Third, or Kings Own, Regiment of Dragoons* (London: Clowes and Sons 1836), p.46.

into being from October to November 1745 and were clothed and fed by noble grandees. They were officered by recalling 75 officers on half pay and commissioning a further 398, which caused uproar amongst the officers of regular regiments who had to pay for their commissions whilst these were given for free. Since noble families raised them, they inevitably bore their names, with regiments such as Halifax's, Granby's and Bedfords' Regiments of Foot alongside Montagu's 9th Horse. Many of these noble regiments wore blue, although not all: Earl Gower's Regiment of Foot, for example, wore red, although its facings are unknown, whilst Lord Harcourt's was also in red faced with yellow and Berkeley's in red faced with green.[6]

The wealthy landowners were supported in this by the formation of 'Local Associations' in towns across the country. These were associations of businessmen and traders who collectively paid for the raising of regiments of infantry or cavalry through subscriptions. The Liverpool association, for example, agreed: 'to form eight hundred or a thousand men into companies of one hundred each, to find them with new blue frocks, hatts, shoes and stockings and to maintain them for two months certain'.[7] The first of the regiments raised by the Loyal Associations was raised by the Lord Lieutenant of Derbyshire and were nicknamed the Derbyshire Blues after the colour of their coats. They formed the basis for the other regiments that followed, such as the Yorkshire Blues and Liverpool Blues. The Yorkshire Blues carried company colours, each with the coat of arms of York, a white shield with a red St George's cross with five heraldic lions on the cross (one on each arm one in the centre). Above the shield was the word 'Religion' with 'and Liberty' underneath.

In Scotland, volunteer regiments were also raised with the Argyll Militia and the Glasgow Volunteers being involved in the Falkirk campaign. It appears that, whilst equipped by the Government, these units did not receive any formal uniform and fought in civilian clothes, using only a black cockade in their hats to distinguish them from the Jacobites.

These new regiments were raised and clothed by their patrons, but it was down to the Government, and specifically the Board of Ordnance, to furnish them with arms. This was more easily said than done, with most not receiving arms until late into the rebellion. In October 1745, Lord Malton wrote to complain that: 'the Yorkshire companies have not yet got a single firelock amonst them, except a few old rusty musquests'. Lieutenant General Wentworth noted that those troops raised in Doncaster had 'scythes fixed upon poles in the manner of pikes, which would make them formidable and such a weapon in a good hand may very well deal with a Highland broadsword'.[8]

Despite their high level of enthusiasm, volunteer units still lacked unit cohesion, discipline and, most importantly, training. As such, they made good

---

6 Andrew Cormack, 'The Noblemen's Regiments' in Andrew Bamford (ed.), *Rebellious Scots to Crush: The Military Response to the Jacobite '45* (Warwick: Helion & Company Limited, 2020), p.78.
7 Speck, *The Butcher*, p.70.
8 Both quotes from Speck, *The Butcher*, pp.70-71.

garrison troops and were used for local policing, searching travellers and the houses of suspected Jacobite sympathisers. However, they were not generally considered battlefield troops. In November 1745 the Duke of Bedford's infantry entered Lichfield where one witness was less than impressed: 'for this regiment was represented to be the forwardest of them, yet neither officers nor men know what they are about. So how it will do against any enemy God only knows'.[9] With the notable exception of Kingston's 10th Light Horse, which is discussed later, all of these regiments were disbanded in 1746 when the rebellion ended.

There is little point in discussing all of these volunteer regiments at length, as most did not see active service to any great extent, coupled with the fact that uniform and organisational details are sketchy. However, mention should be given to those volunteer units that did see action during the Jacobite rebellion.

Kingston's 10th Light Horse was raised on 1 October, 1745, by Evelyn Pierrepoint, Duke of Kingston-Upon-Hull, at a cost of over £8,526. This huge sum was met by contributions from wealthy individuals and through corporate subsidies from the towns of Mansfield and Newark. Some individual's contributions were substantial, such as that provided by Richard Wilson, who paid for the troopers coats at £2 12s 6d each and '247 cloaks in the Hussar style'. The Board of Ordnance provided 252 broadswords. They were also issued with:

> [A] pair of standards and case viz: silk and embroidering, the Dukes arms double; ditto or the county arms, two large crimson tassels; two yellow ditto; four and five eights yards of crimson fringe, four and three eighths yards yellow ditto; and a pair of standard poles fluted with gilt spikes; ticking cases and packing cases.[10]

The regiment comprised six troops of 40 officers and men, the senior troop commanded by the Duke in person. It also had a lieutenant colonel, major, three captains and a captain lieutenant.

The regiment performed so well that it was retained by the Duke of Cumberland at the end of the rebellion and placed on the establishment as the 15th Dragoons. It was disbanded at the end of the War of the Austrian Succession in 1748. The uniform details for this regiment are presented in the appendices alongside those of the other dragoon regiments, namely a red dragoon- style coat faced green with buff waistcoat and breeches. However, this is based on a Morier painting from 1748, shortly before the regiment was disbanded. It is possible that it adopted a red coat when it was placed on the regular establishment to conform to the clothes and equipment of other regiments of dragoons.

Three other non-regular cavalry units were involved in an action against the Jacobite rebels at Clifton in December 1745, namely the Georgia Rangers, the Yorkshire Hunters, and Cumberland's Hussars.

---

9   Duffy, *Fight for a Throne*, p.346.
10 Duffy, *Fight for a Throne*, p.347.

The Georgia Rangers were raised by Brigadier General James Oglethorpe who, as well as being an officer in the army, was also Governor of the American Colony of Georgia. He had raised a unit of mounted troops to patrol the borders of his American province and they were aboard ship in 1745 awaiting transport when the rebellion broke out. They were quickly disembarked and sent to support the regular troops against the Jacobites. Interestingly, there is some evidence to suggest that they had some Native American Indians amongst their number, who had come over from America to aid with recruiting. It has proved impossible to locate any direct evidence to support this but it is an intriguing possibility. The Rangers numbered two troops each of one captain, two lieutenants, a cornet, four quartermasters, two musicians and 60 private men. These troops wore 'Montero' style leather jockey caps along with green dragoon coats with green facings. The colour of the breeches is not known with any certainty.

The Yorkshire Hunters were formed in York on 24 September 1745 and were made up of the fox hunting gentry of the surrounding estates. An eyewitness account describes them on parade:

> The Gentlemen who composed the first Rank, were all dress'd in Blue; trimm'd with scarlet, and Gold Buttons, Gold Lac'd Hats, light boots and saddles, etc., their Arms were short Bullet Guns slung, Pistols of a moderate size and string plain swords. The second and third ranks which were made up of their servants, were dress'd in Blue, with Brass buttons, their Accoutrements all light and serviceable, with short Guns and pistols, and each with a Pole-Axe in his hand.[11]

A surviving print held in the National Library of Scotland entitled: 'A View of the Royal Hunters and the Gentlemen Independents of York…' shows both the infantry and cavalry regiments on parade on a common outside York before departing to take part in the campaign. The cavalry are shown with full lapels and cross belts and carrying a square guidon, all features of a horse regiment and not dragoons. The guidon bears the image of flames from which lightning bolts are springing. As the image is not in colour, we can only speculate on the colour of the guidon. However, the field is lighter than the dark border and darker fringe. Musicians are shown holding a large circular hunting horn. Whilst jackets were blue, waistcoats were either white or buff with buff breeches. Boots are the tight riding type rather than the bucket topped dragoon style.[12]

Cumberland's Hussars were a small unit of Hanoverian hussars who served as the Duke of Cumberland's personal bodyguard. They were present throughout the Jacobite campaign and, although not mentioned directly, probably accompanied him throughout the War of the Austrian Succession. They wore a brown Hussar fur hat with a red bag and white lace. The waistcoat and breeches were also red with white lace, whilst the hussar style

---

11   Bamford, (ed.), *Rebellious Scots to Crush*, p.155.
12   Reid, *Cumberland's Army*; see also a contemporary print in the Walter Blaikie Collection, National Library of Scotland: Jacobite Prints and Broadsides.

jacket was green, laced white. The dolman, so unique to hussars, which was worn draped over the shoulder, was also green, laced white, with a brown fur collar and cuffs. Leatherwork was buff and they carried curved swords in the hussar style.[13]

---

[13] For further discussion of these units, see Reid, *Cumberland's Army*; Bamford, (ed.), *Rebellious Scots to Crush*.

11

Physicians and Surgeons

Medical Provision in the Army of George II

By the beginning of the reign of George II the British Army recognised its responsibility for the health and wellbeing of its soldiers both at home and on campaign. Having the army fit for service made sound military and economic sense, as it was cheaper to pay for the treatment of a sick soldier than it was to recruit and train a replacement for a man dead or discharged unfit. This resulted in the increased establishment of military hospitals and the encouragement of trained medical professionals into the service.

There is an established view that medical practice in the eighteenth century was crude and ineffective and that those who practised it had little knowledge of what they were doing. The large number of deaths in military hospitals, and amongst the wounded after battle, has been taken as proof of medical incompetence or an uncaring attitude from those in high office. In fact, most medical practitioners in the British army did their utmost to treat the men under their care, using the best practises proscribed at the time. There is no doubt that knowledge was lacking, especially regarding the infection of wounds and the transfer of disease, but this was not through want of trying. Most surgeons had the best interests of their patients at heart. However, the inefficiencies of the eighteenth-century military are seen most sharply in relation to the provision of medical care, especially in the aftermath of battle.

Recruitment[1]

Whilst some posts as regimental surgeons were purchased, the War Office preferred to appoint regimental medical staff, hoping to ensure that those taking up the posts had at least a modicum of medical knowledge. However,

---

1 Summary from Christopher Duffy, *The Military Experience in the Age of Reason* (London: Routledge & Kegan Paul Ltd, 1987), Hayter (ed.), *Eighteenth Century Secretary at War*; Sarah Fatherly, 'Tending the Army: Women and the British General Hospital in North America, 1754—1763', *Early American Studies*, Vol.10, No.3 (Fall 2012), pp.566-599.

despite the War Office's best efforts, not everyone who held a medical appointment was always suitably trained.

Medical practitioners identified themselves as being either physicians, dealing with every day ailments and disease, or surgeons, who amputated limbs or removed bullets from injured men. In practice, both functions were interchangeable whilst serving on campaign. At the top of the military pecking order were the Surgeon General and the Physician General, both heads of their respective professions. Physicians were next in line, often working in permanent military or civilian hospitals. Next came surgeons, with regimental surgeons often having to work their way up to permanent positions as hospital surgeons. Hospital surgeons were considered more competent and better qualified than regimental surgeons, as time spent with the regiment was seen as an apprenticeship. Below these were apothecaries, who maintained medical supplies and made up the various prescriptions required by physicians and surgeons alike. At the bottom of the pile were mates, who assisted the surgeons and physicians with their work. Although these men were essentially hired help, they often had 'on the job' training and could become competent surgeons or physicians themselves. In the case of an outbreak of disease or distemper in the army, or on campaign, soldier's wives were often drafted in to act as nursing staff on a temporary basis. If this were to happen, an experienced nurse or military wife would be appointed as matron to manage the nursing staff and the organisation of the laundry, food and bedding on the wards. This freed the surgeons from this managerial role and allowed them to get on with treating the sick.

Pay was very good compared with the rank and file, with regimental surgeons being paid 10 shillings a day and 5 for a competent mate. In addition, those sent out on campaign could expect to have their expenses covered. When Lord Barrington ordered the recruitment of two extra surgeons, three surgeon's mates and three apothecary's mates as 'additional officers to the hospital for the service of the land forces in North America' in April 1756, they were given six months' pay up front 'to enable them to purchase necessaries'.[2] Those placed in charge of permanent hospitals on campaign were also paid more for the extra responsibility. Chief Surgeon William Young was placed in charge of hospital established during the campaign to Martinique in 1757, 'for which extra trouble you are allowed ten shillings p day beside your pay as master surgeon'.[3]

Military surgeons and physicians were treated as officers when on home service or on campaign and were given food and lodgings accordingly. They were commissioned and as such could wear the uniform of the regiment, which many clearly did. Whilst this meant that they enjoyed the comforts of the officers' mess when on campaign, it also meant that they shared the same hardships and dangers. Dr Buchanan, who served on the Dettingen campaign wrote: 'we talked so much of decamping every day, that for Six nights I did not put off my cloaths, nor boots, lay on the ground & happy if I

---

[2] Hayter (ed.), *Eighteenth Century Secretary at War*, p.335.
[3] Hayter (ed.), *Eighteenth Century Secretary at War*, p.335.

could get a little straw in a Soldiers tent'.[4] Dr Robert MacKinly had to run for his life, being chased by Indians, following the massacre of Braddock's army on the Monongahela in 1756 during which: 'he not only lost his Baggage, medicine chest with the instruments sent him by the Government, but all his own stock which was very considerable'.[5]

Training

Young men entering the military medical field had to know very little compared with what we might expect today. Some may have completed a formal education in medical matters whilst others may have served an apprenticeship with a serving surgeon or physician. They were expected to be able to correctly diagnose common diseases through clearly identifiable symptoms, and to prescribe the relevant treatment. There was an expectation that all medical practitioners would try to improve their knowledge of the subject as new discoveries were made or better techniques invented, but this was not always the case and once appointed the incumbent's ability was rarely officially tested.

Service in the military was viewed as the best means of advancing one's knowledge and ability, as service in in one short campaign abroad would likely expose the practitioner to more disease and injury than he might expect to see in years as a parish doctor. For this reason, many physicians and surgeons served with the military, if only for a short time, in order to gain experience before moving on to a civilian post. The Government actively encouraged medical professionals to serve by recognizing service in the army or navy as sufficient credentials to obtain a license to practice as a civilian, something which was usually only in the gift of the Company of Surgeons to grant. Despite opposition, this was enacted into statute in 1749, making service with the army the best way to bypass the otherwise lengthy and expensive civilian route to gaining a license.

Further training once in post was scant, with most learning from their peers. For example, Dr Buchanan recorded that there were meetings between the various regimental surgeons during which successful treatments and procedures were shared:

> I'm intimately acquainted with the greatest part of the Regimental Surgeons of our Army…We have a weekly Club were all are welcome to come, the chief Subject of conversation relates to our own business; it being a standing rule with us, that if any thing remarkable happen'd during the last weeks practice, it's to be made publick for the good of the Society; by this means we know the practice of the whole army during the Campn, & in winter quarters that of the Garrison.[6]

---

4 Buchanan, *Regimental Practice*, p.263.
5 Hayter (ed.), *Eighteenth Century Secretary at War*, p.333.
6 Buchanan, *Regimental Practice*, p.20.

Physicians were also expected to keep abreast of medical developments by reading books and pamphlets, although there was no requirement for them to do so. Whilst most surgeons took their responsibilities seriously this was not universal, and it was perfectly possible for a surgeon to take on his role with the regiment and be just as clueless to the cause of disease and the treatment of wounds when he left as the day he joined. The only saving grace for this was that surgeons – good or bad – rarely stayed with the army for any great length of time, preferring to do their apprenticeship before taking on a job as a parish doctor or a permanent role in a hospital.

General Practice

The first time the new recruit might meet the regimental surgeon was for a physical examination when he joined his regiment. Insanitary living conditions, poor diet and childhood disease meant that not every man brought in by the recruiting sergeant would pass muster. The surgeon would check the recruit for ailments and either pass or reject him. From then on, the surgeon would expect to deal with all of the soldier's complaints, from the common cold and flu to headaches, stomach upsets and accidental injuries. Dr Reide wrote that, 'Surgery forms a very small part of a regimental surgeon's duty, except in an active war',[7] and this seems to be confirmed by a veteran regimental surgeon who stated that: 'in full seven years, he had never met with near 100 properly chirurgical cases in the whole regiment; though in that course of time, near 2000 men had gone through the regimental books'.[8]

A common theme amongst medical men at the time was that illness was due to an imbalance of humors within the body and drawing the 'illness' out could cure this. Bleeding was the most common remedy, with patients being cut and a quantity of blood drained from their body. The belief that bleeding was good for you was prevalent amongst all ranks. Buchanan reported that: 'on every slight fall or bruise the trooper thinks himself neglected if he is not blooded'.[9] Officers were often angry if a soldier returned from seeing the surgeon having not been bled, and Dr Hamilton complained of 'the murmurs of officers, if men are not so soon cured of their complaints as their anxiety would have them'.[10] This attitude went all the way to the top. The Duke of Cumberland issued an order following advice from his master surgeon that: 'Dr Pringle recomends to the Regtal Surgeons timous bleeding in the feverish & Pleuritick disorders, if for the future such patients are sent to the Hospitals without bleeding, complaint will be made of the Surgeons'.[11] Unfortunately, the widespread and often unnecessary use of bleeding as a panacea often

---

7   J. Johnson, *A View of the Diseases of the Army in Great Britain* (London: J. Johnson, 1793), p.284.
8   Buchanan, *Regimental Practice*, p.48.
9   Buchanan, *Regimental Practice*, p.209.
10   Robert Hamilton, *The duties of a regimental surgeon considered: with observations on his general qualifications, and hints relative to a more respectable practice* (London: J. Johnson, 1798), p.58.
11   Buchanan, *Regimental Practice*, p.10

had the reverse effect, with the blood loss weakening the patient further and reducing their body's ability to fight infection.

The other favoured method for treating all kinds of disease involved prescribing medicines that caused 'evacuations', again following the theory that illness was inside you and the best cure was to get it out, by whichever orifice possible! It also appears that soldiers generally only felt that medicine was working if it had a strong and obvious effect. Again, Buchanan wrote that 'Troopers love to be worked heartly, & so much the better if it operates upwards & downwards, & seldom blame a strong vomite but will always find fault with a weake one'.[12] In 1755, Surgeon William Kellett of the 39th Foot wrote: 'The method of cure is very simple & regular, consisting of evacuations of all kinds… not only internally but outwardly apply'd to the nose to promote violent sneezing and by that means give a shock to the Nerves and assist them in throwing off whatever oppresses them'.[13] Other 'cures' included blistering, where a hot knife or blistering agent was touched to the skin and the subsequent blister snipped and the pus extracted. This was used to cure many ailments such as headaches and even gout.

Other common aliments were breaks and fractures, especially amongst the cavalry regiments where, as one surgeon recalled;

> Broken-shins are very common amongst us, from kicks by the horses…the flesh often stripped from the bone & laid bare some inches, as was the case of Burry of Cpt. Gilbert's, his horse running against a post, the tibia was bare three inches, the fleshy part hanging down, being almost ready to drop off; Instances happen dayly both to Troopers & Ban-men.[14]

Anyone not fit for duty through injury or illness ran the risk of being accused of malingering by their superiors and their fellows in the ranks, who often did not take well to having to do extra duty to cover for them. Buchanan remarked that 'their Comrades think nothing of a broken shin, saying they have had as much at foot ball & cured it with a leafe of tobacco; grudge doing duty for their lame Comrade & often oblige him to do his Duty before he is well'.[15] As a result he often had to give their superior officer a certificate to excuse the men from duty and prevent him being pressured to return to work. That said, there were plenty of soldiers prepared to do a little malingering to get out of their duties:

> Some pretend to be sick or Lame & uncapable of Duty…These are not easely detected, tho sometimes discovered by making them drunk, & carefully observing their motions. A Stiff Knee is a common complaint, but upon being fudled, can dance, jump, & cut capars…[16]

Not surprisingly, such men were soon put back on duty.

---

12 Buchanan, *Regimental Practice*, p.79
13 Guy (ed.), *Colonel Samuel Bagshawe*, p.169.
14 Buchanan, *Regimental Practice*, p.281.
15 Buchanan, *Regimental Practice*, p.207.
16 Buchanan, *Regimental Practice*, p.196.

It is interesting to note that soldiers struck down with an illness were not keen to be left behind by the regiment whilst they recovered, as they did not want to be separated from their unit. Given that they were billeted in an area where they did not know anyone and where the local populace was often not well disposed toward the military, the thought of the regiment moving on without him worried the soldier greatly. In 1743, Dr Buchanan recorded that one soldier, who was recovering from yellow fever was: 'greatly low-Spirited, & despairing of doing well, & fearing being left behind, which is always the case with Soldiers & greatly prevents recovery, their Mind being never easie'[17] Indeed, when Corporal Todd became ill whilst posted at home, he preferred to follow behind the regiment at his own pace rather than remain behind in hospital.

Finally, it is worth discussing the issue of mental illness amongst eighteenth century rank and file. In battle, men might see comrades killed and wounded next to them in some of the most horrific ways imaginable, with limbs lost to roundshot and wounds caused by musket, bayonet and sabre. Advancing in line toward the enemy knowing that one could be killed at any moment must have been incredibly stressful and, even if the battle was won, the aftermath of the battlefield would hardly be pretty. The idea that eighteenth century soldiers must have suffered some form of Post-Traumatic Stress Disorder has sometimes been dismissed by historians who believe that these men came from a hardier age, where death was more common in everyday life whilst the killing of animals on a daily basis, either for food or humanely disposing of them when injured, inured men to death and the sight of blood.[18] Yet it is clear from the writings of Dr Buchanan and other regimental surgeons that soldiers did suffer depression and mental health issues as a result of their battle experience. One wrote:

> Soldiers sometimes take a melancholy turn, become lowe spirited, senseless & childish, avoid company, cry or mutter to themselves, love to be solitary. Upon asking their case, they tell long stories about their past & present condition, are in great fear of being some way or other lost.[19]

Given the lack of knowledge surgeons and physicians had about basic infections and disease, it is a massive leap to expect them to have any understanding of Post-Traumatic Stress Disorder or mental illness associated with combat stress, which were not effectively diagnosed until this century. Their treatment is, given everything we know, unsurprising. The prescription was usually a 'heartie bottle',[20] which they found solved the problem in the short term.

---

17 Buchanan, *Regimental Practice*, p.295.
18 See for example Duffy, *Military Experience in the Age of Reason*, p.248.
19 Buchanan, *Regimental Practice*, p.327.
20 Buchanan, *Regimental Practice*, p.327.

Military Hospitals

A soldier with a serious illness that could not be treated in his camp or lodgings would be sent to the hospital for treatment. Likewise, when the army was deployed overseas, one or more semi-permanent hospitals would be established in major towns close to the area of the campaign for the same purpose. When a battle occurred, men would be initially treated in makeshift field hospitals before making the long, and often painful, journey back to the main hospital. The hospital was generally run by a master surgeon or physician who was paid an extra sum on top of their normal wage for doing so. The hospitals intial set-up costs where met by the War Office or, when overseas, by the Commander-in-Chief from the budget allocated to him for the camapign. Once they were up and running, however, they were expected to be maintained by charging the regiment for the soldiers' treatment. The War Office were clear that: 'You are to charge the paymaster of his regiment five pence per day Stoppages from the day of his Entry to the day of his discharge or death, reckoning the first and last day only as one day'. This money was to be used to supply necessary medicines, bandages and so on and also to employ nurses, if they could be found. When the patient arrived from his unit he was to present a signed certificate detailing: 'his Name and the company he belongs to, and of the cloaths sent with him and specifying his ailment. This is to be signed by the Surgeon or his Mate and an officer of the company the patient belongs to; And you are not to admit him with any of his arms or Accoutrements'.[21]

Modern readers might be forgiven for thinking that hospitals during this period where a desirable place for a sick soldier to go, but this was far from the truth. Hospital buildings were not very big and were often overcrowded and lacked sufficant ventialtion. The bedding was usually filthy, the food and water bad and little or no proper sanitation. Medical practitioners did not know about germs or how diseases spread between patients, and as a result patients usually became more ill on arrival at hospital than they had been before. Any infectious diseases or viruses spread like wildfire through the overcrowded, cramped rooms. One of the worst was 'hospital fever', later identified as epidemic typhus, which was also common in jails and other unsanitary places were men were crowded together. This led Dr Buchanan to write that: 'Among the chief causes of sickness and death in an army [is] what is intended for its health and preservation, the Hospitals themselves'. He recommended that 'Surgeons should not send triffling cases to an hospital: those who go for slight Surgery cases are in great danger of catching some distemper of the house viz. fever, small pox &c'.[22] The conditions were often compounded by the lack of nursing staff, as it was difficult to employ people to work in such conditions. Not only was the work undesirable, but the nursing staff ran the risk of catching any infections that may be going around the wards. During an epidemic of flux and fever in 1743, 'the Nurses dyed so

---

21 Hayter (ed.), *Eighteenth Century Secretary at War*, p.335, Barrington to Master Surgeon William Young, 17 February 1757.
22 Buchanan, *Regimental Practice*, p.196.

fast that 33 private Soldiers were obliged to nurse their Comrades'.[23] It was noted that married men, whose wives came to the hospital to attend them, were more likely to survive an illness than those without. One report notes how the wives would be on hand to change dressings, clean bedding, empty bed pans and: 'apply a warm … Dishcloath to the Throat, & sometimes a hot loafe in the event of their husbands' suffering an attack of quinsy'.[24]

The terrible reputation hospitals had amongst the men made it difficult to get soldiers to go there. Dr. Buchanan recorded: 'Our men had taken a dislike to the hospital (and) would rather suffer the injuries of the weather in the field, or think themselves happy if they got into a Boners out-house & lye on straw'.[25] In 1757 Corporal Todd was sent to the hospital at Portsmouth and immediately sought leave from his Colonel: 'to let me march with the Regiment, for I told him the Hospital would kill me to remain in it'.[26]

---

23 Buchanan, *Regimental Practice*, p.283.
24 Buchanan, *Regimental Practice*, p.123.
25 Buchanan, *Regimental Practice*, p.295.
26 Cormack and Jones (eds), *Journal of Corporal Todd*, p.36.

12

The Train

Logistics and Supply in the British Army

There is a military maxim that states; 'Amateurs talk tactics, professionals talk logistics'. Supplying food and forage to an eighteenth-century army was no easy task. Contemporary estimates suggest that an army of 22,000 infantry and 5,000 cavalry would contain 36,000 people and 20,000 horses.[1] The logistics of moving, housing and supplying an army of this size was a mammoth undertaking but which was essential to a successful campaign.

The commander-in-chief in the field did not get involved with logistics: as Humphrey Bland explained, 'the Intendant of the Army has the entire management of it, and by that means leaves the General at full liberty to think of the military Operations only'.[2] Logistical responsibilities fell to three men: the Quartermaster General, the Commissary General and the Wagonmaster General. These senior officers would be present at staff meetings along with the other general officers. The commander-in-chief would outline his strategy for the coming weeks and it would be their responsibility to make sure that the logistics were in place to make that plan come to fruition. Sometimes, as we will see, the expectations of the commanders far outstripped the logistical capability of the commissariat.

The Quartermaster General

The quartermaster general was a post held by a senior officer on the staff of the commander-in-chief. Essentially, it was his job on campaign to ensure that the troops were provided with quarters, either in tents or billeted in inns or local people's houses. In some respects, this was very similar to the role

---

1 Statistics and overview summarised from Rogers, *British Army of the Eighteenth Century*; Gordon E. Bannerman, 'Abraham Hume and the Supply management of the British Army during the '45', *Journal of the Society for Army Historical Research*, Vol. 92, No. 372 (Winter 2014), pp.268-285; M.K. Ritchie, 'The Troubles of a Commissary During the Seven Years War', *Journal of the Society for Army Historical Research*, Vol.36, No.148 (December, 1958), pp.157-164.
2 Bannerman, 'Abraham Hume and the Supply management of the British Army during the '45', p.269.

'A representation of the march of the Guards towards Scotland, in the year 1745', more commonly known as 'The March of the Guards to Finchley'. Engraving after Hogarth's famous painting. (Anne S.K. Brown Collection)

of the regimental quartermaster when the regiments were based at home. However, as might be imagined, finding lodgings for several thousand men was a lot more complicated than a single regiment, especially on foreign soil.

Having been told the route of march by the commander-in-chief, the quartermaster general would, along with his staff, begin to identify the potential camp sites for the advancing army for the end of each day, as well as towns or villages along the route which could be used as billets. The quartermaster general's staff would then approach each regiment and assign them a place in the column, which would also be conveyed to the officer in charge of the wagon train. When the columns set out the following morning the quartermaster general and his staff would ride ahead of the vanguard to the next camp location and begin to mark out the ground allocated to each regiment using ropes and camp colours.

As the columns marched into camp, the quartermaster general would then ensure they went to the correct location. Once all the regiments were in their positions, he would begin to plan the next day's advance and, again, convey that to the regiments. Those who were lucky enough to be assigned billets in houses, or even to be under cover in barns or outbuildings, would be shown to their locations by the quartermaster general's staff, who would also ensure there were no disputes about the best lodgings.

Put in basic terms such as this, the quartermaster general's job seems fairly straightforward and uncomplicated. However, as we shall see, the size of the armies deployed during this period, especially in Europe, and the baggage, wagons, and horses they brought with them made this job far from simple!

The Commissary General

In other European armies, the position of intendant, or commissary general, was a permanent one, allowing an individual and his staff to build up experience in the provisioning and mobilisation of large bodies of troops in preparation for war. In the British Army, however, the regimental agents, alongside the War Office, were responsible for feeding and housing the various regiments during peacetime and it was only as the army was gathering for deployment overseas that a commissary general was appointed. Given how important this role is, it seems astounding that no thought was given to the need for a competent commissary general until the day war began!

The commissary general was a civilian post, which held no equivalent military rank. This was because the appointee worked directly for the Treasury and not for the army. Not surprisingly, the first problem the Treasury had when looking for a suitable candidate was that no-one had any experience of doing the job. Like all other posts in Georgian England, there was always a whiff of nepotism about potential candidates. The Earl of Stair was commander-in-chief of the forces in England when the Jacobite Rebellion broke out in 1745 and he proposed his nephew for the role, even though he had never served with the army, or even the Treasury, before.[3]

For most of the War of the Austrian Succession, this role was filled by Abraham Hume who was appointed to the role of 'Commissary General of Stores, Provisions and Forage to his Majesties Forces' in 1743 and served until the end of the war. Britain's initial involvement in the Seven Years War in Europe consisted of limited raids on France and so a military man, Lieutenant General George Howard, temporarily filled the role. When Britain committed troops to the land war in 1758, the Treasury selected Thomas Orby Hunter, a well-respected Member of Parliament who had a reputation for financial competence. He served until June 1760 when Michael Hatton, a Treasury Official, replaced him.

The position of commissary general was held 'at his Majesties pleasure', meaning it could be rescinded at any time. If the incumbent survived the stress and pressure of the job, he could expect to be dismissed as soon as hostilities ended. No effort was made to debrief him or to garner any of his experience to pass on to a potential replacement. All commissaries, it seems, had to learn their trade from scratch.

The commissary general attended daily meetings with the senior officers, and his tent was usually posted close to that of the commander-in-chief so that he would be on hand if required. The commander would share with

---

3 Bannerman, 'Abraham Hume and the Supply management of the British Army during the '45', p.273.

him his plans, and most importantly his intended route of march. It was the commissary general's role to ensure that magazines were established along the route that would feed and supply the army as it advanced, and in this he worked very closely with the quartermaster general. He was also responsible for the provisioning of the horses with feed, sufficient waggons for the men and equipment, and was 'responsible for providing the army in every situation and with him rests the direction and control of every article of expence'.[4] Two deputies, who held the position of 'Commissaries General of Supply', aided him in this task. One usually attended 'to the mode of supplying the army, and watching it in all its parts, while the whole attention of the other is taken up in superintending the accounts and bringing them regularly forward'.[5]

Beneath them were a number of Assistant Commissaries, whose job it was to 'distribute the bread, Forage, Straw, Fuel and candle to the Troops, and every other extraordinary which the service might require'.[6] The selection of men to do this job, and how many were required, seems to have been rather haphazard. Surviving letters to Hume from his superiors at the Treasury state:

> It is impossible for me to say what number of people may be necessary or what wages to give them'. They go on to suggest: 'suppose at each place where magazine's are to be made that it will be proper to have one head Clerk …and to have one or more person's under him to assist. I suppose a head Clerk may be had at about 7s 6d p day, and those under him at 5 s p day and what labourers may be necessary at the current price of the country…[7]

Finally, a commissary of accounts was appointed by the Treasury to examine the accounts of the commissary general who, it appears, had precious little discretion when it came to spending Parliament's cash.

With regard to the supply of food and wagons to the army, the commissary general did this by issuing contracts to private individuals or companies, who would then undertake to provide the necessary goods. A surviving example of a contract states: 'The undersigned engages to furnish for the service of his Britannick Majesty one hundred good waggons with one driver and four good horses to each, able to draw on unpaved roads 1500 pounds and on paved roads 3000 pounds weight'.[8] This arrangement ensured that the contractor, not the army, would be responsible for the upkeep of the wagons and to replace any that were lost or damaged.

When the goods were supplied, the commissary staff would check them and then issue a receipt to the contractor, who would take this receipt to the paymaster general. He would then either pay the contractor in cash or issue a promissory note for the amount, which could be exchanged with several respectable banks in Europe. For the period up to 1759, all such

---

4 Haviland Le Mesurier, *The British Commissary: In Two Parts. A system for the British Commissariat on Foreign Service* (London: T. Egerton, 1801), p.5.
5 Le Mesurier, *The British Commissary*, p.9.
6 Le Mesurier, *The British Commissary*, p.9.
7 Hayter (ed.), *Eighteenth Century Secretary at War*, p.120.
8 Le Mesurier, *The British Commissary*, p.99.

receipts had to be counter signed either by the commissary general or by the commander-in-chief. This piece of unnecessary paperwork was designed to prevent fraud but in practice slowed down the payment of contractors and often interrupted supplies to the men, as the contractor would, quite rightly, not supply any further goods until his payment was received.

The commissary staff had to be constantly on their toes, as the contractors often cut corners to increase their profits, supplying inferior goods or insufficient quantities. An example of this was recorded by Commissary Halsey in his diary of 1760, where he: 'received undoubted information that Beuilly Reunicken of Dippenaw…being under contract for a large quantity of forage for supplying the magazine of Osnabruk, had sent about 120 wagon loads of hay to that magazine, so insufficient and of so bad a quality that it was rejected'.[9]

The system described above was essentially how the logistical supply of the British Army was carried out throughout the War of the Austrian Succession. In the early years of the Seven Years War, Britain's only commitment to the war in Europe was a financial one, paying subsidies to its Prussian ally and financially supporting the 12,000 Hessians and Prussians that made up the army in Germany. However, in 1758 Parliament voted to take on the direct funding for the 38,124 troops belonging to Hanover and its allies of Buckeburg, Saxe-Gotha and Wolfenbuttel, while in July the commitment was further extended by a dispatch of 8,716 British troops to Germany. In December, the Treasury took over the role of the Hanoverian commissariat as well, so that by the beginning of 1759 the Treasury was paying for, and undertaking to supply, over 60,000 soldiers campaigning on the continent. This constituted a major administrative headache, as each of the different nations that made up the allied force had different logistical practices. For example, Hessian troops were issued 2lb of bread a day, whilst British troops were issued 6lb every four days. Hanoverian troops were paid 'Fleisch Geld' or meat money to top up their rations, whilst none of the other nations were. The books were further confused by the use of ducats to account for some purchases by the regiments and the use of Louis d'Or by others, not to mention the several different types of measure used for forage, flour, and oats amongst the different nationalities.

The individual appointed to sort out the supply problem was Thomas Orby Hunter, who was appointed as 'Superintendent of Extraordinaries' in 1758. Hunter immediately faced a huge logistical problem and had insufficient staff to deal with it effectively. The system of having one commissary general with two assistants and a small team of assistant commissaries was insufficient to get the job done even when faced with supplying the small British army on its own. To now try to deal with the supply of a polyglot army of such enormous size required a complete overhaul in its approach.

To begin with, Hunter brought many wagons into public ownership, buying them outright and giving them to the various regiments for their use. This cut out a good deal of administration with no need for constant

---

9   Ritchie, 'The Troubles of a Commissary During the Seven Years War', p.164.

wrangling with contractors for their supply and upkeep. He also created military bakeries in towns and cities along the marching route that worked alongside their mobile equivalents to produce the army's daily bread. This was such an essential part of the logistical supply chain that Hunter could not continue to rely on an ad hoc system for bread production. Hunter also increased the size of the commissariat. He appointed 13 senior commissaries to help administer the army, creating for each a specialist role such as accounts, inspection of magazines, transport and so on. By end of 1760 this was increased to 18, in 1761 there were 27 and by 1762, when the army had reached 96,000 men, there were 41. This reduced the ratio of senior commissaries from one for every 5,416 troops in 1759 to one for every 2,362 by 1762. There was a corresponding increase in the junior staff under them as well.[10]

To fill these posts, the Treasury was once again faced with a small pool of candidates none of whom had any real experience. In order to attract the best people to the role, the wages for the commissariat were increased substantially. Whilst Hume had received £3 a day whilst in post, Hunter was granted £10 a day, along with a generous lump sum when he took on the role in order to cover his expenses. As Lieutenant General George Howard had continued to receive his army pay as well as his £3 a day for being a commissary general, Hunter was also to receive the daily pay of a general officer. This made him the highest paid official in the army after the commander-in-chief, which indicates that the Government had finally realised how important the role was. The senior commissaries were to be paid £5 a day, which was more than the Lieutenant General of the Ordnance, whilst their junior officers, deputy and assistant commissaries received £2 and £1 respectively, some of the highest wages in the army and certainly more than would be obtained in most occupations at home. Although the post was temporary and was only contracted until the war's end, this increase in wages had the desired effect and many capable individuals were drawn to work with the commissariat.

In 1761, Hunter also streamlined the system for paying contractors, allowing senior commissaries both to hold a quantity of cash, which could be used to pay contractors on the spot for smaller sums, and to sign promissory notes and warrants without reference to the commissary general or the commander-in-chief. This released the administrative logjam and contributed greatly to the smoother running of the army.

Despite all of these reforms, the commissariat appears to have been understaffed and overworked throughout the war. As well as having to be constantly alert for fraud and theft from amongst their contractors and their own military, officials of the commissariat were also under pressure from their high command and their political masters to get the job done. Hunter wrote to the Secretary at War in 1760, proclaiming: 'I do with great truth assure your Grace that though I rise every morning at six o'clock and give a constant and close attention to my business till midnight, I find the time too

---

10   H.M. Little, 'The Emergence of a Commissariat during the Seven Years War in Germany', *Journal of the Society for Army Historical Research*, Vol.61, No.248 (Winter 1983/4), p.206.

short to despatch what is already under my care'.[11] Ultimately, all of Hunter's good work was undone, as the whole system was disbanded at the end of the war and had to be learned again when war broke out in America in 1775.

The Daily Bread

The supply of bread to the army was absolutely essential to maintain it in the field and proved one of the biggest logistical headaches for the Commissariat. If an army was based in or near a town then either the contractor, or the army, could requisition the bakery ovens for military use. During the 1746 campaign in Scotland, for example, the Duke of Cumberland ordered magazines to be established at Perth. Amongst other necessities he ordered: 'all the flower they can, that the Ovens at Perth may be kept constantly employed'.[12]

Where a town was not available, mobile bakeries were attached to the army to do the job instead. Based at a camp or magazine, mobile bakeries could produce the required amount of bread before being dismantled, moved and rebuilt at the next camp. The army usually baked enough bread for four days, marching three before rebuilding the ovens on the fourth and having a day of rest whilst more bread was baked.

A commissary of the bakery was appointed who was responsible for the accounting of the flour and would also record the issue of bread to the various regiments in the army. He would then produce the accounts as required. During the Seven Years War in Germany, the Commissary of the Bakery employed four assistants, one accountant, one master baker, eight head bakers, 188 journeymen bakers, one joiner, four carpenters (one master, three journeymen) eight bricklayers (one master and seven journeymen) and one surgeon. In charge of the wagons and horses were one sergeant major, four sergeants, 70 wagon drivers, four farriers and smiths, two collar makers, two wheelwrights and one veterinary surgeon; a total staff of 301. In total, the bakery for the entire allied army consisted of 1,500 men.[13]

In the early part of the century, mobile ovens were entirely made of brick, but later they had a brick base with an arched metal frame that could be covered with clay to seal in the heat. These were much easier to erect and lighter to transport. Each double oven required about 660 bricks and weighed about 2670lbs. A double oven would bake 300 three-pound loaves per batch and could make five batches in 24 hours (1,500 loaves) making rations for 3,000 men. Twelve such ovens would make 36,000 rations in 24 hours.

Whilst this is certainly a huge achievement, it must be remembered that this would only be enough to feed an army of 30,000 men and its dependants for one day. The mobile bakeries had to get ahead of the army and be in

---

11 L. Namier & J. Brooke (eds), *The History of Parliament: the House of Commons 1754-1790* (London: History of Parliament Trust, 1964) p.414.
12 Bannerman, 'Abraham Hume and the Supply management of the British Army during the '45', p.278.
13 Le Mesurier, *The British Commissary*, p.20.

a position to produce bread prior to the army's arrival and then keep producing it after the army had left, sending the bread after them to the area of operations. Only then would it pack up and move. Once the army was in close proximity to the enemy, the mobile bakeries would set up at the last safe magazine point and produce bread to send forward.

Packing up the bakeries was not an easy matter. The bricks for the 12 double ovens required ten wagons to transport them. In addition, wagons were also required for the troughs used to knead the dough and the huge canvas tents – 32ft long and 24ft wide – that were used to make the bread in. This allowed the bread to be made whatever the weather. There were a further four of these tents used to cool the bread in and another four to hold the sacks of flour, as well and other equipment, such as kettles, lamps, weights, boards and pails. When one adds to this the equipment needed for the men, including their tents and blankets, 96 camp kettles, 300 canteens and so on, the mobile bakery was a convoy of wagons all on its own. However, its role was so crucial to the army that commanders went out of their way to make sure that it was never placed in danger. For example, the bakery that moved with the army of Prince Ferdinand in Germany was considered so important that it had an escort of 400 infantry.

There were no specially designed wagons used to transport bread, which was usually carried in four wheeled 'ammunition waggons', which could hold up to 210 loaves. These were open sided and designed with only a rail to retain the casks of ammunition. When used as bread wagons they had wickerwork panels inserted and a canvas tilt. It is not surprising however, that the bread did not travel well in such a vehicle, especially along muddy cart tracks. In 1761, Corporal Todd complained that, 'the roads is so very deep that our bread waggons cannot get up at the time that it is due, but some times it is 2, 3 or 4 days past & when it comes it is mostly mouldy, not fit to eat, but with those that is almost famish'd is glad to get it any ways'.[14]

The Wagon Master General

Wagons were essential for the movement of men, equipment and supplies and the eighteenth-century British Army needed a constant supply of both them and the horses required to pull them. Broadly speaking, it was usual for one contractor to be given the job of supplying the horses, wagons, and drivers to keep the army moving. He would then sub-contract out the work to other agents, whilst retaining overall responsibility for effective supply. This was complicated from 1758 onwards when the combined army in Europe needed separate wagon contractors for the many different allied contingents. This was one of the reasons why wagons began to be purchased by the Treasury to reduce the need for so many contractors.

Wagons could not be brought from home and used on European roads. Most roads had ruts cut into them by the continuous passage of wagons,

---

14   Cormack and Jones (eds), *Journal of Corporal Todd*, p.217.

so that wagons were forced to use the existing ruts to traverse the road. Unfortunately, the span, or interval between the wheels of wagons, varied in different countries making it essential that wagons were bought or hired locally so that they would run on local roads. Artilleryman John Muller explained: 'Even every county in England observes a different width, which is very inconvenient for those who travel in carriages. The artillery carriages are made like those in Flanders, which is four feet eight inches'.[15]

The commissariat would assign an assistant commissary to be 'Inspector of the Train', who reported weekly to the commissary general on the condition of the wagon train and would highlight any deficiencies. An army officer, often referred to as the 'Wagon Master General', would be appointed by the quartermaster general, to command the train and to ensure that it moved successfully between camps. The contractors were thus placed under military command, as one recorded: 'The discipline of the service was maintained by obliging every contractor to obey the orders of the Officers appointed to command the train and rendering him responsible for the conduct of every individual employed under his contract'.[16] Although the army undertook to provide food for the wagon drivers and forage for the horses, the upkeep of the wagons and replacements for damaged wagons fell to the contractor.

Each regiment was allowed 20 wagons and no more than 82 horses, being four for every wagon with two spare. This was the maximum number of wagons and horses that the army would supply, and provide forage for from the magazines. However, this was not the total number of wagons or horses in the regiment. Officers often brought their own horses, both for riding and as 'Bat' or packhorses to carry their kit. Some officers might also bring their own wagons on campaign, especially if a wife or mistress accompanied them, or if they had a particularly large entourage of orderlies or servants. For example, when he went on campaign in 1747, Lord Albemarle required 60 horses to move his personal baggage, tents and servants, whilst King George II, when he led the Dettingen campaign, brought '13 Berlins, 35 wagons, 54 carts and 662 horses' to move his personal belongings and his staff.[17] Officers paid for forage for these extra horses directly to the agent, unless some could be found locally. However, campaigning soon took its toll on the horses, whilst contingencies of the campaign might require each regiment to travel more lightly, reducing the number of wagons available to each. Whatever the reason, we see regiments on campaign in Germany in 1759 returning on average about 40 horses each as serviceable, reducing the number of serviceable wagons for each to ten.[18]

At first glance twenty seems like a large number of wagons for each regiment, but when one considers how much kit was required to be transported between camps, it is surprising that they only needed 20! A standard foot regiment numbering about 700 men would need to carry 160 standard tents, 12 bell tents, 160 tin kettles and bags, 160 hatchets, their

---

15 Rogers, *British Army of the Eighteenth Century*, p.87.
16 Le Mesurier, *The British Commissary*, p.27.
17 Orr, *Dettingen 1743*, p.44.
18 Returns listed in Hayter (ed.), *Eighteenth Century Secretary at War*, pp.170-175.

drum cases and powder bags, 700 water flasks, haversacks, and knapsacks: before beginning to count food for the men and forage for the horses, which was usually only enough to last two or three days' march.

Although the allocation of wagons for the infantry and the cavalry were similar, different units had different requirements. During the Seven Years war in Germany the Commissariat were allowed 180 horses for 30 waggons (six each), eight for two caissons, six for two forge carts and 10 in reserve making 204 horses in total.[19] The list of wagons and equipment required by the artillery is, not surprisingly, even longer. In 1747 Colonel Muller of the Royal Artillery recorded the makeup of the British artillery train in Europe. As well as ammunition tumbrels, the guns themselves, spare limbers and carriages for the guns, there were also mobile forges, pontoon wagons, laboratory wagons, entrenching tools and so on. In total there were 267 wagons and 1,509 horses for a train consisting of six 12-pounders, six 9-pounders, fourteen 6-pounders and twenty-six 3-pounder guns.[20]

As well as the fighting arm of the army, wagons and horses were also required for the support arms. The field bakeries were required for supply, as were the provision train, which consisted of 900 six-horse wagons during Prince Ferdinand's campaign in late 1759. Next came the field hospitals, with their surgeons and mates, and after them the carriages and wagons of the sutlers, traders, prostitutes, and other civilians who followed an army on campaign. Wagons were also required to carry spare equipment for the wagons and the equipment needed to feed and groom the horses. One surviving list records: '128 sets of harness for the fore horses, 66 sets ditto for the shaft horses, 130 portable managers, 203 pickets, 194 picket cords, 34 Windlasses, 60 Drag Chains for 30 waggons, 35 small hatchets, 35 Greasing Pots, 6 lanterns, 5 Spare fore wheels, 5 spare Hind wheels, 35 Hoes'.[21]

This was not the end of the military need for wagons and horses, as there was a constant stream of supplies going from the last safe magazine to the area of operations. A magazine would not be established close to the enemy for fear it would be captured, and the field bakeries would be similarly established at the last safe magazine. Along with bread, all other necessaries were sent forward, the empty wagons often returning with sick and wounded men. These supply columns were huge and ran pretty much daily up and down the agreed routes between the magazine and the army. During Prince Ferdinand's campaign in Germany, for example, 9,600 wagons were required just to transport the forage for the armies 80,000 horses from the magazine at Cassel to the seat of operations. Wagons were constantly in demand, due to damage, theft or enemy action making any loss hard to replace. Halsey recorded one such loss in his diary: 'we had the misfortune of losing all the transport we expected from Paderborn, some taken, some deserted and about 9… escaped toward Hamelin. I fear it will be some time before wagons

---

19 Summary from Le Mesurier, *The British Commissary*, p.25
20 Royal Artillery, *Seven Years War*, at <http://www.kronoskaf.com/syw/index.php?title=Royal Atillery>, viewed 1 October 2020.
21 Le Mesurier, *The British Commissary*, p.87.

can be collected to supply this loss and enable the regular furnishing this Corps with oats'.[22]

The Impact of Logistics on the Eighteenth-Century British Army

It is easy for armchair generals, when reading about the various campaigns of the War of the Austrian Succession or the Seven Years War, to criticise British generals for being 'plodding'. Historians also fall into this trap, sometimes referring to Cumberland having been 'caught napping' by his French opponent, Maurice de Saxe, who is often described as stealing a march on him in the 1745 campaign in Flanders. These criticisms are usually made without the appreciation of the logistical restrictions the army was under. In 1746, for example, the Duke of Cumberland, keen to pursue the Jacobite army, complained that the Commissary Assistant in charge of the magazine at Perth, a Jacob Gomez Serra, was: ' a man no way of an equal Capacity for such an undertaking, tho I hope honest, who had failed to provide above four days bread, thus preventing the army from marching'.[23] Cumberland was no doubt frustrated at being unable to pursue the Jacobites, but he could not leave until sufficient bread was baked to keep his army supplied until it could reach its next magazine. Spoiled foodstuffs, broken down wagons, poor roads, corrupt agents and incompetent commissaries could all combine to slow or even halt an army, all of which would be beyond the power of the commander-in-chief to correct. When asking why an army was slow to respond to the enemies' movements, it is easy to blame the commander for not being dynamic when, in truth, his hands were likely tied by logistical issues.

One example will suffice to demonstrate how eighteenth-century logistics could ruin a campaign. In 1758, a 7,000 strong British force was marching south from Emden when they encountered heavy rain for several days. The commissary, Micheal Hatton, was forced to admit that: 'the bread for want of covered waggons is dissolved, though I bought the best coverings I could, as is the two days bread the men had in their knapsacks, and I am afraid there is not a dry cartridge in the army. We have bread at Coesfeld… but that can't be got to us, nor we can't get to that'.[24] Without bread to feed the army or dry powder to fight, this force had become 'combat ineffective' without a shot being fired.

---

22   Ritchie, 'The Troubles of a Commissary During the Seven Years War', p.160.
23   Bannerman, 'Abraham Hume and the Supply management of the British Army during the '45', p.278.
24   Jeremy Black, *European Warfare in a Global Context* (London: Routledge, 2006), p.62.

13

The Army on Campaign

Rumours of war might well be rife amongst the patrons of the Public Houses and Inns where soldiers were stationed, but the first they would know for sure that they were being deployed was when the messenger arrived with their 'marching orders'. The soldiers would be ordered to march to a particular location, where they would meet up with the other companies or troops of their regiment and from there they would march to join the army. The marching orders for the Scots battalions deployed to America in 1757 read:

> The Highland battalions should march as soon as they are in readiness, from their present quarters to Port Patrick and be there embarked for Donachdee. You will acquaint the Lord Lieutenant that they should be disembarked at Donachdee and march thro Ireland to Cork, to be there embark'd on board such transports as will be there to receive them…[1]

At this point the regimental wagons and all of the camp followers would pack up and move with the regiment.

Assembly Point

The various regiments of the army would be ordered to gather in a large open space close to the ports from which they were expected to depart. In 1758, troops gathering for the Rochefort expedition encamped on the Isle of Wight whilst those gathering to oppose the Jacobite advance in 1745 were gathered on Finchley Common, which was still being used as a place to encamp soldiers as late as 1780. The camp was set out as it would be if the army were on campaign, with the quartermaster general designating the area set aside for each regiment's tents, before latrine pits were dug, firewood gathered, and sentries posted. At this stage the sentries were as much to prevent desertion as anything else. This would be the soldiers' introduction to life on campaign, as the routines established here would reflect the daily rhythms they would

---
1   Hayter (ed.), *Eighteenth Century Secretary at War*, p.43.

come to expect when they arrived overseas. Once the regiments joined the camp, there would be no opportunity to leave it to purchase food locally, so the men had to make do with their issued rations or purchase additional items from the authorised camp sutlers, although this captive market soon drove prices up.

Camp equipment would now be issued from the stores of the Board of Ordnance. Cooking pots and utensils were issued, along with canteens, blankets, and tents for those who did not have them. For the officers, there was slightly more kit to collect. Lord Ligonier wrote to Lord Harrington to advise him what his ADC should bring on the Flanders campaign in 1745: 'As for his equipage: a bed, some clothes, a couple of horses for himself and for what servants he desires to have is enough …a good groom is absolutely necessary'.[2]

New recruits would join the regiment on a daily basis, or they would receive drafts of men from other regiments to bring those deploying overseas up to strength. Every day, the regiments would practice their drills, marching and deploying, wheeling, and forming lines and columns. The infantry would also practise the firing drill. Prior to deploying to France, Todd's regiment was: 'March'd 4 miles to Bull Marsh to be reviewed by Lieutenant General Honeywood. We went through our Evolutions etc and fired only 12 rounds. It came on very wett & rainy so that the General dismist us before we had done & march'd back to our quarters all very wett & dirty'.[3]

Senior Officers now took the time to form the regiments into brigades and practised drilling and manoeuvring these larger bodies of men. Opportunities to do this during peacetime were rare and very few senior officers had much experience on handling Brigades, let alone whole battle lines or wings of an army. Major General Grant wrote to Jeffrey Amherst about one such training session:

> This morning for the first time I joined the whole together & made them form from the line of march to the front, rear & flanks in different ways by signals. This I intend to practise every day while we remain here that those evolutions may be familiar to them if it should be necessary to put them in practice upon real service.[4]

For old sweats who had been on campaign before, this flurry of extra training was a nuisance. Before the attack on Cherbourg, Todd recorded: 'been constantly kept exercising every day since General Bligh took the command, that he gives us a deal more trouble than is necessary for all the troops here are old and expert in their duty and fit to face any enemy that comes before them'.[5]

---

2 Whitworth, *Field Marshal Lord Ligonier*, p.94.
3 Cormack and Jones (eds), *Journal of Corporal Todd*, p.38.
4 Grant to Amherst, Moncks Corner, March 30, 1761 from Edith Mays, *Amherst Papers, the Southern Sector, 1756-1763* (Maryland: Heritage Books, Inc. 1999), p.221.
5 Cormack and Jones (eds), *Journal of Corporal Todd*, p.64.

The army's camp would be a hive of activity, with supplies and additional regiments coming in, men and horses training and sorting equipment, Sutlers going about their business all combined with the daily life of the regimental wives and children, who went about their own business of cooking, washing, and playing.

Transport

The army would now be embarked onto transport ships. Only those women shown on the regimental returns were allowed to travel on board ship with the army at this time, and many men would have to say goodbye to their wives and families who were forced to stay behind. Those being deployed to America, India, or some other colonial conflict, faced many weeks of tedious travel, often confined below decks for long periods with unsanitary living conditions and poor rations. Disease, especially scurvy, was usually rife and many soldiers thanked their stars when their eventual destination hove into sight. However, even short Channel crossings were not easy, fraught as they were with storms, high winds and potential enemy action. On one such short journey, Gunner James Woods recorded another type of danger: 'Mr Buck, mattross, was missing in the third watch. Looked all over the ship. Could not find him. We supposed that as he went to the heads of the ship to ease himself he fell overboard'.[6]

Marching to War

Having arrived in the theatre of operations and spent time resting and establishing some order to the ranks, it was now time to march out to face the enemy. As discussed in the chapter on logistics, every regiment had a large number of wagons and horses to accompany it, on which was carried their supplies and camp equipment. Not surprisingly, moving such a huge number of men and wagons from one place to another was not easy. An infantry column of 24 battalions with four batteries of artillery attached could stretch back along a road over seven miles (11.7 kilometres). With their baggage wagons added, the column would become about 20 miles long (32 kilometres), which, if marching one behind the other, would take about 12 hours to pass a single point. If one was to add 24 squadrons of cavalry to the column it would become over 35 miles long, or 56.3 kilometres! Given that the armies deployed in Europe during both the War of the Austrian Succession and the Seven Years War were frequently larger than this, the logistical challenges involved in moving an army from A to B becomes obvious. This was not helped by the fact that roads in eighteenth-century Europe were little better than tracks, and the passage of so many horses and wagons could churn up what little road there was and turn it into a quagmire.

---

6   Whitworth (ed.), *Gunner at Large*, p.37.

Choke points such as bridges or defiles, poor weather conditions, or broken-down wagons, all conspired to slow the armies' progress.

The most efficient method was to divide the army into at least three marching columns. The columns on the left and right flanks would contain a mix of cavalry and infantry along with their regimental wagons. In the middle would be the column containing the artillery and the support arms. Each column would be preceded by an advance guard, to alert the main body to any ambushes, and followed by a rear-guard, to prevent any surprise attacks on the rear of the column by enemy light troops. Cavalry scouts would also be designated to ride out ahead and to the flanks of the army to act as a first line of alarm should the enemy appear, but also to keep in contact with the friendly columns travelling to the left or right. Columns generally marched for three days and then rested for the fourth.

It was the job of the quartermaster general to plan a route for each of the columns that took it from its current camp and converged by the end of the day on a suitable location that allowed all three columns to camp in close proximity to one another. This route, often following parallel roads or tracks some miles apart, would then be conveyed to the Wagon Masters, who would decide the order of the march. This would be communicated to the various regiments the night before the march to ensure that the lead regiments, and their wagons, were ready to set off at the appointed time. Even a short delay in getting the first units on the road could have a huge knock on effect on those coming behind and may result in some regiments not making it to their new campsite until after dark.

The regimental drums would beat around dawn the following day, waking the men, who would wash and shave and cook breakfast if available. The drummers would then beat 'assembly' at which time the tents and camp equipment would be packed away onto the wagons and the troops gathered at their allocated positions in the column. When each regiment was gathered on the road and ready to march this was signalled by a ruffle of drums, beginning at the back of the column and rolling forward until it reached the wagon master at the head of the column, who then gave the order to proceed.

Pioneers from the various regiments were gathered together and often went ahead of their column to make repairs, or clear the roads where necessary to allow the wagons to pass unobstructed. If the column was making its way across open ground, the pioneers would be expected to cut gaps in hedgerows or break down enclosure walls, as the crossing of these kinds of obstacles by those at the head of the column could bring the rear of the column to a standstill.

The modern reader may well imagine the army marching along with columns of soldiers in ranks and files, drums beating, flags flying and the officers riding at their head. In truth, the army's advance was a fairly leisurely affair. The pace was not great and the men walked in small groups or with their families, some of whom would be riding on the regimental wagons. The men chatted, smoked their pipes and passed the time of day. Although the wagons and artillery would have to stick to the roads, cavalry and infantry units could move off the muddy tracks and walk alongside them in the fields or open ground to either side. Moving in formed 'Columns of March', where men marched in step, side by side, was reserved for the approach to battle.

Although the men would sometimes be able to put their kit on the wagons, they still had to carry much of their equipment themselves. The musket, bayonet, cartridge pouch, haversack with its contents of spare clothing, toiletries, and foodstuffs, as well as any other items they men may have to carry that day, such as shovels or tent poles, made for a heavy load. When marching in the hot summer weather, it was not surprising that some men dropped out of the march and had to be carried on the wagons or were left behind to catch up to the column at their own pace.

The quartermaster general would ride ahead of the column to the site of the new camp and by the time the head of the column snaked into sight, the allocated area for each of the regiments would be clearly marked out with lengths of rope and 'Camp Colours' stuck in the ground delineating the ground for each regiment in turn. As the regiments arrived in camp the men would line up next to their wagons to unload their equipment. Todd recalled; 'All our camp equipage was serv'd out, the tents number'd & the men tented five men to each tent by the roll. Serjeants & Corporals had each a tent by themselves'.[7] Tents were expected to be pitched in neat rows with officers' and NCOs' tents placed at the end of the rows as befit their rank.

Duties now began to be allocated by the regimental adjutants. After the tents were pitched, latrines were dug and the men began to disperse within the camp area to cut grass or straw to use as bedding. Campfires were set and soon the communal camp kettles would be hung over them and food cooked for the evening meal. On campaign, the men would usually be issued four days' worth of food, which they were expected to carry on their person. A new four-day ration would be issued from the regimental wagons on the morning of the fifth day. The regimental wagons would be replenished in turn when they reached the established magazines along the route.

Some soldiers would be selected for sentry duty, with infantry performing the role of pickets around the perimeter of the camp itself and cavalry being posted further out as a 'Grand Guard' to give early warning of an enemy advance. Within each regimental camp there was a 'Quarter Guard', intended: 'rather for preserving the peace and tranquillity within the regiment, by quelling all disputes that may arise, either between officer and officer, or amongst the soldiers, than for security against the enemy'.[8]

After the meal, those not allocated guard duties were free to do as they pleased. Some would gather round the campfire to smoke their pipes and chat, perhaps taking the opportunity to delouse the seams of their clothes. 'When you looked into the tents you found that only a few of the men were idle; the rest were cleaning a musket, or out doing the laundry, cooking, repairing breeches, mending shoes or carving something from wood to sell to the peasants'.[9]

---

7   Cormack and Jones (eds), *Journal of Corporal Todd*, p.14.
8   Duffy, *The Military Experience in the Age of Reason*, p.162.
9   Duffy, *The Military Experience in the Age of Reason*, p.164.

Those officers not allocated some duty, would retire to their mess tent to while away the evening drinking and playing cards. Colonel Russell of the Coldstream Guards described the scene in a letter home during the Dettingen campaign:

> [W]e meet every night at 6 o'clock, have two tables of whist at a shilling or two, then have a cold collection of almonds, raisons, figs, macaroons, butter and cheese, drink a very thin Moselle wine, without water, laugh and be merry until half after ten and then we all retire to our respective homes. It is the only place I have yet been in that an officer can live on his pay, if it may be called living at all.[10]

Senior officers lived even better when on campaign. A lieutenant general during the Dettingen campaign in 1743 was allowed to draw 60 men's rations per day to stock his table, to which the various senior officers of his command might attend. This excess appalled the Duke of Cumberland, and when he took command in 1745 he reduced this amount to 30 men's rations a day instead. Indeed, the Duke was considered quite frugal in his approach to campaigning, bringing only 140 tons of personal baggage with him from England, including furniture, tents, silverware, and decanters. After all, one cannot keep a table without its necessaries!

The officers' mess was arranged much like it might be in the Regimental barracks: 'One might think it was at Pontacks' Colonel Russell wrote of the Guards officers dining during the Dettingen campaign, 'a long table well set out and illuminated, never less than four or five and twenty officers and the music of our regiment playing all the time'.[11]

Sometimes, entertainments would be organised. These usually occurred on the days when the army was resting, but evening entertainments were not unknown. Horse racing was common, with the associated gambling that invariably accompanies it. Lord George Sackville wrote of the Duke of Cumberland's attempts to amuse the men during the Jacobite campaign in 1745:

> The Duke endeavours to divert the camp every evening by giving plates to be run for by the little horses taken from the rebels; sometimes the ladies ride and sometimes the men, but as saddles are not allowed of you may imagine few go round the course without tumbling, especially the ladies who are commonly half drunk to raise their spirits.[12]

That evening, the quartermaster general would once again pass the destination of the next day's march to the regimental commanders and to the wagonmaster general, who in turn would once again pass the order of march. The following morning the army would go through the routine again. Unless circumstances dictated otherwise, the army would march for three days and

---

10 Orr, *Dettingen 1743*, p.37.
11 Whitworth, *Field Marshal Lord Ligonier*, p.85; Pontack's Head Tavern, in Abchurch Lane, London, was at that time famed for its French cuisine.
12 Whitworth, *The Duke of Cumberland*, p.94.

rest for one, marching in the format described above until they came close to the enemy or entered 'enemy' territory.

So long as the weather stayed good, the campaign life was not too arduous. However, living under canvas for several months, especially for those more used to being quartered in Inns and barracks, took its toll. The men's tents were made from heavy canvas, which proved to be something of a mixed blessing. Whilst the canvas performed well at keeping out the rain, during hot days the tents became unbearably hot but in the evening did not retain the heat but instead became very cold. Dr Buchanan, who served in Germany with the Blues, recorded that this did not bode well for the men's health:

> [O]ne can scarcely believe how desagreably hot a tent is on a warm day. I have much adoe to bear it whilst I ask a sicke man how he does, being almost ready to faint. They are changeable from heat to cold to a surprizing degree, the perspiration sometimes greatly promoted and then suddenly checked.[13]

During the course of the campaign, tents wore out and often, by the autumn, no longer even fulfilled their primary purpose of keeping out the rain. In particularly bad weather, the men were ordered to 'hurdle' their tents, as Corporal Todd described during the campaign in 1760: 'The weather coming on both very wet and cold Lord Granby gave orders for the men to make huts to cook & sit in the day time & to hurdle their tents and thatch them over with anything they can find…'[14] 'Hurdling' was the process of bending light branches or small trees over the tent, higher than the canvas, and then thatching it with straw. This provided a further roof to keep the rain from soaking the canvas of the tent and causing it to sag or leak. This had the advantage that the tent could be collapsed without disturbing the roof, allowing the damp tent to be laid out to dry when the rain stopped and then re-erected under the hurdle again. Corporal Todd records a similar construction being made to act as a kitchen during bad weather:

> [I]t is very bad cooking out of doors; each company has orders to make a cooking place of Long, small trees set up over end with their tops fasten'd together & the thick ends well out at the root so that the place may contain the whole company when off duty…[15]

It was not surprising that with so many men living together in such close confines, disease began to spread. Lessons had been learned from previous campaigns and it had been noted that the use of latrine pits, dug well away from the regiment's campsite, reduced the instances of some diseases, although it was not completely understood why. Dr Pringle, Chief Surgeon to the Duke of Cumberland, made the requirement for latrine pits very clear and issued orders to the effect that: 'Let there be some slight penalty, but

---

13 Buchanan, *Regimental Practice*, p.257.
14 Cormack and Jones (eds), *Journal of Corporal Todd*, p.205.
15 Cormack and Jones (eds), *Journal of Corporal Todd*, p.212.

strictly inflicted, upon every man that shall ease himself anywhere about the camp but on the privies'.[16]

Despite precautions, illness was common amongst the men with colds, flu, and 'ague', or shivering, occurring regularly due to the men living outdoors in all weathers. Not all the men suffered to the same extent. Dr Buchanan noted during an outbreak of ague: 'the foot more subject to it than the horse, being more exposed to the injuries of the weather in doing Duty, having no watch-cloaks. Our Troopers have a good warm cloake & strong boots, & less duty'.[17] Perhaps not surprisingly, 'None of the Officers have been ill of this desease, nor any of their Servants; a plain proof that…it rather proceeds from the Soldiers manner of life'.[18] Buchanan put this down to the officers 'being less exposed to the injuries of the weather, have good dyet good wine and water for their common drink, good lodgings, good fire, [and] are warmer cloathed than the men.'[19] It is interesting to note that for the campaign season of 1745, Buchanan observed: 'When the weather become dry & warm, the ground dry, Complaints were much the same as last Season, but having little or no fatigue, the weather was not so excessive hot, they were neither so frequent nor violent'. His view for this decline in cases of 'ague' and flu was because 'The men were accustomed to a Campn life'.[20]

Camp Followers and Sutlers

As discussed elsewhere, every regiment had a number of official and unofficial camp followers, who usually consisted of the licensed sutlers, or traders, who provided the men with additional food, alcohol and other necessaries, such as spare shirts and so on, along with the wives and children of the soldiers. When the regiment arrived in theatre, the camp followers played a significant role in helping to set up the new camps. The official sutlers would set up shop, supplying the needs of the vast mobile market the army provided. It was the role of the regimental major to issue a license for the sutler to sell to the regiment and also to check the weights and measures used by them to ensure they were not cheating the men. A licensed sutler would often rent or purchase wagons and horses locally, and was allowed to draw forage for a maximum of 14 horses if he was with an Infantry battalion, 12 in a dragoon regiment and 15 in a regiment of horse. Sutlers would then join the wagon train as the army advanced.

However, the presence of such a large mobile market with money to spare did not escape the attention of local tradespeople as well. It was not long before local farmers and merchants would appear as the army made camp to sell their produce, often undercutting the licensed sutlers, much to their annoyance. Although only licensed sutlers were supposed to be in camp, the sheer size of

---

16   Buchanan, *Regimental Practice*, p.201.
17   Buchanan, *Regimental Practice*, p.33.
18   Buchanan, *Regimental Practice*, p.35.
19   Buchanan, *Regimental Practice*, p.25.
20   Buchanan, *Regimental Practice*, p.25.

the military encampments made enforcement difficult, if not impossible, and was not helped by the fact that the men actively encouraged other sellers to enter the camp as a foil to the often massively overpriced goods sold by the licensed sutlers. Very soon local people would be a regular feature of camp life, selling excess produce such as eggs and poultry, or game such as rabbits or fowl. It was also not long before more organised entrepreneurs and unlicensed sutlers would appear, selling locally brewed alcohol or providing entertainment, which usually involved gambling. Large numbers of women also began to follow the army, hoping to make money through prostitution or by cooking and cleaning for the soldiers. An orderly book return for August, 1756, for the British army in America, showed it was attended by 140 tradesmen, including 18 tailors, 25 shoemakers, two stocking weavers and 70 weavers.[21] Inevitably, more undesirable types of people were also drawn to follow the army, hoping to take the opportunity to thieve or to follow in its wake looking for opportunities to loot abandoned houses or farms along the way. Ultimately, if there was a battle, they hoped to make money by looting the dead and wounded and recovering property from the battlefield, such as muskets and lace-covered uniforms. Such a myriad of extra people also had the unfortunate side effect of allowing enemy spies to mix in with the army with relative ease. Whilst the recognised camp followers and licensed sutlers could march with the army, either with their regiment or as part of the baggage train, this huge train of unauthorised camp followers could not, and had to follow behind the army's rear-guard or follow a parallel route. When the army camped, they would often camp nearby or alongside the army's campsite if space allowed.

Even small armies attracted a substantial number of civilian 'hangers on'. Prior to beginning his campaign in the Highlands in 1746, the Duke of Cumberland had to issue an order to forbid any camp followers to come with them, writing:

> Whereas it has been found by experience that the army's being followed by great numbers of idle and ill-designing people is attended with very great inconvenience to it, and may prove fatal to themselves; and whereas the attendance of such great numbers upon the army is not only a great incumberance but consumes very much of the provisions and forage which may be necessary to support the army.[22]

As the army moved closer to the enemy and raids on the baggage by enemy forces became more likely, the bulk of the traders and unlicensed sutlers began to drift away. For them, the risk of losing their goods, or even their lives, outweighed the lure of the potential profit to be made. Corporal Todd bemoaned their loss during the autumn of 1761 whilst on campaign in Germany:

> [A]ll sorts of provisions is excessive dear & scarce now, as here is nothing to be had for money, for the most part of the Sutlers & followers of the army is gone

---

21 Kopperman, 'The British High Command and Soldiers Wives in America 1755-1783', p.21.
22 Bannerman, 'Abraham Hume and the Supply management of the British Army during the '45', p.275.

from us since we have been so long under arms pursuing the enemy that none of them thought themselves safe a long with us.[23]

However, the more immoral and less desirable traders hung on, as the prospect of battle offered more potential gains.

Foraging

When on campaign, the army was expected to supplement its rations by 'living off the land'. This was essentially the practice of obtaining livestock, forage or other essentials from the local population of the towns and villages the army passed through.

When in friendly country, it was essential that the local population be treated well. To this end, rates are established for goods and the local peasants paid promptly in cash or promissory notes to avoid any ill will. When he was Commissary General, Abraham Hume demanded this practice be followed as, 'Differences with the peasants will thereby be avoided and the army will draw forth all their resources with good will, instead of forcing part from them with the point of the bayonet'.[24]

However, despite the army's best efforts, in many cases the local population where not happy with this arrangement. In the first instance, they might not want to give up their livestock, forage or goods in exchange for a promissory note, especially if it was deemed insufficient for the goods being taken. As a result, farmers and merchants often hid their livestock, horses, wagons and any other goods they could when they heard of the approach of the army. Corporal Todd, when campaigning in Germany in 1761, was sent out with a foraging party to look for hidden livestock:

> At length we came to a fine thick shady place in the wood where we perceived nine horses tied to the trees eating grass…We directly unloosed them and each of us took one to lead…back into the village where we saw some waggons as we came, & I went to the Burgomaster & demanded two men to drive the wagons for us up to the regiment.[25]

Generally speaking, however, there was no widespread looting of the countryside. The soldiers were confined to their camp with strict penalties for any found roaming outside, and whilst an area might be stripped of firewood, straw, and so on when an army marched through it, the local population would at least be spared the depravations that might be inflicted on them from an enemy army. Soldiers caught looting or committing criminal acts were dealt with harshly. The Duke of Cumberland's order book, written at Stirling in 1746, states: 'Any man who is found plundering will be hung on

---

23 Cormack and Jones (eds), *Journal of Corporal Todd*, p.195.
24 Bannerman, 'Abraham Hume and the Supply management of the British Army during the '45', p.30.
25 Cormack and Jones (eds), *Journal of Corporal Todd*, p.146.

the spot by the Provost. No soldier to presume to search for arms without an order'.[26] Similar summary justice was common during the campaigns in Flanders and Germany. After all, these were the people who the army was fighting to protect.

However, when the army was marching through enemy territory, things were very different. Individual soldiers were still not allowed to leave camp or to engage in looting or any criminal acts of their own volition. This was just as strictly enforced as if the men had been in friendly territory, as much to maintain discipline as for any other reason. However, the scouring of the enemy's countryside for supplies was an accepted military tactic of the time, as it not only boosted the supplies of one's own army but it also deprived the enemy of them. The difference was that this was organised 'foraging' and authorised by the high command. Whilst on campaign in France in 1758, Corporal Todd wrote, 'We have very strick'd orders, both officers and men, not to presume to stir out of the line to Marraud upon any pretence whatsoever, as a Foraging party will be order'd out for that purpose'.[27]

The foraging party would be led by an officer and contain as many men as were required for the service. It would scour the area of livestock, portable goods, and drink, which were taken back to camp. Local Farmers or merchants would not be paid for these items and would think themselves lucky to escape with their lives if they challenged the soldiers. Todd later recorded:

> [W]e live well as the Captain of the Provost Guard brings plenty of beasts & sheep into camp & we kill & dress what we please… and there is very large cellars stock'd with Wine, Brandy & Cyder. We knocks the heads of large casks out & lades our kettles, Canteens or anything that we can find.[28]

When an enemy town was encountered it was accepted practice to ask it to offer up a contribution of supplies to prevent wholesale looting. If a town was to be 'searched' and its provisions removed, it was customary to allow wealthy residents to pay a sum to the army to prevent their houses being 'searched', or looted. If this sum was paid, sentries would be placed outside the house known as the 'Safe Guard', which appears to be the origin of this term.

Whether the army was campaigning in friendly or enemy territory, there was only so long the local area could sustain so many thousands of men and horses. Before long, the locals had no more food to sell, or have forcibly removed from them, whilst the whole area would very soon be short of forage for the voracious appetites of the horses. An army had to keep on the move if it was expected to supplement its rations from the local area, and those who did not soon used up everything the area had to offer.

---

26   Whitworth, *The Duke of Cumberland*, p.77.
27   Cormack and Jones (eds), *Journal of Corporal Todd*, p.72.
28   Cormack and Jones (eds), *Journal of Corporal Todd*, p.79.

Ravaging

George II reigned during a period often described as the 'Age of Reason', one that embodied enlightenment and civilised behaviour. Wars, it is often thought, were fought in a similar vein, with pleasantries being exchanged between opposing generals, armies undertaking to look after each other's wounded, and prisoners undertaking 'upon their honour' not to fight again if given parole. This sort of behaviour suggests a more gentlemanly type of warfare from the later practice of 'total war' which brought death and destruction to everyone in its wake. However, it is important not to get carried away with this view of eighteenth-century warfare, as it was just as cruel and the suffering just as great as in any other war. Equally we must ensure that we do not sugar coat our view of how the British Army could behave when given free rein to do so.

The ravaging of an area involved the burning of houses, driving off livestock, removing all portable goods of value and burning the rest, and was a tactic available to commanders if they felt it was justified. Strategically, this policy was designed to remove any logistical value that area may have for the enemy, and would be described in modern terms as a 'scorched earth' policy. It was also employed to force an enemy army to come to battle in order to protect the lands that were being 'ravaged'. However, the cruelties and suffering inflicted on the civilian population who were unlucky enough live in that area were enormous and those not killed trying to protect their homes might very well die soon after from starvation or exposure.

For example, when James Wolfe was besieging Quebec in 1759, he wrote of his intentions to ravage the area around the city to his commander, Jeffrey Amherst, as early as March that year. He stated that if the city 'is not likely to fall into our hands…I propose to set the town on fire with shells, to destroy the harvest, houses and cattle both above and below, to send off as many Canadians as possible to Europe and to leave famine and desolation behind me'.[29] This policy was designed to starve the city over the coming winter making it easier to besiege should the British army return the following year. Whilst the siege was going on, Wolfe sent expeditions up and down the St Lawrence River on a regular basis, burning farms, destroying crops and driving off or making prisoner the local population. On just one expedition in September, Captain Scott recorded:

> Upon the whole, we marched fifty two Miles, and in that distance, burnt nine hundred and ninety eight good Buildings, two Sloops, two Schooners, Ten Shalloops and several Batteaus and small Craft, took fifteen Prisoners (Six of them Women and five of them Children) kill'd 5 of the Enemy, had One Regular wounded, two of the Rangers kill'd and four more of them wounded.[30]

---

29   Trevor Royle, *Culloden: Scotland's Last Battle and the Forging of the British Empire* (New York: Pegasus, 2017), p.253.
30   Royle, *Culloden*, p.256

During 1758, the British army carried out raids on the French coast that were designed to force the French army to commit troops to coastal defence. On such raids, the aim was more to destroy and plunder than it was simply to forage. Corporal Todd remembered:

> [B]eing upon Duty on a High Eminence from which we could discover plainly 22 towns or villages all on fire this night…This looks Dreadfull & the Conflagration all this makes is astonishing. To hear the poor Inhabitants crying and running about, they know not where, by losing their all & even in great danger of their lives…[31]

Later, he wrote:

> And at four o'clock in the afternoon the Captain of the Provost Guard return'd with great number of cattle, as cows, hogs, sheep & fowls etc and every man had orders, that was on duty, to dress and cook what they pleas'd…we scarce have a tent but all there Canteens is full of Wine, Brandy or Cyder. And here is several large houses with great Cellars full that we can go & get what we please, but Orders is given that if any man be found intoxicated he will be severally punished, as we are in the Enemys Country.[32]

During these expeditions, 'enemy' goods and property were generally seen as fair game. Todd wrote soon after the above entry: 'Here is plenty of good houses in the suburbs and villages all around, that we are in hopes of seeing what is in them by and by'.[33] Stealing from the enemy in these circumstances was not just practised by private soldiers, but the officers often led by example. Lieutenant General Hawley was billeted in the house of a Mrs Gordon in Aberdeen, during the Jacobite rebellion. When he left, he ordered that her china and anything of value be packed up and shipped down to London. Mrs Gordon was understandably furious and wrote to the Duke of Cumberland, as he had assured her that her house would not be plundered, but to no avail. This example makes an interesting point about the army's behaviour during the Jacobite Rebellion. Whilst passing through England and the lowlands of Scotland, it behaved very much as if it were in 'friendly' lands, with no looting or 'foraging'. However, when the army marched into the Highlands, that mood changed and the soldiers began to behave as if they were now entering 'enemy' territory. This is reflected in the general orders issued to the troops, who were often given leave to ravage the land as they marched, with one order reading: 'all Cattle, Victual, Forrage, Arms taken from the rebels belong as a reward to those who take them'.[34]

---

31 Cormack and Jones (eds), *Journal of Corporal Todd*, p.94.
32 Cormack and Jones (eds), *Journal of Corporal Todd*, p.74.
33 Cormack and Jones (eds), *Journal of Corporal Todd*, p.74.
34 Bannerman, 'Abraham Hume and the Supply management of the British Army during the '45', p.276.

Winter Quarters

When the campaign drew to a close, the men were withdrawn into winter quarters, there to wait out the bad winter weather and be ready for the renewal of the campaign in the spring. The men were not expected to spend a winter under canvas, and were thus billeted in local towns and villages along the 'front line' with the enemy often doing the same in the towns and villages in the area they held.

As always, the local people were not happy about having soldiers billeted in their houses for the coming months. James Wolfe met with hostility when on campaign in 1743: 'The people were I was billeted refused to let me in, so I went to the townhouse and complained and this gentleman took me and another officer that was with me to his house'. He was 'one of the civilest men I ever met in my life'.[35]

In 1743, Captain Philip Brown's squadron of the Kings Own Regiment of Horse took 12 days to make the journey from England to Ostend and then marched the 11 miles to Bruges to join the army, arriving at one in the morning, only to find the doors of their billets also locked. 'We was obliged to break open the doors of my Inn before we could gain admittance, after which enquiring for a bed they said we must lay in the kitchen, but we took the liberty to take possession of the Landlords'.[36]

The bad weather and the scattered nature of the various companies of the regiment made it impractical to use this time for drill or training, and instead the men spent much of the winter in idleness. Many officers applied for leave to return to England, but for those who remained the time passed slowly in their billets. Whilst stationed in Ghent in 1742, Lieutenant Richard Davenport of the Horse Guards wrote:

> Here is nothing of diversion but playing billiards and going to a little French theatre, which I do almost every night for seven pence, without understanding at all what passes. I am heartily tired of this place, the people are disagreeable and cheat us in everything; as for the women, I have not seen one that is so handsome as my laundresses sister… except the foot soldiers wives who look like angels.[37]

Inevitably, the men turned to drink to pass the time and as a result, fights and squabbles emerged not only between the soldiers, but often between them and the populace they were billeted on. One report from 1742 reads:

> Lord Stair receiving daily complaints of disorders committed by drunken soldiers and particularly those of the Foot Guards, recommends it to the commanding officers to endeavour to surpress that scandalous practice so prejudicial to the Service and to the mens health.[38]

---

35 Ernest Sanger, *Englishmen at War; A Social History in Letters 1450-1900* (Stroud: Alan Sutton, 1993), p.131.
36 Orr, *Dettingen 1743*, p.27.
37 Orr, *Dettingen 1743*, p.28.
38 Orr, *Dettingen 1743*, p.29.

Inevitably, the men's days revolved around food, or very often the lack of it. Supply wagons were usually delayed by bad weather and worse roads, whilst the area the men were billeted in quickly became devoid of any food that could be purchased, even if the men could afford the sky-high prices. The British contingent housed in Paderborn for winter quarters in 1760 found the area around the town had been scoured clean of any forage. One commissary wrote:

> This scarcity was increased by the difficulty of the roads, and probably in some degree by the avarice of contractors, over whom…so strict a watch had not been kept as is at all times necessary for that sort of people. But whatever were the causes of this scarcity, it was bitterly felt by the troops and was accompanied by diseases which thinned them extremely.[39]

The men had no choice but to hunker down and wait out the winter, ready for the campaign to begin again in the New Year.

Spies, Lies, and Deserters: Intelligence Gathering on Campaign

At home, the Cabinet and the War Office were generally very well informed about strategic matters going on overseas. This information was gathered by ambassadors and envoys sent to the courts of the other powers, as well as from those bribed or blackmailed into passing information. The British Government was well aware of the French plans to invade England in 1744-1745, for example, and usually knew which ports the invasion ships were gathering in. However, the role of eighteenth-century spies on a strategic level is not the purpose of this section. Instead we are going to look at the ability of the military, specifically the army on campaign, to gather intelligence about the enemy army in front of it.

Pushing out in front of the army as it advanced were the cavalry vedettes, whose role it was to alert the rest of the army to enemy movements. This would consist of a thin line of cavalry, either as individuals or in pairs, operating close enough to see one another but spread out sufficiently to cover as much ground as possible. They would hope to detect any enemy ambush before the vanguard of the advancing columns stumbled into it, or make the columns aware of any hazards or issues about the terrain that may cause a problem, such as a destroyed bridge for example. Infantry, operating in skirmish formation, would also perform the same role if moving through wooded terrain, or over ground that cavalry found difficult. Infantry did not perform the role as well as cavalry, for they could not get back to the main column as quickly to warn them of danger. However, these infantry and cavalry outposts were not an intelligence gathering system, but rather a trigger to alert the army to danger. They did not contribute to the commander's knowledge of the whereabouts of the enemy until they stumbled into them.

---

39   Ritchie, 'The Troubles of a Commissary During the Seven Years War', p.157.

That said, these outposts did speak to local people and could gather useful information about the local terrain, the state of roads and river crossings as well as some information about the enemy army if it had passed that way recently. This information often had to be taken with a pinch of salt if passed by the populace of an enemy country, however. Indeed, the army suffered this problem when campaigning in the Highlands of Scotland, where one frustrated officer wrote: 'There is no trusting to any people in the country to give intelligence…the Presbyterian Ministers are the only people we can trust'.[40]

The role of scouting ahead of the army and looking for information about the enemy fell to the light cavalry in most European armies. These were independent-minded men, usually led by dashing commanders, who actively went looking for enemy units, operated behind the enemy lines and disrupted supply routes or attacked baggage wagons. Acting as scouts they could report back on the location and likely march route of the enemy and count his approximate numbers. The value of having light cavalry was demonstrated to the Duke of Cumberland during the Jacobite Campaign, when Kingston's Light Horse performed very well in gaining intelligence about the Jacobite army, but the cuts made after the War of the Austrian Succession ended reduced the army's ability to develop an effective light cavalry arm. In 1755, light cavalry troops were added to existing regiments, as discussed above, but it was 1759 before full regiments of light horse were raised. The British Army was late to identify the value of these troops but got there in the end.

The majority of information about the enemy obtained by the British Army on campaign in Europe was gained through spies. This may seem rather incongruous alongside our view of British officers, who, we might imagine, would not stoop to such dastardly behaviour! In fact, it appears that spies were not only employed but were actively encouraged. Whilst there was no eighteenth-century equivalent of MI6, with a director and civil servants controlling the recruitment and deployment of these individuals, it was the responsibility of a member of the command staff to run these agents, collect their information and pay them for their trouble. Although their techniques might be rudimentary, there was certainly no shortage of money with which to encourage men to undertake the work.

During the War of the Austrian Succession, the role of collecting intelligence fell to the Duke of Cumberland's personal secretary, Sir Everard Fawkener, who held the surprising title of Postmaster General. Since 1707, the Post Office held the monopoly on the carrying of post within the British Isles, and all post coming into the country or out of it went through their hands. A special department was set up within the Post Office that intercepted and read the post from French ambassadors or suspected French spies as well as all sorts of other communications that may have held intelligence value. Code breakers worked within this part of the Post Office to decipher those messages written in code and, as a result of their efforts, both the King and

---

40   Whitworth (ed.), *Gunner at Large*, p.77.

the Cabinet remained remarkably well informed. It is probably no surprise, therefore, that the Postmaster General should be on the Duke of Cumberland's staff on campaign, accompanying him on the Fontenoy campaign in 1745, as well as on the subsequent campaign against the Jacobites, before returning with him to Europe until 1748. During 1745 Fawkener spent an estimated £35,000 on what was entered into the accounts as 'secret service money', and when Jeffrey Amherst took over its management in 1748 his 'secret service' bill rose to £80,000 for that year alone.[41] Clearly, whilst spying had its dangers it also appears to have been well rewarded.

There were so many people moving in and out of an eighteenth-century military camp, from sutlers to local people selling their wares, prostitutes and entertainers, as well as the wives and families of the soldiers themselves, that it must have been relatively simple for spies to move unnoticed amongst the troops and pick up information about the coming campaign. Certainly, French spies are often mentioned being discovered and executed during both the War of the Austrian Succession and the Seven Years War. In May, 1747, Gunner James Woods recorded in his diary: 'The same day at 4pm a French captain, who was taken up as a spy, was hanged near Flemings Regiment'[42] whilst in 1761, Corporal Todd related a most unusual case of one spy discovering another:

> The two men that was taken up as spies in the Brunswicks Camp, the 24th instant, being tryed by a General Court martial & found guilty was sentenced to be hanged by the Captain of their Provost Guard. And they were executed accordingly, as one of our spies affirm'd that he had seen them frequently in the Enemys camp as such. This seems sharp work to us, as one spie Detects Another & they not knowing how soon it may be their own case…[43]

Indeed, so suspicious must the staff have been of spies within the camp that they undertook manoeuvres simply to fool them into false reporting. On one occasion Todd's regiment: 'Loaded the baggage & form'd the line of battle for two hours, then pitched our tents in the same place. This was Occation'd for to blind the Enemys Spies & to take any of them that could be found in our camp.'[44]

Information was also obtained from deserters from the enemy army. Most of those who deserted were rarely in possession of significant intelligence, being mostly private soldiers, but their information about the general state of the enemy's army was still useful. During the Seven Years War one report read: 'Several Deserters came from the enemy & informs us that they are in great want of alsorts of Necessarys & that Numbers of their men fall sick daily, that all their hospitals are full.'[45]

---

41   Whitworth (ed.), *Gunner at Large*, p.112.
42   Whitworth (ed.), *Gunner at Large*, p.39.
43   Cormack and Jones (eds), *Journal of Corporal Todd*, p.185.
44   Cormack and Jones (eds), *Journal of Corporal Todd*, p.180.
45   Cormack and Jones (eds), *Journal of Corporal Todd*, p.231.

In Canada in 1760, a French army marched against Quebec to retake it after its loss to Major General Wolfe the previous year. Whilst this army was disembarking at Pointe-aux-Trembles, a French soldier was swept away by the river and thought lost. However, clinging to a lump of ice, he was plucked from the river further downstream by British soldiers who immediately took him before their commanding officer. Warmed by the fire and a generous helping of hot brandy, the Frenchmen told Major General Murray that he was part of French main force, which even now was marching toward Quebec. Murray was thus able to gather the British forces and deploy them to meet this threat.

During campaigns in the eighteenth century, the commanding general and his staff could not afford to be behind the lines relying purely on intelligence reports to inform their battle plans. Often, they had to go out on scouting missions themselves, with a small cavalry escort, to see the lay of the land or to reconnoitre the enemy positions. On one occasion in 1761, Todd recorded:

> This morning HSH Prince Ferdinand, the Marquis of Granby & several other Generals rode along our line and up to the rising ground upon our left, where some of our Piquets were posted. They seemed to be reconiting [sic] the Enemy upon several hills, where they could get any prospect by having their telescopes out for that purpose.[46]

By use of their light troops, the information of the local populace and deserters, and by use of their own spies, the British high command had an identified structure for gathering intelligence whilst on campaign. How effective these techniques were is debatable, but at least the army was aware of the need for intelligence and was actively taking steps to obtain it rather than stumbling blindly forward toward the enemy.

The Approach to Battle

Eventually, as a campaign progressed, the two enemy armies would end up in close proximity to each other at which point they would begin to manoeuvre into the best position for the coming battle. Light troops from both armies would now be engaged on a daily basis in skirmishing with the enemy, driving in their foraging parties and piquets whilst protecting their own. They would also attempt to drive off enemy scouting parties whilst at the same time scouting the enemy positions themselves. This war of manoeuvre, feints, and probes could go on for some days, and soon took its toll on the men. Dr Buchanan recorded on the Dettingen campaign that the Blues:

> [W]ere ordered out over night, in order to cover the foragers nixt day, were obliged to lye on their arms in the open field, stand to their arms all nixt day, &

---

46   Cormack and Jones (eds), *Journal of Corporal Todd*, p.184.

return to Camp at night & often wet to the skine, & some accidents of Gunshot wounds from skirmishing with the Enemies out parties.[47]

Corporal Todd mentions skirmishing with the enemy almost daily prior to battle, such as in July, 1761, when he wrote: 'Encamp'd near Hilbeck & this morning there was some smart Skirmishing at our advance posts & several Kill'd upon both sides…'[48] and again in September he recorded, 'this morning a party of our Green Yeagers advanced to the Enemys grand guard, whereof a smart Skirmish ensued that several was Kill'd upon the spott, & the Yeagers took 14 horses & brought them off into our camp & sold them to the sutlers'.[49]

That said, the common soldiers of both armies do not appear to have held too much animosity toward each other. Often, the night before battles or when the armies were encamped close by each other, the sentries and piquets would agree not to fire on one another. Indeed, as Todd records, this often went further:

> [T]he Enemy seems very agreeable as several of us Last night upon the advance posts bought Geneva [gin] off some of their Centrys [sic] at a moderate price as there is only a small ditch in some places betwixt our line of Centrys & theirs so that any may be handed over easily. And they have orders not to fire upon any Centry upon his post, the same as our Centrys has. And they are ready to either Buy, sell or Exchange anything they have with [us] as Bread, Liquor etc.[50]

This good-natured exchange between the armies could not last forever, however, as inevitably, the day of battle would arrive.

---

47 Buchanan, *Regimental Practice*, p.311.
48 Cormack and Jones (eds), *Journal of Corporal Todd*, p.173.
49 Cormack and Jones (eds), *Journal of Corporal Todd*, p.199.
50 Cormack and Jones (eds), *Journal of Corporal Todd*, p.187.

14

The Experience of Battle

At some point in the campaign, the commanders of both armies would draw the series of manoeuvres, feints, marches and counter marches to an end. It is possible that one army had been out manoeuvred, perhaps by having its supply lines cut or its escape route back to friendly territory threatened. In such cases, the outmanoeuvred army would retire and give ground to the enemy who in turn would move forward and consolidate their gains. This may seem to be an unsatisfactory outcome to a season's campaigning, but in truth the seizing of land, towns and fortresses was considered just as important as winning battles. Both sides recognised that at some stage the war would end and prizes won during the war would make valuable bargaining chips in the inevitable peace negotiations. However, if neither side was outmanoeuvred, and both had the will to engage, then a battle would be inevitable.

Battles in Europe were rarely joined without prior notice, with neither side moving quickly enough to organise a large-scale surprise attack. Instead, both sides moved their armies slowly into place, and men might be told during the evening that a battle was likely on the following day. On those instances when the British army was in a prepared defensive position, such as at Rocoux in 1746 or Lauffeld the following year, then the men would see the enemy troops forming in the distance and be well aware of what was about to happen.

Orders would now be issued to the army to prepare for battle. Men would store their kit on the battalion wagons and carry only what they needed. Richard Kane wrote:

> When he finds that there is no avoiding coming to battle, he is to order the soldiers to lay down their knapsacks, tent poles and what is cumbersome and the Serjeant sends them to some place out of the way, where a Serjeant with a few men takes care of them. If we win the day, they will be safe. If not, tis no matter what becomes of them.[1]

---

1   Kane, *New System of Military Discipline*, p.113.

At this point, light 6-pounder or even 3-pounder cannon would be detached from the artillery train and sent to join individual battalions to act as battalion guns. The men who had been identified as labourers to assist the gunners would now fall out and perform this duty. Gunner Woods noted one such deployment in his diary prior to Lauffeld: 'Two short sixes were sent to every foot regiment which lay in the field with a detachment of artillery to every two guns with one officer'.[2]

The camp followers and families would stay with the wagons and the supplies in the rear whilst the soldiers prepared to march. This would be the last opportunity for the soldiers to say goodbye to their loved ones, push some food into their pockets, check their canteens were full and ensure that they had a full cartridge box. The men would then fall in for inspection. The sergeants would now move among the men, checking their kit. Corporal Todd remembered: 'Every man was ordered to examine his firelock well, to see that he had a good flint fixed fast & was properly loaded, and not to fire until he had orders from his officer'.[3] Having checked the men's cartridges and their muskets, the sergeants would fall into the ranks and the order would be given to form march column. At the beat of the drum, the men would step off to battle.

Command and Control on the Battlefield

The commander-in-chief was in charge of the army and directed its deployment and movements on the battlefield. To assist him, he would appoint a general officer to be in charge of the first line of infantry, one for the second and, if it existed, one for the third line, including the reserves. The same would be done for each wing of the cavalry.

In the British army of the eighteenth century the seniority of rank was as follows. Other than the commander-in-chief, who might be a field marshal like Stair and Wade, or captain-general like Cumberland, the highest rank was that of general, who could often command an entire army or a large portion of it. The general would be aided by lieutenant generals, who served as his immediate subordinates and who would be assisted in turn by major generals. Beneath these were the colonels of the regiments who were often given command positions, or, indeed, might hold general rank themselves, leaving their individual regiments to be commanded by their lieutenant colonel. As Humphrey Bland put it:

> The General of the Horse, or the General of the Foot have not any fix'd Duty ; but when a considerable Body of Troops is order'd out upon any Service, they are generally appointed to Command them ; in which case they have always one or more Lieutenant-Generals, several Major-Generals, and Brigadiers under them,

---

2 Whitworth (ed.), *Gunner at Large*, p.51.
3 Cormack and Jones (eds), *Journal of Corporal Todd*, p.165.

the Number of whom are generally proportion to the number of Troops, or as the Service … may require.[4]

For the coming campaign, from three to five infantry battalions or a similar number of cavalry squadrons would be placed together in a brigade, which would often be commanded by a major general or brigadier general. This brigade would stay together for the rest of the campaign under the command of the same officer, assuming they were not killed or wounded. This provided consistency in command, logistics and so on.

Until 1746 the position of brigadier general appears to have been a substantive rank between colonel and major general. However, during the period of peace that followed the end of the War of the Austrian Succession, the rank of brigadier general fell out of use, with no new colonels appointed to the rank and those who already held it being promoted to major general. Thereafter, the rank appears to have been a temporary one, granted almost exclusively to those posted overseas and relinquished as soon as their posting ends. For example, in 1759 all three of Wolfe's subordinate commanders at Quebec were granted the temporary rank of brigadier general, with each commanding one of his infantry brigades.[5]

The commander-in-chief employed a number of aides de camp on his staff at the beginning of every campaign, who were usually picked from promising young officers from various regiments. They had to be bright, good horsemen and had to be able to communicate the wishes of the commander clearly and effectively if asked questions in the heat of battle. For this reason, officers selected as aides often went on to do well in the army as commanders in their own right, such as James Wolfe, who was aide de camp to Henry Hawley during the Jacobite campaign.

When the commander-in-chief issued an order his adjutant, who would always be next to him, wrote it down. This would then be handed to an aide who would be instructed to take it to the particular general it related to. If possible, the commander-in-chief would explain the order verbally to the aide, to ensure that he understood it. The aide would then ride to the general it was intended for and deliver the orders. He would wait in case the recipient had any questions that needed to be clarified, in which case the aide would do so verbally. As we shall see, these clarifications needed to be concise and in the spirit of what the commander-in-chief intended. The aide would then be expected to return to the commander-in-chief to be tasked again. A similar system was then employed by subordinate generals to communicate with their brigadier generals and in turn by them to the colonels of the regiments. In cases of urgency, the commander-in-chief or the brigade commanders might ride over to the officer in question and personally deliver the orders. A good example of this occurred at Fontenoy in 1745, where the Duke of Cumberland had to ride over to his right flank to personally deliver orders to

---

4   W.B.R. Neave-Hill, 'The Rank Titles of Brigadier and Brigadier General', *Journal of the Society for Army Historical Research*, Vol. 47, No. 190 (Summer 1969), p.98.
5   Neave-Hill, 'The Rank Titles of Brigadier and Brigadier General', p.98.

THE EXPERIENCE OF BATTLE

Brigadier General Ingoldsby, who was being somewhat tardy with their execution.

There are not many accounts written by aides about exactly how they went about their business and as a result we have to assume than in most cases the system worked reasonably well. Clearly, if an aide was hit by a stray bullet or roundshot, the message might not be delivered and examples of this happening during the Seven Years War do exist. However, to really showcase how the system was supposed to work it is best to give an example where it failed.

At the Battle of Minden in 1759, Lord George Sackville had been placed in command of the cavalry on the allied right flank. At one point in the battle, the British infantry had advanced in the centre and crushed a French cavalry attack, sending them fleeing back toward their lines.

'The Right Honble Lord George Sackville: Lieutenant General of His Majesty's Forces, Lieutt. General of the Ordnance, Colonel of the Second Regiment of Dragoon Guards, Commander in Chief of the British Forces on the Lower Rhine, & One of the Lords of His Majesty's Most Honourable Privy Council &c.' Engraving by McArdell after Joshua Reynolds. (Anne S.K. Brown Collection)

The allied commander, Prince Ferdinand, now issued orders that the allied cavalry should advance to exploit the retreat. His adjutant handed the order to Captain Edward Ligonier, an experienced officer and a good horseman. He immediately rode to find Sackville, to whom he delivered the order: 'To advance with the cavalry. The enemy was in confusion and the commander hoped to profit from it'. Sackville immediately drew his sword and ordered the cavalry to advance. However, Sackville could not see any French troops from his current position and he began to lead the cavalry too far to the right. Ligonier, still at Sackville's side, was able to advise him to move further to the left. However, by this time Prince Ferdinand had seen the incorrect movement from the hill above, and he sent a further aide to correct the error. This aide was Lieutenant Colonel Charles Fitzroy, who was asked by Prince Ferdinand to go to Sackville and hurry on the British cavalry, which he did. Arriving at Sackville's side he now delivered the order that the British cavalry were to advance to the left. Sackville called a halt to the advance. He had both Hanoverian and British cavalry under his command. Was he just to advance the British to the left? If so, what of the Hanoverians? Fitzroy was insistent that it was the British cavalry who were to advance, but Ligonier, who was still with Sackville, disagreed saying he should advance the whole force. Sackville was unconvinced and now decided to ride over to see Prince Ferdinand himself to clarify. Whilst he was away, a third aide, named Captain Winzingerode, arrived and spoke to Sackville's second in command, the

Marquess of Granby. Winzingerode was in an excited state and asked why the cavalry was not advancing, as he was aware that the opportunity to ride down the retreating French was fast disappearing. Having understood the situation, Granby now ordered forward just the British cavalry, leaving the Hanoverian cavalry in place. He had not gone far before orders came from Sackville for him to halt. Sackville had by now clarified that he was to take all of the cavalry forward, and upon seeing Granby going forward with just the British, sent an aide to order him to stop. By the time Sackville had returned to the cavalry, and they had been re-formed and marched off together in the right direction, the opportunity was lost. Sackville was subsequently court martialled for disobeying orders, which is why we know so much about the movement of the aides de camp on this particular day. The court martial records do give a good indication about how orders were delivered during battle and make clear the need to employ cool-headed aides to carry them.[6]

Deploying for Battle

Before discussing how the eighteenth-century British army ideally deployed for battle, it is important to stress that none of the battles of the War of the Austrian Succession, the Seven Years War, or any of the overseas battles in which British troops were engaged occurred in so formal fashion as this. Contact with the enemy has a habit of throwing a spanner in even well-oiled military machinery.

The Cavalry Screen

Before the army could deploy, ideally a protective screen of cavalry would be deployed to the front of the army to protect it from the sudden advance of enemy cavalry. Infantry and artillery were at their most vulnerable when in columns, marching and forming on the battlefield, and a sudden rush of cavalry could catch them in the incorrect formation and sweep them away. Once the infantry and artillery were in place, the cavalry would retire. Some would now deploy on the flanks, to protect the long infantry lines from being attacked by enemy cavalry in the flank and rolled up, whilst some would go to the rear to act as a reserve. The reserve would be used to chase and run down the fleeing enemy in the event of a victory, or to cover the retreat from enemy cavalry if things went less well.

A cavalry squadron of two troops in three ranks would occupy a frontage of about 120 yards when moving, which would reduce to about 90 yards if they were stationary and deployed 'boot to boot'. The guidon of the squadron would be placed on the right of the first line where all the men of the squadron could see it. It would then be used to control the movement of the cavalry, with all of the men keeping pace with the guidon bearer going

---

6 Summary from Piers Mackesy, *The Coward of Minden: the Affair of Lord George Sackville* (London: Penguin Books Ltd, 1979).

forward and using it as a fixed point when wheeling right, or to keep pace when wheeling left. It is not clear if the guidon was moved to the front of the regiment once in position and ready to charge or if it remained at the end of the front rank. The commander of the squadron would be at the front with either his drummer, in the case of dragoons, or trumpeter, for horse, and would use the musician and the sound of his voice to command the regiment. If multiple squadrons of the regiment were present, the regimental commanding officer would stand at the front-centre, accompanied by his musician and the regimental guidon bearer. The cavalry squadrons would deploy in chequerboard formation, leaving about 200 yards between each squadron. They had to be deployed in this formation to be able to respond to enemy cavalry attack, and could not deploy in the scattered skirmish formation that they would use if deployed on piquet duty around a camp or when the army was on the march. A skirmish formation like this would not stop close formation enemy cavalry and would be swept away. The only drawback to this deployment was that these close formations of cavalry were vulnerable to artillery fire if forced to deploy too close to the enemy. Relating events at Dettingen in 1743, the *London Gazette* noted how the infantry battalions were deployed before moving forward through the intervals in the cavalry to their positions on the battlefield:

> His majesty ordered the foot that was coming up to the right, into the wood and some Battalions posted to cover that flank and as fast as they arrived he placed the infantry, British and Austrian and 4 battalions of Hanoverians, who all marched through the intervals of the horse, from the mountain to the main in two lines, which were supported by the cavalry of the right wing, also in two lines.[7]

Deploying the cavalry to cover the infantry whilst they formed was not always necessary. At Culloden, for example, the flat open nature of the terrain and the lack of enemy cavalry, allowed the army to deploy about two miles from the battlefield before marching to it in formation. Equally, the close nature of the terrain at Fontenoy, the previous year, had made it very difficult for the cavalry to deploy in a defensive screen. As the cavalry debouched from the wood that edged the battlefield, they found that the ground was broken by fields that were surrounded by hedges and walls, as well as a deep sunken road that made effective deployment of the cavalry impossible. Jeffrey Amherst wrote:

> [T]he infantry, on his arriving on the plain, was very much surprised at the disposition General Campbell had made, for instead of advancing in the plain & drawing up his squadrons in a good front with proper intervals… he had clustered them all together with their arses in the hedges, and some enclosed by the hedges & their flanks to the enemy.[8]

Clearly, deploying cavalry was not as easy as it might seem.

---

7   Orr, *Dettingen 1743*, p.54.
8   Kent Archives, U1350 Journal of Sir Jeffrey Amherst, 1745.

THE ARMY OF GEORGE II

John, Earl of Craufurd, who held a cavalry command at Fontenoy. Engraving by and after Thomas Worlidge. (Anne S.K. Brown Collection)

Once the infantry was deployed, they would move forward through the intervals between the cavalry regiments to their place on the battlefield or the cavalry would retire through the intervals between the infantry regiments. However, cavalry retiring in panic sometimes did not manage this. When the Blues fell back in disorder at Dettingen, following defeat by French cavalry, they burst through the deployed infantry battalion behind them. An officer of Peers' 23rd Foot (the Royal Welch Fusiliers) wrote: 'we were obliged to make an interval to let the Blues through us. Brigadier Huske, who was at the head of our Regiment, exhorted them… to return to their charge, but to no purpose: and we were forced to let them pass'.[9]

The Cavalry Battle

British cavalry squadrons throughout this period of the eighteenth century charged enemy cavalry and engaged them with the sword. This may seem a fairly obvious statement, but some European cavalry formations, certainly at the beginning of this period, were still approaching the enemy at the trot and firing pistols before closing with their swords. The Duke of Marlborough had not favoured this approach as he felt it was not only ineffective but reduced the impact of the charge. This doctrine was adopted by all regiments of British cavalry when encountering enemy horse, even those designated as dragoons, which by definition should have acted as mounted infantry. Indeed, many of the most successful British cavalry charges of the period involved dragoon regiments.

Upon sighting the enemy horse, British cavalry squadrons would form into two lines with intervals between the squadrons on either side and behind. The intervals were designed to allow the cavalry deployed behind the first line to wheel and move into different positions on either flank, or to have sufficient room to change formation and retire if required to do so. They also allowed infantry to advance between the deployed squadrons if required.

Cavalry would now drop any surplus kit, if it had not already been left on the regimental wagons prior to the battle. The men would only need their weapons and perhaps a water bottle for the next few hours and they did not want to carry anything that might impede them in the coming melee or slow their horse. Corporal Todd remembered seeing a cavalry squadron of the Scots Greys dumping its kit prior to a cavalry skirmish in Germany in 1761:

> An aide de camp with orders from the Marquis of Granby for the cavalry in our column to throw away all their tent poles, Kettles & all sorts of baggage to lighten

---

9 Orr, *Dettingen 1743*, p.60.

themselves as much as possible & to make a charge upon a large body of the Enemys cavalry who seemed to stand firm about a mile to our front... So they Clap'd Spurs to their horses & fell to galloping from us.[10]

The two opposing cavalry forces would then simply charge at one another with the intention of beating the enemy in combat and driving them off. In the majority of cases, one side or the other gave way before swords were actually crossed, but even if the two sides did collide, the horses generally passed between each other, with the men swiping at each other as they passed. Although swords were capable of inflicting very serious wounds, casualties in cavalry regiments were usually much lower than in the infantry, as cavalry melees were not protracted with one side gaining the ascendancy quite quickly after the opposing sides collided. It was generally accepted that squadrons of horse had an advantage over squadrons of light horse or dragoons. Horse regiments were often mounted on larger horses, sometimes wore cuirass or similar armour, and were often regarded as consisting of better trained troops. Whilst this might have been true of some European armies, as far as the British cavalry went there was little difference between the horse, dragoon and dragoon guard regiments in how they performed in cavalry battles. At Dettingen, for example, the Blues were easily beaten by their French opposition and turned back in disorder, whilst dragoon regiments took on, and defeated, French household cavalry regiments. Even the new light cavalry regiments, introduced at the end of the Seven Years War, performed well against enemy cavalry despite having lighter mounts than the horse.

One of the largest cavalry charges of the period occurred at Lauffeld in 1747, where the French had managed to turn the allied army's left flank. With the allied infantry in retreat, the French moved 150 squadrons of cavalry into position to pursue them, hoping to turn retreat into a rout. Seeing the danger, Lieutenant General John Ligonier gathered 60 squadrons of British, Hanoverian, and Hessian cavalry to oppose them. Taking the initiative, Ligonier ordered a charge that caught many of the French cavalry regiments at the halt, resulting in the French being defeated and driven back. Ligonier rallied his troops and led four squadrons of British dragoons on a further charge that, despite early success, was eventually overcome by French numbers. Ligonier was captured during this charge, and the Scots Greys who accompanied him took 40 percent casualties in killed and wounded. Although the allied cavalry was eventually driven back, the charge had shattered the French attack and saved the retreating allied infantry from disaster.

The Infantry Deploy

Ideally, each infantry regiment would march onto the battlefield, wheel smartly from column into line and deploy three ranks deep, with the colours front and centre. Each company would have a three-foot gap between it and

---

10 Cormack and Jones (eds), *Journal of Corporal Todd*, pp.155-156.

the next, in which stood the NCOs. The grenadier company would usually be on the right, but often this veteran company was split and placed with half at each end of the line, in order to provide reassurance to the new men and stiffen the resolve of the battalion by their example. The officers would be placed in the gaps between their companies, with the colonel 'on foot, with his sword drawn in his hand, about eight or ten Paces in Front, opposite the centre, with an expert drum by him'. The colonel, a contemporary was keen to point out, 'should appear with a cheerful countenance, never in a hurry or by any means ruffled; and to deliver his orders with great calmness and Presence of Mind'.[11] When stationary, the sergeants stood in the gaps between the companies as their role would be to supervise the men whilst firing, to ensure they took their time reloading, fired low, and so on. When the battalion was moving they marched behind their men 'where they are assisting the officers in seeing the platoons do their duty'.[12] The drummers were divided in three groups and placed on the right and left of the battalion and also in the centre in line with the sergeants. The major and the adjutant were positioned on the flanks where they could observe the behaviour of the battalion as a whole and ensure the ranks were kept straight and that the battalion advanced as a body

All the regiments of foot would now deploy into line in their battlefield positions. Brigades would be deployed with the most senior regiment on the right, the next most senior on the left with the junior battalion in the centre. For example, the First Brigade at Culloden consisted of the 1st Royal Regiment on the right, the 14th Foot on the left and the 34th Foot in the centre. The brigade with the most senior battalion in it would often be given the place of honour on the right of the front line. At Fontenoy in 1745, for example, the right of the first line was held by the Guards Brigade, with the 1st Foot Guards on the right, the Coldstream Guards on the left and the 3rd Foot Guards in the centre. Generally speaking, the foot would be deployed in two lines with an equal number of battalions in each line, although three lines was also acceptable where space was tight. A battalion of about 600 men would occupy a frontage of about 200 yards when deployed in three ranks. In an ideal situation, military theorists of the time suggest that each battalion would leave a gap of about 200 yards between it and the next battalion in line. When the second line deployed, their battalions would deploy opposite the gaps left by the first line, so that from the air the deployment would look like a chequerboard.

The gaps between the battalions in the first line would often be filled by deployed artillery. Even a four-gun battery of light guns could occupy a space of about 80 yards, which allowed sufficient space for limbers to be brought up, turned and the gun deployed without encroaching into the space of the next gun. As discussed above, this allowed the cavalry deployed in the rear to move up, passing through the gaps and the deployed artillery to counter attack any enemy cavalry who may be attacking the infantry to the front, as happened at Dettingen in 1743. At this battle, Major Charles Colville

---

11 Kane, *New System of Military Discipline*, p.111.
12 Kane, *New System of Military Discipline*, p.114.

of Campbell's Regiment stated: 'We likewise formed our foot in two lines, leaving proper intervals for our horse drawn up in the rear'.[13] Also, artillery roundshot, when it struck an infantry battalion, would often carry on through to strike battalions deployed behind it, and so by deploying in chequerboard fashion the casualties from enemy roundshot could be reduced.

However, the constraints of the battlefield meant that it was not always possible to deploy with such large gaps between battalions. At Culloden the gap between the first rank battalions could have been as little as 21 yards (20 metres) which is likely given that only two 3-pounder guns were deployed between each battalion in the front rank. Occasionally, other factors would prevent this ideal deployment. At Fontenoy, the three Guards battalions began the battle up to their full strength of nearly 1,000 men, whilst the other battalions in the army paraded around five or six hundred. Subsequently, when the first line deployed, Jeffrey Amherst saw that: 'there was not quite room enough for the regiments of the front line so the General ordered the battalion of Royal to fall in between the two lines as a Corps de Reserve'.[14]

Once in line, the men would now stand in silence as the rest of the army moved into position. Most had written their wills the night before and had left them with the Chaplain, or sent them home, as one soldier recorded: 'I sent a letter to Preston with my will & power in it, sign'd by my Lieutenant Collonel, that if any pay or prize money be due to me, my mother may know how to look after it…'[15] Some men, like Corporal Todd, kept alcohol in their water bottles, which they could now use to have a shot of 'Dutch courage', whilst others turned to God. Private Sampson Staniforth was in the ranks of infantry waiting for the order to advance at Fontenoy when he:

> [S]tepped out of the line and threw myself on the ground and prayed that God would deliver me from all fear and enable me to behave as a Christian and good soldier. Glory be to God he heard my cry and took away all my fear. I came into the ranks again and had both peace and joy in the Holy Ghost.[16]

This time spent waiting, especially if under artillery fire, would be frustrating for the men, and it appears that officers regularly ordered the men to cheer, or give a 'huzzah' to keep their spirits up and, hopefully, to dispirit the enemy. At Dettingen, for example, the Household Cavalry, spent a good deal of time under artillery fire, at which point Colonel the Earl of Crawford rode along their line: 'shouting "Never fear, my boys, this is a fine diversion"…Then he ordered us to huzza and brandish our swords, and soon after the Monsieurs light hearts seemed to fail them suddenly'.[17] An officer at the same battle remembered: 'Our army gave such shouts before we were engaged, when we were about a hundred paces apart before the action began, that we hear

---

13 Orr, *Dettingen 1743*, p.55.
14 Kent Archives, U1350 Journal of Sir Jeffrey Amherst, 1745.
15 Cormack and Jones (eds), *Journal of Corporal Todd*, p.66.
16 Abel Stevens, *The History of the Religious Movement of the Eighteenth century Called Methodism* (London: Alexander Haylin, 1859), Vol.I, p.180.
17 Orr, *Dettingen 1743*, p.62.

by deserters it brought a panic among them'.[18] This 'general huzza' amongst the army appears to be confirmed by Lord Stair, who was quoted as saying: 'When I give the signal. Let the huzza be general through the line and-my life for it – the victory is ours… If I can't beat them by firing, I can beat them by Huzzaing'.[19]

The Infantry Advance

The time had now come for the infantry to advance. The colours would be moved out in front of the battalion. There would be a ruffle of the colonel's drum at which point the battalion would stiffen to attention, expecting a word of command. The colonel: 'then gives the Word, March; at which time the Drum beats to the March: and when the battalion has got within four or five paces of him, he turns to the enemy and marches slowly down'.[20] The colour party would march several paces out in front of the line. All those on the left of the colours would look slightly to their right, so they could see the colour party, whilst those on the right would look left. Using the colour party as a guide, the line would advance, keeping pace and distance with the colours.

Of course, it was not as easy as this. There was clearly a lot of pushing, with both sides of the line tending to drift toward the colours. This led to the inevitable 'bunching' in the centre. This was made worse when under fire, as gaps in the line were to be filled, in theory, by the ranks behind. Men were understandably loath to fill a gap created by a friend who had just had his head carried away by roundshot! The response to the NCOs' cries to 'Close Up!' was to do just that, with the files moving together, again causing men to 'bunch' toward the centre. This meant that invariably, the advancing line had to be regularly stopped to re-form and re-dress the ranks.

The infantry would soon come under long range artillery fire, with roundshot bouncing through the ranks. After the battle of Fontenoy in 1745, Captain Charles Hamilton remembered, 'I was forced to be very civil and made a great many bows to the balls, for they were very near me, for both my right and left hand men were killed and all around me there were men and horses tumbling about, but thank God none touched me'.[21]

At Minden, the British battalions advanced into a heavy cannonade, as Captain Thompson wrote afterwards:

> I saw heads legs and arms taken off, my right hand file of men not more than a foot from me were all by one ball dashed to pieces and their blood flying all over me; this I confess staggered me not a little but on my receiving a contusion in the bend of my right arm by a spent musket shot, it steadied me immediately,

---

18   Orr, *Dettingen 1743*, p.65.
19   Orr, *Dettingen 1743*, p.65.
20   Kane, *New System of Military Discipline*, p.117.
21   Sanger, *Englishmen At War*, p.138.

THE EXPERIENCE OF BATTLE

British grenadiers assaulting French field works outside Louisbourg, 1758. Watercolour by Richard Simkin. (Anne S.K. Brown Collection)

all apprehensions of hurt vanished, revenge and the care of the company I commanded took over.[22]

As the battered battalions got closer, the opposing artillery would switch to partridge shot, sometimes called grapeshot, which, when fired, had an effect much like a giant shotgun. This type of artillery fire caused the most casualties amongst those it was used against. At Fontenoy, Charles Hamilton recorded: 'The foot were very sadly cut to pieces, for ye French put grape shot in their cannon & cut them down just as if they were shearing corn.'[23] It was just as effective when used against cavalry, as a British artillery officer witnessed at Minden:

> We drew up ten guns close to the six Regiments on the right and there waited undiscovered till the enemy came almost within a pistol shot…and when they were just going to gallop down sword in hand amongst the poor mangled Regiments, we clapt our matches to the ten guns and gave them such a salute as they little expected. Our balls…had the desired effect for we mow'd them down like standing corn.[24]

---

22 Sanger, *Englishmen At War*, p.167.
23 Sanger, *Englishmen At War*, p.138.
24 Sanger, *Englishmen At War*, p.169.

It is hard for the modern reader to imagine how on earth the infantry battalions could continue to advance in the face of such destruction. At least, one might imagine, the cavalry could cover ground quickly and hope to reduce the amount of fire they might take. For the infantry, advancing at a slow steady pace, the constant artillery fire must have been galling, but against all odds they often succeeded. For example, Captain Wortley of Bligh's 20th Foot, recorded his own regiments advance at Melle in 1745, where they:

> [R]eceived the fire of twelve pieces of cannon which were in our front. Our regiment marched up to the cannon with so much conduct and bravery that they soon beat off the enemy, broke the whole battery and turned four pieces of their own cannon against them. But having no gunners, they could neither make a proper use of them, nor spike them.[25]

After what must have seemed like an age, the infantry battalion would now see the enemy battalions getting closer, and might well start to come under musket fire. Again, long-range musket fire was not very effective as the musket was a very inaccurate weapon. Corporal Todd remembered advancing against the French 'who were posted upon the top of a rising ground…And as we March'd up the hill (they) fired a whole volley upon us & then set up a shout, but scarce Kill'd us a man, their shot flying over us'.[26]

During the advance, the men kept their muskets upright against their shoulder, marching as if on parade. They were not expected to march forward with their weapons lowered by their waists, bayonets fixed and pointed at the enemy, as is often depicted by Hollywood. This, the argument went, made them too prone to firing before they were ordered to, as Bland explained:

> In advancing toward the enemy, it is with great difficulty that the Officers can prevent the Men… from taking their arms, without orders, off from their shoulders and Firing at too great a distance. How much more difficult must it be to prevent their firing when they have their arms in their hands ready cock'd and their fingers on the trickers [sic].[27]

When the commanding officer, or the brigade commander if moving as part of a general advance, decided that it is time to return fire, he would give the order to halt. The drums would stop beating the march and the whole battalion would come to a stop. The colour party would pass to the rear of the battalion to clear the way for firing. The drums would now give a ruffle, which will indicate to the soldiers that firing was about to commence. At this point: 'the two Rear Ranks close forward, keeping their thumbs on the cocks and their arms well recovered; and the Front Rank kneels, placing their butts on the ground by their Left Feet, where all are to wait for the next word

---

25 Emily Symonds, *Lady Mary Wortley Montagu And Her Times* (Whitefish: Kessinger Publishing, 2010), p.196.
26 Cormack and Jones (eds), *Journal of Corporal Todd*, p.182.
27 Blackmore, *Destructive and Formidable*, p.100.

of command'.²⁸ The men would then raise up one arm, bent at the elbow to create the necessary room to fire, before undertaking the process known as 'locking up'. To do this, the second rank man would place his left foot between the feet of the kneeling man in front of him, whilst the third rank man placed his left foot between the feet of the second rank man. This had the effect of moving each man slightly to the right of the man in front, giving each one room to fire his musket. Half an arm's length was estimated to create a nine-inch gap between the files, but such a tight formation allowed little room for reloading, with both the back rank and middle rank having to take a step backwards to do so. By 1756 the 'locking up' drill had changed with the second rank man now stepping back, placing his right foot in line with that of the kneeling front rank man, which allowed him to fire over his head. The rear rank soldier stepped to the right so that his right foot was behind the left heel of the man in front. This allowed him to fire through the gap created between the man in front and the man next to him. This also had the effect of creating a 21-inch gap between the files that now allowed the men to load without having to step back to do so. This is estimated to have increased the rate of fire and also to have made the whole exercise easier to learn. The soldiers would now wait for orders. All the weeks of going through the platoon firing evolutions on review were about to be put to the test.

Infantry Firepower

The flintlock musket had an effective range of 450 paces or 300 yards, but would be unlikely to hit the proverbial barn door at this range. The best results could be obtained at distances of 100 yards or less with real execution being done at 50 yards.

The battalion fired using a system of platoons, with each firing in an allotted sequence to maintain a steady rolling fire. Generally, under this system, the fire of the front rank was held in reserve, in case the enemy made a sudden advance on the battalion, or extra firepower was suddenly needed to drive off an attack by horse, for example. The front rank of the two centre companies, however, did fire along with the platoons, in order to preserve the life of the colonel, who was standing out in front. Richard Kane's manual instructed the colonel: 'to take special care that he keep opposite the two Centre platoons…when it comes to the turn of the centre platoons to fire, that both he and the drum step aside, and return as soon as they have done, otherwise they must fall by their own fire'.²⁹ If the centre platoons of the front rank reserved their fire and then fired all at once with the rest of the front rank, the colonel and his drummer would have nowhere to go and would undoubtedly be hit.

The signal for each platoon to fire came by a beat or ruffle of drums. The noise of the musket fire, combined with the shouts and screams of battle, not to mention the disorientation caused by the clouds of acrid smoke that

---
28   Kane, *New System of Military Discipline*, p.117.
29   Kane, *New System of Military Discipline*, p.113.

Close-up of musket lock, showing the brush (suspended by a chain form the soldier's cross-belt) used to keep the pan clear during prolonged firing. (Reconstruction by Richard Marren Craft Workshop – photograph © Alan 'Kael' Ball)

would quickly form around the battalion meant that the colonel's voice could soon become lost. By keeping the drummer near him, he could continue to give the order to fire verbally and by use of the drum combined.

The first shot given by the line was widely considered to be its best. This was the shot loaded casually whilst in camp and fired with a new flint. Prolonged firefights led to a breakdown in fire discipline, blunted flints, and badly loaded weapons being fired through a pall of gun smoke. For this reason, the 'first fire' was husbanded by colonels, with some even believing that the army which fired first would lose the fight, as it would allow the enemy to advance closer to give their first fire. The first volleys delivered by the British line at Fontenoy in 1745, for example, almost completely destroyed the French force opposite them.

After the first volley, the sergeants alongside each platoon would now take over, telling their men 'softly what they are to do, but so as none must hear them but their own men.'[30] At the command 'Load' the private brought his weapon back and held it suspended across his chest with his left hand while he pulled the lock back to the half cock position with his right. Reaching into his cartridge box he would pull out a cartridge, a twist of stiff paper containing a lead ball weighing just over an ounce and seven drams of black powder. Biting off the end furthest from the ball, and tasting the bitter saltpetre, he

---

30   Kane, *New System of Military Discipline*, p.118.

THE EXPERIENCE OF BATTLE

1745 plate showing drill movements for loading and firing. (Anne S.K. Brown Collection)

would shake a little of the powder into the pan of his musket, close the pan, and drop the butt of the musket to the ground. He then poured the remainder of the powder down the barrel, followed by the ball and finally the paper, which prevented the ball rolling out of the barrel again. Taking his ramrod from its position below the barrel, he would ram home the ball and wad to seat it securely. Looking along the line, a man might very well see veterans not drawing the ramrod but simply knocking the butt of their musket firmly on the ground to seat the ball and powder down the barrel. This so called 'tap loading' certainly saved time but often did not seat the ball and powder as securely, resulting in less range and power when fired.[31] However, if the fire fight was already at close range then this made little practical difference. Commanders were keen to ensure that every ball counted and preferred that the men did not tap load. This led Bland, in his drill book, to be clear that, if the men 'are not press'd too close by the Enemy, the ramming down of the cartridge should not be omitted in Service'.[32]

The soldier would then replace his ramrod and return his musket to the ready position. At the command 'Present' he would point his musket at the enemy. Sergeants would now remind the men to aim low, usually around the enemy's knees, as the kick of the musket would cause the barrel to rise dramatically and inexperienced units often fired their shots well over the heads of the enemy. The final command would be 'Fire' after which, in the blinding smoke and noise of the other ranks or platoons firing in order, the private would go through the loading process again. Well-trained units could expect to fire two or three rounds a minute. Kane declared that the soldier: 'continues his firings as fast as he can, until he obliges them [the enemy] to give way',[33] and that was essentially what happened, with volley after volley being fired into the enemy until he was forced to retire. The first battle of the War of the Austrian Succession, as far as the British were concerned, was at Dettingen. With neither men nor officers having been in battle before, the lack of experience told. The platoon firing system quickly broke down as Colonel Russell of Duroure's 12th Foot witnessed:

> [We] were under no command by way of Hyde Park firing, but the whole three ranks made a running fire of their own accord…The French fired in the same manner…without waiting for words of command and Lord Stair did often say he had seen many a battle and never saw the infantry engage in any other manner.[34]

Those that did keep their discipline seemed to do better. An officer of Peers' 23rd Foot wrote:

> Our people imitated their predecessors in the late war gloriously, marching in close order as firm as a wall, and did not fire till we came within sixty paces, and still kept advancing; For when the smoak blew off a little, instead of being among

---

31 For a discussion of tap loading see Blackmore, *Destructive and Formidable*, p.105
32 Blackmore, *Destructive and Formidable*, p.105.
33 Blackmore, *Destructive and Formidable*, p.103.
34 Orr, *Dettingen 1743*, p.64.

their living we found the dead in heaps by us; and the second fire turned them to the right about, and upon a long trot.[35]

James Wolfe was in no doubt that: 'a cool well levelled fire with the pieces carefully loaded is much more destructive and formidable than the quickest fire in confusion'.[36]

The British firing had much improved when it was next tested at Fontenoy and by the time of the Seven Years War, the strength of the British army was in its fire discipline, which was by then far superior to their French enemies.

Infantry versus Cavalry

At Dettingen, Fontenoy and, most famously, at Minden, the British infantry were attacked by massed squadrons of French cavalry. Humphrey Bland, when writing his drill book, was very clear that infantry who kept their formation and controlled their fire, had nothing to fear from cavalry: 'If foot could be brought to know their own Strength, the Danger which they apprehend from horse would soon vanish; since the fire of one platoon, given in due time, is sufficient to break any squadron'.[37]

As the squadrons approached the infantry, often at trotting pace, the first volleys were usually enough to bring down many men and horses from the front ranks, causing the ranks behind to stumble or pull up. In his drill manual, Kane explained that the:

> Fire of one rank will stop and disorder horse; and then a second and a third on the heels of it will certainly send them a packing…nor has it been known that ever a body of horse alone, without the assistance of foot, brake in upon a body of foot that with calm resolution made their regular fires.[38]

The most famous example of infantry destroying cavalry occurred at Minden in 1759, when six battalions of British infantry were attacked by, and destroyed, 72 Squadrons of French cavalry. One eyewitness to the attack wrote:

> The French charged them with a least 20 squadrons, but by their steadiness and bravery, keeping their fire till the enemy were close up to them, gave them such a terrible fire that not even lions could have come on; such a number of them fell, both horses and men that it made it difficult for those not touched to retire. This charge over, a second and third came on and were repulsed in the same manner.[39]

---

35   Orr, *Dettingen 1743*, p.64.
36   Blackmore, *Destructive and Formidable*, p.124.
37   Blackmore, *Destructive and Formidable*, p.100.
38   Kane, *New System of Military Discipline*, p.126.
39   Sanger, *Englishmen At War,* p.167.

Even if the cavalry did force their way through the barrage of fire and manage to get amongst the infantry, the resulting melee did not always go their way. Horses were loath to run onto the phalanx of waiting bayonets and usually shied away, whilst those that did crash into the infantry often found themselves at a disadvantage. During the Battle of Dettingen, for example, French cuirassiers charged Campbell's 21st Foot (Royal North British Fusiliers), and, despite taking casualties, still managed to charge home. A number of the infantry lay down on the ground to avoid the blows of the cavalry sabres, but as the French passed through them, the Scots stood up again, the rear rank facing about, and then fired into the rear of the French cavalry. Major Colville remembered: 'tho we gave them a very warm reception, yet a good many of them broke through us with more courage than conduct, for as they could not stop their horses, we faced upon them and brought them down very fast. So that few, or none of them, went back'. [40] When the battle was over, the King called to Lieutenant Colonel Sir Andrew Agnew, commanding he regiment, stating that he saw: 'the Cuirassiers get in among your men this morning, Colonel'. 'Oh Aye your Majestee' replied Sir Andrew, 'but they dinna get oot again'.[41]

Cavalry were at their most effective when charging infantry in the flank or rear. A line attacked in the flank was lost, as it could not fire or face the enemy and could quickly be rolled up. This was the abiding fear of all generals in this period, and turning an opponent's flank was every general's aim. Cavalry could also be effective if the infantry were not in their line formation, were caught perhaps in column, or changing from one formation to another. Under such circumstances they could not lay down the volume of fire required to stop a mass of men and horses who then crashed into the infantry and often swept them away. Similarly, if infantry were broken by musket or cannon fire and were in retreat, they were in no position to fend off a determined cavalry attack and it was often then that cavalry could wreck the most havoc on infantry regiments.

The Tipping Point

Winning the infantry firefight came down to who could maintain their fire whilst ignoring their own casualties for the longest time. Soon after firing commenced, the soldiers would be surrounded by a pall of smoke, deafening volleys, screams of the wounded and the shouts of their officers. Around them could see their wounded and dead comrades whilst from the front, through the smoke, they would see the flashes of the enemy volleys and hear the shots whiz past. All of the soldier's senses would be overwhelmed and he had to rely on his training to keep going through the motions of loading, presenting, firing and then loading again. Confusion would reign and only the most disciplined troops could stand it for long.

---

40 Orr, *Dettingen 1743*, p.59.
41 Orr, *Dettingen 1743*, p.59.

THE EXPERIENCE OF BATTLE

Contemporary records are full of tales of near-death experiences during battle, and of some very lucky escapes. Major John Reid of the 42nd Highlanders was twice wounded during an assault on a French position in Martinique in 1762, with one ball causing 'a violent contusion on one thigh which for several days threaten'd a mortification' whilst the other hit him in the jacket pocket and was stopped by 'a bunch of keys and some Spanish Dollars'.[42] Cornet Wortley acted as an aide de camp to Major General Sinclair at the Battle of Fontenoy in 1745, and as such was in the middle of the action all day. He wrote to his Father when the battle was over to let him know he was alright:

> I received a shot in my clothes and had my shoulder notch shot off (and musket) shots clattered on my furniture behind me and against my pistols before me. Some were, I suppose, partly spent…I was twice thrown from my horse by a cannonball…when I got up I was a good deal stunned, either from my fall or the wind of the ball or both! The ball was so near to me that everybody was surprised to see me alive.[43]

At some point, one side would give way and start to fall back or reach a tipping point when they would simply break and run. This could happen after a sustained fire fight, as happened at Dettingen, or after a single powerful volley, as happened at Quebec. Either way, musket fire was usually the cause, as French contemporaries testified. Marshal Noailes wrote to Louis XV after Dettingen about the British battalions, claiming: 'Their infantry was closed and held themselves brazenly, they conducted a fire so lively and so sustained that the old officers never had seen anything like it, and so superior to ours one could not make any comparison'.[44]

However, if firepower was not enough, the British army was happy to advance with the bayonet in order to force a decision. A line of screaming men advancing with bayonets fixed was usually enough to convince a wavering enemy that it was time to leave. James Wolfe recorded this as an accepted tactic, writing: 'If the firing is ordered to begin by platoons, either from the wings or from the centre, it is to proceed in a regular manner till the enemy is defeated or till the signal is given for attacking them with bayonets'.[45]

Volleys followed by a sudden bayonet charge appear to have happened at battles such as Lauffeld, where the British fired one volley before 'leaping in among them immediately after it, thus struck them with such a terror that they gave way'.[46] Although melees did occur, they were usually short-lived affairs, as most men dreaded being stabbed by a bayonet. It was recognised that hand-to-hand combat was still necessary to defeat an enemy ensconced behind earthworks or in prepared defences, but examples of long drawn out close quarter fighting between infantry battalions on the battlefield are

---

42 McCulloch, *Sons of the Mountains*, p.273.
43 Symonds, *Lady Mary Wortley Montagu And Her Times*, p.423.
44 Blackmore, *Destructive and Formidable*, p.121.
45 Blackmore, *Destructive and Formidable*, p.124.
46 Blackmore, *Destructive and Formidable*, p.104.

extremely rare. Whether the tipping point came as a result of firepower, or a sudden charge, the victorious soldiers would now advance to their enemies' position.

Pursuit and Consolidation

If victorious, the army would advance and take the ground once held by the enemy. Cavalry would now move forward to begin the pursuit, hoping to turn the enemies retreat into a rout and perhaps overrun their baggage or guns. For the infantry, most simply collapsed where they stood, or rested on their arms, grateful to have survived the day. The defeated army would now retire back toward its last safe magazine, covered by a screen of cavalry, leaving the victors in charge of the battlefield.

15

'The Butcher's Bill'

The Aftermath of Battle

It may be stating the obvious somewhat, but when a battle ended the victor was left in charge of the field of battle whilst the vanquished retreated back along their line of supply. For the British Army during the War of the Austrian Succession, the only times it was victorious and held the field in Europe were at Dettingen in 1743 and at Culloden in 1746. The other major engagements at Fontenoy (1745) Roucoux (1746) Falkirk (1746) and Lauffeld (1747) were all defeats. Indeed, even the 'victory' at Dettingen was a pyrrhic one, with the British having to retire the following day due to a lack of supplies, leaving their wounded to the mercy of the French. It was not until the British contingent joined the allied army led by Prince Ferdinand of Brunswick in Germany during the Seven Years War that this trend was reversed, with victories such as those at Minden (1757) and Emsdorf (1760). As a result, whilst we have lots of contemporary accounts of retreats, detail of army procedure after victory is, at least in the early period, harder to come by.

    Those that held the battlefield may have won, but any immediate personal feelings of joy or elation at being victorious and, more importantly, having survived the day, were soon replaced by feelings of exhaustion as the adrenaline left the soldiers bodies and the realisation of their situation set in. Most would not have eaten since they left camp and often even basic necessities, such as water, could not be found. The wounded were scattered all across the battlefield and their moans and cries for help were soon the only sounds left as the guns stopped firing. A witness to the battlefield at Dettingen wrote to his wife: 'My dear, tis a very shocking thing to see the poor souls that are lying upon the ground and to hear their cries'.[1] Dr Buchanan had evident sympathy for the horses of the army, noting in the wake of Fontenoy: 'The wounded horses would not foresake their Regmts though they had lost their Riders, & followed so long as they could walk, & some had only three legs to stand on'.[2]

---

1   Orr, *Dettingen 1743*, p.67.
2   Buchanan, *Regimental Practice*, p.277.

Those leaving the ranks to go to the aid of their wounded comrades were still not safe from enemy fire. Armies used artillery to cover their retreat and so roundshot continued to bounce across the battlefield even after the outcome was decided. At Dettingen, Sam Davies, whilst looking for the body of his master, Major Honeywood, witnessed one such incident:

> When I came a little higher I saw some of our men lay on the ground, some dead, some wounded, some without arms, some without legs. I saw one Fryer of our Regiment… he was afoot, the other men asked them to fech them some water from a well that was by them. He had been several times and as he was going again a cannon ball came and went into his back, takes his left breast away and his hart gumpt on the ground.[3]

Most regiments camped on the battlefield and had to wait for their regimental wagons to come up. These were often delayed as the wagons for the wounded took priority and as a result the men often camped with no equipment. A trooper from the Household Cavalry wrote of the aftermath of Dettingen: 'before we were engaged we threw our baggage away so that we were obliged to lie with our horses in our hands in the open fields.'[4] whilst Doctor Pringle recorded the miserable state of the army after the same battle:

> [W]hen the action was over we encamped near to the field of battle. Had violent raine for Sixteen hours, & few tents pitched, many having lost their tent poles, tent pins &c: & no straw. Were obliged to lye on wet ground. Many men were wet to the skine especially such as were on duty. We had no provision; some men had not broke bread these eight & forty hours… the wounded were left in the field that night, excepting a few taken up by the enemy… in the most unhappy & deplorable condition imaginable, without provisions for the troops, remedies for the sick & wounded, or any means of Reposing themselves, of which they were in so much want …the night passed amidst the Groans of the dying, & the complaints of those who survived them.[5]

Carrion Crows

Remarkably, the recovery of the wounded from the battlefield did not begin straight away. In fact, very often men were left overnight with recovery operations not beginning until early the following day. As a result, many who could perhaps have survived, died of exposure or bled out from their wounds. This was not the only danger they faced. As soon as the battle was over, and sometimes even before it had fully finished, the battlefield began to be invaded

---

3 Sanger, *Englishmen At War*, p.135.
4 Orr, *Dettingen 1743*, p.68.
5 Sir John Pringle, *A View of the Diseases of the Army in Great Britain, America, the West Indies, and on Board of King's Ships and Transports, from the Beginning of the Late War to the Present Time. Together with Monthly and Annual Returns of the Sick, and Some Account of the Method in Which They were Treated in the Twenty-Ninth Regiment, and the Third Battalion of the Sixtieth Regiment* (London: J. Johnson, 1793), p.35.

by the worst followers of both armies. Scavengers and looters, they robbed the dead and wounded of anything of value, squabbling amongst themselves for the best pickings and often finishing off any wounded men who resisted. This was such an accepted feature of battlefield that no-one seems to have taken any action to prevent these people going about their business. During the retreat after Fontenoy, one officer saw: 'two camp sutlers…one of whom was busy slitting the gold lace from a dead officer when a cannonball came whistling and shore her head away. Upon which, without sound uttered, her neighbour snatched the scissors and deliberately proceeded'.[6]

Invariably, when wounded men were found, they had been stripped of their valuables and often even of all their clothes by looters. One British officer remembered after Dettingen: 'When the body of General Clayton, who had led the Allied left wing so steadily, was found, it was completely naked and Major Philip Honeywood was found by his servant, still alive, but also stripped'.[7] Indeed, Major Honeywood's servant left a diary record of the event:

> [A]t last they finds my master on the ground naked for two Frenchmen had stripped him of his clothes, watch and money and left him for dead under a tree [he is] as well as he could [be] considering he lay four hours naked upon the cold ground… he has six wounds, two cuts on the head, a stab under his right arm with a bayonet. One ball went in at his body, out at his back, another ball in at his back…[8]

Corporal Todd found much the same scene in Germany during the Seven Years War:

> This morning at 4 O'clock all our pioneers, camp colour men & a large detachment was ordered to march into the wood…to bury all the dead, which we found numbers of them stripped naked by the boars & the followers of the army…Large holes was made & 20 or 30 thrown into the holes or pits together, both of the enemys & our own men.[9]

The Jacobite Cavalry had to fire their weapons in the air to drive off the local people who had come to loot the battlefield of Falkirk in 1746, with one Jacobite noting: 'there were a great many officers killed, for Goold watcheses were at a chape reat [sic]'.[10]

The retreating army often had to leave behind their more seriously wounded troops, hoping that they would be treated well by the enemy. In Europe this was often the case, as cartels had been signed between the various states agreeing that prisoners and wounded men would be treated

---

6   Thomas Carlyle, *The Works of Thomas Carlyle* (Miami: Palala Press, 2015) p.103.
7   Orr, *Dettingen 1743*, p.67.
8   Orr, *Dettingen 1743*, p.67.
9   Cormack and Jones (eds), *Journal of Corporal Todd*, p.169.
10 Geoff B. Bailey, *Falkirk or Paradise: The Battle of Falkirk Muir 17th January 1746* (Edinburgh: John Donald Publishers, 1996), p.160.

well. Leaving friends behind, however well they might be cared for, did not sit well with the men. Lieutenant Colonel Charles Russell of the 1st Foot Guards wrote after Dettingen:

> To our great shame be it spoken, we left the field of battle the next day and the village where our sick and wounded lay, without taking proper care to bring 'em with us; so that when we came hither the French seized upon 'em as prisoners of war and lucky for 'em took care of 'em, which is more than we had done…[11]

The medical staffs of both armies were to be given free passage to assist the wounded and any interference with them was considered to be against the rules of war. After the Battle of Fontenoy, the light troops of the French army were alleged to have taken the British surgeons prisoner when they were on their way to assist the wounded who remained on the battlefield. In an anonymous letter published in the *Gentleman's Magazine*, a person claiming to be an army surgeon stated that the French light troops would not let them treat the wounded: 'altho' the barbarians saw hundreds continually imploring our assistance. In this unprecedented way we remain'd three days, numbers dying every hour, because we had nothing to dress them with'.[12] The Duke of Cumberland wrote personally to the French commander, Maurice de Saxe, to complain about this treatment as it was considered to be extremely bad form.

Field Hospitals

This period saw the introduction of mobile field hospitals which followed the army on campaign and were often the first place were wounded men would be brought for care. The British Army had some wagons dedicated to moving wounded men from the battlefield to the rear area hospitals, but all too often there were far too few wagons for the numbers of wounded involved and men had to rely on their colleagues, or just as often on the enemy, to carry them to the nearest field hospital for treatment. Even as late as 1761, a report to the Secretary at War identified: 'one great impediment to the cure of the sick is the want of a sufficient number of carriages with each Brigade to transport them'.[13] Transport in the unsprung carriages along the back lanes and pothole filled roads to the clearing station must have been agony for the wounded, as one Surgeon recognised: 'when they were flung in waggons and drove along the causey to Lisle, Valenciennes, &c. In this jolting journey you may easily conceive the misery of these poor wretches, most with their legs, arms, &c., shatter'd to pieces'.[14]

---

11 Sanger, *Englishmen At War*, p.137.
12 Francis Henry Skrine, *Fontenoy and Great Britains share in the War of the Austrian Succession 1741-48* (Knighton: Terence Wise, 1997), p.218.
13 Hayter (ed.), *Eighteenth Century Secretary at War*, p.342.
14 *London Magazine: Or, Gentleman's Monthly Intelligencer*, Volume 14: 1745, p.288 A letter from a British Surgeon in the Army dated June 1745.

Most wounded men relied on their comrades carrying them back to the hospital in blankets or on horses secured for the purpose. When Major Bagshawe lost his leg to roundshot during the 1746 expedition to Lorient, he had to be carried back to the hospital and described the ordeal:

> I was obliged to be carryed the day after the amputation Eleven miles, lying on a bolster between two poles, & eight of these miles in the night through woods that catcht hold of me every now & then & the worst road I think can be travelled after this several days on a rolling sea more distressful than the former…I have been twice since in danger of bleeding to death & twice that all our physicians and surgeons said it was ten to one against me.[15]

It has been estimated that up to a third of wounded men died due to neglect on the battlefield or in transit to field hospitals before even reaching medical help.[16]

The temporary field hospital was like a modern clearing station, where the wounded would be temporarily treated before being transferred to a permanent hospital, which would have been established further to the rear. Given what we already know about well-established hospitals during the eighteenth century, it will come as no surprise to the reader to learn that temporary hospitals were far from conducive to good treatment and swift recovery. Dr Buchanan described the temporary hospital he saw at Dettingen:

> Here our hospital was in great disorder as their baggage was not yet arrived from Flanders, the Sick lyeing on straw only in Barns, Stables, outhouses, &c: there was commonly a Dunghill before the Door where all their Pots, Bedpans, &c: were emptied, & stinke abominably in warm weather, & great swarms of vermine are dayly produced; those Dunghills are lower situated than the Street, & when raine falls the common Channel empties… itself into the Dunghills, carrying much filth along with it, & after raine the stench was almost insufferable.[17]

Not all temporary hospitals looked like this, however. Buchanan also saw the field hospital erected by the Hanoverian contingent of the allied army on the same campaign:

> The Hanoverians had their hospital baggage in the field; their hospital was soon put in good order; their men in good houses, lye on palliases stuffed with Straw, have good coverings; their dressings are very neat of drawn lint, wounds cleaned with fine Spunge, soaked in warm water & brandy, use the caustic on the first appearance of proud flesh…hospital medecines are carried on a large waggon, divided into many different partitions, & opening at many places; any particular medicine may be easely got at, the whole easely packed & unpacked.[18]

---

15   Guy (ed.), *Colonel Samuel Bagshawe*, p.54.
16   Duffy, *The Military Experience in the Age of* Reason, pp.170-172.
17   Buchanan, *Regimental Practice*, p.281.
18   Buchanan, *Regimental Practice*, p.284.

French field hospitals were also much better than the British ones, with a much higher survival rate amongst wounded men treated by the French after the battle of Fontenoy than amongst the British. However, the state of the British field hospital speaks more of the failure of logistics and the inability of the army to get its medical wagons to the front than it does about the medical capability of its surgeons.

Once inside the hospital, Buchanan wrote: 'its impossible to describe the variety of wounds from Cannon Shot, small arms, swords & Bayonets'. He began to treat the wounded as best he could, but: 'having no assistant… avoided amputations as much as possible'.[19] Medical knowledge amongst the surgeons working in the temporary hospital varied, with some experienced surgeons working alongside new surgeon's mates. Medical instruments were not sterilised or even washed between patients and there was little or no anaesthetic to ease the pain of those undergoing invasive surgery or even amputation. Some surgeons did not think it necessary to clean a wound or remove all foreign matter before stitching it closed, leaving the patient vulnerable to infection at a later stage.

John Hunter was an army surgeon from 1760 to 1763, during which he served on the Belle Isle campaign. He observed that treatment for gunshot wounds often involved brutal exploration and enlarging of the wound in order to extract the bullet, which introduced more infection into the wound and often led to excessive bleeding and death. Instead he proposed only removing bullets if they were in easy reach of the surgeon and instead had wounds cleaned and bound, leaving the lead shot still in the body. John Jones, who was a surgeon during the French and Indian War and who went on to be Professor of Surgery in Kings College, New York, proscribed the application of 'nothing but dry, soft lint to recent wounds' and stated that 'Bullets were removed only if within easy reach of the surgeon. If a wound had to be closed, a piece of onion was placed in the cavity before closure, and the wound reopened in 1 to 2 days'.[20] Other, similarly bad ideas were common practice amongst surgeons in the British Army, making it a wonder anyone survived at all.

Cannon fire and musket balls often caused compound fractures in bones, which could not be repaired by eighteenth-century medicine, making amputation the only option. Fortunately, if that is the right term, this was an area in which military surgeons were well practised. The surgeon would cut around the limb to be removed with a sharp knife, peel back the flesh and then cut through the bone with a saw designed for the purpose. The invention of the screw tourniquet in 1718 had made thigh amputations possible and much reduced the risk of death when carrying out amputations below the knee. However, death from amputations was still high, especially when one adds the individuals who survived the initial operation but subsequently died from infection in the following days or weeks. Many surgeons became

---

19 Buchanan, *Regimental Practice*, p.267.
20 Peter Jackson-Lee, *Courage After The Battle – The story of how Armed Forces Personnel survive their mental and physical injury after leaving the Armed Forces* (London: Brown Dog Books, 2019), p.6.

very skilled at carrying out amputations, such as that carried out on Major Johnstone of the Horse Guards, for example, who:

> Received a Cannon shot on the left anckle, the bones smashed to pieces & the foot hanging by the great tendon, the large arterie bleeding at … full stream. I stiched the artery, cut off the anckle, dressing dry with proper bandage &c: leaving the amputation of the leg to a more convenient opportunity. It's surprising how some people bear pain better than others, this Gentleman never changed his voice or altered his Countenance; when I told him You must loose your leg, he answered cooly, that shall be the work of another day.[21]

Transfer to Permanent Hospital

The wounded soldiers would be moved as soon as possible from the temporary field hospital to a more permanent structure. This was usually done using wagons, but Dr Buchanan records that after Dettingen: 'the Sick were brought down the Rhine in Barges; suffered much from cold & wet & bad provisions, were Sick, faint & weake, pains in all their bones, Limbs numb & threatning a mortification'.[22]

The permanent military hospital at least had the facilities and correct medical equipment required to treat the wounded, as it had been established for this purpose and had time to prepare to receive the patients. Dr Pringle described the hospital used in the town of Ath:

> [A]fter the action of Fontenoye the Sick & wounded were sent to the Hospital at Ath, the Soldiers barracks being fitted up for that purpose, & are the most commodious we have yet had, each apartment containing only Six or Seven beds, a proper fire place, are well aired, & each roome seperated by a wall, & our sicke recovered well.[23]

According to Pringle, about 600 wounded were sent to this hospital, which was opened the day after the battle. In all it treated 991 patients, of whom only 59 died, a surprisingly low percentage given that some of the patients had been seriously injured. A good example is Cornet Davis of the Blues, who was thrown from his horse at Fontenoy. He was described by his surgeon as: 'much bruised, being draged & trampled, vomiting blood, urine bloody & was blooded, &c: went to Aix la chapelle for the benefit of the warm bath and recovered dayly'.[24]

Most deaths occurred as a result of infections, which medical science at the time did not understand. As a result, a variety of foul mixes were applied to wounds to prevent them becoming infected, including wood tar, chlorine, tincture of benzoin, silver nitrate, and various alcohol solutions,

---

21 Buchanan, *Regimental Practice*, p.267.
22 Buchanan, *Regimental Practice*, p.258.
23 Pringle, *A View of the Diseases of the Army*, p.35.
24 Pringle, *A View of the Diseases of the Army*, p.35.

many of which did more harm than good. Despite the facilities and the better conditions, some wounds could not be treated. Dr Buchanan noted:

> [C]ontusions from cannon balls seldom recover, tho at first they appear to be trieffling, yet soon spread upwards & downwards, commonly attended with large Emphysema over the whole body, as happened to Campbell of Cptn Gilbert's from a bruise on the outside of the right knee; face & body greatly swelled, his very eyes were shut up. & this was the case with many.[25]

Similarly, surgeons lacked the skill to remove bullets lodged deep in the body without killing the patient in the process. Captain Charles Vanbrugh was wounded by a musket ball at Fontenoy and carried to a hospital by his friend Captain Yorke. Despite being seen by a surgeon, there was little they could do:

> [W]e found yesterday the ball so fixed to the main bone of the thigh that it was in vain to attempt the taking it out; however, with the assistance of the best surgeon in the army we made an incision upon the part yesterday, but without success. I saw him a few hours before he died and kissed him, I was sure for the last time… the last words he spoke was concern for his mother and his regret in leaving me; nothing else affected him in dying.[26]

Prisoners

A treaty agreed between the French and British governments during the War of the Austrian Succession, and replicated by many European nations during the Seven Years War, made provision for prisoners. The first article stated that the wounded of either side were not to be made prisoners but should be properly cared for. Other articles included a provision for prisoners to get the same bread ration as their captors and be allowed to send a letter to their family giving the news that they were safe. Prisoners could then be traded on a 'like for like' basis for prisoners held by the other side. If the enemy held no prisoners of a suitable rank for a direct exchange, a ransom could be paid to secure their release instead. The tariff for ransom and exchange had been agreed and each rank had its set value laid down, from a Marshal of France (25,000 Florins) all the way down to a simple private. Chaplains, surgeons, and civilian volunteers were not to be made prisoners but were to be released unharmed.

The articles also stated that prisoners were not to be forcibly enlisted into their captor's army, although this did not stop both sides from trying. Deserters from the French army were enlisted into the British army in America, whilst Corporal Todd recorded regular visits from recruiters during his period of captivity in 1761, who attempted to enlist him and his men into the Irish Brigade: 'And the officers told us we had better Inlist, as

---

25 Buchanan, *Regimental Practice*, p.267.
26 Sanger, *Englishmen at War*, p.139.

they would give us Large Bounty Money & then we should live as we ought'.[27] Both Todd and his men refused.

During the Jacobite rebellion, French troops who were serving in the army of the Pretender were dealt with according to the treaty obligations. However, the Jacobite Highlanders were considered to be British subjects and as such were treated as rebels, being treated badly if they were taken prisoner at all. James Wolfe was clear about this: 'We had the opportunity of avenging ourselves and I assure you as few prisoners were taken of the highlanders as possible'.[28] Sir Everard Fawkener gave clear instructions to troops operating in the Highlands after Culloden: 'I am to inform you that HRH treats all prisoners born subjects of His Majesty as traitors and rebels: and all others as prisoners of war… Likewise that if you hear of any persons yet in arms against His Majesty you endeavour to put them to the sword'.[29]

British officers who were captured by the French could expect to be treated like gentlemen. The soldiers involved in their capture realised that taking a general or a colonel prisoner could result in a cash reward for them, either from the individual there and then, or from their subsequent ransom. Sir John Ligonier was taken at the Battle of Lauffeld in 1747, after which he wrote;

> The soldier who captured me would have had his head broken if I had still had a loaded pistol. He knocked off my hat and, taking his off to salute me, said: "General you are my prisoner and I bid you welcome". He had six others with him and I gave him my purse. Without dismounting they led me off toward the King, who was quite close…But when I came to the King he greatly reassured me saying, with a charming smile, "Well General, we will have the pleasure of your company at supper tonight".[30]

Ligonier's coach and all his belongings were captured by the French as the defeated British retreated, but the King returned all of these to him and he continued to dine with the King and the senior French officers until paroled. It seems that even in captivity, officers always came off better than their soldiers.

Booty

The private soldiers of the army had few opportunities to benefit financially from their success in battle. On the battlefield itself, when enemies were killed and positions taken, the advancing troops had no time to stop and go through the pockets of the dead or wounded men that they were marching over, although occasionally this did occur. For example, in 1745, Sergeant MacLeod of the Black Watch stopped to go through the pockets of a French

---

27 Cormack and Jones (eds), *Journal of Corporal Todd*, p.233.
28 Sanger, *Englishmen at War*, p.153.
29 Whitworth, *The Duke of Cumberland*, p.89.
30 Sanger, *Englishmen at War*, p.142.

colonel who he had killed whilst assaulting Fontenoy and was rewarded with a find of 175 ducats. Occasionally the baggage train of the enemy force was overtaken by the pursuing army and, in these cases, loot might be also be obtained by the common soldiers. After the Battle of Dettingen there was a great deal of baggage left behind by the retreating French forces and one officer remembered how: 'pleasant to see many of our common soldiers strutting in Hats and feathers & fine gold trimmings which they have taken from their conquered enemies'.[31]

Usually the only way for men to gain a financial bonus was to capture a senior enemy officer or to perform a heroic act, such as the taking of an enemy colour in battle. After the battle of Culloden, Cumberland rewarded men who had captured colours with 16 guineas, whilst at Dettingen the King offered £150 for every captured enemy colour! During the landings on Barbados in 1762, Private Daniel Gunn of Montgomery's Highlanders distinguished himself by single-handedly capturing four French grenadiers, despite being 'scarce five foot high but a broad well set man'. Major General Monckton presented him with a guinea for each of his prisoners, at which he declared that if he had known they were worth that much, 'by the Lard, I wad ha brought twa more of them'.[32]

Occasionally, some soldiers were rewarded with prize money simply for taking part in a campaign. Those involved in the taking of Havana had private payments made to them from the enormous ransom paid for the city by the Spanish Government. The British commander netted £132,000, with bounties paid to other officers on a sliding scale down to the common soldiers who received £2 10 shillings each. Every man who fought at Culloden was given a cash bonus to make up for the hardships of the campaign: 376 sergeants got 19 shillings each, (normally their pay was 1 shilling a day) 6,602 privates received 9 shillings, 6¾ pemce; 402 Corporals and 252 drummers got pay outs somewhere in between while the Argyll Militia and 20 Subaltern Officers received £100 between them. Cumberland also gave £1,640 for the relief of widows and orphans of men killed at Culloden.

However, such incidents were rare and the only thing most men walked away with after a battle was their lives, for which they were extremely grateful.

---

31 Orr, *Dettingen 1743*, p.67.
32 McCulloch, *Sons of the Mountains*, p.272.

16

'La Guerre Sauvage': The Army in the American Colonies

One might assume that a landmass the size of America was large enough to contain both British and French ambitions. However, war between the French colony of New France, stretching from maritime Canada to the Ohio valley, and the thirteen British colonial states along the east coast of North America was inevitable. Usually, the two colonies had gone to war when their parent countries did so in Europe, resulting in King William's War (1688–1697) Queen Anne's War (1702–1713) and King George's War (1744–1748). However, the war that would finally settle the matter began in America. The policy of successive French-Canadian Governors had been to build a line of forts from Louisburg in the north, sweeping in an arc around the Appalachian Mountains and ending up at the Mississippi, where they joined the French colony of 'La Louisiane'. To the French, the Appalachian Mountains thus formed the border between French-claimed land and British territory, hemming in the fledgling British colonies and denying them any westward expansion. When the French began building a fort in the Ohio Valley in 1753 the Governor of Virginia, Robert Dinwiddie, sent a young officer named George Washington to demand that they leave. When they refused, Washington returned in 1754 with a mixed force of regular soldiers and Provincial volunteers to forcibly eject them but was defeated at the Battle of Great Meadows (also known as Fort Necessity). The Duke of Cumberland was determined that the French should not be allowed to curtail British expansion, writing to Dinwiddie: 'None of your preparations, none of your military measures are of any effect till the Government has fixed the bounds of the French in America. How far they should come and no further.'[1]

Regular troops were then sent to the colonies by both sides. The British war did not get off to a good start when a British column under Major General Braddock was defeated at the Battle of the Monongahela in 1755. However, under successive commanders the British army soon began to adapt to the conditions of fighting a campaign in the vast wilderness of North

---

1 Whitworth, *The Duke of Cumberland*, p.161.

THE ARMY OF GEORGE II

Nova Scotia Ranging Company, 1755 (left). Hatman, Colonel William Shirley's or the Cape Breton Regiment of Foot, 1746-49 (right). The latter regiment was a short-lived unit which ranked as the 65th Foot for its brief lifetime; an equally short-lived successor was ranked as the 50th from 1755 to 1757. Artwork by Derek Fitzjames. (Anne S.K. Brown Collection)

America and Canada. They modified their uniforms, changed their training and method of fighting, and learned new skills to overcome substantial logistical challenges. William Pitt also committed the might of the British exchequer to the war, paying not only for regular troops to be transported to America, but also for the raising of substantial Provincial forces and units of Rangers. This money also bought the co-operation, or sometimes just the neutrality, of the numerous Native American tribes that were also major players in the conflict. By early 1758 the British had 44,000 men under arms in America, estimated to be more than the entire white male population of New France, making victory almost inevitable. The Royal Navy prevented significant French reinforcements arriving to assist and in 1760 Major General Jeffrey Amherst overcame significant logistical challenges to co-ordinate the approach of three British columns on the French capital of Montreal. Victory in the French and Indian War secured North America for the British and ended French ambitions on the continent.

Recruitment in the Colonies

The British colonies had something of a labour shortage in the middle of the eighteenth century, with an unskilled labourer able to earn two or three shillings a day, much more than the 6d paid to regular soldiers after stoppages. This made recruitment from the populace very difficult, and recruiting parties who used underhand tactics to enlist colonists were made very unwelcome. In 1756, a Philadelphia mob attacked a recruiting party, beating the sergeant to death in the scuffle, whilst there were riots in Wilmington, Delaware, the following year in which recruiting parties were beaten and driven out of town. This forced recruiters to look overseas to fill the ranks, with the promise of land in the new colonies upon retirement. Recruitment for the new 60th Royal American Regiment was carried out not only in Britain and Ireland but also in Holland, Germany, and Switzerland. Recruiters also enlisted German Protestants from amongst the French Prisoners of war being held in Portsmouth. These men were also promised farm plots in the colonies when they eventually mustered out, making it a tempting offer for those wanting a new start. Recruiters were allowed extra money 'for the passage of a small number of Women and Children, which he will be indispensably Obliged to take for the success of the Affair and the acquisition of proper men'.[2] This policy was designed to appeal to unemployed married men or those who wanted a new start for themselves and their families overseas. Figures for 1757 show that the policy was reasonably successful, with 607 foreign nationals being recruited into the regulars in America in that year alone.

Regular Regiments in America

Regular regiments deployed to America began to alter the appearance of their uniform almost as soon as they landed. The 44th and 48th, which landed with Braddock in 1755 were initially issued waistcoats and breeches of Osnabruck linen to help them cope with the hot weather. This was buff coloured, and often the men chose not to wear their heavy wool coats whilst marching in the summer heat.

No significant changes were officially ordered to the soldiers clothing until 1758, during the Ticonderoga campaign on Lake George. For this campaign, Lord Howe ordered the men of the 55th Foot to adjust their uniform to suit the needs of forest fighting, adjustments which were soon followed by the rest of army in that theatre. Hats were no longer turned up into a tricorne, but instead had the brim cut down. Hair was cut short and never powdered. Soldiers coats were cut short, with one commentator stating: 'Regulars as well as provincials have cut their coats so as scarcely to reach their waists',[3] and the issue leggings were often replaced with Indian style mittasses. The men began to carry tomahawks and knives for close fighting whilst the issue sword and any other unnecessary kit was left behind in camp.

Some regular soldiers began to go out on patrol with the Native Americans and the better Ranger companies, and in most cases they dressed either in the Native American fashion or in a manner much closer to the Rangers as, not surprisingly, the red coat did not provide a great deal of camouflage. The adoption of Indian dress was welcomed by officers, with Colonel Bouquet writing: 'I have been long in your opinion of equipping numbers of our men like the Savages and I fancy Col Byrd of Virginia has most of his best people equipt in that manner'.[4] For his part, George Washington was equally enthusiastic: 'Soldiers in such a dress are better able to carry their provisions

---

2   Peter Way, '"The scum of every county, the refuse of mankind": Recruiting the British Army in the eighteenth century' in Erik-Jan Zürcher (ed), *Fighting for a Living: A Comparative Study of Military Labour 1500-2000* (Amsterdam: Amsterdam University Press, 2013), p.3.
3   Letter from Camp, 12 June, 1758, in *Boston Evening Post* quoted in Parkman, *Montcalm and Wolfe*, p.345.
4   David L. Preston, 'British soldiers and Indian Warriors from Braddock to Forbes's Campaigns, 1755-58', *Pennsylvania History: A Journal of Mid-Atlantic Studies*, Vol.74, No. 3 (Summer 2007), p.15.

are fitter for the active service we are engaged in and less liable to sink under the fatigues of a long march'.[5]

When Major General Wolfe besieged Quebec in 1759, many of the regiments with him had come directly from England and had only been involved in the siege of Louisbourg the year before. As such, many of them had not made the adjustments to their uniforms as those fighting on around Lake Champlain had. However, as the campaign wore on, it appears that these troops also adopted the same uniform changes so that by the end of the war most British regulars would have cut down hats, short coats, and light equipment rather than appearing as they might have done in Europe.

60th Royal American Regiment of Foot[6]

As well as the British regular regiments there were also regular battalions raised entirely in the colonies. First, and best known of these, was the 60th Royal American. Established by Royal Warrant in December 1755, the Regiment was originally designated as the 62nd but with the disbanding of the 50th and 51st in 1757, it was re-designated as the 60th. Although it did have colonists amongst its ranks, many of the recruits for this regiment came from the foreign recruiting outlined above, including a high number of Swiss and Germans. During the campaign, any non-French prisoners of war captured by the British were offered an opportunity to enlist, which many accepted.

Being a royal regiment, it wore red coats with blue facings, turn-backs and breeches. When on campaign, the men wore an undress uniform that had no lace. On their dress uniforms, lace would be white. Grenadiers wore a standard mitre with a blue front band with white lace. There appears to be no evidence that they wore a bearskin cover over their mitres, which they are often depicted wearing in modern representations. Drummers wore the Royal Livery of a red coat with blue cuffs, lapels, turnbacks, and breeches. The 60th appear to have cut down their hats and coats in line with other regular troops during the war.

Recruiting went well and the regiment finished the war with four battalions. As it was raised to fight in America, there was much less emphasis on platoon firing in line during training and much more focus on skirmish warfare and light infantry tactics. There is evidence that some of the first battalion were issued with rifled carbines for more accurate aimed fire in close woods rather than the standard Brown Bess musket.

---

5   Preston, 'British soldiers and Indian Warriors', p.15.
6   Summary from Ruth Sheppard (ed.), *Empires Collide; the French and Indian War 1754-63* (Oxford: Osprey, 2006); Carman, *British Military Uniforms*; Carl Franklin, *British Army Uniforms from 1751 to 1783* (Barnsley: Pen and Sword, 2012).

80th Regiment of Light Armed Foot[7]

In December 1757, Lieutenant Colonel Thomas Gage submitted a proposal to raise, at his own expense, a 500 man regiment of 'light armed foot' provided that the crown reimburse him and commission him a colonel. Approval was obtained and the regiment was subsequently formed on May 5 1758. Later that year it fought at the Battle of Ticonderoga before joining Amherst's force the following year for his more successful advance on the same location. It then remained with Amherst for the advance on Montreal in 1760. The regiment was disbanded in 1764. Although raised as 'light armed foot' Gage appears to have sold the commissions with more concern for his personal patronage, as only four of the 19 officers joining the regiment had any previous light infantry experience.

The regiment wore distinctive brown jackets with brown cuffs and lapels. There were no turnbacks as their jackets were cut short in light infantry style. Waistcoat and breeches were red and gaiters were brown. They wore cut down hats and carried a minimum of equipment. Drummers wore the same brown jackets as the infantry. The regiment appears not to have carried any colours on campaign but whether any were actually commissioned is unclear. There was no grenadier company.

95th Regiment of Foot[8]

In 1760 several independent companies were raised in England to be sent to America. The aim was for these men to be split up and used to reinforce regiments already posted there. However, as the Cherokee War in the southern states progressed, eight of the companies were sent to South Carolina under the command of James Grant of the 40th Foot. Initially formed into two battalions, they were brought together to form the 95th Foot in 1761. During the campaign they were found to be 'troublesome' with the various independent companies not working well together. To make matters worse, they were poorly trained and disciplined. The regiment was disbanded in 1763, having served a short time in the Caribbean, and its fit men distributed amongst surviving older regiments still in America.

They were initially clothed entirely in red with no lace, allowing for coloured cuffs and lining to be added when they reached their respective regiments. Although the 95th was granted grey facings, it is unlikely that they had these facings and linings added during the Cherokee campaign. It appears that one of the eight companies was trained as a 'light infantry' company, but whilst it is likely that a grenadier company was formed it is less likely that it was issued with distinctive grenadier caps, as the regiment was formed on an ad hoc basis in theatre before immediately going on campaign.

---

7 Summary from Sheppard (ed.), *Empires Collide*; Carman, *British Military Uniforms*; Carl Franklin, *British Army Uniforms from 1751 to 1783* (Barnsley: Pen and Sword, 2012).
8 Summary from Sheppard (ed.), *Empires Collide*; Carman, *British Military Uniforms*; Carl Franklin, *British Army Uniforms from 1751 to 1783* (Barnsley: Pen and Sword, 2012).

The Light Infantry

From the beginning of the campaign, British officers recognised the need to train regular troops in the 'skirmish' style of warfare practised by the Native Americans and the French. In 1756, the Duke of Cumberland wrote to Lord Loudon: 'I hope that you will in time teach your troops to go upon scouting parties; for till regular officers with men that they can trust learn to beat the woods and to act as irregulars, you will never gain any certain intelligence of the enemy'.[9] Brigadier General Forbes was equally supportive, recognising: 'in this country we must comply and learn the art of war from Enemy Indians or any thing else who have seen the country and Warr carried on in it'.[10]

Initially, officers and men were sent out with the Rangers and their Native American allies to learn how to traverse the wilderness, live off the land, track the enemy and lay ambushes. The men learned quickly, and very soon each regiment had a core of trained light infantry who could deploy as scouts or to go on patrol when the regiment was in camp. These troops were then used to train others and a nucleus of the new 'light infantry' companies that were formed. In January 1759, Amherst wrote to Lord Ligonier stating his intention to increase the light infantry of each British regiment to company size which:

> [S]hall consist of 1 Captain, 2 Lieutenants, 1 Ensign, 4 Sergeants, 1 drummer and 100 rank and file in the battalions of 1000 men; and of 1 Captain, 1 Lieutenants, 1 Ensign, 3 Sergeants, 1 drummer and 70 Rank and File in the regiments of 700…this will make a fine light alert corps for this country and I intend that they should all be good marksmen and that all the regiments likewise will be well practised in firing ball.[11]

The light infantry companies were extremely effective as they combined the scouting and backwoods fighting skills of the Rangers with military discipline, being able to take orders and fight as a coherent unit. When asked what troops were best to undertake actions against Native Americans, Thomas Gage was in no doubt, writing in 1759: 'The light infantry of the regiment headed by a brisk officer, with some of the boldest rangers mixed in with them, to prevent their being lost in the woods, will be the most likely people to effect this service'.[12]

The light infantry adapted their uniform to suit the wilderness. A contemporary account described the light infantry uniform:

> [T]he sleeves of the coat are put on the waistcoat and instead of coat sleeves he has two wings like the Grenadiers… He has no lace but the lapels remain. His knapsack is carried very high between his shoulders as the Indians carry their pack. His cartouch box hangs under his arm on the left side, hung with a leather strap and his

---

9   Whitworth, *The Duke of Cumberland*, p.171.
10   Preston, 'British soldiers and Indian Warriors', p.15.
11   Middleton (ed.), *Amherst and the Conquest of Canada*, p.17.
12   John Grenier, *The First Way of War: American War Making on the Frontier, 1607–1814* (Cambridge: Cambridge University Press, 2008), p.138.

horn under the other arm hanging by a narrower web…his canteen down his back, under his knapsack and covered with a cloth. He has a rough case for his tomahawk, with a button and it hangs in a leather sling down his side… between his coat and waistcoat. His hat is made into a cap with a flap and button with as much cloth as will come under his chin and keep him warm when lying down.[13]

So, basically, the waistcoat now had the coat sleeves on it. When they put the jacket on, it had no sleeves but the shoulders stuck out a bit, where the sleeves have been removed, looking a little like the wings on a Grenadier uniform. This coat retains the lapels, which could be folded across for extra warmth in winter. Hats were cut down as the regulars did, or were discarded in favour of leather 'jockey' style caps. They cut their coats usually to waist length and wore Native American mittasses or buckskin leggings instead of their issue gaiters. Footwear was also usually moccasins or similar locally made shoes rather than the issue buckled leather style. As they travelled without the support of wagons or pack trains, the men had to travel light and carried backpacks in addition to their ammunition pouches. Most of them carried knives or tomahawks for close quarter work.

Light Companies were often issued with captured French trade muskets, as these were lighter and considered more accurate than the standard issue musket. Amherst was an enthusiastic supporter of this practice, writing to Governor Whitmore in 1759: 'As soon as the operations of the campaign are fixed I shall rob you of some of the light French arms for the light infantry'[14] and again to Colonel Morris in 1759 to inform him:

> I have cut the French arms shorter which makes them much lighter and handier for the light infantry. I shall send you… seventy five firelocks which are for the three Sergeants inclusively and you will deliver …the French firelocks you have that they may be shortened as the others, for I shall want more firelocks I believe than what I have.[15]

The success of the regular light infantry companies shows the versatility of the eighteenth-century British soldier more than any other aspect of this war. Within a few short years the Light Infantry were able to learn and then master this new form of warfare, and by 1760 were able to defeat even Native American forces in the woods of North America.

Militia and Provincial Regiments

The regular British Army in America was initially very small and completely unable to meet the demands placed on it by the colonial assemblies, all of whom demanded regular troops to protect the frontier from French and Indian incursions.

---

13 Stuart Reid, *Quebec: The Battle that Won Canada* (Oxford: Osprey, 2003), p.16.
14 Middleton (ed.), *Amherst and the Conquest of Canada*, p.16.
15 Middleton (ed.), *Amherst and the Conquest of Canada*, p.48.

Each of the colonies could call upon every able-bodied man to turn out as a militia to oppose any military threat to the state. However, these men would bring their own weapons, had little official training and would only remain in the field for a short period until the danger had passed. Most of them had never been in combat and were not trained soldiers and as a result their performance in battle was mixed. George Washington wrote in August 1756 of one defeat that was entirely due to:

> [T]he dastardly behaviour of the militia, who ran off without one half of them having discharged their pieces, although they were appraised of the ambuscade by one of the flanking parties before the Indians fired on them: and ran back to Ashbys Fort, contrary to orders, persuasions, threats etc. [16]

The militia lacked discipline and were always notionally under the command of the colonial Governor and not the local military commander, and as such could come and go as they pleased. This led Washington to declare:

> Militia, you will find, sir, will never answer your expectations, no dependence is to be placed upon them…when they are ordered to certain posts for the security of stores, or the protection of the Inhabitants, will, on a sudden, resolve to leave them, and the united vigilance of their officers cannot prevent them.[17]

The short-term nature of their deployment and the ambiguous system of command made the use of the American militia unattractive to the British regular commanders although large numbers of them did serve for short periods at various times during the war.

Instead, each of the colonies was encouraged to raise Provincial regiments from amongst their population to support the regular battalions. Recruiting into the Provincials, however, proved just as difficult. Fortunately for the army, the economy of the colonial provinces was not particularly cash rich, with many transactions taking place through barter or exchange of labour for goods. For young men in the colonies it was hard to raise the money required to buy and run a farm. However, in 1756 a private signing on with a Provincial regiment was offered £1 12s per month plus subsistence paid at 8d per day, making 52 shillings per month in cash. By the end of the war, pay had gone up dramatically with some troops being paid nearly double this amount. Thus, the average American private could expect to muster out at the end of the year with £15 in his pocket, which, depending on location, could buy between 30 to 150 acres of unbroken or frontier land. Well worth the risk for any enterprising young man. Compare this to the British regular who received, on average, 5 shillings a month!

---

16 John B. Russell (ed.), *The Writings of George Washington: Being His Correspondence, Addresses, Messages, and Other Papers, Official and Private, Selected and Published from the Original Manuscripts; with a Life of the Author, Notes and Illustrations*, (Jared Sparks: American Stationers' Company, 1833) Vol.II, p.167.

17 Russell (ed.), *The Writings of George Washington*, Vol.II, p.97.

'LA GUERRE SAUVAGE': THE ARMY IN THE AMERICAN COLONIES

The men who joined the Provincials were generally from families who owned land or were involved in business, and were not usually driven to join the army by poverty or destitution. Rather, they were young men with ambitions to make their way in the world, and their service in the regiment was merely a means to an end. As a result, few would re-enlist for more than one campaigning season. Which brings us neatly to a rather unusual aspect of the Provincial regiments. They were raised at the beginning of a campaigning season under contract to the Provincial Assembly to serve just for that year's campaign or occasionally just for a specific expedition. When that campaign or expedition was finished the regiment was disbanded and the men went home. Although aware that they were fighting for the King of England, they regarded their employer as their state, with which they had signed a contract. There are a number of examples of Provincial regiments staging protests or simply marching home, or 'deserting' as the British saw it, when their contracts had expired or if they thought their terms of enlistment had been breached. For example, in July 1758 Colonel Partridge's Provincial Battalion marched out from Fort William Henry in protest over short rations and were only persuaded to return when promised full rations would be restored.[18]

Field officer of the 2nd Connecticut Regiment, 1760. Watercolour by Herbert Knötel. (Anne S.K. Brown Collection)

This had two main effects. Firstly, there was little continuity from year to year, as the same men, from privates through officers, were unlikely to re-join the regiment for more than one campaign. Even if some did, the regiment would have to start from scratch in terms of training and experience every year, meaning that no Provincial regiment could ever improve in its performance. The other effect was that the British regulars found the Provincials unreliable, as they could refuse to follow orders or pack up and leave at any time if they felt their contracts had been infringed.

Provincial colonels and officers often brought their own friends and relatives with them to join the regiment, and it was not uncommon for an officer to have a brother or other relatives in the ranks, all having joined together. This had the effect of making discipline in the ranks much less harsh than it was with the regulars. Provincial officers were often on first name terms with their men and shared their campfires and food. They would explain why certain things had to be done and tended to take their men with them through example rather than by enforcing discipline. There was no instance of more than 30 lashes being handed out within a Provincial regiment, and even then only for the most serious of offences.[19]

---

18 Anderson, *A People's Army*, p.252.
19 Anderson, *A People's Army*, p.125.

Some of the ruling assemblies fully supported the war, such as **Connecticut**, which voted for troops every year the war lasted despite not being on the front line. In 1758, for example, it raised and paid for 5,000 men who were organised into four battalions of 12 companies. **Massachusetts** also enthusiastically supported the war and raised six battalions every year from 1756. Despite its size, **New Hampshire** voted funding for Provincial troops and Rangers and by 1759 one third of all able-bodied men of military age in the colony were serving with the British military in some capacity. **New York** raised 1,000 men in 1757, and over 2,000 every year after that. Some states, however, pleaded poverty. **Georgia**, for example, raised only one company of 40 Rangers to contribute to the war in 1756. These were used to police the colony's own borders but funds were withdrawn for even this small number of troops and by 1758 the Governor had to pay them from his own pocket. Despite Governor Dobbs' willingness to supply men, he wrote of **North Carolina** that: 'the misfortune of this province is that we have no cash; Our paper currency is at great discount and though we can raise and pay men in the province, yet we have no credit to pay them out of the province'. As a result of the lack of pay and supplies, one observer wrote; 'The North Carolina troops are in a pitiable condition, and lack health, uniforms and everything. I have never seen such misery'.[20] Although 450 men were raised in 1754 to assist Washington, they arrived too late to take part in the campaign. The lack of supplies led to desertions, which became so bad the regiment was disbanded. This sorry state of affairs continued throughout the war, with the state providing less than 100 men every year.

Pennsylvania suffered tremendously during the war from Native American raids into the colony, yet it found it uniquely difficult to deal with this issue as the colony was founded on the pacifist teachings of the Quaker religion and Quakers held the majority in the ruling assembly. They were loath to back any motions to raise troops for the defence of their villages and towns even when the attacks became widespread, preferring instead to attempt negotiations. In 1755 Governor Morris managed to pass the Supply Act which allowed the raising of full-time troops to build frontier forts to protect the settlers, but this had the added advantage that the troops did not disband at the end of the campaigning season and also that the troops remained to man the forts once built. By 1758 there were three battalions protecting the frontier which, despite being called 'Ranging Companies' appear to have been trained and equipped as regular infantry, Rangers being more acceptable to the assembly than regular troops. It is another peculiar fact that the troops were supplied with uniforms, but not guns, instead being given an allowance of; '7/6 for the use of a gun & a blanket or half that sum for either of them'.[21] The assembly, it would appear, did not mind giving an allowance for a man to bring his own weapon but would not buy and issue weapons to the men.

---

20 John R. Maass, *The French & Indian War in North Carolina: The Spreading Flames of War* (Mount Pleasant: Arcadia, 2003), p.4.
21 William A. Hunter, *Forts on the Pennsylvania Frontier* (Harrisburg: The Pennsylvania Historical and Museum Commission, 1960), p.195.

'LA GUERRE SAUVAGE': THE ARMY IN THE AMERICAN COLONIES

Private, the New York Regiment 1756. Watercolour by Herbert Knötel. (Anne S.K. Brown Collection)

Private, Hoar's Massachusetts Regiment, 1761. Watercolour by Herbert Knötel. (Anne S.K. Brown Collection)

Private, the Augusta Regiment (Pennsylvania) 1757. Watercolour by Herbert Knötel. (Anne S.K. Brown Collection)

Corporal, the Pennsylvania Regiment 1760. Watercolour by Herbert Knötel. (Anne S.K. Brown Collection)

THE ARMY OF GEORGE II

Despite all the inducements, recruitment in some states was slow. In 1758, for example, **Massachusetts** raised only 4,500 men despite voting to raise six battalions and had to impress 2,500 men from the militia. Recruitment was also slow in **Maryland**, where the Provincial Regiment there never numbered more than 300 and for the first years of the war was barely company strength. In 1756 **New Jersey** raised one battalion of 500 men nicknamed the 'Jersey Blues' and supplemented it with another battalion in 1759. They were equipped with blue coats faced red with red turnbacks. They appear to have had blue waistcoats and breeches. From 1757 they wore a shorter coat described as: 'dark drab turned up with middle drab cloth'. Drab is generally described as light brown, the colour of undyed wool, and so we can assume this mean light brown with cuffs in a lighter shade again. Breeches were buff or buckskin. All leatherwork was natural leather in colour but was the same as that issued to British regulars. In 1758 the regiment was ordered to trim their hat brims to 2.5 inches and they were no longer cocked. Officers were not issued their uniforms and had to purchase their own. To begin with they followed the pattern of the British regulars, wearing red coats with blue or green facings. By the end of 1757 the officers were wearing dark forest green coats with green facings and trimmed with silver lace. Waistcoats and breeches may well have been buff, or drab as the soldiers wore.

Left: Grenadier Company officer, New Jersey Regiment (Jersey Blues), 1758. Watercolour by Herbert Knötel. (Anne S.K. Brown Collection) Right: Private in marching order, New Jersey Regiment (Jersey Blues), 1758. Watercolour by Herbert Knötel. (Anne S.K. Brown Collection)

'LA GUERRE SAUVAGE': THE ARMY IN THE AMERICAN COLONIES

Rhode Island voted for a regiment of Provincial regulars for every year of the war, usually numbering about 500 men but in 1758 providing a full battalion of 1,000 men. These troops were employed in the battle of Ticonderoga, at Fort Carillon and in the eventual advance on Montreal.

South Carolina spent much of the war trying to deal with Cherokee incursions into the colony and what small numbers of troops they raised spent their time patrolling the frontier. Despite voting sufficient money for a 700-man battalion in 1757, recruits were slow to join and the regiment was forced to draft those with: 'no visible lawful means of maintaining themselves and their families and all sturdy beggars and all strolling or straggling persons'.[22] Even using this measure the numbers never rose above 500 and by the time the regulars moved south in 1760 to take part in a campaign against the Cherokee, one British officer said: 'We have not a single man with us that is of any consequence in the Provincials'.[23]

In 1754 Governor Dinwiddie of **Virginia** ordered the formation of a full-time regiment. Although it was initially supposed to consist of volunteers, recruits were not forthcoming and Dinwiddie ordered a draft of men instead. However, one could avoid the draft by providing a substitute or paying a £10 as an exemption fee. This meant that the ranks were filled with Virginias poor, who Washington described as 'loose, Idle Persons… quite destitute of House, and Home', as well as a number of men listed as of African or Native American ancestry. Washington did drill them in standard infantry tactics and also ensured that they: 'regularly practiced in Shooting at Targets, in order that they may acquire a Dexterity in that kind of firing'.[24]

Private, the Virginia Regiment 1758. Watercolour by Herbert Knötel. (Anne S.K. Brown Collection)

Provincial battalions appear to have been organised in line with British regulations. Units would have included drummers, although not all battalions seem to have formed a distinct grenadier company. There was little opportunity to train the newly raised Provincials, even if there had been experienced men within their ranks who could carry out such training. As a result, most battalions reached the front line with not even the basics of drill or fire discipline. Although regulars were often assigned to them in an effort to get them up to speed, there was a limit to what could be achieved before the campaign started.

---

22   Lawrence Cress, *Citizens in Arms: The Army and Militia in American Society to the War of 1812* (Carolina: The University of North Carolina Press, 1982), p.59.
23   Daniel J. Tortora, *Carolina in Crisis: Cherokees, Colonists, and Slaves in the American South* (Chapel Hill: University of North Carolina Press, 2015), p.121.
24   John C. Fitzpatrick (ed.), *Writings of George Washington from the Original Manuscripts* (Charlottesville: University of Virginia Library, 2001), p.170.

When actually encountering the enemy, the Provincials do not seem to have done too badly. The idea of not taking cover when fired on seemed alien to the young Americans, who often went prone or took cover to return fire rather than standing in ranks. This happened at the Battle of the Monongahela, where provincial soldier Tom Faucett defended this tactic: 'we knowd better than to fight Injuns like you red backed ijits [because] we wouldn't stand up rubbin shoulders like a passel o' sheep and let the red skins make sieves outen us.'[25]

Although uniform was issued to most provincial regiments, the frequency of orders reminding soldiers of the need for uniformity suggests many thought it was optional. There are descriptions of Provincial soldiers in a variety of clothing as well as a selection of different hats, which seems to have been common through the ranks. Major Hawkes of the Massachusetts Regiment wrote in his general orders: 'Except those on duty, it is expected that the commissioned officers do not wear scotch bonnets but wear something that they may be distinguished as officers.'[26] In 1755, Washington ordered his officers:

> [T]o provide himself as soon as he can conveniently, with a Suit of Regimentals of good blue Cloath, the Coat to be faced and cuffed with Scarlet, and trimmed with Silver: a Scarlet waistcoat, with silver lace, blue Breeches, and a silver-laced Hat, if to be had for Camp or Garrison Duty. Besides this, each Officer to provide himself with a common Soldiers Dress, for Detachments, and Duty in the Woods.[27]

Coats were usually cut short on campaign, but officers may have retained full dress coats which would have red turnbacks. This uniform would have arrived in time to be worn by the regiment when it accompanied Braddock's column.

Colours certainly existed for each of the Provincial Regiments but not for the Ranging Companies. In truth, little is known about the Provincials colours, and since the regiments were often distributed in small groups on various fronts, it is difficult to know where the colours might have been and if they actually saw action. Based on what we do know, each battalion would have carried the Union Flag, with its unit designation in the centre enclosed by a garland, and then a Colonel's Colour, which would have been either the facing colour of the battalion or a colour significant to the state. This Colonel's Colour would have a small Union Flag in the upper corner next to the flagstaff and usually bore the name of the state or the states emblem. For example, the Virginia Regiment had a white Colonel's Colour with the letters 'VA Regt' enclosed by a garland, whilst the Maryland Regiment carried a yellow and black Colonel's Colour, these being the colours of the Calvert

---

25 Paul E. Kopperman, *Braddock at the Monongahela* (Pittsburgh: University of Pittsburgh Press, 1977), p.139.
26 Brown, Thomas, Eastburn, Robert, Hawks, John and Putnam, Rufus, *Narratives of the French & Indian War: Ranger Brown's Narrative, The Adventures of Robert Eastburn, The Journal of Rufus Putnam-Provincial Infantry & Orderly Book and Journal of Major John Hawks* (London: Leonaur, 2008), p.43.
27 Russell (ed.), *The Writings of George Washington*, Vol.II, p.41.

family who raised the regiment. It can be assumed with a fair degree of certainty that, where colours existed, they would have been carried before the Ticonderoga campaign, as the regulars were carrying theirs.

Ranger Companies[28]

Ranger companies had always been required to police and protect the scattered settlements of the thirteen colonies and Provincial Governments had raised and paid for them to perform this task from the early 1700s. Some of these units were recruited from frontier settlements, incorporating men who were familiar with the frontier terrain and hardened to its life, whilst others were recruited from newly arrived immigrants or even overseas, such as those members of the Georgia Rangers recruited in Britain. The more successful Ranger companies included a high proportion of Native Americans in their ranks, as these men could teach the new recruits the indigenous way of war, as well as the basics of scouting and living off the land. Gorham's Rangers, for example, contained 60 Native Americans led by Provincial officers when it was first raised in 1744.

With the rapid increase in British military numbers in Canada and North America during the French and Indian War, the high command saw the need for a corresponding increase in the numbers of Rangers to provide light infantry support. Rogers' Rangers, for example, became an independent company in 1755, and was so successful that by 1756 it had increased to three companies. By 1757 it had risen to seven companies and numbered over 750 men.

This need for more Rangers resulted in a recruitment drive, with potential Rangers being offered much higher pay than their contemporaries in Provincial line regiments. Rangers were paid 3 shillings a day, more than service in Provincial line regiments and much more than a British regular soldier, who could only expect 5 shillings a month! These disparities in pay made new recruits gravitate toward the Rangers, where they were employed whether they had any suitable experience or not. Many of the recruits were newly-arrived immigrants from Ireland and Scotland who had never even seen a Native American, let alone have the ability to track one through the woods. Rufus Putnam, for example, was encouraged to undertake ranging duties for his Provincial battalion in exchange for increased pay and rum ration: 'the General…told us if we would still stand as Rangers we should have three dollars per month allowed us, extraordinary, and half a pint of rum when we scouted. The rum we got sometimes; but the money we never see'.[29] He had no experience of fighting in the wilderness or even of wilderness navigation, which he proved soon after by becoming lost for three days whilst on patrol along with two of his colleagues and almost freezing to death before they found their way back to camp.

---

28 Summary from Sheppard (ed.), *Empires Collide*, and Parkman, *Montcalm and Wolfe*.
29 Dawes (ed.), *Journal of General Rufus Putnam*, p.62.

The men sent to act as Rangers on the Quebec expedition in 1759 had little practical experience and seem to have been not much better than brigands. James Wolfe described them as 'six new raised companies of North American Rangers- not complete, and the worst soldiers in the Universe'.[30] These men were not particularly effective at scouting but enthusiastically undertook the ravaging of French lands, looting and murdering to an extent that appalled the regular officers. Colonel Fraser reported how two rangers had murdered and scalped two French children who they were supposed to be bringing in as prisoners: 'The wretches boasted of it on their return… but I believe this barbarous action proceeded from the cowardice and barbarity which seems so natural to a native of America'.[31]

However, much as they complained about the Rangers and their effectiveness, the British military had no choice but to use them. Efforts to train British regulars to act as Rangers were not initially successful, with Chief Surgeon, Richard Saunders Huck, noting in 1758:

> [A]lthough it has been pretty much in vogue lately to decry all Rangers, and Rogers has come in for his share of discredit, parties therefore of regular troops commanded by such officers as were judged properest for that service have been sent out to procure intelligence but returned without effecting anything.[32]

Whilst some Rangers, such as Gorham's and Rogers', continued to do good service and were effective against the enemy, for the majority it was recognised that they had to be led by regulars to be effective. British regular light infantry units, commanded, or accompanied by, Rangers, proved to be the most effective combination, providing the local 'know how' with military discipline. Although Rangers were employed up to the end of the war and beyond, it is in this joint role that they performed best.

Initially raised along regular lines, Rogers' Rangers consisted of 60 privates, three sergeants, an ensign, and two lieutenants. However, there seems to have been no hard or fast rules about the size of command structure of a ranging company. Barnard's Rangers, for example, totalled only 40 men, whilst the newly raised Rangers accompanying Wolfe were 'not complete', suggesting they never reached their paper strength. Rangers often went out on scouts with as few as six or seven men, or on larger raids were numbers could be over 100. It was generally the case that men designated to be Rangers practised shooting at marks to improve their aim and learned how to reload from a kneeling or prone position.

Some of the Ranging companies were issued with uniforms. Gorham's Rangers, for example, were issued with red coats with brown linings and cuffs, brown waistcoats and leather caps. The idea of having brown linings was to reverse the coats when on campaign. This need for camouflage is reflected in the use of short green jackets by Rogers' Rangers, who also wore

---

30   Reid, *Quebec*, p.16.
31   Oliver Warner, *With Wolfe to Quebec: The Path to Glory* (Toronto and London: Colins, 1972), p.113.
32   Grenier, *The First Way of War*, p.138.

'LA GUERRE SAUVAGE': THE ARMY IN THE AMERICAN COLONIES

Rogers' Rangers, summer dress, 1758. Watercolour by Herbert Knötel. (Anne S.K. Brown Collection)

Rogers' Rangers, winter dress, 1758. Watercolour by Herbert Knötel. (Anne S.K. Brown Collection)

green waistcoats and breeches with Indian leggings. Officers were permitted to have silver lace on their jacket, but it is unclear if this would be worn on campaign. One description left of Rangers during the 1759 campaign in Quebec has them wearing a black jacket with blue cuffs and lapels and black leggings. The Scots bonnet appears to have been popular headgear, although stocking caps, cut down tricornes, or round hats were also seen. One British officer favoured the montero style leather cap which he thought: 'much more convenient, & less troublesome than hats in our excursions thro' the woods & by water'.[33] However, on campaign, Rangers wore what they pleased and it is unlikely that strict uniform codes were enforced. Henry Pringle of the 27th Foot wrote of Rogers' Rangers that: 'They dress & live like the Indians, & are well acquainted with the woods… [they] carry their provisions & blankets upon their backs',[34] suggesting that many wore Indian garb well into 1757.

---

33 Gary Zaboly, *American Colonial Ranger: The Northern Colonies 1724-64* (Oxford: Osprey, 2004), p.60.
34 David L. Preston, 'Make Indians of our white men: British soldiers and Indian Warriors from Braddock's to Forbes Campaigns, 1755-1758', *Pennsylvania History: A Journal of Mid-Atlantic Studies*, Vol.74, No. 3 (Summer 2007), p.294. See also Zaboly, *American Colonial Ranger*, p.56.

THE ARMY OF GEORGE II

Gorham's Corps of Rangers, 1761. Watercolour by Herbert Knötel. (Anne S.K. Brown Collection)

James Smith was captured at Braddock's defeat and lived as a captive amongst Native Americans for five years. During Pontiac's Rebellion he was asked to raise a company of Rangers to help defend the frontier. He chose as subalterns 'two of the most active young men…who had also been long in captivity with the Indians' and dressed his rangers: 'uniformly in the Indian manner, with breech clouts, leggings, mockesons and green shrouds'. They wore red handkerchiefs on their heads and 'painted [their] faces red and black, like Indian warriors'.[35]

Many Rangers preferred shooting with loose ball and a powder horn rather than with fixed cartridges, although they are sometimes shown wearing 'belly box' style cartridge boxes. They carried a tomahawk and a knife rather than a bayonet for close quarter fighting.

Native American Allies

The relationship between the British military and the Native American Indians was never a particularly happy one. Unlike the French, who treated the various tribes as allies, the British viewed them as native auxiliaries who were expected to obey orders and to work for an agreed wage. The Native Americans viewed themselves as independent nations who provided warriors to support the Europeans only when it suited them to do so, or where they saw political or military advantage. The warriors themselves expected to receive regular 'gifts' of food and arms to keep them in the field, and they usually dispersed after gaining a significant victory over the enemy. This made them very unreliable allies in British eyes, although they recognised that their skill at woodland warfare was essential to eventual victory.

Although the British had the support of the Iroquois Six Nations of tribes, this was as much due to political machination by the Native Americans as anything else. Playing the British off against the French kept the Six Nations in a controlling position in the Ohio Valley and, although native warriors were employed by the British throughout the campaign, the attitude of most Native Americans toward the British was one of neutrality. Whilst the British recognised the natives' skill at scouting and ambush, commanders would rather employ Rangers and light infantry to perform this role, as the natives

---

35   Preston, 'British soldiers and Indian Warriors', p.20.

were felt to be too unreliable. However, they did go to great lengths, through agents such as William Johnson, to bribe and encourage the native peoples not to join the French, as every indigenous warrior in British employ was one lost to the enemy. Major General Jeffery Amhurst wrote in 1759 of his new allies: 'I know what a vile crew they are, and I have as bad an opinion of those lazy rum drinking scoundrels as anyone can have: I shall however, take them into his majesties service for this next campaign, to keep them from doing mischief elsewhere'.[36]

Native Americans dressed as they pleased, usually wearing a breechclout, leggings of cloth or deerskin, known as mittasses, and soft leather moccasin shoes. They wore elaborate war paint, which was usually significant to the individual warrior rather than uniform across a tribe or war party. However, it does appear that those employed by the British were: 'distinguish'd by a Yellow Fillet or Yellow Ribband and some carry their matchcoats on a pole; Any Indians having the above Marks and Signals are to be received as friends'. Abraham Bosomworth, an officer in the Royal American Regiment, reported that these badges were: 'very conspicuous & easily seen at a distance in woods'.[37]

Medical Support

Civilian doctors and surgeons were already present in the colonies serving the various communities of settlers. However, these were fairly well scattered and did not exist in the numbers that would soon be required for a military campaign.

In April 1756 a hospital was established in Albany, where Lord Loudon ordered the building of a facility capable of taking 300 patients and supplied it with ten tons of supplies shipped from London. It was staffed by 11 commissioned officers – a hospital director (James Napier) two surgeons, two apothecaries, three surgeon's mates, and three apothecary's mates – with three civilian personnel: a matron, a steward, and a clerk. The civilian staff remained at Albany but the surgeons and apothecaries travelled with the armies. The hospital was also staffed with women from the 44th and 48th Foot, who served as nurses, with women from other regiments also being employed there as they arrived in theatre. The presence of a clerk enabled detailed records to be kept of patients coming in and out of hospital and also to keep track of how long they had been there. This greatly improved efficiency and allowed the correct billing of the various regular and Provincial regiments for the services of the hospital.

The matron was ordered to 'to see that the nurses keep their wards clean, that they behave themselves soberly and regularly and give due Attendance to the patients'.[38] The surgeons remained with the army and set up a field hospital at Crown Point during the Ticonderoga campaign. This, it appears,

---

36   Middleton (ed.), *Amherst and the Conquest of Canada*, p.196.
37   Preston, 'British soldiers and Indian Warriors', p.16.
38   Fatherly, 'Tending the Army', p.582.

was just as badly overcrowded and under-supplied as those in Europe, acting only as a clearinghouse, where patients were given initial treatment before being sent by boat down the lake to Fort William Henry and on to Albany. John Frost, a Provincial soldier, went to the field hospital to look for wounded friends: 'We went in to see them that were alive. And of all the smells that I ever smelt there never was none that smelt so bad'.[39]

Over all, medical provision appears to have been no better than in Europe, although the permanent hospital in Albany does appear to have been well run and as a result had a lesser mortality rate than similar facilities in Europe.

The majority of deaths amongst British soldiers in America occurred through disease. Many were stationed in frontier forts in all weathers where poor nutrition, coupled with poor hygiene and sanitation, meant that outbreaks of dysentery, flu, and fevers were common. In addition, diseases such as measles and smallpox were already present in the colonies and were picked up by soldiers passing through settlements or carried to forts by civilian traders. Sometimes, the climate did not agree with the new arrivals, especially those deployed to the southern states. When a Montgomery's 77th Highlanders arrived in South Carolina, for example, they had only 16 men out of action from the whole battalion, but within a month 'there were over 500 sick [and] still greater numbers must have perished if some of the inhabitants of this town had not, out of compassion, received nearly 200 of them into their houses'.[40]

Logistical Challenges

As outlined elsewhere, the eighteenth-century British Army required a lengthy supply train in order to function properly. When the men arrived in America it quickly became clear that the infrastructure of the new colonies not as developed as it was in Europe. Whilst the 13 British colonies had large areas of cleared farmland and established towns, the vast wilderness beyond them was covered in ancient woodland, lakes, mountains, and fast-flowing rivers with few recognisable paths let alone roads. The British thus had to overcome significant logistical challenges before they could even come to grips with their enemy.

The French practised *La Petite Guerre* or a form of guerrilla war, where small groups of lightly-armed French troops and their North American Indian allies would attack the established farms and settlements along the frontiers. They also ambushed supply columns and attacked isolated garrisons. By carrying out his type of warfare they hoped to tie down the British military protecting the frontiers and to prevent armies moving toward the settlements like Quebec or Montreal by disrupting their supply lines. The British strategy involved advancing their armies through the wilderness to capture French forts, settlements, and ultimately the capital, Montreal, and

---

39 Fatherly, 'Tending the Army', p.594.
40 McCulloch, *Sons of the Mountains*, p.209.

thus win the war. This required moving large numbers of men and supplies across some of the toughest terrain in the world.

To begin with, there were no roads outside the 13 colonies, just dirt paths and hunters' trails. For the army to get anywhere they usually had to construct their own road as they went. The soldiers had to undertake backbreaking labour, clearing forests to allow the wagons to pass and building forts to protect the supply route. These roads had to be cut through some of the toughest terrain imaginable, as Lieutenant Archie Robertson wrote in 1758 whilst attempting to build a road to Fort Duquesne with Forbes force. Robertson knew that 'the public are greatly surprised at the slowness of our proceedings: but please allow me to acquaint you that none can form any idea of the hardships and difficulties we undergo in forcing roads over hills and swamps for near 200 miles except those that undergo the labour'.[41]

It was not uncommon for progress to be as slow as two miles a day. In Europe, local people might be employed to assist with this sort of building work, with carpenters or manual labourers paid by the army to assist. In the wilderness of America and Canada, the men had to learn these trades 'on the job' and to become self-sufficient. Colonel Bouquet said that his soldiers had to be: 'taught to throw up entrenchments, make facines and gabions, as well as to fell trees, saw planks, construct canoes, carts, ploughs, barrows, roofs, casks, bateaux and bridges, and to build ovens and loghouses... become tolerably good carpenters, masons tailors, butchers, shoemakers etc'.[42]

The roads created were made from felled logs laid side by side and covered with dirt, or, if the land was flat, simply by clearing the trees and undergrowth so that the wagons and artillery could pass. However, passing along even these cleared paths and 'cord wood' roads took its toll on the wagons, which often had to have wheels or axles replaced due to the rough going. A lack of trained carpenters made repair difficult. Of the 73 supply wagons that made the journey to Fort Littleton in 1758, only 33 would still serviceable to continue on to supply the army. It took three days to ferry just 30 wagons across the Susquehanna in Pennsylvania in 1758, and often columns would be delayed whilst they waited for the water level in fords to reduce so they could cross. Bouquet, who led the advance to Fort Duquesne on the Ohio alongside Brigadier General Forbes, was acutely aware of the vulnerability of large trains of wagons following clearly defined routes, stating that it: 'weakens our line of march and keeps the troops tied to a convoy which they cannot lose sight of'.[43]

However, these roads had to be followed as the regular British troops could not navigate their own way through the dense woodland without Rangers or Native Americans to guide them. When they tried to do so, they quickly became lost, as one officer of the 44th Foot recorded, when advancing on Fort Carillon in 1758, where he encountered: 'dark woods and

---

41 McCulloch, *Sons of the Mountains*, p.67.
42 Matthew C. Ward, '"The European Method of Warring Is Not Practiced Here": The Failure of British Military Policy in the Ohio Valley, 1755–1759', *War in History*, Vol. 4, No. 3 (July 1997), p.257.
43 Ward, '"The European Method of Warring Is Not Practiced Here"', p.257.

The Death of General Wolfe. Engraving by Augustin Le Grand after Benjamin West. (Anne S.K. Brown Collection)

swamps that were almost impassable, till at length, having lost our way, the army was obliged to break its order of march, we were perplexed, thrown into confusion and fell upon one another in a most disorderly manner'.[44]

Using the waterways to travel could be just as dangerous without skilled pilots. The fast-flowing rivers had many waterfalls and strong currents that could catch out inexperienced navigators. The weather also caused problems for both armies, especially in winter when temperatures could plunge as low as -20 degrees, which the soldiers often had to endure without any proper winter clothing or shelter. Heavy snows fell and frostbite was common, whilst many soldiers simply died of exposure. Captain Henry Pringle of the 27th Foot was separated from Rogers' Rangers after the Battle of the Snowshoes and wandered lost in the wilderness for two days:

> [T]he wind pierced us like a sword; but instead of abating it increased together with a freezing rain, that incrusted us entirely with ice…we made a path around a tree and there exercised all night, though scarcely able to stand or prevent each other from sleeping. Our guide, notwithstanding repeated cautions, straggled from us where he sat down and died immediately.[45]

---

44   John Knox, *An Historical Journal of the Campaigns in North America for the Years 1757, 1758, 1759, and 1760* (Toronto: Champlain Society, 1914), p.257.
45   Brown et al, *Narratives of the French & Indian War*, p.57.

Such harsh conditions drove men to desperate measures. Ranger Thomas Brown became lost with a companion in winter whilst attempting to reach Crown Point:

> After we had travelled twenty two days, fifteen of which we had no provision except roots, worms and such, we were so weak and faint that we could scarce walk. My companion gave out… [and] next morning he died… I finally came to this resolution: To cut off his bones as much flesh as I could and tie it up in a handkerchief, and so proceed as well as I could.[46]

Despite initial setbacks, the difficult terrain, the severe weather, and the hostile enemy, the British Army was still able to traverse the wilderness to take the French forts on the Ohio and on Lake Champlain. Eventually, after the fall of Quebec, three British columns were able to advance from the Ohio, along Lake George, and down the St Lawrence to arrive before Montreal in 1760, forcing the surrender of New France. The French and Indian War is best remembered for battles such as Quebec and Fort William Henry, but this was a war not won by open battle, but through logistics.

The Experience of Combat

The French and Indian War was fought initially in two theatres: In the north, around Lake Ontario, the St Lawrence River and the Lake George/Lake Champlain approach to Montreal, both armies concentrated their regular forces and the majority of their Provincial and militia units. This was where the larger battles and sieges of the war were fought. In the west, especially along the Virginia and Pennsylvania frontier, was fought what the French referred to as *La Guerre Sauvage* or the Indian War. In this theatre, various Native American tribes were encouraged by the French to raid across the frontier into the British colonies, attacking settlers' farms, towns, and even isolated forts. Based at Fort Duquesne in the Ohio Valley, the French military provided the native war parties with supplies to carry out the raids, hoping that these constant incursions would tie down British regulars and Provincial regiments in attempting to secure the 500-mile frontier.

In 1756, Robert Dinwiddie Governor of Virginia wrote to Major General James Abercromby, advising him that he had 'come in to a Country cover'd with woods and sometimes unaccessable Mountains, etc. The European Method of Warring is not practised here'.[47] This was a massive understatement. The experience of battle in Canada and America could not have been more different for soldiers trained to fight in the European manner. Although European style battles did occur, such as at Quebec in 1759 or St Foy in 1760, for much of the time the men were engaged in a guerrilla war with raiding French and Native American war parties. The Native Americans fought in a way completely foreign to British soldiers, and with their war whoops and

---

46 Brown et al, *Narratives of the French & Indian War*, p.57.
47 Ward, '"The European Method of Warring Is Not Practiced Here"', p.247.

terrifying appearance, they struck fear in men newly arrived in the colonies. William Smith recorded the Native American style of fighting in 1764:

> [S]uppose he had made the dispositions usual in Europe for a march, or to receive the enemy: and that he is then attacked by the savages. He cannot discover them, though from every tree, log or bush he receives an incessant fire and observes that few of their shots are lost. He will not hesitate to charge those invisible enemies, but he will charge in vain. For they are as cautious to avoid a close engagement as indefatigable in harassing his troops: and notwithstanding all his endeavours, he will still find himself surrounded by a circle of fire which, like an artificial horizon, follows him everywhere.[48]

Colonel Henry Bouquet confirmed this, writing: 'Indian tactics in battle could be reduced to three principles: surround the enemy, fight in scattered formation, and always give ground when attacked'. He stated that native peoples had: 'no very respectable opinion of our manner of fighting them, as, by our close order, we present a large object to their fire and our platoons do little execution as the Indians are thinly scattered and concealed behind bushes or trees'.[49]

Unlike in Europe, where wounded men or prisoners could expect to be treated decently by their enemy, the harsh frontier environment bred a harsh form of warfare that often shocked British soldiers with its barbarity. Prisoners could expect to be killed out of hand, or face hideous torture at the hands of victorious Native American warriors. Wounded men could also expect no quarter, as no enemy would want to carry them through the wilderness to get aid, and even the dead were not safe from mutilation. In 1757, Rufus Putnam of the Massachusetts Provincial Regiment had a particularly gruesome find when out with a search party attempting to locate the wounded from a skirmish the day before:

> [T]hey found that two of those wounded men… were carried off and the third they found barbecued at a most doleful rate… with his nails all pulled out, his lips cut off down to his chin and up to his nose and his jaws laid bare: his scalp was taken off, his breast cut open, his heart pulled out and his bullet pouch put in the room of it.[50]

The war in America saw significant changes to the British forces that were sent there to fight it. European tactics clearly were not going to work in the wilderness against an elusive foe such as the Native American tribes and their French allies. However, this war more than any other shows the British soldier's adaptability to changing circumstances. After a disastrous start, the British Army changed its tactics, adapted its uniform and developed

---

48 Colin G. Calloway, *The Victory with No Name: The Native American Defeat of the First American Army* (Oxford: Oxford University Press, 2014), p.110.
49 Adam Bancroft, *Savages In A Civilized War: The Native Americans As French Allies* (Auckland: Golden Springs Publishing, 2015), p.91.
50 Brown et al, *Narratives of the French & Indian War*, p.67.

new light infantry skills to face, and then overcome, their enemy. British soldiers also learned new skills, building roads and forts, navigating rivers and scouting across the wilderness alongside provincial Rangers and Native Americans. By the end of the war, the British regiments in America had become a formidable fighting force, as their subsequent deployment against French and Spanish colonies elsewhere would soon prove.

17

John Company: Service in India[1]

The conflict between France and Britain for dominance in India is a long and involved story, made all the more complex by the inclusion of the political machinations of the various Nawabs and Indian Princes, vying for control of the various provinces that made up Moghul India. This chapter focuses on the British regiments sent to fight there along with the Indian forces raised to support them, and deals with their uniform, logistical supplies and other day-to-day issues rather than the campaigns in which they fought.

The Honourable East India Company (HEIC) had been granted exclusive rights to trade in India by Queen Elizabeth I in 1600 and was further granted a monopoly on the trade by James I. They were given permission to 'employ troops in war, erect forts, acquire territory, form alliances and govern with complete authority' by King Charles II in order that the trade routes, ships and company employees could be protected. It was, after all, a long trip back and forth from India to England and the company employees could not be expected to return to seek the King's blessing for every skirmish or land dispute. By the beginning of the eighteenth century, the HEIC had holdings in the presidencies of Bengal, Bombay and Madras, protected by a small number of European troops and locally employed mercenaries. The trade between India and Great Britain was lucrative and it made the HEIC, its directors and shareholders, very wealthy and the company did not want to reduce this profit by having to raise or maintain an army.

However, the HEIC was not the only European trading company trying to corner the Indian market. Also well-established were the French Compagnie des Indes Orientales and the Dutch Vereenigde Oost-Indische Compagnie. All of these trading companies employed locally-raised private armies to protect their trade from pirates and brigands but during the early period

---

1   Summary based on Philip Mason, *A Matter of Honour: An account of the Indian Army its Officers and Men* (London: Purnell Book Services Ltd, 1974) and Bruce Lenman, 'The Weapons of War in Eighteenth Century India', *Journal of the Society for Army Historical Research*, Vol.46, No.185 (Spring, 1968), pp.33-43.

these were little more than mercenaries who were not trained or supplied by the Europeans and were less-than-reliable in open battle.

At the time, India was a patchwork of semi-independent states all notionally loyal to the Moghul Emperor but actually vying to control more land to expand their influence. The three European companies traded with the blessing of the local ruler, often paying a tax on the traded goods. At the beginning of the period, this relationship between the European companies and the various Nawabs and local rulers was one of master and supplicant, as *Colonel* Bussy of the French Compagnie des Indes Orientales described:

> We never appeared before him [the Nawab of Arcot] but as supplicants, carrying presents which he continually exacted from us… and as for the Nizam himself, he deigned not to write to any European Governor and hardly honoured with a look the rich presents he brought.[2]

Major Stringer Lawrence, who re-organised the British forces in India. Mezzotint by R. Houston after Joshua Reynolds. (Anne S.K. Brown Collection)

The French were the first European power to deploy trained European regulars alongside drilled Sepoys when they took Madras from the British in 1746. Although it was returned to British control as part of the peace treaty in 1749, its fall served as a wakeup call to the HEIC, which now employed Major Stringer Lawrence to overhaul their army. Although their home countries were at peace, the French and British forces in India continued their conflict by fighting a proxy war, sending their forces to support opposing sides in Indian dispute for the inheritance of the title of Nawab of Arcot. Nasir Jung was supported by the British whilst Chanda Sahib was supported by the French. The presence of disciplined French and British forces caused a shift in the balance of power, as this conflict showed that small numbers of drilled troops could defeat the much larger Indian forces with relative ease. Indian rulers now competed to have the French or British on their side, as they recognised that without them their armies could not prevail.

By 1756, France and Great Britain were once more at war in Europe and consequently open war broke out once again in India. This time both sides deployed armies consisting of trained Europeans and sepoy troops alongside irregular Indian allies. The war did not begin well for the HEIC with the capture of Fort William at Calcutta by Indian forces in 1756. Despite there being a substantial recruitment and training programme for sepoys taking place in Madras, the HEIC holding in Bengal had not followed suit and as a result the garrison forces there were easily over run. The 146 prisoners from the garrison were held overnight in one small prison cell, the so-called

---

2   Mason, *A Matter of Honour*, p.17.

THE ARMY OF GEORGE II

Major General Robert Clive (1725-1774). Engraving after unknown artist. (Anne S.K. Brown Collection)

'Black Hole of Calcutta', during which all but 23 died of suffocation. After this setback, the HEIC sent trained troops from Madras, along with the first British regular forces to arrive in India, the 39th Foot, to Bengal to recapture Calcutta. The commander, Robert Clive, not only managed this but also completely defeated the Nawab's French-backed forces at Plassey in June 1757. The British victories continued, with the capture of the French settlement of Chandannagar the same year and ultimately the defeat of the French forces at Wandiwash in 1760. By 1761 the French centre of trade at Pondicherry fell into British hands, effectively ending French ambitions in India. Dutch ambitions to curtail HEIC expansion in Bengal were also dealt a crushing blow when their army was defeated at Chinsurah in 1759.

Although battles were important, the strategic aim of war in India was the control of land. By controlling the wealth-producing areas, taxes could be raised and armies funded for the next campaign. Seizing land from one's enemy reduced his access to taxes and hence there was a corresponding reduction in the army he could field the following year. Land was controlled by the taking and garrisoning of forts and towns that were then used to exert control over the local populace, hence ensuring the collection of taxes. A claimant to the title of Nawab usually had little to offer his potential European allies except the promise of land grants upon his accession. Hence the HEIC was often paid through grants of land in the Presidency in which it supported the local ruler. The smallest land grant, called a Jaghir, was worth around £190,000 a year in Madras whilst the French lands in the Northern Circars seized by the British at the end of the Seven Years War was estimated to be worth £490,000 a year. This constant land expansion by the HEIC resulted in it effectively ruling large areas of the country and moved it from being supplicant to king-maker. By 1761 the HEIC armies were the predominant military power in India and the company commanded a staggering level of wealth compared with other Indian rulers. The trading company that did not initially want to pay for an army now had one which they could use to demand trade concessions and payments from Indian rulers who, if they refused, found themselves deposed and a more compliant ruler installed in their place. The land grants gained from grateful rulers the HEIC had supported, or the lands seized from those who had supported the French, gave the HEIC significant wealth and political power in India, which formed the basis of the British Empire.

The Army in India

The HEIC was in India to trade and to make profit. The raising and maintaining of an expensive army were not conducive to profit-making, and so the trading posts and forts of the early HEIC holdings were protected by mercenary bands or locally employed men with little training or equipment. In 1747, for example, Madras was protected by 3,000 locally raised 'Peons', of which only 900 had matchlock muskets, the rest having swords and spears. However, the unreliable nature of these troops required the HEIC to recruit European battalions which were better armed, trained and disciplined and hence could be relied upon to protect the HEIC holdings. It was not initially envisaged that these battalions should be used for anything other than coastal defence, but as the nature of the war with the French and Dutch companies expanded, so did the need for trained troops who could travel inland and fight in pitched battles. It was the successful use of trained and disciplined Indian troops by the French that eventually forced the HEIC into following suit, raising sepoy battalions of their own.

Recruitment

The holdings of the HEIC were located in three different areas of India: Madras, Bombay and Bengal. Madras established a European Battalion in 1742, which went on to fight throughout this period, being present at Arcot in 1751, Plassey in 1757, Condore in 1758, and Wandiwash in 1760. In 1758 the Madras Europeans were organised into two battalions, both numbering about 500 effectives. Bombay also had a European battalion, which had previously existed as independent companies until 1742, when these were brought together to form the Bombay European Regiment. The first European battalion of infantry was formed in Bengal in 1756 after the destruction of the garrison during the siege of Calcutta.

In 1759, the HEIC estimated that it required 2,000 new recruits every year just to maintain its European battalions, due to death, desertion or retirement of those already serving. However, it was difficult to recruit Europeans to come to India to serve as soldiers for two reasons. Firstly, India had a reputation as being the graveyard of European soldiers, due to the high death rate from disease. Many colonial postings had a reputation as being practically a death sentence due to disease, but India's reputation was particularly bad. Secondly, the HEIC was always competing with the regular army for recruits, with many recruiting parties scouring the country for likely volunteers, especially during times of war when demand was high. During the year 1754-55 the company recruited 1,001 men from Britain but after war broke out in Europe they managed only 488 for the following year. When the Seven Years War was at its height, the HEIC managed to recruit only 202 men in 1759 and 197 the following year.[3] This often forced the HEIC recruiters to use some pretty underhand tactics to get recruits on board ship to India. When the promise of a generous bounty failed, some recruits were basically kidnapped or press-ganged into the service, a practice that became known as 'crimping'. The recruiters were also forced to take men who would

---

3 Summary from Mason, *A Matter of Honour*, pp.34-38.

not normally make the grade for the British Army, either through ill health or bad character.

Not surprisingly, the men of the European battalions were not exactly the cream of the crop, with one officer accusing many of the European recruits of bringing:' insolence, mutiny, profligacy, debauchery and disease into their Armies in India'.[4] The HEIC was not averse to employing foreigners to make up the difference. These could be recruited from European sailors or traders or anyone who found themselves in India without employment. In 1751 two companies of Swiss mercenaries were recruited directly, each consisting of four officers, six sergeants, six corporals, a drum major, two drummers and 120 rank and file. Sickness and desertion meant that by 1754 these troops could no longer function as independent companies and they were integrated into the Madras European Regiment. A check of the roster list for the HEIC European battalions shows not only British and Swiss in its ranks, but also Germans and even French deserters.[5]

The inability of the HEIC to properly recruit Europeans led to the British Government sending regular British Regiments to India to support them. The loss of the trade concessions to the French would be a substantial hit to the British economy, which the Government was not prepared to risk. To this end, the 39th, 79th, the 84th and 89th Regiments of Foot all served in India along with a detachment of the Royal Artillery.

Sepoy Regiments

The recruitment of sepoy infantry was initially forced upon the HEIC because their enemies were doing so. However, it actually made perfect sense. The local Indian recruits did not suffer as badly from sickness as the European recruits did and they were already acclimatised to the hot weather. From the Company's point of view, they were also cheaper to employ and there was no shortage of good recruits.

The first drilled sepoy units were formed in the Madras presidency, under Major Stringer Lawrence, who was essentially the architect of the new HEIC army. Indian recruits were required to be 5'7" tall and needed to meet the standard requirements for European soldiers in terms of health, with agricultural labourers being preferred as they were considered hardier than city folk. The Madras presidency was a significant wheat growing area, which resulted in no shortage of recruits who met the height and health requirements. However, in Bombay and Bengal, where rice was the staple diet, many men did not meet the height requirement, forcing the army to take whatever men they could. These were rarely Bengalis with most coming from Behar, Oudh, Rohilkand, the Punjab, and even Afghanistan. The Bombay

---

4   Robert Johnson, 'True to their salt: Mechanisms for recruiting and managing military labour in the army of the East India Company during the Carnatic Wars in India', in Erik-Jan Zürcher (ed), *Fighting for a Living: A Comparative Study of Military Labour 1500-2000* (Amsterdam: Amsterdam University Press, 2013), p.276.
5   Stuart Reid, *Armies of the East India Company* (London: Osprey, 2009), p.42.

Army was equally dependant on northerners coming from Rajputana, Oudh and Behar, as they had only a small land holding in this trading post to draw from and, again, many did not meet the minimum requirements.

Recruits were taken from across the Indian caste system, with men being employed who might be regarded as 'untouchables' in other walks of life. This seems to have been the case except in the Bengal Army, where only the highest castes were admitted and constant care was taken to avoid any breach of caste restrictions. The overruling of the caste system was just one method used to exaggerate a 'special status' held by Sepoys. They were allowed to eat certain foods that perhaps only those higher on the social ladder might be allowed, were considered members of a warrior caste by their association with the army, and were dressed in a smart uniform, all of which enhanced the sepoys' self-esteem. Given that most of the men were not locally recruited, they already felt separate from the rest of society, with their HEIC regiment becoming their new home. All religions were recruited and served alongside each other with all religious practices tolerated by the Company. In fact, the European officers forbade Christian missionaries to go among the men during this time for fear that they might cause unrest. One officer was keen to allow religious freedom, as the Sepoys 'fidelity and affections we have hitherto secured by an unremitted attention not to offend their religious scruples and superstitions'.[6]

When a Sepoy joined the new companies, or battalions, he was obliged to swear an oath of allegiance to the HEIC. A copy of the oath taken in 1766 survives and begins:

> I … do swear to serve the Honourable Company faithfully and truly against all their enemies while I continue to receive their pay and eat their salt. I swear to obey all the orders I receive from my commanders and officers, never to forsake my post, abandon my colours or turn my back to my enemies…[7]

This oath was taken in front of the rest of the troops and was seen as a solemn undertaking by the soldiers, who also swore not to betray their comrades. This further bound the sepoy to the HEIC.

Sepoys were allowed to bring their families into camp. This was often not just a wife and children but also a grandparent or cousins. Unlike in Europe, where wives and family were tolerated but not encouraged, there seems to have been no reluctance to allow sepoys to bring their families to camp where they could be cared for and fed. Indeed, in 1762, when sepoy troops were embarked for Manila, arrangements were made to pay the men in advance so that their family could be provided for in their absence. A sepoy's pay was six rupees a month, worth around 12 shillings, which was about average for soldiers serving with Mughal lords in India at the time. NCOs, such as havildars (sergeants) and naiks (corporals), were paid more, with havildars, for example, being paid eight rupees a month. What was different about Company pay was that it was regularly issued and could be

---

6 Johnson, 'True to their salt', p.275.
7 Mason, *A Matter of Honour*, p.66.

relied upon. The problem with serving Indian lords was that pay was often in arrears and, if one's lord was defeated in battle, all debts would not be paid and one's employment would be effectively ended. In addition, Indian lords tended to only employ armies during the campaigning season, meaning that men were often only employed for eight months of the year, whilst a sepoy received pay all year round.[8]

From his wage the sepoy could expect to have deducted half a rupee a month, or six rupees a year, for clothing. The uniform cost 4.5 rupees, leaving a surplus of 1.5 rupees per private sepoy. This extra cash was awarded to the European officers of the battalion and amounted to about 2,000 rupees each for the three captains and 300 each for the subalterns. This was considered an extra allowance for the European officers who commanded sepoy regiments as it was felt that: 'officers appointed for this duty should have some extraordinary allowance for their trouble'.[9] In addition, the sepoy would also be deducted one fanam (one-twelfth of a Rupee) each month which went into a fund to provide for the families of sepoys killed or disabled in action. Sepoys with the cash to do so, could purchase promotions if they became vacant. These were not very expensive, with an NCO's position costing about a week's wages. However, candidates were generally judged on merit and length of service rather than solely on the ability to pay.

The recruitment and training of the sepoy battalions was in many ways similar to that of soldiers in Britain. Shared isolation, regular pay, continuous employment, and the camaraderie of the ranks transformed what could have been an alienating experience into a positive one and gave the Sepoys an esprit de corps not often found in the soldiers of the Moghul armies or the other European sepoy regiments. The inclusion of their families in the regimental camp and the allowances made to support them in the event of the sepoy's death or injury further strengthened the soldiers' bond with the regiment, with many viewing the HEIC as their 'Nizam' and the regiment as their home.

Organisation

HEIC European Regiments were organised in the same way as regular British regiments, with ten companies, one of which was designated as a grenadier company. However, in practice this was purely aspirational, as these battalions rarely numbered more than 500 men. In 1757, the Bengal European Regiment numbered only 250 men although it did reach 1,000 men in 1760, when it took in drafts of French, Dutch, and German prisoners who obtained their freedom by serving the HEIC. The European regiments do not seem to have served as full battalions, and were instead sent out as individual companies, with two companies of the Bombay Regiment sent to assist Lawrence in 1752, for example, or in 1756 when two further companies were sent to Bengal.

---

8   Mason, *A Matter of Honour*, p.65.
9   Mason, *A Matter of Honour*, p.64.

JOHN COMPANY: SERVICE IN INDIA

In 1755, regulations for the sepoy companies required each to consist of one subadar (captain), four jamadars (lieutenants), eight havildars (sergeants), eight naiks (corporals) and one hundred private soldiers. In 1758, the independent companies were formed into two battalions and further battalions were ordered to be raised, so that by the end of 1759 there were five battalions in total and by 1765 there were 10.[10]

Each battalion consisted of nine companies each of 120 men, with one company being designated as a Grenadier company. Listed alongside the private soldiers are 'Tom Toms' or drummers, and trumpeters. Attached to each sepoy regiment were two European commissioned officers and three European sergeant majors, who were there to supervise the Indian officers and NCOs and to: 'make them keep up a good command amongst the Sepoys and support them well in it'.[11] Also shown on the returns was a commandant, who was essentially a native Indian who worked as the agent for the regiment, procuring uniforms, transport, food and so on. He also worked as something of a cultural advisor to the European officers, advising them on matters of religion or the caste system as it affected the men.

The Company refused to pay for a cavalry arm during peacetime, as a cavalry trooper cost twice as much to maintain as an infantryman. Instead they hired Indian mercenaries when war broke out to perform this role.

Elements of the Royal Artillery arrived in India with the first regulars in 1756, and are listed as consisting of three companies. The officers shown as part of the expedition include one major, three captains, two captain lieutenants, three first lieutenants, three second lieutenants and ten lieutenant fireworkers. It is not clear exactly how many mattrosses were in the expedition.[12]

British cannon were brought from England but the carriages were made in India, with the emphasis on them being sturdy and above all light. This was probably to do with the width of the artillery limbers and carriages having to match the ruts in the roads in India, much as they had to do in Europe, and since this distance was not known it was thought best to manufacture the carriages in country. The manufacture of the barrels, along with the mix of powder and the types of shells used were kept a closely guarded secret from their Indian allies, with one order stating: 'no foreigner…no Indian, black or person of a mixt breed nor any Roman Catholic' [to be] allowed in the

Sepoy officer, 1757. Watercolour by Charles Lyall. (Anne S.K. Brown Collection)

---

10 Mason, *A Matter of Honour*, p.62.
11 Johnson, 'True to their salt', p.280.
12 Whitworth, *Gunner at Large*, p.72.

Laboratory room where the powder was made'.[13] This was because the British artillery was substantially better than the artillery used in India at the time, and much better served, and the HEIC did not want its enemies discovering their secrets.

Uniform

In theory, HEIC European Regiments wore uniforms similar to the regular army. The Bombay European Regiment wore a red coat lined green with green cuffs and lapels until 1768 when the facings changed to blue. The Madras and Bombay troops appear to have worn red coats lined buff, with buff lapels and cuffs. They also had buff waistcoat and breeches with all lace being white. The regular British regiments arriving in India were not issued any specific uniform to better cope with the climate and, in theory, would have appeared as they did in Europe.

In practice, however, clearly the soldiers would have made changes to their uniform to suit the hot climate they now found themselves in. Unfortunately, very little can be said with any amount of certainty about the uniforms worn in India during this early period. Stringer Lawrence gave orders in 1748 that each captain should be responsible for clothing his company in: 'a pattern coat and hat, or cap, suitable to the climate'. The captain was to reclaim this money through stoppages on the men's wages as happened in Europe. Doubtless the red woollen coat retained cuffs and lapels but perhaps lacked lining and may well have been cut short. The hat was very likely worn with the brim turned down as was sometimes worn in Europe to keep the sun off. An illustration of an artillery matross from the time shows him wearing a 'solar topee', a broad brimmed hat which consisted of a rattan framework over which was stretched cotton or linen. A list of equipment issued to troops at Trichinopoly in 1755 included locally made soft leather 'Pariar' shoes, coarse shirts, coarse stockings, and gingham breeches and waistcoats. At this time, gingham was blue and white stripped and was similar to that issued to men working on-board ship as marines. This would make sense as it is unlikely that the men would wear waistcoats of red wool, as were worn in Europe, and the use of gingham material for the waistcoat and trousers would certainly be more suited to the climate. The fact that trousers such as this were already being worn by troops assigned on board ships shows that it was already common practice and something the men may have had made during their journey to India or soon after arriving. As regards equipment, the European battalions would have carried leatherwork similar to that issued to the regulars.[14]

Officers would have appeared on dress parade exactly as regular officers would have in Europe, with a crimson sash and gorget to denote rank. When on campaign they no doubt put the dress coat away and wore something much more practical as most officers did in other theatres. Listed amongst the possessions of Captain Robert Bannatyne, who was killed at Conjeveram

---

13 Mason, *A Matter of Honour*, p.30.
14 Summary from Reid, *Armies of the East India Company*.

in 1759, are 'five pairs of old gingham breeches' as well as two old regimental coats and his dress embroidered one.[15] This suggests the officers wore gingham trousers just as the men did, and wore less formal dress coats, saving their best for parade.

The sepoys initially had no uniform to speak of. This would not be unusual as most troops employed by the Company up until then had received no issued uniform or equipment. Stringer Lawrence's new sepoy companies were drilled in the use of the flintlock musket and there is frequent mention of them using their bayonets, so it is safe to assume that their equipment matched that of the regular European regiments. In April 1756 there is an order from the President of Fort St George acquainting the board with his success in persuading the sepoys to wear 'an uniform of Europe Cloth' as this 'would serve at once to give them a more martial appearance and take off a considerable quantity of woollen goods'.[16] This is typical of the Company as it not only solved the problem of providing uniform but it also shifted some wool which was clearly not popular amongst the shoppers in India. Sepoys in Bombay were not issued red coats until 1760.

The sepoys wore short, waist length red coats, with no collar or lapels, with a white shirt. White shorts were worn, reaching to mid-thigh, which had a coloured vandyke edging. A sash was tied around the waist, which was white although it may have been the colour of the facings for NCOs. Legs were bare, as were the soldiers' feet, although occasionally sandals are shown. A white turban was worn which, on the surviving contemporary prints of Bombay Sepoys, has a feather inserted in it. More elaborate turbans were adopted by the early 1770's but for the bulk of the war in India the Sepoy turban was rather plain.

The original direction was that all the sepoy regiments should have the same facing colour. However, this appears not to have been instigated, as the seven battalions raised by the Madras presidency are listed in September 1759 as wearing: 1st blue, 2nd yellow, 3rd green, 4th black, 5th red with the 6th initially wearing yellow and the 7th green, both faced red.[17] A directive in 1760 instructed all of the sepoy regiments to adopt red coats with blue facings, but the European officers resisted this, stating this would damage regimental pride if all were forced to look the same. It appears that this argument may have won out, as William Hickey, when he was bound for India in 1768 to take up a position in the HEIC, was advised to take with him a few yards of cloth of different colours so that he might make up the facings on his jacket to suit the regiment to which he was to be attached.[18] The sepoy battalions carried one Regimental Colour, which was the colour of the facings, along with the flag of the HEIC presidency.

---

15 Reid, *Armies of the East India Company*, p.42.
16 Johnson, 'True to their salt', p.269.
17 Reid, *Armies of the East India Company*, p.20.
18 Patrick Cadell, 'Uniforms of the Madras Army', *Journal of the Society for Army Historical Research*, Vol.27, No. 112 (Winter 1949), p.171.

Daily Life

The daily life of a soldier in India could actually be more comfortable than his life in Europe. Even the poorest of private soldiers could afford to engage servants or pay to have his laundry done or other daily chores. When on the march, the men had their servants carry their packs and no water bottles were necessary as young boys acted as water carriers for the army, going along the lines filling cups from water skins and handing them to the men as required. Hence, the soldiers marched with just their weapons and their cartridge boxes and bayonets, which was just as well in the sweltering heat.

The men were allowed a daily issue of 1½ pounds of beef or mutton, 1½ pounds of rice or 1 pound of biscuit, two-fifths of a pint of arrack, a measure of salt, and firewood to cook with.[19] Substituting rice for bread was not popular with the men but logistically it was much easier to boil rice than it was to set up ovens, grind flour and bake bread, which slowed up European armies considerably. Arrack is a strong alcoholic drink made from the fermented sap of coconut flowers or sugarcane and it became the standard drink for British soldiers deployed to India during this period. It was cheap and easily obtained by the men, but its very high alcohol content did not always suit new arrivals used to beer. For example, Gunner James Woods recorded in 1755 that: 'We are having to send a great many of our men every day to the hospital occasioned by their drinking new arrack.'[20]

Initially, soldiers with the HEIC had been contracted only to serve as coastal garrisons, and when the army began to be used as a field army in the interior, the men rightly objected, seeing this as a breach of contract. This resulted in the HEIC making an extra payment to officers and men to cover additional expenses incurred by campaigning on the interior, including the cost of transport, hire of tents, and the purchase of all kinds of personal supplies which they would not have otherwise have needed. This compensation was known as the 'batta' or field service allowance. This payment was extended to include all regular troops who arrived in India, with Woods recording being paid his in January, 1756: 'Received the Batta allowed by the Honourable E.I. Company for the quarters etc from 30 November 1755 to this day, which was to each Captain and captain / Lieutenant for a month of 31 days 100 rupees'[21] In 1766 the European officers in the Bengal Army threatened to resign en masse when Robert Clive deprived them of 'Batta' payments, which by that time supplemented their wages by up to 50 percent.

Medical Support

The biggest threat to European soldiers came from illnesses such as cholera, typhoid and smallpox, as well the natural hazards of heat, snakebites, and

---

19 G.J. Bryant, 'British Logistics and the Conduct of the Carnatic Wars (1746–1783)', *War in History*, Vol. 11, No. 3 (July 2004), p.283.
20 Whitworth (ed.), *Gunner at Large*, p.96.
21 Whitworth (ed.), *Gunner at Large*, p.98.

the constant plague of flies and mosquitoes and the dangers they posed. European soldiers fell ill and died in their droves upon arrival in India, which is not surprising given the conditions in some of the garrison posts. One eyewitness recorded that Madras was:

> [B]uilt upon a low, flat and sandy beach, and surrounded almost entirely by stagnant swamps, or ponds of stagnant water, which are not only a receptacle for every sort of corruption and filth, but have their edges, as well as the beach on the other side, covered at all hours of the day with the natives, in the act of relieving nature from their burdens, to take advantage of the water for washing afterwards, which is their invariable custom. What a source of putrid exhalations under a vertical sun![22]

A military hospital existed in Madras as early as 1664, but it was never enlarged, so that by 1756 the same building was still being used even though by this time it was clearly inadequate. A larger, more suitable hospital was not built until 1771 and it appears that the Presidencies of Bengal and Bombay were equally poorly served. Hospitals and regimental surgeons had to rely on shipments of medicine chests from Europe for many of their medical supplies. These supplies were hard enough to come by during times of peace, but during war the enemy's capture of merchant and military shipping destined for India made the situation worse. Add to this the Indian tactic of disrupting British supply lines, and the number of sieges the British troops were involved in, and it becomes clear why it was that some medical necessities were so scarce. Even when they did arrive, they were often still not of much use, as one surgeon recorded his medicines: 'much damaged on account of the careless and injudicious Package of them'.[23] European surgeons had no idea how to treat the various diseases which afflicted those troops newly arrived from Europe, resulting in the death of most. Contemporary diarists, such as Gunner Woods who served in India, rarely passed a week without recording the death or serious illness of a comrade. Of the 22 officers of the Royal Artillery that went to India in 1755, only two returned.

Although European troops continued to be treated, often ineffectually, by European surgeons, the sepoy troops did not put much faith in European medicine. They preferred to use 'Bazaar Medicines' or herbal remedies provided by village doctors. The sepoy preferment for native doctors led to the appointment of a 'Doctor' to each sepoy battalion in 1765, who was to have the pay of a Havildar. How much the European surgeons used these 'Bazaar Medicines' is unclear, but with European medicines in such short supply it seems very likely that they did.

In common with military medical provision in Europe, field hospitals either did not exist or were poorly provided for. Following the British victory at Wandiwash, Colonel Eyre Coote wrote:

---

22 Pratik Chakrabarti, '"Neither of meate nor drinke, but what the Doctor alloweth": Medicine amidst War and Commerce in Eighteenth-Century Madras', *Bulletin of the History of Medicine*, Spring 2006, pp.1–38.
23 Chakrabarti, '"Neither of meate nor drinke, but what the Doctor alloweth"', p.5.

> Such a multitude of poor objects, and not in my power to give them the least assistance for want of every one necessary requisite for an hospital…If it is possible to send surgeons and proper people from Madras to attend the wounded here who are very numerous, you may by that means save the lives of many gallant men, several of whom have not been dressed since the day of action.[24]

There was little medical help available for the European troops, and even less for the sepoys, who were generally treated only after the Europeans had been seen. For example, after the Battle of Changamah in 1767, Joseph Smith wrote: 'I wish on these occasions of service the hospital was amply provided with surgeons. We could then afford some succour to the poor and brave Sepoy who is wounded and loses a limb in the service. It would be a great encouragement to them to do their duty with spirit'.[25]

It seems that the wounded had to rely on care by their comrades and their servants, with the few regimental surgeons badly overstretched. Although not explicitly mentioned, local Indian healers from the supply train were no doubt employed to tend to the sepoys, brought off the field by their comrades.

Logistics and Supply

The southeast or Carnatic region of India, where much of the conflict took place during this period, had been settled for centuries. In the eighteenth century it was well populated and richly cultivated, and had a system of roads described by some as better than those in Europe. Although there were no navigable waterways, HEIC armies could also be supplied by ship at various locations along the coast. This made wagon trains much easier to move and made supplies much easier to come by.

In the First Carnatic War, the conflict was restricted to British and French forces, with the Indian Nawabs generally remaining neutral. This allowed both sides to buy food and transport directly from the Indian towns and villages as they moved around. During most Indian conflicts, armies passing through an area would raid local villages and steal crops as they came across them. As a result, the peasants would bury the food and run off as soon as they heard an army was nearby. The HEIC took a different approach, paying a fair price for food at local villages as the army progressed. This very civilised approach to war was actually driven by practicalities. In the first instance, the HEIC did not want to upset the rulers of the area its troops were passing through by raiding or stealing crops. Also, the HEIC armies lacked cavalry and so could not forage widely for food as other Indian armies could. Equally, the Company's administrators were not particularly enamoured with the idea of burning and looting lands which they hoped, at the end of the conflict, to either take charge of or begin trading with. A happy populace with all its fields and houses intact will be able to pay taxes or start trading much quicker than those whose fields were destroyed. This had the

---

24 Chakrabarti, '"Neither of meate nor drinke, but what the Doctor alloweth"', p.6.
25 Mason, *A Matter of Honour*, p.69.

knock-on effect of building the HEIC reputation for fairness, meaning that many within the civilian population brought goods to them to sell, making supplying the army even less of an issue.

During the Second Carnatic War, the responsibility for supply fell to the much larger Indian armies that the French and British were supporting. Indian armies in this period were supplied by a mobile market that the Nawab encouraged to follow the army. Instead of supplying the men with food, he paid them in cash and they bought what they needed from the merchants and sutlers who followed in their wake. The Nawab then taxed the profits of the merchants by way of a fee as compensation for his labour in organising and policing the bazaar. This often meant that the civilian train following the army was many times that of the fighting men, as it included not only the merchants and sutlers but often the families of the soldiers as well as those desperadoes and thieves hoping to profit from the aftermath of a battle. When one adds to this the soldiers' servants, labourers, and wagon drivers, it made for a prodigious supply train. For example, when Sir Eyre Coote started on a campaign with 6,000 Sepoys his army attracted 15,000 followers, whilst a later Indian led army of 12,000 soldiers had a following of 40,000 people.[26]

However, this mobile bazaar was not under martial law, nor was it contracted in any way, and as a result it could melt away if the going got tough. Equally, it was very vulnerable to attack by raiding enemy forces and could quickly disperse if the merchants and sutlers within it felt they had more to lose than to gain by staying with the army. Even when travelling with an Indian army employing such a huge mobile bazaar, the HEIC continued to issue food to its own men. This was partly driven by the merchants' reluctance to sell beef to the HEIC troops, as a result of which the HEIC troops usually drove a herd of cattle with them. The troops continued to use the bazaar for luxury food items or for alcohol, with the merchants happy to extend credit to the Europeans and the sepoys, as they knew the HEIC would pay its troops if the campaign was a success or not.

The only area of logistics that was troublesome for all armies fighting in India during the eighteenth century was the lack of bullocks to pull the huge number of carts and guns that the army brought with it. Contemporary reports often bemoan the fact that bullocks were not to be had for any amount of money and the lack of them restricted the movements of the army. Captain Munro of the HEIC wrote that: 'Bullocks, money and faithful spies are the sinews of war in this country'.[27]

The Experience of War

In many ways the experience of war in India was very similar to that in Europe. The British troops deployed in three ranks, practised the same fire discipline, and moved and manoeuvred on the battlefield in much the same

---

26 Summary from Bryant, 'British Logistics and the Conduct of the Carnatic Wars'.
27 Bryant, 'British Logistics and the Conduct of the Carnatic Wars', p.280.

way. What was very different was the scale of the battles they fought, often involving small numbers of well-trained HEIC or British troops facing many times their number of enemy forces. For example, at Arcot in 1751, Robert Clive defeated a Franco-Indian force of 11,000 men with 200 European infantry, 300 Sepoys and three guns, whilst at Plassey, Clive again defeated an army of over 35,000 men with fewer than 3,000 Europeans and Sepoys, admittedly helped by the defection of much of his opponent's army.

Indian armies of this period invested heavily in their cavalry, as serving with the infantry was considered to be for peasants. As a result there were generally three types of cavalry on the battlefield; Siladars, or minor nobles, who brought their own men and equipment; Ekadars, or 'holders of one', who were often mercenary cavalry each of whom brought his own horse and armour; lastly the Pendharis, or Pindarris, who made up the light horse. Both the Siladars and the Ekadars invested heavily in their horses, armour and equipment and whilst they did not mind facing enemy cavalry, they were loath to ride into the fire of disciplined infantry lines or to face the three ranks of bayonets that awaited them if they did manage to close. Equally, the Pindarris were little more than bandits, useful for scouting and raiding enemy supply lines but were just as unwilling to charge steady lines of disciplined troops. Whilst some effort was made by the French and Dutch to train sepoy troops, often the majority of the infantry facing HEIC armies were badly trained and equipped, and were either mercenary soldiers with no loyalty to the cause beyond the money they were being paid, or pressed men from the lands owned by the Indian lord they served. Not surprisingly, they quickly faltered and fled under fire. One area where the Indian forces always seemed to be well supplied was in cannon, often deploying large numbers of guns of very heavy calibre. For example, Mir Kasem deployed 133 guns against the British 30 guns at Buxar in 1764. However, Indian artillery was very often poorly served and was usually very heavy and not manoeuvrable once deployed. Indian powder was not as good as that used by the British, whilst the guns themselves were not well designed or made, making them unreliable in battle. As a result, the artillery arm of the Indian armies was more for show than for effect.

The HEIC was successful in its campaigns in India because it was wealthy and well-administered. The HEIC administered the provinces under its control much more efficiently than the local powers, whilst its trade provided it with an additional, reliable, source of income. Therefore, they could raise and pay for armies much more efficiently than the local rulers and keep them in the field for longer. Since the HEIC armies were maintained all year round, and not disbanded at the end of every campaigning season, training and discipline could be maintained whilst a sense of pride and belonging developed in the sepoy regiments in particular. This improved their fighting ability, making them more than a match for the mercenaries or pressed men in the Maratha armies. HEIC artillery was better made and served than the Indian guns, albeit that the latter were usually present in larger numbers and in larger calibres than the British. They only area the HEIC army was weak was in cavalry, which had as much to do with a reluctance to part with cash as anything else. That said, there was usually enough mercenary cavalry for hire at the beginning of every campaign to make up the shortfall. It is important to stress that the HEIC could not have succeeded in India without the sepoy regiments. Some historians, especially those writing before the Second World War, promote a view that the sepoys only performed well when led by British officers, or that the Europeans regiments bore the brunt of all the fighting, neither of which views stand up to scrutiny. The Indian troops were hardy, resilient and brave and the emerging British Empire could not have been built without them.

18

Colonial Regiments in the Rest of the Empire

Lord Barrington, then Secretary of War, wrote to the Prime Minister in 1759 to discuss recruits for the overseas posts then garrisoned by British troops. As well as the armies deployed in India and America, he mentioned the troops deployed in Germany and in the garrisons of Minorca and Gibraltar. He then went on to list the other overseas postings to which British soldiers had been sent, which included garrisons in Guadeloupe, Jamaica, and Antigua, St Augustine and Grenada, and a garrison in Senegal, apparently much reduced through sickness.[1] Troops would soon be dispatched to Cuba, when the Spanish entered the war on the side of the French, and to take French-held Martinique. It is beyond the scope of this book to discuss all of these expeditions and overseas garrisons, other than to talk in general terms about them as they relate to the British army sent to attack or garrison them.

These overseas postings were not popular amongst British soldiers for two main reasons. Firstly, there was no limit to how long a regiment might be away from home. It was cheaper for the Government to simply keep a unit in one location and occasionally send out new recruits to keep it up to strength than it was to bring entire regiments back and send new ones out. For this reason, garrisons in the colonies often felt they had been forgotten by the Government, and for good reason. The 38th Foot was sent to the Caribbean in 1716, for example, and did not return home to England until 1765! In July 1730, the War Office finally drew up a system of rotation for foreign service, with one of the stated aims being: 'to relieve soldiers of despair of ever returning home'[2]. This was applied straight away, and the following year the 39th Foot was sent to put down a rebellion in Jamaica and was returned to England in March 1732. However, despite its good intentions, the War Office soon began to slip back into its old habits as the years go by and although the intention existed to bring troops home, there does not seem to have been any timescale set for how long regiments could be posted overseas before they had to come home.

---

1 Hayter (ed.), *Eighteenth Century Secretary at War*, p.53.
2 Atkinson, 'The Army under the Early Hanoverians', p.145.

As discussed elsewhere, the second reason for not wanting to go to some of the more exotic overseas postings was the change in climate and the inevitable sickness it brought with it. Death rates amongst British troops in the Caribbean and West Africa were very high and many recruits viewed a posting there as a death sentence, preferring to desert rather than board the ship. For this reason, it became common practice to withhold details of the regiment's destination until all the men were safely aboard. Officers were just as desperate to avoid these postings as their men, and the War Office was inundated with requests for transfers when the Regimental postings were announced. Lord Barrington wrote:

> One Captn. Fish ordered to Guadalupe, has friends who plague me to write to get him some exchange to save him from going, to make him a Major, or get him a Company in another Regiment, or procure him a leave of absence, are, they think, as easy for Ld H as to take a pinch of snuff.[3]

Recruitment

Regiments that were posted overseas were allowed to recruit in Britain to fill their depleted ranks. Officers were dispatched to raise recruits for the garrison in Gibraltar, often being allowed to pay a bounty of £5 to each prospective new recruit as an incentive. Even then, recruiting was slow, with the Garrison Commander complaining in 1737 that he could not get his: 'officers to bestir themselves to obtain recruits'.[4] The War Office directly recruited for those regiments too far away to send back recruiting parties. However, Lord Barrington recognised that as soon as the recruit's posting became known, he declined, preferring to take a post with a regiment based at home or serving in Germany. As a result, he wrote, 'Recruits in general come in slow…I almost despair of getting any more Volunteers for the Regts at Jamaica & Antigua, where 750 men are needed to complete three Regiments'.[5] Indeed, it seems like all of the overseas garrisons were in need of recruits. When Barrington wrote to Newcastle in 1759, he listed 3-400 required for Senegal, 6-700 required for Guadaloupe, on top of the men he needed to send to Germany, America, and India, not to mention: 'The number of Effectives wanting to compleat the Army at home are near 8000 men'.[6]

To supplement the garrisons, soldiers being posted home were often given incentives to remain in the colony instead. When Hayes' and Newton's Regiments were ordered home from Jamaica in 1731, the men were offered £10 each as an incentive to transfer to the Independent Companies that were raised and permanently based there. Grants of land or money were commonly offered to entice troops to remain in the garrison, as even those

---

3   Hayter (ed.), *Eighteenth Century Secretary at War*, p.285.
4   Atkinson, 'The Army under the Early Hanoverians', p.146.
5   Hayter (ed.), *Eighteenth Century Secretary at War*, p.352.
6   Hayter (ed.), *Eighteenth Century Secretary at War*, p.352.

who mustered out of the army would still provide an experienced militia force if required.

Uniform

It will come as no surprise to the reader to learn that troops in overseas garrisons adapted their uniform to suit the climate. However, whilst modifications were made, the basic red wool coat appears to have remained in use. The medical theory at the time was that sweating was good for you, as it brought out impurities, and regimental surgeons actually recommended the troops continue to wear wool rather than switch to linen so they would sweat copiously and hence fend off disease.

However, modifications from parade dress clearly had to be made. Troops leaving for foreign service from 1761 were ordered to have linen linings fitted into their coats. This applied, apparently, even to those going to the Mediterranean, as the 11th Foot left that year for Minorca with brown linen linings fitted. Sometimes, even linen linings were not cool enough and drastic measures had to be taken to make the coat fit for tropical climates. In 1762, Major General Monckton issued orders to the new troops arriving in Barbados which read:

> The Commanding Officers of the Corps will order the linings to be ript out of the mens coats, the lapels taken off and the skirts cut shorter'. He further advised: 'providing the men with something that is thin to make sleeves for their waistcoat, as the troops may be ordered to land in them.[7]

Often those who were already in theatre, or who had served abroad elsewhere, instructed the new arrivals as to how best to adapt their kit. Major Grant of the 42nd Highlanders had been campaigning in America and on Guadeloupe and was amused to see a new battalion come ashore in the Caribbean:

> The 76th… landed in white spatterdashes, gorgets & spontoons and sashes, and trusted their provisions to their servants. We older campaigners, accustomed to backwoods expeditions, took care to equip ourselves with haversacks containing our provisions and were ridiculed by the Gay Gentlemen for so doing, but in two days the note was changed…[8]

It is not possible to say with any certainty exactly how uniforms were modified over the years in each of the overseas posts other than to take the lead from what happened elsewhere. Hats usually had their brims let down to keep the sun off the soldier's faces and necks. Coats were discarded and sleeved waistcoats worn, or the men did not wear a waistcoat and instead wore just their uniform coat with the lining stripped out. Breeches were

---

7   McCulloch, *Sons of the Mountains*, p.271.
8   McCulloch, *Sons of the Mountains*, p.272.

usually discarded in favour looser fitting trousers like those worn on ship, whilst soft leather shoes or local footwear were worn.

Daily Life

Initially, the men found much to wonder at when they arrived at their overseas postings. One soldier on campaign in Cuba wrote: 'We grew familiar with the scorpions, Toads, Santipieds & Tarantulas, or rather spiders as large as my hand, but among the lesser species, the variety was without end'.[9] Gunner Woods was equally amazed by the 'crocodiles and great serpents' he encountered in Madagascar, as much as by the natives, who: 'go mostly naked with nothing but a bandage round their middle and a cloth between their legs and tucked in'.[10]

However, after the initial period of excitement passed, the men soon settled into the monotony of garrison life. One soldier wrote of his time in the West Indies: 'Occasionally mounting guard, attending parade morning and evening, with the injurious and often unnecessary fatigue of a field-day, constitute the whole duty of a soldier in a West India island, even in time of war'.[11]

As a consequence, many turned to drink as the only form of relief. Rum was cheap and easily available in the West Indies and one regimental surgeon blamed its frequent consumption for the subsequent levels of illness and poor discipline amongst the troops. Just as in other theatres, the army often promoted drinking alcohol for 'health reasons'. Spruce beer was given to the men, as it was believed to stave off scurvy, whilst the water was often so bad that the men had to turn to alcohol as the only source of liquid. During the Havana campaign, for example, the soldiers were required to dig trenches and man defences in the heat of the day and on a diet of 'salt pork and rum'. One soldier recorded that the 'bad water brought on disorders that were mortal' and so the men would not drink it. As a result 'you could see the men's tongues hanging out like a mad dogs'. Rum was the only thing the men could drink and it became quite common to find: 'Officers and soldiers drunk every hour of the day'.[12]

The real fear for men posted overseas was of disease, and every overseas posting seemed to take a toll in men much higher than those lost to action. During the campaign to take Cartagena de Indias in modern day Columbia in 1741, for example, the British lost nearly 9,000 men to yellow fever and other diseases. Assuming the new arrivals could survive the first few months in their new homes, they usually adapted to the local conditions, but many still became ill due to the lack of fresh fruit and vegetables at some postings, which weakened the men and brought on scurvy. A couple of examples will suffice to illustrate this point.

---

9   McCulloch, *Sons of the Mountains*, p.280.
10 Whitworth (ed.), *Gunner at Large*, p.85.
11 Kopperman, 'The British High Command and Soldiers Wives in America', p.23.
12 McCulloch, *Sons of the Mountains*, p.279.

When the 35th Foot relieved the 31st at Pensacola they were in 'perfect health and spirits'. But within less than six weeks the men were afflicted with 'Fluxes, Yellow Fevers, black vomits and coups de soleil' so that 'a Captain, Lieutenant, Surgeon, two Volunteers, five officers wives out of six, ninety five men and above forty women and children were swept away and the rest left in a lanquid and dispirited state'.[13] More serious still was the case of the Highland Battalions sent to take part in the campaign in Cuba. Of the 2,075 all ranks that were mustered for the campaign, 1,245 would die of malaria and yellow fever, whilst only 480 men returned fit for duty, the rest being ill when they arrived back in America. This did little to lessen the reputation of a posting to an overseas colony as a death sentence for soldiers.

The Experience of Battle

Clearly, whilst some colonial battles played out along European lines, other campaigns were very different in terms of the forces deployed against the British and the tactics used. After taking the city of Manila in the Philippines in 1762, British forces set about trying to subdue the surrounding land, which was easier said than done. Many Filipinos fought a guerrilla war against the British with few firearms and often with only bows and arrows. In one attack, a British officer wrote: 'Although armed chiefly with bows, arrows and lances, they advanced up to the very muzzles of our pieces, repeated their assaults and died like wild beasts, gnawing on the bayonets'.[14] However, on the whole the majority of forces encountered during these expeditions were French or Spanish regular troops supported by locally raised militias, and fought in the European manner. During the campaign against Havana in 1762, for example, a British force of infantry was advancing across open country when 700 Spanish cavalry suddenly surprised and attacked them. Captain David Dundas recorded that the infantry:

> [W]ith the greatest steadiness and presence of mind, had faced about, wheeled forward, were in 2 lines, and in readiness to give them a fire of 500 light infantry at a distance of 60 yards. This checked their career, they ceased to advance, the troops reloaded, recommenced a fire and the enemy went back as fast as they came.[15]

He went on to say that this was lucky, as the light infantry 'had left their bayonets on board ship; accustomed only to act in the woods, they never dreamt of such an adventure on open ground'.

---

13 Hayter (ed.), *Eighteenth Century Secretary at War*, p.355.
14 Nicholas Tracey, *Manila Ransomed* (Liverpool: Liverpool University Press, 1995), p.47.
15 McCulloch, *Sons of the Mountains*, p.278.

19

Leaving the Army

Although the term of enlistment in the eighteenth-century British Army was technically for life, not many soldiers could expect to serve out their time. The constant raising and then reducing of regiments with the coming and ending of war meant that for most soldiers their military life could come to an abrupt end when their regiment was reduced in size, or even disbanded altogether.

When an infantry soldier mustered out, he was entitled to fourteen days subsistence pay to get him home. In addition, he was given three shillings for his sword and bayonet. Mounted troops were entitled to six days pay if they retained their horse and saddle or twelve days pay if they did not.[1] The 23rd Foot, for example, was reduced by two companies in November 1748 and the discharged men 'paid 14 days subsistence, with the usual allowance of 3 s for their sword'.[2]

Those whose regiments were reduced whilst overseas were encouraged to either join the locally-raised forces or to settle in the colony to provide an experienced local militia. Many Scots soldiers took this option at the end of the French and Indian War in America and they were enthusiastically supported in this by the British Government, who were keen not to have unemployed soldiers wandering around in England. In a letter to the Duke of Newcastle dated September 1760, the Secretary of War wondered:

> [W]hether as many soldiers as possible should not be disbanded there, if a general peace be concluded before they are removed from that part of the world. The reason is this. In time of peace reduced soldiers are a burthen to the mother country, because for one that takes to industry at home, ten takes to evil courses.[3]

Soldiers who left the army fit and well were expected to go on to find gainful employment elsewhere, and neither the regiment nor the War Office felt any responsibility toward them. Some went on to work as labourers or returned

---

1   Cormack, 'These Meritorious Objects of the Royal Bounty', p.77.
2   A.D.L. Cary (ed), *Regimental Records of the Royal Welch Fusiliers* (Uckfield: Naval and Military Press, 2015), p.109.
3   Hayter (ed.), *Eighteenth Century Secretary at War*, p.58.

to their trade, if they had one, whilst others found alternative civilian employment. The Mutiny Act of 1713 permitted retired soldiers to take up a trade within the county in which the soldier had been born and protected the man for three years from arrest for debt or the confiscation of his stock in trade.[4]

However, just as many re-enlisted in other regiments, as a certain level of recruitment was always required simply to replace natural wastage within the regiments retained on the establishment. Hence, soldiers who wished to continue serving the colours could always find ways of doing so, either in the regular army, the East India Company, or other overseas forces.

When a regiment was reduced, the best and most experienced soldiers were often retained by the Colonel to provide a cadre of troops who could then train new recruits when the regiment was inevitably increased in size when war broke out. As a result of this, it was possible for soldiers to spend most of their lives in the service, as Colonel Bagshawe noted with some incredulity about some men in his regiment: 'there is in this regiment, and in the same company, a Captain, Lieutenant, a serjeant and a drummer whose ages put together exceed 340 and who have been more than 200 years in the service'.[5] However, soldiers could not remain with the regiment indefinitely, and at some point they would have to be mustered out.

Obtaining a Pension

To qualify for a pension, the soldier would first of all have to be recommended to the Board at Chelsea by his regiment. For this to happen, the soldier would have to meet a number of criteria.

First of all, he would have to have been invalided during service to the extent that he could no longer serve in his capacity as a soldier. For example, there were those who had been injured in battle or who had lost limbs through accidents, and this rule applied regardless of the applicant's length of service. For example, Trooper Robert Murray of Ligonier's Horse had served less than a year when he was disabled at the Battle of Dettingen, whilst Thomas Sudds blew his hand off cleaning his firelock after only six months service and was pensioned in July 1735.[6] Some soldiers, however, had ailments that were caused by the hardships of campaigning over many years that were still considered severe enough for them to be invalided out of the service. The 93rd Foot discharged a '63 year old soldier named John Bowland, discharged for consumption', along with Matthew Wheatley, aged 60, who was 'infirm and Unable to learn his exercise'. Other, younger, men were discharged for being lame, having 'obstinate and Scorbutick ulcers' or, in the case of Private Keith Carr, discharged for being 'very infirm & much troubled with worms'. Privates William Grace was discharged as he suffered epileptic fits, whilst

---

4 Cormack, 'These Meritorious Objects of the Royal Bounty', p.145.
5 Guy (ed.), *Colonel Samuel Bagshawe*, p.37.
6 Cormack, 'These Meritorious Objects of the Royal Bounty', pp.85-86.

Private John Knowlan, aged 50, was described, apparently by someone with a sense of humour, as being afflicted by 'Piles of many years standing'.⁷

The second means of qualifying for a pension was to have completed 20 years' service. This rule had been first set out by the War Office in 1685 and stated that those: 'disabled by wounds in flight or other accidents', or 'as having served the Crown 20 years … [and] are become unfit ffor service' were duly qualified'.⁸ However, by 1738 the pressures placed on the hospital prompted the Commissioners at Chelsea to change this requirement, stating:

> The Commissioners … having observed that many Invalid soldiers make pretentions to the Pension on the merit of twenty years service in the Army although not disabled thereby, 'Tis their Opinion that no persons serving in Great Britain or Ireland are properly entitled to the said Pensions Except such as are by age or wounds or by Distempers contracted in the Service become disabled from doing Duty.⁹

In other words, it was no longer enough simply to have served 20 years but the soldier also had to have a disability. This resulted in some soldiers serving well beyond their time. Trumpeter John Wood of the 4th Regiment of Horse celebrated his 80th birthday in post whilst Private George Murray of the 6th Foot served 55 years before receiving his pension at the age of 79.¹⁰ To offset this, regimental recommendations began to use terms such as 'unfit and unable to march', 'incapable of his duty' or sometimes simply 'worn out' to describe men who were now too frail to continue soldiering but had no obvious injury. For example, in 1762 Private Spicer Harris was commended to Chelsea as he was 'quite worn out in the service'.¹¹

The final criterion for a regimental recommendation was that the soldier should have an exemplary disciplinary record. There are a number of courts martial cases recorded for the 1st Foot Guards were clemency was requested for the defendant based on their previous good conduct, apparently in the knowledge that a conviction might negate any chance of their obtaining a pension. For example, Lambert Scriven was convicted of missing guard duty and having dirty kit for which he should have received 200 lashes, but he was successfully reprieved as he had been: '18 years in the regiment and never to a court martial before'. John Bellgrave received a similar plea for mercy after being convicted of missing a Field Day 'in regard he has an extraordinary good character having never been confined since he was in the Regiment'. This seems to be borne out by the register in Chelsea, as none of the men admitted bore the scars of flogging or suffered disabilities as a result of such harsh discipline.¹²

---

7 Guy (ed.), *Colonel Samuel Bagshawe*, p.202.
8 Cormack, 'These Meritorious Objects of the Royal Bounty', p.104.
9 Cormack, 'These Meritorious Objects of the Royal Bounty', p.105.
10 Cormack, 'These Meritorious Objects of the Royal Bounty', p.112
11 Guy (ed.), *Colonel Samuel Bagshawe*, p.202.
12 All from Cormack, 'These Meritorious Objects of the Royal Bounty', p.82.

If he met all of the above criteria, the soldier would be given a recommendation for a pension from his regiment that would not only list the soldiers name, regiment, rank and detail of his service, but which also included a description of the soldier himself, to avoid fraud. Having been recommended, the soldier would now have to make his way to London to make his claim before the admissions board of the Chelsea Hospital. From 1726 onward, those awaiting a board would be housed at the expense of the War Office in villages on the outskirts of London. Registering the men for this accommodation allowed the War Office to assess when enough men had gathered to make it worthwhile for a board to sit.

Once called, the board would look at each applicant's regimental referral and also have him examined by a surgeon from the Hospital. It was only if this surgeon confirmed that the soldier was disabled, as detailed in his referral, would his pension be granted. Indeed, not all of those referred by their regiments passed muster. For example, in 1741 Horse Grenadier Bates Howard, was recommended for a pension as he suffered from 'colds' due to sleeping out when guarding horses put out to the new grass, but he was ordered to return to his troop.[13] Thomas Bateman was discharged from Frazer's Marines with a broken collar bone after 12 years' service in that regiment and the Foot Guards, but was returned to his regiment as unqualified having recovered from his injury. Equally, in 1744 John Ainsworth's lameness was found unconvincing and he was sent back to Cholmondeley's Foot.[14]

However, most recommendations were justified and approved by the board. Indeed, from 1713 to 1755 only 1,301 applications were rejected out of the 25,026 regimental recommendations.[15]

Having been granted his pension of 5d a day, things were still not straightforward for our retiring soldier. Pension payments were made in arrears on 25 December and again on 25 June. In theory, the longest a soldier would have to wait to collect his first payment was six months, but in fact these payments were often delayed. In the 37 years between 1719 and 1755 inclusive, pensioners had to wait 12 months between payments on 32 occasions with only 10 occasions when the wait was for six months.[16] This meant that a soldier might have to wait up to 17 months to obtain his first payment. As a result, pensioners had to borrow money to tide them over and when their payment was eventually made, they would usually have to use all of it to pay off their outstanding bills. This meant that pensioners were almost always in debt. It was not until 1754 that the Duke of Cumberland was able to force the treasury to begin to pay pensions six months in advance, rather than in arrears, which went some way to improving their lot.

In order to collect his pension, the soldier had to present himself in person at the appropriate office in Whitehall, as no system existed to send small amounts of money to individuals around the country. This was often impractical, as soldiers would have to travel from all over the Britain, as well

---

13   Cormack, 'These Meritorious Objects of the Royal Bounty', p.41.
14   Cormack, 'These Meritorious Objects of the Royal Bounty', p.88.
15   Cormack, 'These Meritorious Objects of the Royal Bounty', p.88.
16   Cormack, 'These Meritorious Objects of the Royal Bounty', p.192.

as from Ireland, to do so. Perhaps not surprisingly, many out-pensioners sold their pensions to agents, who collected the sums for them and in return gave them a line of credit with shopkeepers, merchants and traders in the area of the country they intended to settle. Agents usually took a percentage of the value of the pension in return for this service and the pensioner rarely profited from it.[17]

Whilst the pension was certainly better than no income at all, it was not considered sufficient to live on and most of those in receipt of it still had to find some form of work to survive.

Making a Living

Those discharged early from the military as invalids could continue to serve by joining the Invalids Regiment. Raised in 1719 under Colonel Edmund Fielding, the Invalids were originally intended to provide garrisons for the many forts and castles that made up the defences of Great Britain. Soon after it was raised the regiment provided companies to garrison Portsmouth and Plymouth as well as sending a garrison to Jersey and Gibraltar. The Regiment was made 'Royal' in 1741 and in 1751 it was designated as the 41st Foot. The Invalids Regiment gave old soldiers the opportunity to continue to be paid, clothed, housed and fed by the army when otherwise they might have been out on the streets. For the Government, the Invalids Regiment provided a cadre of experienced soldiers who could still perform useful service and released fit soldiers from garrison duty for service elsewhere.

Older men who left the army without a pension and with no prospect of joining the Invalids Regiment faced an uncertain future. Many suffered from ill health brought about by many years of military service and most, by modern standards, would be considered alcoholics, such was the drinking culture within the army of the time. Finding alternative employment was therefore difficult and, for those without families to go home to, even finding somewhere to live was a struggle. For this reason, many old soldiers and their families were force to turn to charity for help or to resort to vagrancy to scratch a living. Local Parish records are full of entries listing 'relief' money paid from Parish coffers to help soldiers in need. For example, Berkhamstead Parish Constables accounts for 1747-9 show a total of 25 soldiers helped along with three described as 'a disbanded soldier'. In five of the cases the soldier had with him a wife or children, or just a child, and various sums from 6d to 1s were provided. Gifts were also made to 'an old Soldger 91 years of age' and to assist 'a Soldgers wife and 2 children with a pass'.[18] Court records from February 1732, relate to an incident of theft, allegedly committed by the wife of an ex-soldier discharged from the 7th Foot in January 1730. Her defence shows what poverty they had been driven to, as it describes: 'John Knight, her husband, was a pentioner to Chelsea Hospitall and that they had travelled

---

17   Cormack, *'These Meritorious Objects of the Royal Bounty'*, p.269.
18   Screen, *'Eighteenth Century Army at Home'*, p.230.

about the country since the end of February, 1732, Selling of Mousetrapps in order to the bettering their living in the world'.[19]

Life in the eighteenth-century British army was not an easy one, but was certainly better than some alternative careers of the time, and the treatment of those no longer able to work in eighteenth century society was not much better in other walks of life. For many soldiers, the end of their service in the army opened doors to a new life in America, Canada, India or the Caribbean, where they went on to make a success of their lives. The end of military service did not doom all old soldiers to a life of poverty and vagrancy, but it remains a fact that throughout this period, on into the Victorian era and, some might argue, up to the present day, the reintegration of retired soldiers back to society has never been adequately provided for. We need to look around at the issues surrounding modern soldiers returning to society before we judge the Georgians too harshly.

---

19   Screen, 'Eighteenth Century Army at Home', p.230.

Epilogue

When setting out to write this book I had originally planned the subtitle to be 'The Army that forged an Empire', implying that during this period the foundations were laid for an effective, adaptable and progressive army that would go on to carve out the British Empire. However, as my research went on, it became clear that that the 'Army', defined in this case as the institution of command, infantry, cavalry, artillery, logistics and support arms, was no better off at the end of the reign of George II than it was at the beginning. In terms of actual numbers, after the Seven Years War was over the British establishment was returned to its 1749 level of 30,000 men, a number insufficient to meet its new commitments to police the colonies in America, Canada, and the Caribbean, as well as garrison the Mediterranean and African possessions, support the HEIC in India, and garrison its various forts and magazines in Britain and the Channel Islands. The army began the reign overstretched and ended the reign in a similar manner.

Lessons learned about the provision of logistics during the campaigns in Europe and America were forgotten, as the men who had implemented the changes retired and did not pass the learning on. Indeed, the same lessons were being relearned as late as the Crimean War. Whilst medical provision remained constant, it was never very good to begin with and the soldiers who fought in the American War of Independence were no better served than their predecessors.

Reforms to the uniform and appearance of the army were implemented successfully, which did enforce uniformity and established the army as the possession of the Crown and not the independent colonels of the regiments. However, by the time of the American War of Independence the uniform itself had followed the European trend and aped the short jackets and general appearance of the Prussian army. This was clearly a backward step as the soldiers hated these uniforms, which provided no warmth or cover for them in bad weather, and found the cut and design more for show than practicality. Given all of this, it is hard to make a convincing argument that the British Army on the death of George II was any better in real terms than it had been at his ascension.

Yet an Empire, or at least the basis of one, had undoubtedly been won. The British were now sole masters in America and Canada, had substantial holdings in the Caribbean, in India, Africa, and the Mediterranean and had retained the King's holdings in Hanover. In every theatre in which the army had been engaged, it had ultimately won. Given how overstretched it was in terms of manpower, its lack of funding and its poor logistical support, how can this have been possible?

The answer, I would contend, lies with the men themselves. The high command was very far from the 'upper class twits' of popular imagination, and was instead staffed with capable and professional soldiers. They led by example, putting themselves in harm's way and sharing in the hardships on campaign of the private soldiers. The junior officers and senior NCOs were not discharged when regiments were reduced in size, but retained, so they provided a veteran cadre on which a new regiment could be built. They passed on their experience and skills to new recruits and as a result the regiments were able to perform much better on the battlefield than newly raised regiments had any right to.

Credit should also be given to the individual soldier. In each theatre of operations, the British soldier adapted to the prevailing conditions to overcome his enemy, and in no campaign was this more obvious than in America. Here, the infantry adapted their clothing and equipment and learned from the experienced Rangers and from their Native American allies. They also adapted their training to suit the terrain, learning new 'light infantry' tactics, scouting and marksmanship. Called upon the build roads, forts and settlements out of the wilderness, they rose to the challenge and conquered the harsh terrain and severe weather conditions. This could not have been done with unwilling or ill-disciplined troops.

The British soldier adapted and overcame despite the shortages of money and support services. This was a pattern that would repeat itself in the years to come and, some might argue, continues today. It was not the British Army, as an organisation, which laid the foundation for the Empire, but the indomitable spirit of the British soldier.

Appendix I

Infantry Uniforms 1742-1760

Regiment*	Facings	Lace 1742	Lace 1751	Notes
1st	Blue	Plain white	Plain white	Royal; gold officer lace.
2nd	Green	Black & yellow	White edged with oblique green stripes	Silver officer lace.
3rd	Buff	Red & buff	Edged blue, red & buff	Silver officer lace.
4th	Blue	Blue zigzag	Blue zigzag	Royal; silver officer lace.
5th	Pale Green	Plain white	Plain white	Silver officer lace.
6th	Yellow	Red zigzag	Edged 2 red zigzags	Silver officer lace.
7th	Blue	Red zigzag	Edged blue line	Royal Fusiliers; silver officer lace.
8th	Blue	2 blue stripes	Edged yellow	Royal; gold officer lace.
9th	Dark Yellow	Red zigzag & yellow	Edged blue centre red worm	Silver officer lace.
10th	Yellow	No lace	Red stripe and edged 2 blue zigzags	Silver officer lace.
11th	Green	Yellow & green	Edged green & red	Gold officer lace.
12th	Light Yellow	Yellow stripe	Central yellow stripe	Gold officer lace.
13th	Yellow	Yellow zigzag	Edged blue/red zigzag	Silver officer lace.
14th	Buff	No lace	Red zigzag edged 2 blue stripes	Silver officer lace.
15th	Yellow	No lace	Edged alternate yellow & blue	Silver officer lace.
16th	Light Yellow	Red worm	Yellow zigzag within red edging	Silver officer lace.
17th	Grey-White	Grey-White	Edged with 2 blue stripes with 2 blue inner zigzags	Silver officer lace.
18th	Blue	Yellow	Blue worm	Royal; gold officer lace.
19th	Green	Green & yellow	Edged red & blue stripe	Gold officer lace.
20th	Yellow	Plain white	Thin blue and red stripes.	Silver officer lace.
21st	Blue	Blue worm and yellow edge	Edged yellow with blue zigzag	Royal North British Fusiliers; gold officer lace.
22nd	Buff	Buff stripe	Edged alternate blue & red stripe	Gold officer lace.

THE ARMY OF GEORGE II

Regiment*	Facings	Lace 1742	Lace 1751	Notes
23rd	Blue	Yellow & blue stripe	Edged black and red lines	Royal Welch Fusiliers; gold officer lace.
24th	Olive Green	Green stripe	Edged green	Silver officer lace. White coat lining after 1751.
25th	Yellow	Red and green	Edged blue, yellow & red	Gold officer lace.
26th	Yellow	No lace	Edged two yellow lines	Silver officer lace.
27th	Buff	2 yellow stripes	Edged yellow with blue zigzag	Gold officer lace.
28th	Yellow	Plain White	Edged yellow & 2 black zigzags	Silver officer lace.
29th	Pale Yellow	No lace	Edged blue & yellow, with blue worm	Silver officer lace.
30th	Yellow	Plain white	Blue edged	Silver officer lace.
31st	Buff	Yellow zigzag	Green stripe	Silver officer lace.
32nd	White	Green stripe	Edged Black & Black Zigzag	Gold officer lace.
33rd	Red	Plain white	Plain White	Silver officer lace; White coat lining after 1751.
34th	Yellow	Blue and yellow	Yellow edged & blue worm	Silver officer lace.
35th	Orange	Plain White	Edged red, yellow zigzag	Silver officer lace.
36th	Green	Edged green	Edged green	Gold officer lace.
37th	Yellow	Yellow	Yellow white yellow stripe, with blue zigzag	No lace on lapels; silver officer lace.
38th	Yellow	Plain white	Edged 2 green stripes with yellow central stripe	Silver officer lace.
39th	Pale Green	Edged green	Green waved line	Gold officer lace.
40th	Buff	Black worm	Edged 3 buff/ black/ buff lines	Gold officer lace.
41st	Light Green	Plain white	No lace for privates	Invalids. 'Royal' after 1741 with change to blue facings. Gold officer lace.
42nd (43rd until 1748)	Buff	No lace	Edged red with central red line	'Black Watch' Highlanders; gold officer lace. 'Royal' after 1758 with change to blue facings.
43rd (54th until 1751)	White	Plain white	Edged red with central blue stars	Silver officer lace.
44th (55th until 1751)	Yellow	No Lace	Edged blue zigzag and black zigzag with central yellow stripe between	Silver officer lace.
45th (56th until 1751)	Green	Black stars	Green stripe and green stars	Silver officer lace.
46th (57th until 1751)	Yellow	No lace	Yellow stripe with two blue zigzags	Silver officer lace.
47th (58th until 1751)	White	Blue stars	Edged blue/ yellow/ blue zigzags	Silver officer lace.

APPENDIX I

Regiment*	Facings	Lace 1742	Lace 1751	Notes
48th (59th until 1751)	Buff	Edged green	Edged green & yellow line with central blue wavy line	Gold officer lace.
49th (63rd until 1751)	Green	N/A, raised 1743	Central yellow stripe and blue scroll pattern surround	Gold officer lace.

* During the War of the Austrian Succession, the number of regiments of foot rose to 66, including those listed above. The original 42nd was raised to garrison Georgia, and the 44th-53rd were the ten Marine Regiments. These and the regiments numbered as 60th-62nd and 64th-66th were disbanded at the end of the war, at which time the survivors were renumbered as shown in the table.

Appendix II

Infantry Regiments Raised During the Seven Years War

Regiment*	Facings	Lace**	Notes
50th	Black	Edged black	Silver officer lace. Raised 1755 as 52nd.
51st	White	Green worm	Gold officer lace. Raised 1756 as 53rd.
52nd	Black	Red & yellow worm	Silver officer lace. Raised 1755 as 54th.
53rd	Scarlet	Red worm	Gold officer lace. Raised 1755 as 55th.
54th	Popinjay Green	All yellow	Silver officer lace. Raised 1755 as 56th.
55th	Green	All yellow	Gold officer lace. Raised 1755 as 57th.
56th	Purple	Pink worm	Silver officer lace. Raised 1755 as 58th.
57th	Yellow	Edged black	Gold officer lace. Raised 1755 as 59th.
58th	Black	All yellow	Gold officer lace. Raised 1755 as 60th.
59th	Purple	All yellow	Silver officer lace. Raised 1755 as 61st.
60th	Blue	Edged blue & blue worm	Royal American, silver officer lace. Raised 1756 as 62nd.
61st	Buff	Edged Blue	Silver officer lace. Raised 1756 as 2/3rd; numbered as 61st 1758.
62nd	Buff	Blue/yellow/blue worm	Silver officer lace. Raised 1756 as 2/4th; numbered as 62nd 1758.
63rd	Dark Green	Edged green stripe	Silver officer lace. Raised 1756 as 2/8th; numbered as 63rd 1758.
64th	Black	Edged yellow	Gold officer lace. Raised 1756 as 2/11th; numbered as 64th 1758.
65th	White	Edged yellow/blue/red	Silver officer lace. Raised 1756 as 2/12th; numbered as 65th 1758.
66th	Lime Green	Edged crimson & crimson worm	Gold officer lace. Raised 1756 as 2/19th; numbered as 66th 1758.
67th	Yellow	Lime green worm	Silver officer lace. Raised 1756 as 2/20th; numbered as 67th 1758.
68th	Dark Green	Edged yellow & black worm	Silver officer lace. Raised 1756 as 2/23rd; numbered as 68th 1758.
69th	Willow Green	Yellow and black stripe	Gold officer lace. Raised 1756 as 2/24th; numbered as 69th 1758.
70th	Dark Grey	Edged blue	Gold officer lace. Raised 1756 as 2/32nd; numbered as 70th 1758.
71st	White	Black and red stripe	Silver officer lace. Raised 1756 as 2/3rd; numbered as 71st 1758. Disbanded 1763.

APPENDIX II

Regiment*	Facings	Lace**	Notes
72nd	Red	Edged red; blue worm	Gold officer lace. Raised 1756 as 2/33rd; numbered as 72nd 1758. Disbanded 1763.
73rd	Green	Blue and yellow worm	Gold officer lace. Raised 1756 as 2/34th; numbered as 73rd 1758. Disbanded 1763.
74th	Dark Green	Edged yellow and red	Silver officer lace Raised 1756 as 2/36th; numbered as 74th 1758. Disbanded 1763.
75th	Red Buff	Green and yellow	Buff coat lining: Gold officer lace. Raised 1756 as 2/37th; numbered as 75th 1758. Disbanded 1763.
76th	Green	Green worm	White lining: Gold officer lace. Raised 1756 as 61st, renumbered 1758. Disbanded 1763.
77th	Green	Plain white	Highlanders. Silver officer lace. Raised 1756 as 62nd, renumbered 1758. Disbanded 1763.
78th	White	Plain white	Highlanders. Gold officer lace. Raised 1757 as 63rd, renumbered 1758. Disbanded 1763.
79th	Yellow	Plain white	Silver officer lace. Raised 1757 as 64th, renumbered 1758. Disbanded 1763.
80th	Dark Brown	None	Light Infantry. Raised 1758, disbanded 1763.
81st	Blue	No lace	Invalids. Raised 1757, disbanded 1763.
82nd	Blue	No lace	Invalids. Raised 1757, disbanded 1763.
83rd	White	Not known	Raised 1758, disbanded 1763.
84th	Blue	Red worm	Gold officer lace. Raised 1758, disbanded 1763.
85th	Blue	Plain white	Royal Volunteers. Raised 1759, disbanded 1763.
86th	Orange	Black stripe	Raised 1758, disbanded 1763.
87th	Green	Red worm	Highlanders; gold officer Lace. Raised 1759, disbanded 1763.
88th	Green	Plain white	Highlanders; silver officer lace. Raised 1760, disbanded 1763.
89th	Buff	Not known	Highlanders; silver officer lace. Raised 1759, disbanded 1763.
90th	Green	Not known	Irish Light Infantry. Raised 1759, disbanded 1763.
91st	Black	Black worm	Gold officer lace. Raised 1759, disbanded 1763.
92nd	Black	Edged plain white	Donegal Light Infantry; silver officer lace. Raised 1760, disbanded 1763.
93rd	Grey	Grey worm	Silver officer lace. Raised 1760, disbanded 1763.
94th	Dark Blue	No Lace	Silver officer lace. Raised 1760, disbanded 1763.
95th	Red	No Lace	Gold officer lace. Raised 1761, disbanded 1763.
96th	Buff	No lace worn in India	Silver officer lace. Raised 1760, disbanded 1763.
97th	Gosling Green	White and black	Silver officer lace. Raised 1760, disbanded 1763.
98th	Green	White	Silver officer lace. Raised 1761, disbanded 1763.
99th	Not Known	Not Known	Raised 1761, disbanded 1763.

THE ARMY OF GEORGE II

Regiment*	Facings	Lace**	Notes
100th	Buff	Not Known	Highlanders. Raised 1760, disbanded 1763.
101st	Pale Yellow	Not Known	Highlanders. Raised 1760, disbanded 1763.
102nd	Not Known	Not Known	Raised 1761, disbanded 1763.
103rd	Not Known	Not Known	Raised 1761, disbanded 1763.
104th	Blue Cuff white turnbacks	White	Gilt officer lace. Raised 1761, disbanded 1763.
105th	Dark Blue	Gilt	Highlanders; gold officer lace. Buff waistcoats. Raised 1761, disbanded 1763.
106th	Black	Not Known	Wore black caps with brass plates. Raised 1761, disbanded 1763.
107th	Dark Blue	Not Known	Gold officer lace. Raised 1761, disbanded 1763.
108th	Not Known	Not Known	Raised 1761, disbanded 1763.
109th	Not Known	Not Known	Raised 1761, disbanded 1763.
110th	Dark Blue	Not Known	Raised 1761, disbanded 1763.
111th	Pompadour	White	Silver officer lace. Raised 1761, disbanded 1763.
112th	Dark Blue	Not Known	Raised 1761, disbanded 1763.
113th	Dark Blue	Not Known	Highlanders; silver officer lace. Raised 1761, disbanded 1763.
114th	Dark Blue	Not Known	Highlanders; silver officer lace. Raised 1761, disbanded 1763.
115th	Not Known	Not Known	Raised 1761, disbanded 1763.
116th	Not Known	Not Known	Invalids. Raised 1762. Re-numbered in 1764 as 73rd. Disbanded 1769.
117th	Not Known	Not Known	Invalids. Raised 1762. Re-numbered in 1764 as 74th. Disbanded 1770.
118th	Not Known	Not Known	Invalids. Raised 1762. Re-numbered in 1764 as 75th. Disbanded 1770.

* Between 1754 and 1756, the numbers 50th and 51st belonged to two regiments raised in New England (see Appendix III). When these were disbanded, the junior regiments were renumbered, with the 52nd becoming the 50th, the 53rd becoming the 51st and so on. To avoid confusion, this list details the regiments **after** the re-numbering.

** All lace was white and had a colour added to distinguish the various regiments. Some lace was edged with a colour, some were edged alternately with white and a colour and some had a worm, or twist, of the colour through the lace.

Appendix III

British Regiments Serving in North America

Regiment	Arrived	Facings	Breeches	Waistcoat	Notes
40th	1717	Buff	Red	Red	Officers buff waistcoat and breeches.
47th	1750	White	Red	Red	From 1758 red facings.
45th	1750	Dark Green	Red	Red	
50th	1754 (raised locally)	Red	Red	Red	Disbanded 1756.
51st	1754 (raised locally)	Red	Red	Red	Disbanded 1756.
44th	1755	Yellow	Buff	Buff	Issued buff linen in 1755 on arrival; officers wore yellow waistcoats.
48th	1755	Buff	Buff	Buff	Issued buff linen in 1755 on arrival.
60th	1755	Blue	Blue	Red	No lace on service uniform.
35th	1756	Orange	Red	Red	Officers orange waistcoats.
42nd	1756	Buff		Red	Facings blue after 1758; bearskin grenadier caps.
1st	1757	Blue	Blue	Red	
17th	1757	Light Grey	Red	Red	
22nd	1757	Buff	Red	Red	
27th	1757	Buff	Red	Red	Officers buff waistcoat and breeches.
43rd	1757	White	Red	Red	
46th	1757	Yellow	Red	Red	Officers yellow waistcoats.
55th	1757	Dk. Green	Red	Red	Officers buff waistcoat and breeches.
77th	1757	Green		Red	Bearskin grenadier caps.
78th	1757	Buff		Red	Bearskin grenadier caps.
15th	1758	Yellow	Red	Red	
28th	1758	Yellow	Red	Red	

THE ARMY OF GEORGE II

Regiment	Arrived	Facings	Breeches	Waistcoat	Notes
58th	1758	Black facings/ buff turnbacks	Red	Red	Officers buff waistcoat and breeches.
80th	1758	Brown	Red	Red	All ranks wore brown coats faced light brown.
95th	1760	Red	Red	Red	No grenadiers.

Appendix IV

American Provincial Regiments

Regiment	Coat	Facings	Breeches	Waistcoat	Notes
Connecticut	Red	Yellow	Red	Yellow	Blue coats faced red from 1760.
Georgia	Blue	Red	Blue	Red	Raised only one unit of rangers. Uniformed after 1758.
Maryland	Red (single breasted)	Black	Red	Red	Civilian clothes until 1756. 1757 onwards, uniform as shown.
Massachusetts	Blue	Red	Red	Blue	Senior officers wore a red coat faced red.
New Hampshire	Civilian	Civilian	Civilian	Civilian	No uniform issued.
New Jersey	Blue	Red	Blue	Red	Coats cut short. Yellow trim on Tricorne.
New York	Brown	Tan	Buckskin	Buckskin	Officers wore red coats faced green until 1756. 1757 Green coats faced light green.
North Carolina	Civilian	Civilian	Civilian	Civilian	
Pennsylvania and Delaware	Green	Red	Buff	Red	Coat cut short.
Rhode Island	Civilian	Civilian	Civilian	Civilian	
South Carolina	Blue	Buff	Red	Buff	After 1759 blue coats faced red, blue breeches red waistcoat.
Virginia	Blue	Red	Blue	Red	Coats cut short; brown gaiters.

Appendix V

Special Distinctions and Badges Displayed on Regimental Colours

Regiment	Distinction / Badge
1st	The Royal Cipher within a circle that bears the motto of the order of the Thistle. Crown and thistle three corners.
2nd	Queen's cipher within a garter with the motto: *Pristinae virtutis memor* and a lamb in three corners.
3rd	A Green Dragon in the centre with the motto *Veteri Frondescet honore*. Crown with a rose and crown in three corners.
4th	Royal cypher in the centre with the lion of England in three corners.
5th	St George and the Dragon centre with a rose and crown in three corners
6th	An Antelope in the centre with a rose and crown in three corners.
7th	Tudor Rose within a crowned garter. White horse in three corners.
8th	White Horse within a Garter centre with the motto: *Nec Aspera Terrant*. Royal Cipher and crown in three corners.
18th	A Harp below a crown centre with the motto: *Virtutis Namurcensis Praemium*. Rampant Lion arms of Namur three corners.
21st	A Thistle within a circlet bearing the motto of the order of the thistle. Royal cipher and crown in three corners.
23rd	Centre: Prince of Wales's plumes. 1st Corner: rising sun, 2nd Corner: Red Dragon, 3rd Corner: Prince of Wales' Plumes.
27th	A three towered castle and the word Inniskilling centre. White horse three corners.
41st	Rose and Thistle on same stalk centre. Royal Cipher and crown in three corners.

Appendix VI

Heavy Cavalry Uniforms

Uniforms of the Horse regiments (pre 1746)

Regiment	Hat/Coat Lace	Facings	Waistcoat	Breeches	Holster Covers	Horse Furniture	Notes
1st (Blues)	Yellow	Blue	Red	Blue	Red edged as furniture	Red edged with elaborate gold embroidery.	Blue Coats. Red flask cord. Joined the Household Cavalry 1746.
2nd (Kings)	Yellow	Blue	Blue	Blue	Red edged as furniture	Red: Gold scrolled edging. King's coat of arms on saddle cloth.	Blue flask cord. Became 1st Dragoon Guards 1746.
3rd (Queens)	Yellow	White	Buff	Buff	Red edged as furniture	Red: Gold scrolled edging Trophies, flags & drums on saddlecloth.	Buff flask cord. Became 2nd Dragoon Guards 1746.
4th	White	White	White	Red	White edged as furniture	White: Edged Blue & Red ivy leaf pattern. Trophies, flags & drums on saddlecloth.	White flask cord. Became 3rd Dragoon Guards 1746.
5th	Yellow	Blue	Blue	Blue	Blue edged as furniture	Blue: gold scrolled edging Royal coat of arms on saddle cloth.	Blue flask cord. Became 1st Horse 1746.
6th	White	Green	Green	Green	Red edged as furniture	Red: white scrolled edging. Trophies, flags & drums not Royal Cypher on saddlecloth.	Buff flask cord. Became 2nd Horse 1746.
7th	White	Yellow	Yellow	Yellow	Yellow edged as furniture	Yellow edged red. Trophies, flags & drums not Royal Cypher on saddlecloth.	Yellow flask cord. Became 3rd Horse 1746.
8th	Yellow	Black	Buff	Buff	Buff edged as furniture	Buff edged black. Trophies, flags & drums not Royal Cypher on saddlecloth.	Coats lined buff, buff turnbacks. Buff flask cord. Became 4th Horse 1746.

THE ARMY OF GEORGE II

Uniforms of the Horse Regiments (post 1746)

Regiment	Hat/Coat Lace	Facings	Waistcoat/ Breeches	Housing and Holster Covers	Horse Furniture	Notes
1st	White	Pale Blue	Pale Blue	Blue edged as furniture	Pale Blue: edged white/ red/ white.	Musicians in reversed colours and white breeches and waistcoat.
2nd	Yellow	Green	Green	Green edged as furniture	Green: edged yellow/ red/ yellow.	Musicians in reversed colours and white breeches and waistcoat.
3rd	White	Pale yellow	Pale yellow	Yellow edged as furniture	Yellow: edged white/ red/white.	Musicians in reversed colours and red breeches and waistcoat. 1760 issued skullcaps and cuirasses.
4th	Yellow	Black	Buff	Buff edged as furniture	Buff: edged white/ black/ white.	Buff turnbacks on the coat. Musicians possibly in buff coats with red facings rather than black coats. 1760 issued skullcaps and cuirasses.

Household Cavalry Uniforms 1751

Regiment	Hat/Coat Lace	Facings	Waistcoat/ Breeches	Housing and Holster Covers	Horse Furniture	Notes
1st Horse Guards	Gold	Dark Blue	Buff	Red edged as furniture	Red. Edged gold, with red stripe.	No lapels. Gold edged shoulder strap.
2nd Horse Guards	Gold	Dark Blue	Buff	Blue edged as furniture	Blue. Edged gold, with Blue stripe.	No lapels. Gold edged shoulder strap.
1st Horse Grenadier Guards	White	Dark Blue	Buff	Blue edged as furniture	Blue. Edged gold, with red stripe.	Gold Lace for officers. Grenadier caps. No lapels. Gold edged shoulder strap.
2nd Horse Grenadier Guards	White	Dark Blue	Buff	Red edged as furniture	Red. Edged gold, with blue stripe.	Gold Lace for officers. Grenadier caps. No lapels. Gold edged shoulder strap.
Royal Horse Guards (Blues)	Gold	Scarlet Red	Red until 1758, then Buff	Red edged as furniture	Red. Edged gold, with red stripe.	Dark Blue Coats. Full red lapels, cuffs and turnbacks. Red flask cord.

APPENDIX VI

Dragoon Guards Uniforms from 1746

Regiment	Hat/Coat Lace	Facings and Lapels	Waistcoat /Breeches	Housing and Holster Covers	Horse Furniture	Notes
1st	Gold for officers: yellow others	Dark Blue	Blue	Scarlet	Scarlet edged yellow with blue stripe.	Black Horses.
2nd	Gold for officers: yellow others	Buff	Buff	Buff	Buff edged yellow with blue stripe.	Black Horses.
3rd	Gold for officers: yellow others	White	White	White	White edged yellow with blue stripe.	Black Horses. Saddlecloth had 'III DG' inside a wreath of roses and thistles instead of the King's cypher.

Appendix VII

Dragoon Uniforms

Regiment	Hat Edge & Lace	Facings	Waistcoat	Breeches	Holster Covers	Horse Furniture	Notes
1st (Royal)	Yellow	Blue	Blue	Blue	Red edged as saddlecloth	Red edged gold/ blue/gold third each.	Buff waistcoat and red breeches worn until 1753. Blue flask cord. Royal Lace. Holsters & furniture blue until 1751 edged white and yellow.
2nd (Royal North British)	N/A & White	Blue	Blue	Blue	Blue edged as saddlecloth.	Blue edged white/Red/white third each.	Troopers wore mitre cap. Grey Horses. Red flask cord. Holsters & furniture red until 1751 edged yellow and green.
3rd (King's)	Yellow	Light Blue	Light Blue	Light Blue	Light Blue edged as saddlecloth.	Light Blue edged gold/dk blue/ gold.	Blue flask cord. Holster covers and saddlecloth red edged yellow until 1751.
4th	White	Green	Green	Green	Green edged as saddlecloth.	Green edged white/red/white	No flask cord.
5th (Royal Irish)	White	Blue	Blue	Blue	Blue edged as saddlecloth	Blue edged gold/ blue/gold third each	Flask cord buff. Saddlecloth had Harp of Ireland rather than King's cypher. Lace yellow until 1751, then Royal lace. Furniture edged red and white until 1751.
6th (Inniskillings)	White	Yellow	Yellow	1742: Red 1751; Yellow	Yellow edged as saddlecloth	Yellow edged white/blue/ white	Inniskilling castle motif on the saddlecloth. Edging red and blue until 1751.
7th (Queen's)	White	White	White	White	White edged as saddlecloth	White edged gold/blue/gold	Musicians: Royal lace, white waistcoat and breeches. Edgings red/blue/yellow until 1751.

APPENDIX VII

Regiment	Hat Edge & Lace	Facings	Waistcoat	Breeches	Holster Covers	Horse Furniture	Notes
8th	White	Yellow	Yellow	Yellow	Yellow edged as saddlecloth	Yellow edged white/yellow/white	Facings: 1735: Yellow: 1742: Orange: 1751 Yellow. Housings and saddle cloth: Orange edged white in 1742.
9th	White	Buff	Buff	Buff	Buff edged as saddlecloth	Buff edged white/blue/white	Housings and saddlecloth edged red and blue in 1742.
10th	White	Yellow	Yellow	Yellow	Yellow edged as saddlecloth	Yellow edged white/green/white	Housings and saddlecloth edged red and blue in 1742.
11th	White	1742: white 1749: Buff	1742: White 1751: Buff	1742: Red 1751: Buff	Buff edged as saddlecloth	Buff edged white/green/white	Housings white edged gold/blue/gold in 1742
12th	White	White	White	1742: Red 1751: White	White edged as saddlecloth	White edged yellow/green/yellow	Housings and saddlecloth edged red yellow and blue in 1742.
13th	1742: White. 1751: Yellow	Green	1742: White 1751: Green	1742: White 1751: Green	Green edged as saddlecloth	Green edged white/yellow/white	Housings and saddlecloth edged red and blue in 1742.
14th	White	Yellow	1742: White 1751: Yellow	1742: White 1751: Yellow	Yellow edged as saddlecloth	Yellow edged white/red/white	Housings and saddlecloth edged red and blue in 1742.
15th	Yellow	Green	Buff	Buff	Green edged as saddlecloth	Green edged yellow/green/yellow	Raised 1745 as Kingston's Light Horse; re-raised as 15th Dragoons 1746; disbanded 1749. Green patch on collar. Musicians red coats faced green with gold lace.

Appendix VIII

Light Dragoon Uniforms

Regiment	Coat	Cuffs	Waistcoat & Breeches	Holster Covers	Horse Furniture	Notes
15th	Red lined white. White lace	Green	White	Green edged yellow with red stripe.	Green edged yellow with red stripe	Green collar on coat. White turnbacks. White strap left shoulder. White crest and red plume on helmet. Green cloth. Green Lapels.
16th	Red lined white. White lace	Black edged white	White	White edged red and black stripe	White edged red and black stripe	Black collar on coat. White turnbacks. White strap left shoulder. No lapels. Red plume on helmet and black cloth.
17th	Red lined yellow. White lace	Yellow	White	Yellow edged with two white stripes.	Yellow edged with two white stripes	Yellow cuffs, lapels and turnbacks. White strap left shoulder. Red plume and yellow cloth. Disbanded 1763.
18th	Red lined white	White	White	White	Red edged white	Renumbered 17th in 1763. Lace Black and white. No collar but white lapels. 'Or Glory' motto and death's head device on cap. Red plume. Brown fur band. White strap left shoulder.
19th	Red lined White lace	White	White	White edged red	White edged red	Renumbered 18th in 1763. White lapels.
20th	Red lined white	Yellow	White	Yellow edged white	Yellow edged white	Yellow collar. Red plume on helmet and yellow cloth band. White strap left shoulder. Disbanded in 1763
21st	Red lined dark blue. White lace	Dark Blue	Buff	Dark Blue	Blue edged white	Blue collar on coat. Officers had white bearskin holsters. Musicians Tricorne hats and feathers. Green plume. Black cloth. Disbanded in 1763

Colour Plate Commentaries

Plate 1
3rd Troop of Horse Guards, War of the Austrian Succession

This soldier is from the 3rd Troop of Horse Guards, as denoted by the two yellow stripes on his carbine belt and the yellow saddlecloth. The coat has no lapels, unlike other regiments of horse, and was decorated with elaborate gold lace as befits the Kings Household troops. The 3rd and 4th Troops of Horse Guards served in Flanders during the War of the Austrian Succession, being present at both the battles of Dettingen and Fontenoy. Due to cut backs, both troops were disbanded in 1746.
   (Original artwork by Patrice Courcelle, © Helion & Company)

Plate 2
Sergeant, 1st Royal Dragoons, Battle of Dettingen 1743

This image depicts an unidentified sergeant of the Royals who captured the standard of the French Guard Cavalry, the 'Mousquetaires Noirs' in a desperate melee during the battle. The staff of the captured colour is broken as the French cornet who was carrying it had it strapped to his leg, forcing the sergeant to cut the staff off the colour to carry it away. Note the sergeant's blue sash, which was ordered to be worn around the waist after 1745, but which at this time would still have been worn over the left shoulder. Lace for sergeants was edged gilt on the lapels and the cuffs, with a gilt or gold silk aiguillette, which uniquely for the 1st Dragoons was worn on the left shoulder.
   (Original artwork by Patrice Courcelle, © Helion & Company)

Plate 3
15th Light Dragoons, 1760

Raised in 1759 by Colonel George Augustus Eliott, the regiment was officially designated the 15th Regiment of Light Dragoons but was usually referred to as 'Eliott's Light Horse'. The 15th saw significant action in Europe during the Seven Years War, distinguishing itself at the Battle of Emsdorf in 1760 and again at Vellinghausen the following year. The clothing instruction of April 1759 reads:

'a short coat lapelled and turned up with dark green, white lining and white waistcoat with a green collar; white buttons and button holes, two white shoulder straps…white linen breeches; jockey boots and spurs'. In this description it is the coat that has a green collar, not the waistcoat. It is possible that the officers' coats had the lapels edged in white, but the troopers' lapels were not. Note the trooper's sword knot is white, but would be crimson and gold for an officer.

(Original artwork by Patrice Courcelle, © Helion & Company)

Plate 4
Artillery Matross, 1746

The artist David Morier painted a scene depicting the Royal Artillery train in camp at Roermond in Flanders in 1748, and the Matross shown here is based on that painting and on descriptions of the uniform worn by the artillery. The lace on the coat and waistcoat is quite extensive even for this lower-ranked individual, and would have been gold for senior ranks. Practical black gaiters are worn as white ones were too hard to keep clean when working with the guns. This Matross is armed with a musket and cartridge box as he would be expected to defend the guns when they were limbered and moving from place to place and also on the battlefield, should the battery come under attack. The large powder horn is for use when priming the touchhole of the cannon ready for firing.

(Original artwork by Patrice Courcelle, © Helion & Company)

Plate 5
Drummer of the 37th Foot, Battle of Minden 1759

This drummer wears the reversed colours of his regiment, having a yellow coat lined red with red cuffs, lapels and turnbacks. The shoulders of the coat bear the distinctive 'swallow's nest' padding and it is decorated with white lace interwoven with the blue, red and yellow colours unique to this regiment. The false sleeves at the rear of the coat had previously only been worn by drummers of the Foot Guards, but from 1751 were regulation for all drummers. His legs are covered by the much more practical black gaiters that were now common amongst infantry regiments for everyday wear.

(Original artwork by Patrice Courcelle, © Helion & Company)

Plate 6
Highlander, 42nd Foot, Ticonderoga 1758

This image depicts a soldier of the Black Watch, as the 42nd Foot was more commonly known. The distinctive Highland dress includes short coat, plaid and bonnet. Note his pistol, broadsword, dirk and bayonet, which were carried in all theatres at this time, making him formidably armed in addition to his musket. The GR on his cartridge box is common amongst many regiments by the time of the Seven Years War but was considered the right only of the Foot Guards in the early part of George II's reign.

(Original artwork by Patrice Courcelle, © Helion & Company)

Plate 7
Light Infantryman, 55th Foot, North America, 1758

This infantryman wears the adapted uniform ordered by Lord Howe, who was colonel of this regiment when it arrived in America. Sleeves were cut off the coat and attached to the waistcoat, and often the men would just wear the sleeved waistcoat when out scouting or in the summer heat. This soldier is wearing his sleeveless coat over his sleeved waistcoat, buttoning the lapels across for warmth. The shoulders of the coat now stand slightly proud, where the sleeves have been removed, and the fabric is cut to resemble the wings of grenadier coats. He wears practical Indian mittasses instead of gaiters and a cut-down, jockey-style, leather cap, which was designed have the flaps button under the chin, keeping the ears warm on cold nights. Our soldier has the flaps buttoned up to keep them out of the way when patrolling. Howe's uniform adaptions were widely copied by other regiments fighting in North America and became the standard uniform for British light infantrymen in that theatre.

(Original artwork by Patrice Courcelle, © Helion & Company)

Plate 8
Gage's 80th Regiment of Light Armed Foot, North America, 1758

This unit was raised in 1758 as a light infantry regiment and this is reflected in its training and appearance. Learning from the uniform adaptations adopted by the British regular light infantry, Gage's 80th wore short coats, cut down leather caps and either black gaiters or Indian style mittasses as shown here. The exact shade of brown used in the uniform is not known for definite, but this dark shade is based on the best evidence we have. There is no lace and practical black buttons, all designed for camouflage when fighting in the woodlands of North America. The tomahawk was issued, as were the powder horn and pouch for extra ball, should he use up his cartridges. This regiment was trained to fight in skirmish order, using light infantry tactics, and not to fight in line like normal regular battalions. As such, they carried no colours and officers wore little insignia beyond a gorget so as not to present an obvious target to the enemy.

(Original artwork by Patrice Courcelle, © Helion & Company)

Plate 9
39th Foot, India 1757

The 39th sailed for India in April 1755 along with three companies of the Royal Artillery to supplement the Honourable East India Company's army.

The climate was very hot and humid and so the 39th adapted its uniform to suit the weather conditions. This soldier has flattened the brim of his hat to keep the sun off his face and neck. He wears no waistcoat and has cut his woollen coat short. He wears loose-fitting breeches made of gingham fabric, which at this time was blue and white stripes, and no stockings. His shoes are made from soft leather and are locally bought. He carries the minimum of equipment as the rest would be on the baggage or carried by his servant.

(Original artwork by Patrice Courcelle, © Helion & Company)

Plate 10
Officer, 13th Foot, War of the Austrian Succession

The presence of a gorget around his neck, the crimson sash and the silk aiguillette on his shoulder identify this man as an officer. Generally, officers' uniforms would be much better made than the soldiers and have gilt or silver lace. He carries the 'espontoon' that denotes his commissioned status but which was often abandoned on campaign, especially in America, in favour of a fusil or light musket.

(Reconstruction by Pulteney's Regiment – http://www.13thfoot.co.uk/ – photograph © Cath Smith)

Plate 11
Stand of Colours, 13th Foot, War of the Austrian Succession

These are the colours of Pulteney's 13th Foot as they may have appeared prior to the 1747 regulations, displaying the coat of arms and motto of their colonel. After 1747, the coat of arms on both the King's Colour and the yellow Regimental Colour would be replaced with the number of the regiment in gold Roman numerals surrounded by a wreath of roses and thistles on the same stalk. The regulations were designed to bring uniformity to the army and to show that the regiment belonged to the King and not to individual colonels.

(Reconstruction by Pulteney's Regiment – http://www.13thfoot.co.uk/ – photograph © Ellie Wout)

Plate 12
Grenadier, 13th Foot, War of the Austrian Succession

This is a reconstruction of a grenadier of the 13th Foot as he would have appeared during the 1740s. He is wearing practical brown marching gaiters rather than white ones, which were kept for parade. Note the presence of the brass holder on his cross belt originally designed for a slow match to light grenades, but retained as a distinction for grenadiers. His jacket has no 'wings' on the shoulders, which would be introduced later in the period.

(Reconstruction by Pulteney's Regiment – http://www.13thfoot.co.uk/ – photograph © Lucy Bamford)

COLOUR PLATE COMMENTARIES

Plate 13
Hatman, 68th Foot, Seven Years War

This is an image of the private soldier as he would have appeared through most of our period. Note that his hair is not powdered, as it would only be for review, and he carries only the kit necessary for battle. The small sword shown on his left hip was worn more as the sign of a status than as an actual practical weapon for fighting, and although retained in Europe it was often left in camp when campaigning overseas.

(Reconstruction by The Old 68th Durham Light Infantry Society and Display Team – http://www.68dli.co.uk/index.php – photograph © Ellie Wout)

Plates 14 and 15
Fusilier, 23rd Foot (Royal Welch Fusiliers), War of the Austrian Succession

Fusiliers wore mitre caps just as grenadiers did, but lacked the other distinctions, such as the slow-match holder on the cross belt and the later wings on the shoulders of their coats. This soldier wears practical brown gaiters for campaigning. Note the elaborate lace pattern on the jacket that was emerging as the unique identifier for regiments with similar facing colours. This soldier also wears the blue breeches reserved for Royal regiments.

(Reconstruction by Richard Marren Craft Workshop – photograph © Alan 'Kael' Ball)

Plate 16
Officer, 23rd Foot (Royal Welch Fusiliers) c.1740-1760

Infantry officers can immediately be distinguished by the lace on their coat and hat as well as by the crimson sash over their right shoulder. The gold-coloured gorget denotes this officer as belonging to a Royal Regiment as do his blue breeches. Note the privately-purchased hunter-style boots commonly worn by many infantry officers of the time. Although this reconstruction is based on the 23rd Foot, this officer could belong to any one of the several Royal regiments whose officers wore gold lace.

(Reconstruction by Richard Marren Craft Workshop – photograph © Maria Dare)

Bibliography

Archival Sources

Kent Archives, U1350/01/2: Journal of Sir Jeffrey Amherst, 1st Baron Amherst.
The National Army Museum, 1968-07-222-1 Dept APFS, Printed Pamphlet – The Case of General Ingoldsby.
The National Army Museum 1968-07-222-1 Dept APFS, Leather bound manuscript order book.

Published Sources

Anderson, Fred, *A People's Army: Massachusetts Soldiers and Society in the Seven Years War* (Chapel Hill: University of North Carolina Press, 1996).
Bancroft, Adam, *Savages In A Civilized War: The Native Americans As French Allies* (Auckland: Golden Springs Publishing, 2015).
Barrett, C.R.B., *The 7th Queens Own Hussars Volume 1 1688-1792* (London: Leonaur, 2008).
Bailey, Geoff B., *Falkirk or Paradise: The Battle of Falkirk Muir 17th January 1746* (Edinburgh: John Donald, 1996).
Bamford, Andrew (ed) *Rebellious Scots to Crush: The military response to the Jacobite '45* (Warwick: Helion and Company, 2020).
Berkovich, Ilya, *Motivation in War* (Cambridge: Cambridge University Press, 2017).
Black, Jeremy, *Britain as a Military Power 1688-1815* (London: Routledge 2016).
Black, Jeremy, *European Warfare in a Global Context* (London: Routledge, 2006).
Blackmore, David, *Destructive and Formidable: British Infantry Firepower 1642-1765* (Barnsley: Frontline, 2014).
Blackmore, David, *British Cavalry in the Mid-Eighteenth Century* (Nottingham: Partizan Press, 2008).
Brown, Thomas, Eastburn, Robert, Hawks, John and Putnam, Rufus, *Narratives of the French & Indian War: Ranger Brown's Narrative, The Adventures of Robert Eastburn, The Journal of Rufus Putnam-Provincial Infantry & Orderly Book and Journal of Major John Hawks* (London: Leonaur, 2008).
Buchannan, Dr John, *Regimental Practice or A Short History of Diseases common to His Majesties own Royal Regiment of Horse Guards when abroad (Commonly called the Blews)* (Aldershot, Ashgate: 2012).
Calloway, Colin G., *The Victory with No Name: The Native American Defeat of the First American Army* (Oxford: Oxford University Press, 2014).
Cannon, Richard, *Historical Record of the First, or Royal, Regiment of Dragoons* (London: Clowes and Sons, 1840).
Cannon, Richard, *Historical Record of the Third, or Kings Own, Regiment of Dragoons* (London: Clowes and Sons, 1836).
Carlyle, Thomas, *The Works of Thomas Carlyle* (Miami: Palala Press, 2015).
Carman, W.Y., *British Military Uniforms from Contemporary Pictures* (London: Leonard Hill Books Ltd, 1957).
Cary, A.D.L. (ed), *Regimental Records of the Royal Welch Fusiliers* (Uckfield: Naval and Military Press, 2015).

BIBLIOGRAPHY

Chapman, John (ed,) *Bard of Wolfe's Army: James Thompson, Gentleman Volunteer, 1733-1830* (Montreal: Robin Brass Studio, 2010).

Cormack Andrew and Jones Alan (eds) *The Journal of Corporal Todd 1745-1762* (Stroud: Sutton Publishing for the Army Records Society, 2001).

Cress, Lawrence Delbert, *Citizens in Arms: The Army and Militia in American Society to the War of 1812* (Chapel Hill: The University of North Carolina Press, 1982)

Dawes, E.C. (ed.), *Journal of General Rufus Putnam* (Albany: J. Munsell's Sons, 1886)

Duffy, Christopher, *Fight for a Throne: the Jacobite '45 Reconsidered* (Solihull: Helion and Company 2015).

Duffy, Christopher, *The Best of Enemies: Germans against Jacobites, 1746* (London: Bitter Books, 2013).

Duffy, Christopher, *The Military Experience in the Age of Reason* (London: Routledge & Kegan Paul Ltd, 1987).

Duncan, Francis, *History of the Royal regiment of Artillery* (London: John Murray, 1879).

Fitzpatrick, John C. (ed.), *Writings of George Washington from the Original Manuscripts* (Charlottesville: University of Virginia Library, 2001).

Franklin, Carl, *British Army Uniforms from 1751 to 1783* (Barnsley: Pen and Sword, 2012).

Grenier, John, *The First Way of War: American War Making on the Frontier, 1607–1814* (Cambridge: Cambridge University Press, 2008).

Guy, Alan (ed.), *Colonel Samuel Bagshawe and the Army of George II 1731-1762* (London: The Bodley Head for the Army Records Society, 1990).

Graham, Aaron and Walsh, Patrick (eds), *The British Fiscal-Military States, 1660-c.1783* (Oxford: Routledge: 2016).

Hamilton, Robert, *The duties of a regimental surgeon considered: with observations on his general qualifications, and hints relative to a more respectable practice* (London: J. Johnson, 1798).

Hayter, Tony (ed.), *An Eighteenth Century Secretary at War: The papers of William Viscount Barrington* (London: The Bodley Head for the Army Records Society, 1988).

Hunter, William A., *Forts on the Pennsylvania Frontier* (Harrisburg: The Pennsylvania Historical and Museum Commission, 1960).

Houlding, J.A., *Fit for Service: The Training of the British Army 1715-1795* (New York: Oxford University Press, 1981).

Jackson-Lee, Peter, *Courage After The Battle – The story of how Armed Forces Personnel survive their mental and physical injury after leaving the Armed Forces* (London: Brown Dog Books, 2019).

Johnson, J., *A View of the Diseases of the Army in Great Britain* (London: J. Johnson, 1793).

Johnson, William, *The Papers of Sir William Johnson* (Albany: The University of the State of New York, 1939).

Kane, Richard, *A New System of Military Discipline for a Battalion of Foot…* (Uckfield: Naval and Military Press, 2012).

Knox, John, *An Historical Journal of the Campaigns in North America for the Years 1757, 1758, 1759, and 1760* (Toronto: Champlain Society, 1914).

Kopperman, Paul, *Braddock at the Monongahela* (Pittsburgh: University of Pittsburgh Press, 1977).

Le Mesurier, Haviland, *The British Commissary: In Two Parts. A system for the British Commissariat on Foreign Service* (London: T. Egerton, 1801).

Maass, John R., *The French & Indian War in North Carolina: The Spreading Flames of War* (Mount Pleasant: Arcadia, 2003).

Mays, Edith, *Amherst Papers, the Southern Sector, 1756-1763* (Maryland: Heritage Books, Inc. 1999).

McCardell, Lee, *Ill-Starred general: Braddock of the Coldstream Guards* (Pittsburgh: University of Pittsburgh Press, 1986).

McConnell, Charles, *The French are Landing: The Forgotten Invasion of Carrickfergus in 1760* (Carrickfergus: Carrickfergus Publications: 1995).

McCulloch, Ian Macpherson, *Sons of the Mountains. The Highland Regiments in the French Indian War 1756-1767* (Fleischmanns: Purple Mountain Press, 2006).

Mackesy, Piers, *The Coward of Minden: the Affair of Lord George Sackville* (London: Penguin, 1979).

Mason, Philip, *A Matter of Honour: An Account of the Indian Army its Officers and Men* (London: Purnell Book Services Ltd, 1974).

Middleton, Richard (ed.) *Amherst and the Conquest of Canada: Selected papers from the Correspondence of Major-General Jeffrey Amherst 1758-1760* (Stroud: Sutton, 2003).

Tortora, Daniel J., *Carolina in Crisis: Cherokees, Colonists, and Slaves in the American South* (Chapel Hill: University of North Carolina Press, 2015).

Tracey, Nicholas, *Manila Ransomed* (Liverpool: Liverpool University Press, 1995).

Tytler, Alexander, *An Essay on Military Law and the Practice of Courts Martial* (Edinburgh: Murray and Cochrane, 1800).

Orr, Michael, *Dettingen 1743* (London: Charles Knight & Co Ltd, 1972).

Parkman, Francis *Montcalm and Wolfe* (Boston: Little Brown and Company, 1902).

Pringle, Sir John, *A View of the Diseases of the Army in Great Britain, America, the West Indies, and on Board of King's Ships and Transports, from the Beginning of the Late War to the Present Time. Together with Monthly and Annual Returns of the Sick, and Some Account of the Method in Which They were Treated in the Twenty-Ninth Regiment, and the Third Battalion of the Sixtieth Regiment* (London: J. Johnson, 1793).

Reid, Stuart, *Armies of the East India Company* (London: Osprey, 2009).

Reid, Stuart, *British Redcoat 1740-93* (London: Osprey, 1996).

Reid, Stuart, *Quebec: The Battle that Won Canada* (Oxford: Osprey, 2003).

Reid, Stuart, *Cumberland's Army; The British Army at Culloden* (Leigh-on-Sea: Partizan Press, 2006)

Rogers, H.C.B., *The British Army of the Eighteenth Century* (Oxford: Allen and Unwin, 1977).

Royle, Trevor, *Culloden: Scotland's Last Battle and the Forging of the British Empire* (New York: Pegasus, 2017).

Russell, John B., *The Writings of George Washington: Being His Correspondence, Addresses, Messages, and Other Papers, Official and Private, Selected and Published from the Original Manuscripts; with a Life of the Author, Notes and Illustrations* (Jared Sparks: American Stationers' Company, 1833).

Sanger, Ernest, *Englishmen at War; A Social History in Letters 1450-1900* (Stroud: Alan Sutton, 1993).

Schofield, Victoria, *Highland Furies: The Black Watch 1739-1899* (London: Quercus Publishing, 2012).

Sheppard, Ruth (ed.), *Empires Collide; the French and Indian War 1754-63* (Oxford: Osprey, 2006.)

Showalter, Dennis, *Wars of Frederick the Great* (Barnsley: Frontline Books, 2012).

Skrine, Francis Henry, *Fontenoy and Great Britain's share in the War of the Austrian Succession 1741-48* (Knighton: Terence Wise, 1997).

Smyth, B, *A History of the Lancashire Fusiliers* (Dublin: The Sackville Press, 1903).

Speck, W.A., *The Butcher; The Duke of Cumberland and the Suppression of the '45* (Cardiff: Welsh Academic Press, 1995).

Stevens, Abel, *The History of the Religious Movement of the Eighteenth century Called Methodism* (London: Alexander Haylin, 1859).

Sumner, Ian, *British Colours and Standards 1747-1881(1) Cavalry* (Oxford: Osprey, 2001).

Sumner, Ian, *British Colours and Standards 1747-1881 (2) Infantry* (Oxford: Osprey, 2001).

Symonds, Emily, *Lady Mary Wortley Montagu And Her Times* (Whitefish: Kessinger Publishing, 2010).

Warner, Oliver, *With Wolfe to Quebec: The Path to Glory* (Toronto and London: Colins, 1972).

Whitworth, Rex, *The Duke of Cumberland* (Barnsley: Pen & Sword 1992).

Whitworth, Rex *Field Marshal Lord Ligonier* (Godmanchester: Ken Trotman, 2006).

Whitworth, Rex, *Gunner at Large: The Diary of James Wood RA 1746-1765* (London: Leo Cooper, 1988).

Wolfe, James, *General Wolfe's instructions to Young Officers* (London: Franklin Classics, 2018).

Zaboly, Gary, *American Colonial Ranger: The Northern Colonies 1724-64* (Oxford: Osprey Publishing, 2004).

Zürcher, Erik-Jan (ed), *Fighting for a Living: A Comparative Study of Military Labour 1500-2000* (Amsterdam: Amsterdam University Press, 2013).

Thesis

Cormack, Andrew Edward, 'These Meritorious Objects of the Royal Bounty ...' The Administration of the Out-pension of the Royal Hospital, Chelsea in the early Eighteenth Century (Thesis for the degree of Doctor of Philosophy, 2016).

Articles

Atkinson, C.T., 'Grenadier Companies in the British Army', *Journal of the Society for Army Historical Research*, Vol.10, No.40 (October 1931), pp.225-231.

Atkinson, C.T., 'The Army under the early Hanoverians: More gleanings from W.O.IV and other sources in the public records office,' *Journal of the Society for Army Historical Research*, Vol.21, No.83 (Autumn, 1942), pp. 138-147.

Bannerman, Gordon E., 'Abraham Hume and the Supply management of the British Army during the '45', *Journal of the Society for Army Historical Research*, Vol.92, No.372 (Winter 2014), pp.268-285.

Bryant, G.J., 'British Logistics and the Conduct of the Carnatic Wars (1746–1783)', *War in History*, Vol.11, No.3 (July 2004), pp.278-306.

Chakrabarti, Pratik, '"Neither of meate nor drinke, but what the Doctor alloweth": Medicine amidst War and Commerce in Eighteenth-Century Madras', *Bulletin of the History of Medicine*, Spring 2006, pp.1–38.

Cadell, Patrick, 'Uniforms of the Madras Army', *Journal of the Society for Army Historical Research*, Vol. 27, No.112 (Winter, 1949), pp.171–175.

Fatherly, Sarah, 'Tending the Army: Women and the British General Hospital in North America, 1754—1763', *Early American Studies*, Vol.10, No.3 (Fall 2012), pp.566-599.

Garnham, Neal 'Military Desertion and Deserters in Eighteenth-Century Ireland', *Eighteenth-Century Ireland / Iris an dá chultúr:* Vol.20 (2005), pp.91-103.

Gilbert, Arthur, 'Law and Honour amongst Eighteenth century British Army Officers', *The Historical Journal* Vol.19, No.1 (Mar., 1976), pp.75-87.

Gilbert, Arthur, 'The Regimental Courts Martial in the Eighteenth Century British Army', *Albion: A Quarterly Journal Concerned with British Studies*, Vol.8, No.1 (Spring, 1976), pp.50-66.

Kopperman, Paul E. 'The British High Command and Soldiers Wives in America 1755-1783', *Journal of the Society for Army Historical Research* Vol.60, No.241 (Spring 1982), pp.14-34.

Kopperman, Paul E., '"The Cheapest Pay": Alcohol Abuse in the Eighteenth-Century British Army', *The Journal of Military History*, Vol.60, No.3 (Jul., 1996), pp.445-470.

Lenman, Bruce, 'The Weapons of War in Eighteenth Century India', *Journal of the Society for Army Historical Research*, Vol.46, No.185 (Spring, 1968), pp.33-43.

Little, H.M., 'The Emergence of a Commissariat during the Seven Years War in Germany', *Journal of the Society for Army Historical Research*, Vol.61, No.248 (Winter 1983/4), pp.201-214.

Middleton, Richard. 'The Recruitment of the British Army 1755-1762', *Journal of the Society for Army Historical Research* Vol.67, No.272 (Winter 1989), pp. 226-238.

Neave-Hill, W. B. R., 'The Rank Titles of Brigadier and Brigadier General', *Journal of the Society for Army Historical Research*, Vol. 47, No.190 (Summer 1969), pp.96-116.

Neuberg, Victor, 'The British Army in the Eighteenth Century', *Journal of the Society for Army Historical Research*, Vol.61, No.245 (Spring 1983), pp.39-47.

Oates, Jonathan, 'Hessian Forces Employed in Scotland in 1746', *Journal of the Society for Army Historical Research*, Vol.83, No.335 (Autumn 2005), pp.205-214.

Oates, Jonathan, 'Dutch forces in Eighteenth Century Britain: A British Perspective' *Journal of the Society for Army Historical Research*, Vol.85, No.341 (Spring 2007), pp.20-39.

Preston, David L., 'British soldiers and Indian Warriors from Braddock to Forbes's Campaigns, 1755-58', *Pennsylvania History: A Journal of Mid-Atlantic Studies*, Vol.74, No. 3 (Summer 2007), pp.280-306.

Preston, David L., 'Make Indians of our white men: British soldiers and Indian Warriors from Braddock's to Forbes Campaigns, 1755-1758', *Pennsylvania History: A Journal of Mid-Atlantic Studies*, Vol.74, No. 3 (Summer 2007), pp.280-306.

Ritchie, M.K., 'The Troubles of a Commissary During the Seven Years War', *Journal of the Society for Army Historical Research*, Vol.36, No.148 (December, 1958), pp.157-164.

Screen, J.E.O., 'The Eighteenth Century Army at home as reflected in Local records', *Journal of the Society for Army Historical Research*, Vol.88, No.355 (Autumn 2010), pp.217-232.

Sumner, Percy, 'Uniforms and Equipment of Cavalry Regiments from 1684 to 1811', *Journal of the Society for Army Historical Research*, Vol. 13, No. 50 (Summer, 1934), pp. 82-106, Vol.14, No. 55 (Autumn, 1935), pp.125-142.

Ward, Matthew C., '"The European Method of Warring Is Not Practiced Here": The Failure of British Military Policy in the Ohio Valley, 1755–1759', *War in History*, Vol.4, No.3 (July 1997), pp. 247-263.

Online Sources

3rd Kings Own Hussars website at <http://british-cavalry-regiments.eu5.org/3rd.html>.
'87th Foot', *Seven Years War*, at <http://www.kronoskaf.com/syw/index.php?title=87th_Foot>.
'British SYW Artillery', *My Seven Years War*, at <http://crogges7ywarmies.blogspot.com/>.
'Marquis de la Galissoniere: Memoir on the French Colonies in North America December 1750', at <http://www.let.rug.nl/usa/documents/1701-1750/marquis-de-la-galissoniere-memoir-on-the-french-colonies-in-north-america-december-1750.php>.
Royal Artillery, *Seven Years War*, at <http://www.kronoskaf.com/syw/index.php?title=Royal Atillery>.